Sacrificed Lives

Sacrificed Lives

KRISTEVA ON WOMEN AND VIOLENCE

Martha J. Reineke

INDIANA UNIVERSITY PRESS
Bloomington and Indianapolis

The paper used in this publication meets the minimum requirements of American National Standard for Information Sciences—Permanence of Paper for Printed Library Materials, ANSI Z39.48–1984.

Manufactured in the United States of America

Library of Congress Cataloging-in-Publication Data

Reineke, Martha J.
Sacrificed lives : Kristeva on women and violence / Martha J. Reineke.
p. cm.
Includes bibliographical references (p.) and index.
ISBN 0–253–33299–0 (alk. paper). — ISBN 0–253–21128–X (pbk. : alk. paper)
1. Women—Crimes against. 2. Violence. 3. Sacrifice. 4. Kristeva, Julia, date —Criticism and interpretation. 5. Girard, René, date —Criticism and interpretation. [1. Abused women.]
HV6250.4.W65R455 1997
303.6'082—dc21 96–53642

1 2 3 4 5 02 01 00 99 98 97

To Beth

CONTENTS

ACKNOWLEDGMENTS *ix*

1. INTRODUCTION 1

Part I

2. KRISTEVA IN CONTEXT 17
Psychoanalysis, Feminism, and Beyond

3. THE SUBJECT OF PSYCHOANALYSIS 49
Death-Work and Agency

4. IN SEARCH OF THE MOTHER IN MIMESIS 65
From Death-Work to Sacrifice

Part II

5. "THIS IS MY BODY" 105
Abjection, Anorexia, and Medieval Women Mystics

6. "THE DEVILS ARE COME DOWN UPON US" 128
Myth, History, and the Witch as Scapegoat

7. LIFE-SENTENCES 161
The Mother in the Cultural Archives of the West

NOTES *199*
REFERENCES *217*
INDEX *227*

ACKNOWLEDGMENTS

In 1985, I first read the work of Julia Kristeva. No feminist author I previously had encountered spoke to me about women's lives as Kristeva did. I wanted others to hear Kristeva's words and to find them as compelling as I found them. This book was born of that desire. I extend appreciation here to the many persons on whom I have relied while I have been writing about Kristeva. In the absence of their support, I would not have written this book.

I thank conversational partners at UNI with whom I developed the thesis of this book. In the 1980s, I shared ideas that form the nucleus of the book with David Ingram, Alice Swensen, Lora Rackstraw, Marcel Cornis-Pop (who introduced me to the work of René Girard), and Maryline Lukacher, who were members of the "French Reading Group," an ongoing faculty seminar at UNI. David Crownfield, who brought that group together, was an especially valued mentor. Other colleagues at UNI who lent support to this project include Shivesh Thakur and Edward Amend, Department Heads in the Department of Philosophy and Religion during the years that I was writing this book. Students in "Religion and Society" and the "Graduate Seminar in Women's Studies" helped me to fine-tune my argument as we read together many of the works cited in this book. Susan Hill offered important insights during the last stages of writing. Cynthia Goldstein, who never met a sentence that she felt would not benefit from a greater economy of expression, read every draft of this book, encouraging me to seek ever clearer modes of expression. I thank her for her patience, humor, and wise advice.

I thank the Graduate College at the University of Northern Iowa for a series of Summer Fellowships and a Professional Development Leave that supported my writing. My student assistants Christal Frakes, Corrine Bertram, Marnette Doyle, and Victoria Blitsch were valued conversational partners and researchers. The staff of Rod Library, especially interlibrary loan librarians Nancy Judas, Rosemary Meany, and Ed Wagner, provided an exceptional quality of support. On many occasions, when I arrived at their office exhausted after a day of writing, I received an extra boost of energy from the obvious pleasure that they took in their jobs.

I thank also my colleagues within the American Academy of Religion and the Society for Phenomenology and Existential Philosophy who supported this project. Naomi Goldenberg's mentorship was very much appreciated. Ellen Armour and Cleo Kearns made exceedingly helpful suggestions. Members of the Colloquium on Violence and Religion were influential to my efforts to incorporate the work of René Girard into this project.

I thank Robert Sloan at Indiana University Press. I am profoundly appreciative of his commitment to this book through all stages of its development. Thanks also to Tamsin Lorraine, Kelly Oliver, and James G. Williams, who were readers for the press. They offered exceedingly helpful criticisms of various drafts of this book, contributing substantially to its final shape.

I thank my parents, Mary and Lester Reineke, and my sister, Janalee Reineke-Lyth, on whose example and wise counsel—never give up on that to which you have committed yourself—I had reason to rely while writing this book. I express appreciation to my professors at Earlham College and Vanderbilt University for their formative influence on my intellectual development. I acknowledge also Phyllis Baker and Sharon Hels, whose unwavering confidence in me proved inspiring when I fell short of inspiration myself. I thank the staff at Casa Montessori (school and summer day camp) for providing an environment for my daughter in which she thrived during the many hours that I devoted to writing. I thank my husband, Bill Cozart, and my daughter, Beth, for creating a home with me in which hope can be sustained that an economy of violence does not definitively and finally shape human experience. But for that hope, I could not have brought myself to think for so long and with such persistence about sacrifice.

Sacrificed Lives

INTRODUCTION

> I do not believe it is possible for a rational system, based on the data of consciousness, to respond to the evil and horror that exist in the world.
>
> —Julia Kristeva, *Nations without Nationalism*

This is a book about women and violence. I have a compelling interest in the subject, for violence asserts a pervasive presence in my life. It shapes the lives of women students and friends. It shadows my daughter's life and my own. But it shouldn't. Women should not live in fear of violence. Nor should their autonomy and freedom of choice regularly be constrained by its threat. In writing this book, I seek to contribute to the diverse resources of feminist theory in support of feminism's efforts to address the problem of violence. I want to speak to violent constraints on women's lives and enhance the capacity of feminist theory to contribute to feminist interventions on behalf of women's free agency in a culture of violence.

I. Framing the Problem of Violence

Over time, I have seen a constellation of problematic images of aggression emerge and join, shaping for me suggestive interrogative parameters for a discussion about women and violence and forming the impetus for this work. These images constitute the background for my consideration of a theory of sacrifice as a key resource for feminist theorizing about violence.

The first image that informs my reflections on violence emerged from a conversation with a student. At the end of the last night of class one semester, a student stopped by my desk to tell me what the course and her "A" average meant to her. She stated that she had enrolled in college against the strong wishes of her husband, who over a period of years had treated her interest in further education with derision: "you are too stupid to last five minutes in college," he'd said. Recalling the first night of class, she told me that, at its midpoint, she had run out of the room in tears. Having easily succeeded in following my lecture, she was enraged that she had accepted her husband's assessment of her abilities for so many years and was astonished to discover that she was not stupid. Although she had been overcome momentarily by the enormity of her realization, she had returned to class the following week. She now wanted to share with me the full story behind her success: she had lasted more than five minutes in my class; in fact, she had thrived.

Violence, this student reminded me, does not always present itself in terms of physical assault. Violence transpires also as paralysis, an "immobilization in being," as Luce Irigaray observes (1986, 6), which can keep a woman locked in her home for years, unable to assert herself. Why? On what continuum does paralysis merge with other acts of violence? Any exploration of violence against women that will be adequate to the phenomenon must account not only for physical incidents of violence, but also for *paralysis,* which immobilizes women in cultural bonds not of their own making (Irigaray, 1986, 9).

Additional images cluster together in my mind: textual accounts of violence mix with my memories of women's faces, whose makeup unsuccessfully hid their bruises. I am puzzled by this mix. What are the explicit connections to be made between a broken human body and explanations that would make sense of it? In my experience, scholarship about violence invites me wholly to subsume the visceral elements of violence to the controlled reason of analysis. But I find persistently disquieting the disjunctions that I perceive between the life circumstances analyzed in accounts of battering *and* the violence recorded on the body, sometimes bruising and sometimes killing. Despite the plethora of economic, political, educational, and cultural factors that count as explanations for given incidents of violence, the connections between these factors and the violent acts themselves often remain ambiguous to me. After I've read it all, I still find myself asking, "Why her?" and "Why her body?"

I remain perplexed because reports of violence that inspire my questions seem often, in my experience, to be formulaic variations on "he had a bad day so he went home and kicked the dog." However carefully and copiously they are rendered, accounts which highlight the social factors that contribute to violence do not focus on its internal logic as I would wish. When I examine the trajectory of violence, I want to know what drives its apparently inexorable march toward brutality. What *grounds and connects* moves marked out along a path that advances from a "bad day," to "kicking the dog," to "kicking her?" On what bridges does a perpetrator of violence stand when he makes these transitions? Why does he invoke bodies at all? And why are women so often the recipients of the violent gestures that bruise and sometimes kill? Is the pathway of violence sexually differentiated by caprice? If social factors of vulnerability were reassigned, would a different set of victims be found along it? These questions attest to a pattern of *substitutionary violence* that solicits further attention.

As I think about violence, mind-searing images of torture recounted in recent newspaper reports of local criminal proceedings emerge, and force me to reflect also on violence's boundless capacity for extension and elaboration. I find myself seeking a calculus that I might use to measure protracted violence. In the absence of such a calculus, I do not comprehend why threats turn into shoves and punches or why battering gives way to more torturous invasions of the body. But such an instrument of measurement seems not to exist. In accounts of violence against women, generally only a photo or autopsy report attests to battering directly, graphically, *in its minutiae.* Yet, I want to know, once a body is invoked by a perpetrator of violence, why does violence reach down ever deeper into it? Why does shoving give way to violation, to tearing and splitting open the body, to slow torture ending in death? Confronted with the elaboration of violence, I want to know why speech and all its signs wholly fail: what is missing? Why is speech so inadequate that such an act becomes necessary? (Irigaray, 1986, 7). Finally, why is the female body so often the body of choice in such invasions? What accounts for its privileged violation? The investment of violence in *soma,* or flesh, needs to be considered more closely, for ready answers to these questions elude me.

At the same time that I find my attention drawn to the invasive nature of violence—its deep landscape—the extensions of violence on other fronts come to mind as well. I am wary of a myopic vision that would lead me to offer only assessments of localized incidents of violence against women. I attribute my uneasiness to that one aspect of radical feminism (Jaggar/Rothenberg, 1993, 120) which I always have found especially compelling: when considering violence, radical feminists emphasize that women are victimized as members of a group. They remind me that incidents of violence against women do coalesce. As a consequence, when women are ignored as a category of victims, not only is their experience of violence distorted, but also key contributing factors to violence are misread, sustaining an abusive culture. Alert to these concerns, I seek to examine violence against women on a broadly inclusive continuum.[1]

Puzzled about violence and haunted by images I cannot fathom, my ongoing reflections have coalesced around several images: *paralysis, substitutionary violence, and soma.* These images establish an agenda for further inquiry. I want to learn how paralysis becomes a way of life for so many women, radically occluding their agency. I want to examine also the layered, substitutionary representation of violence in order to understand its internal logic. For, if my reflections are to contribute to efforts to free women from the grip of violence, I need to give careful account of paths taken by violence. Along its trajectory are key points of transition—life circumstances conjoined with gestures of sheer brutality—that remain murky. If, in the purported wholly accomplished signs of violence so copiously documented by scholarship, are hidden moments of aggression not yet captured by these signs, I need to account for them, and not only for violence's well-mastered moments.

I am drawn also toward elements that, arising in the actual display of violence, appear to shape it and evoke soma. Violence, I perceive, spans the boundaries of being, moving into, across, and out of the human body. Apparently finding meaning, indeed generating meaning, in that very transgression, violence mandates that, if I am to understand it, I must go where it goes. I must cross the boundaries of being where violence has crossed them, to bring to conscious reflection its previously hidden route of passage. Therefore, in my effort to understand violence against women, I must draw toward that aspect of violence which so often remains concealed: a somatic hinge that embraces sign and act. There, I must attempt to trace the gesture of torture that would probe ever deeper into the flesh of its victim. Finally, if the violence I examine is preferentially visited on women, I need to explore this as well, forging connections among all these themes, so as to account for sexual differentiation common to the aspects of violence I address.

Attuned to these images of violence and aware of their sexually differentiated moments, I seek precise connections among them that enable me to examine violence in the broadest purview. The notion of an *economy of violence* is particularly helpful to my efforts to understand a paralyzing continuum of violence, inclusive of intimate and global relations, whose distinct points regularly are marked by paralysis, battering, and death. On several counts, an economic model of violence invites systematic attention to forms of cultural disorder that have particularly onerous consequences for women.

First, an economic model allows consideration of violence on multiple levels. After all, in a monetary economy, from which this strong metaphor is taken, monetary relations encompass pennies and dimes in a change purse as well as instruments of international finance. Similarly, this model makes readily observable the links between violence in intimate relationships and violence directed against women in groups. Violent incidents do not transpire as isolated acts. They are systematically constituted. Their meaning and value are a function of these connections. If violent elements exhibit a propensity to extend their range of power or a proclivity for dissolution and weakness, they are more readily assessed if their elements are seen in the context of interrelations effected by the system of which they are constituent parts and not elsewhere.

Second, an economic model sheds light on the intractable nature of violence. This model suggests that patterns of sexually differentiated violence are best understood as lived investments, rather than as expressions of deliberate and intentional choices. Therefore, this model honors feminists' sense that critical distance from a culture of violence is achieved only with difficulty. For, just as persons participate in the monetary economy of a given society, in part, because they experience that economy in ways that discourage them from construing their behavior in terms of consent or dissent, so also do humans in a violent society live as persons wholly embedded in its culture and mores.

In an economy of violence and in a monetary economy, persons grant the economy authority in the very act of using its currency and not because they employ an explicit mechanism of consent. As a consequence, an economic model lends credence to the notion that violent elements in a given culture can exert a coercive, immobilizing effect, discouraging opposition and assertions of agency, even when specific agents of coercion are not present. In light of an economic model of violence, Teresa Brennan's wise assessment of the long-standing subjugation of women proves all the more telling: the constitutive factors in women's oppression are intractable but not immutable (1991, 117).

Finally, an economic model offers a refined portrait of feminist politics, suggesting that, because systems that oppress women do exhibit a tendency to produce collusive effects, they cannot be countered by polemical fiat (Brennan, 1991, 118). Instead, if women are to engage effectively in anticollusive politics, they must necessarily establish leverage from within the economy they would contest. They must analyze it as a system in order to locate points of weakness that portend the subversion of relations that economy has forged. In all these respects, the notion of an economy of violence resonates positively with the goal of this project: to engage in a thoughtful, nuanced exploration of sexually differentiated violence, one that is cognizant of the immense challenges posed to those who seek to contest its paralyzing, hegemonic rule.

An economic model helpfully illuminates the landscape of violence highlighting, in particular, its broad expanse and immobilizing features. However, an investigation of substitutionary violence and humans' somatic investments in violence is advanced when this economy is defined more precisely. A more exact specification indicates that these forms of violence are proper to a *sacrificial* economy.

Admittedly, readers may find the terminology of sacrifice disconcerting. After all, sacrifice is most often associated with societies encountered in the panoramic surveys of religion undertaken by scholars such as Frazer, Robertson Smith, and Durkheim. Sacrifice figures prominently in these scholars' catalogues of religious practices in ancient Greece, Israel, Rome, and India as well as in their accounts of rituals in traditional societies which became known to them as a consequence of Europe's colonizing ventures (Jay, 1992, x). Even so, the culture of violence in which women live is most productively understood in terms of a sacrificial economy. Feminist theorists who seek to understand that culture in order to intervene on behalf of women's agency should not relegate sacrifice to societies inventoried by nineteenth-century European scholars in their grand theories of religion. Feminist theorists should invoke sacrifice as a powerfully instructive metaphor for analyses of women's lives.

Analyzing the culture of violence in which women are constrained in terms of sacrificial theory is beneficial because sacrificial theory attends to the themes of violence described above: paralysis, substitutionary violence, and humans' somatic investment in violence. Sacrificial theory considers violence in terms of an economic continuum, inclusive of local and global incidents, whose end points are marked by paralysis and death. Sacrificial theory attends also to the internal logic of violence and its substitutionary path. Moreover, sacrificial theory teaches that sign and body must be invoked under a single rubric if violence is to be analyzed appropriately. The very margins of experience must be investigated, for only at the borders of language and soma, meaning and chaos, can explicit and systematic attention be given to violence's propensity for elaboration and extension. Therefore, in multiple respects, sacrificial theory promises to facilitate feminist theorists' critical engagement with a culture of violence.

The notion of an economy of violence shaped by sacrifice promotes systematic thinking about violence supportive of feminism's concerns. The violence that pervades women's experience mandates such precision in reflection; in its absence, feminists cannot hope to come to terms with the intractable nature of violence. As sustained attention is given in this project to the interrogative themes about violence set forth here, invocation of a sacrificial theory will prove warranted. No longer will sacrifice appear an arcane phenomenon at some distance from the present concerns of women. Because sacrifice will be shown to be a phenomenon with powerful contemporary analogues in women's lives, feminism's need for a theory of sacrifice will be evident. Those who seek to identify and helpfully address the pervasive blight of violence on women's lives will readily observe the compelling relevance of sacrificial theory to their concerns.

The theorist of sacrifice whose work primarily informs this project is Julia Kristeva, for she gives especially close examination in her work to the themes of violence set forth here. She is acutely aware of violence as a symptom of a brutalizing economy, and she is attuned to the protracted nature of violence to which incidents of torture regularly attest. Moreover, Kristeva's specific perspective on sacrificial violence is particularly helpful to feminists. Drawing on the resources of psychoanalysis and linking sexual differentiation in society with patterns of substitutionary violence, Kristeva accounts for how and why culture regularly enacts violence against women. In looking not only at constraints exerted on women in a sacrificial economy—their "penitentiary condition" (1985a, 216)—but also at their potential for *productive* dissolution of bonds forged there, Kristeva seeks, by means of an emancipating grammar, the commutation of women's life-sentences. Drawing on Kristeva, this project attends closely to life-sentences that immobilize women. It focuses as well on possibilities for women's emancipation from the economy in which these sacrificial bonds are forged.

A presentation of Julia Kristeva as a theorist of sacrifice is not without precedent. Both Patricia Elliot (1991) and Cleo Kearns (1993) have framed their reflections on Kristeva in light of sacrificial themes. Kelly Oliver also has had occasion to highlight Kristeva's theory in terms of the organizing paradigm of sacrifice (1993, 40–41). Reading Kristeva in a manner that emphasizes her theory of sacrifice does pose some risk: so tight a focus could skew the reception of her work among persons who are first introduced to it here. Fortunately, the major interpreters of Kristeva (Lechte, 1990; Oliver, 1993, 1993a) explore a broad range of themes and issues in Kristeva's writings. They are crucial resources for students of Kristeva. Although this project does place Kristeva's work under a lens that reflects in acute relief the role of women within a sacrificial economy, readers need not conclude that her work should be read only through this lens. Instead, readers may observe the particular value of this lens to persons who are concerned about constraints on women's agency that emerge at a specific juncture. For persons who wish to explore sexually differentiated violence forged of intimate and social bonds, reading Kristeva as a theorist of sacrifice is highly instructive.

II. Kristeva's Psychoanalytic Theory: A Helpful Resource for Feminists?

Some readers may doubt that Kristeva is a useful resource for reflecting about violence against women because her work is grounded in psychoanalytic feminism. Psychoanalytic feminism is widely criticized in feminist circles as antifeminist in its consequences, if not in its intent. These apprehensions are unwarranted. Feminist theorists can benefit from considering Kristeva's work in lieu of precipitously dismissing it.

The feminist argument against psychoanalytic feminism is succinctly summarized by Patricia Elliot (1995, 42). She notes that feminist critics of psychoanalytic feminism assert that it distinguishes the transhistorical structures on which it focuses (e.g., the unconscious) from socialized patterns of behavior. Because these structures are distinct, their critics do not believe that they share a key characteristic of the social and historical: the capacity for amelioration and transformation. Because psychoanalytic feminists appeal to these structures in their efforts to account for the circumstances of women's lives, they necessarily represent women's oppression as inevitable and social change as impossible, notwithstanding any rhetorical claims they might make to the contrary. Since feminism is committed, by definition, to social change, psychoanalytic feminists are antifeminist.

Kristeva's sacrificial theory is implicated in this criticism because she employs the tools of psychoanalysis to decipher the internal logic of violence and expose a trajectory of violence whose origins lie deep within the social milieu. The structures to which she appeals—linked under a general rubric of the unconscious—are broadly transhistorical. Is criticism of her work along grounds set forth by feminist critics of psychoanalytic feminism well founded? Kristeva is not vulnerable to this line of criticism. Kristeva is wholly cognizant of issues of power and domination within the processes of individual and group identity formation that she identifies. Moreover, she establishes that transhistorical structures, which she associates with the labor of the unconscious, do not exclude options for social change.

Nevertheless, Kristeva does stand fully in the camp of psychoanalysis. Kristeva does make stronger claims about nonhistorically specific, determining factors in subject formation than would the most magnanimous critic of psychoanalytic feminism. After all, the psychoanalytic account might actually be accepted by that critic as an admissible theory of the social construction of identity if work undertaken by the unconscious were understood by all parties in the debate to be restricted to the internalizing of social norms. But Kristeva goes further. She understands that the work of the unconscious not only reflects social relations, but also exhibits a constructive capacity to shape social relations. Kristeva wishes to acknowledge the human subject's history of socialization *and* the distinct psychic processes which inform that history. Because subject creation necessarily involves a social history *and* the labor of the unconscious, neither can be subjected to a reductionism that makes one the repository of the other.

Indeed, far from being the suspect transhistorical structure critics of psychoanalytic feminism condemn, Kristeva cites the unconscious as decisive for agency. As the chapters that follow establish, Kristeva traces to the work of the unconscious the very capacity a given subject exhibits to undermine cultural expectations and to withstand the allure of culture which so often leads to acceptance of its norms. If humans are not ciphers of historical circumstance, as she wishes to submit, they owe their capacity for an autonomy of being to work undertaken by the unconscious. Thus, rather than dismiss the unconscious, Kristeva valorizes it as the human subject's best hope for agency. As a consequence, in dissent from the critics of psychoanalytic feminism, Kristeva emphatically rejects the firmly established association between "the historically mutable and the politically actionable" (Brennan, 1991, 119).

That, for proponents of psychoanalytic theory, such as Kristeva, the unconscious is the motor of human agency and, for the feminist opponents of psychoanalytic theory, if acknowledged at all, the source of human capitulation to conditions of domination suggests an impasse in feminist theory. That feminist theorists who take seriously the work of the unconscious are themselves perceived to be in complicity with forces of domination personalizes the critical impasse at which feminist theorists have arrived and makes all the more urgent thoughtful attention to the current stalemate. Clearly, a nuanced discussion of the issues is in order. Can this project contribute to such a dialogue?

Intending that this project do so, I find suggestive terms for discussion set forth by Teresa Brennan. She observes that critics of psychoanalytic feminism should not conflate psychoanalytic feminists' call for a distinct strategy of political engagement with structures of the unconscious with a condemnation of their very appeal to such structures (1991, 115). Instead, feminist theorists should treat as separate moments in their critical evaluation the case to be made for the structures to which psychoanalytic feminists appeal and the political strategy appropriate to them, if their case is found plausible.[2]

Accepting Brennan's terms, I here contribute to a conversation among feminists concerning the utility of psychoanalytic theory to their concerns. By way of a sacrificial theory, I demonstrate that psychic structures associated with the labor of the unconscious as well as historical or social patterns of socialization contribute to the human experience. Each warrants careful reflection. Not disavowing the possibility that the work of the unconscious may contribute to the acceptance of oppression, I emphasize its role also in the subversion of norms. At the same time, I indicate that patterns of socialization exhibit a potential to both liberate and oppress. Rather than reject one set of influences out of hand, as irrelevant to the political commitments of feminism, because I appeal to Kristeva I suggest ways in which feminist theorists may work together to theorize the positive and problematic aspects of *all* the diverse processes that shape human experience.

III. An Outline of *Sacrificed Lives*

This project sets forth a sacrificial theory in two parts. Part I establishes a context for reading Kristeva and introduces the main features of her reflections on the unconscious. Part I draws on the broad corpus of her writing and offers a close reading of those portions which address violence. Part I closes with a sustained treatment of Kristeva's theory of sacrifice. Part II applies Kristeva's theory to key moments in women's lives in the past which call for sacrificial analysis. The past is chosen deliberately as a point of focus: Kristeva teaches us of the widespread capacity among humans to hide from ourselves our sacrificial interests. Deception is most firmly entrenched at the points within a sacrificial economy where persons are currently invested. As a consequence, novice theorizers of sacrifice who may not readily detect our own complicity in ongoing ventures of a sacrificial economy need to focus on the past. If the work of a sacrificial economy can be exposed there, when we become more advanced students of that economy, we may be able to constructively assess sacrificial violence today.

Chapter 2 places Kristeva's sacrificial theory in context. Its theoretical precursors and founding assumptions, which often pose a challenge for readers unfamiliar with the larger setting out of which her work emerges, are emphasized. In particular, Chapter 2 assesses Kristeva's critical engagement with Jacques Lacan's psychoanalytic theory. Two aspects of his work are shown to be especially significant. First, the world about which Kristeva and Lacan write is a signifying economy: human subjects are creatures of language, dependent for every meaning—including their own—on a world they create when they exchange signs. Second, the subjects about whom Kristeva and Lacan write are not the unified, self-possessed entities whose identity fulfillment American readers like to champion by way of diverse therapies and self-help programs. Kristeva, following Lacan, understands humans to be shaped by a founding and unalterable alienation. On both counts, Kristeva's views position her at some distance from dominant trends in American ego psychology.

Because Kristeva's readers sometimes find her terminology daunting, Chapter 2 introduces and explains her specialized vocabulary. At the same time, this chapter indicates that readers' frustrations with her writing are not generally attributable to Kristeva's willful use of difficult terminology. To the contrary, discomfort with Kristeva's writing usually rests not with her *words* but with the disturbing *world* of violence they evoke (Elliot, 1991, 193).

Chapter 2 concludes with a discussion of another obstacle to readers' appreciative engagement with Kristeva: her coding of sexual difference. Feminist critics of Kristeva often understand her to distinguish between sex as a locus for the physiological or empirical differentiation of bodies and gender as a locus for the representation of these bodies in culture. Maintaining that Kristeva is constrained by a dualistic perspective to assign space for agency to one of two mutually exclusive domains—an arena of the precultural feminine or an arena of cultural representation accessible only to men—these critics assert that she finds no actionable space for women to effect social change. But Chapter 2 demonstrates that Kristeva undermines a sex/gender dichotomy because she recognizes that bodies are always already implicated in signification (Chanter, 1993, 189; Oliver, 1993, 156). Finding that bodies are wholly invested in the historical praxis of human subjects, Kristeva does offer women actionable space for emancipating acts.[3]

Kristeva associates this space with the unconscious. Kristeva's reflections on the unconscious are decisive for her understanding of human subjectivity and the signifying economy in which humans live. They are critical not only for her perceptions of this economy's vulnerability to exploitation and its conscription to a sacrificial agenda, but also for her confidence that this economy, notwithstanding its historic implication in violence, provides grounds for emancipation and resistance. Therefore, Chapter 2 takes a multipronged approach to setting forth key tenets of Kristeva's theory of the unconscious. It challenges suspicions about the unconscious set forth by Kristeva's feminist critics. Kristeva's theory provides compelling testimony that the labor of the unconscious is a primary resource for, rather than obstacle to, assertions of agency by all human subjects, women as well as men.

Chapter 3 offers a detailed commentary on Kristeva's views of the unconscious. A cluster of terms that exemplify its work—the abject, semiotic, negativity, death-drive, death-work, and maternal matrix—are deployed. These elements of the unconscious contribute to aspects of subject formation that establish humans' capacity to become creatures of words and enter the world of language. Two functions of language in the signifying economy are contrasted. One, the more visible, draws on signs to secure humans in the world and reconcile them to estrangement as an ongoing factor in their lives. The other, associated with the unconscious and witnessed only indirectly, at the borders of language, shelters a heterogeneity and excess from which humans draw their capacity for community, creativity, and agency. Because both aspects of language establish subjects as effects, rather than causes, of signifying processes, they attest to a certain fragility in humans. Because humans are vulnerable, when their signifying ventures fail, constraining their agency, they can experience a radical loss of place in the world. Kristeva traces the origins of violence in society to humans' efforts to preserve their positions in the world against such loss.

Chapter 4 follows the trajectory of Kristeva's thought as she tracks violence, trailing it from its origins in processes of subject formation across the broad expanse of the signifying economy. On first glance, she observes that humans' formative processes appear successful, enabling them to resolutely manage their affairs. However, under her close examination, regulation in the social order is exposed as acute, protective control. Under even closer examination, humans appear fully engaged by threat. At that juncture, Kristeva submits that humans exist under the auspices of a sacrificial economy.

Chapter 4 supplements Kristeva's insights with those of René Girard, another major theorist of sacrifice. Aspects of the sacrificial social contract that are implicit or understated in Kristeva's work come fully into view when Girard's theory is compared with hers. The chapter shows that Kristeva's theory of sacrifice speaks decisively to the themes that frame this project's consideration of violence against women: paralysis, substitutionary violence, and soma.

Kristeva's theory of sacrifice illuminates a *paralyzing continuum* of violence. Conceiving of human community in terms of a signifying economy, she perceives that human interactions form a complex and broadly pervasive web of relations that often leave little space for the free exercise of choice. Moreover, Kristeva accounts for diverse expressions of constraint when she detects a basic frailty in that web of relations. For, engaged in proactive reinforcement of positions there, persons create a limiting climate for others, even in the absence of directly coercive acts.

Kristeva accounts also for *substitutionary patterns* of violence in the signifying economy. These patterns emerge when persons exchange civil instruments (signs), which they have used to negotiate places in society, for weapons of raw violence. When persons perceive that not only their formally adjudicated positions in society, but also their very capacity to *be* in the world are at risk, they draw no longer on familiar strategies for claiming space, for example, tools, money, and other instruments of exchange. Conscripting the resources of the unconscious, they invoke extraordinary means. Measuring their choice of weapons against the degree of perceived threat that they discern, persons under siege substitute common instruments for lethal weapons: the very powers of life and death.

Observing these moves, which invoke not only sign but *soma,* Kristeva explains the protracted nature of violence, which draws ever deeper into the human body. When humans seek to bring harmony out of forms of disorder that, experienced as an attack on their very being, threaten to exclude them altogether from the signifying economy which is their home, they turn to the borders of language, site of the unconscious. Resources for agency provided by the unconscious, now in sway to a sacrificial economy, become murderous. For, at the very boundaries of life and death, humans invoke the most ancient of gestures: they cut, kill, and eat bodies to create community. Homing in on the core of a sacrificial economy, these acts show that, when humans are confronted with chaos, they do not always run away. For, if they can capture and master the powers of chaos without capitulating to them, becoming causes rather than effects of language, the world belongs to them.

Even though processes of subject formation associated with the labor of the unconscious appear to dictate neither that humans violently mediate the founding circumstances of their alienated existence nor that they secure their positions in the world against loss by recourse to murder, history chronicles widespread evidence of sacrifice.

When Kristeva surveys this historical record, she achieves her most significant insight: the centrality of *sexual difference* in the work of the sacrificial economy. Kristeva perceives that, when humans seek to identify threats to human existence and community, contain their menace, and achieve redress in the face of radical loss, very often a perceived difference between the sexes is "mobilized" by those who would deny or manage loss by projecting its threat onto women (Elliot, 1991, 207). The differential effects of sacrificial violence on women, documented in the historical record, create bonds—life-sentences—which immobilize women and, under circumstances of radical crisis, place their very lives at risk. Regularly made scapegoats in the sacrificial economy, women's lives are forfeited so that others' lives may be saved.

Where and when does this happen? Part II demonstrates that, if we want to glimpse the sacrificial economy at work, we should look at religion. Why religion? According to Kristeva, the historical record preserves a widespread tendency among humans to hide from their direct view the workings of the sacrificial economy. Religion is a notable exception. Among those conceptual and symbolic systems traditionally called on to uphold the sacrificial economy, religion figures most prominently (1984c, 9, 70), for it regularly submits to public representation that economy's substitutionary, sacrificial mechanism of violence.[4] Indeed, prior to the modern era, religion comprised *the* culturally sanctioned space to confront absolute threats to human community, throttle, and vanquish them. Purification rites, food taboos, and pollution fears comprise a constellation of religious behaviors whose logic is governed by the threat to survival experienced in the ambiguities of human experience, when humans find that the fragile boundaries that have secured their existence need to be redrawn. In religious ritual, humans can confront what eludes them as effects of signifying processes: the very process—menace and promise, life-threatening and life-saving—by which they are bounded from the chaos of origins to be subjects in the world. Moreover, within the sacrificial functions of religion, sexual difference plays a key role, creating and maintaining a climate whose contours, attesting to widespread and pervasive violence against women, regularly subvert their agency and make women scapegoats.

Part II continues a conversation with feminist theorists. It suggests that, because feminist theorists have been inattentive to the cultural space shared by religion and violence,[5] they have been precluded from understanding adequately how women's lives are shaped by and always are vulnerable to violence. Feminist theorists also have not been able to reflect adequately on strategies for escape and survival. Drawing on the evidence of history, Part II proposes that the capacity of feminist theory to contribute to feminist interventions in a culture of violence can very much benefit from a theory of sacrifice attentive to religion.

Although Kristeva's comments on religion prove the initial inspiration for a sustained study of sacrifice, Part II does not emphasize, as she has, religions of indigenous peoples and of the Biblical period. Instead, it uncovers patterns at key moments in the history of Western Christianity. It documents the complicity of the Christian religion in creating and maintaining a culture of sacrifice. Particular interest is taken in the function of sexual difference within the religious practices that are examined. Part II focuses on occasions in the history of Christianity when persons, perceiving that their ongoing commerce with each other is under radical threat of disruption, invoke substitutionary patterns of violence to address this threat. Summoning powerful resources of religion and turning their violence on women, they dramatically amplify ordinary constraints on women's lives, reconfiguring them as sacrifice. Life-sentences imposed on women become death-sentences. Thus, at key moments in the history of Western Christianity, under the conditions of a radically challenged social order, the signifying economy functions as a sacrificial economy.

Part II considers three sacrificial tropes: mystic, witch, and mother. Chapter 5 focuses on the medieval mystics, who, in significant numbers, died from severe asceticism. Notwithstanding these deaths, some scholars argue that the medieval mystics exercised great autonomy and freedom of agency, defying constraints imposed on them by the larger social order. Chapter 5 dissents from this reading and presents manifest evidence that the mystics' lives were shaped by a violent, homicidal agenda. When the mystics died of severe asceticism, they were victims of sacrifice. Of course, the perpetrators of violence disguised their agenda. Indeed, perhaps at no other time in history have agents of sacrifice been more successful in concealing their commitments. Moreover, the mystics' accounts of their lives do suggest that they perceived themselves to be autonomous agents of faith, not victims. However, notwithstanding other scholars' valorization of the mystics' lives, they were primary casualties of the sacrificial economy of medieval Europe.

Chapter 6 addresses the European witch hunts. At first glance, they appear to be an easy case. If women dragged out of their homes and killed to avenge famine, pestilence, and war were not sacrificial scapegoats, who are? Moreover, in contrast to the mystics, who lived in a society that concealed its lethal agenda, agents of death in the society in which women accused of witchcraft lived were brutally direct about their intentions: they *sacrificed* women. However, a sacrificial hypothesis is not easily articulated. Dissembling, in this case, belongs to contemporary scholars of the witch hunts. They refuse to read these events as sacrifice.

Chapter 6 confronts this refusal in order to perceive anew the witch hunts as ventures of a sacrificial economy. Girard serves as a vital resource once again. In assessing the hunts in the wake of the great loss of life that they produced, Girard states that, had our ancestors been as unwilling to label their acts as sacrifice as are today's experts, they never would have put an end to the witch trials (1986, 99). These chilling observations about contemporary scholarship on the witch hunts frame the argument of Chapter 6. Echoing Girard, this chapter asserts that, only if we come to terms with the discourse of sacrifice preserved in the historical records of the hunts, can we hope to act on contemporary instances of sacrifice. For our amnesia in respect to the past suggests a blindness to our present circumstances, which keeps us paralyzed in the grip of violence.

Chapter 7 maintains the goal of addressing widespread, contemporary blindness toward sacrifice while examining the figure of the mother in the cultural archives of the West. Chapter 7 notes multiple incidents of dissemblance and obfuscation concerning sacrificial violence and its female victims. Although these cultural archives purport to preserve, in literature and art, valorizing portraits of mothers, no salutary circumstances for women are detected, only scapegoats. Moreover, these archives directly and unambiguously preserve clear evidence of sacrifice, even though contemporary students of the cultural record are unwilling to label sacrifice as such. Thus, around the figure of the mother coalesce all the ambiguities which are associated with the sacrificial tropes of the mystic and the witch.

Seeking a safe route through the sacrificial economy, Part II seeks further instruction in its ways and tools by which persons might leverage position to confront and challenge its ongoing work. Drawing on the three tropes of sacrifice and exploring their relations, Part II offers persons who are engaged in critical reflection on violence against women vital insights concerning the abusive culture in which women live, and facilitates feminists' efforts to address and challenge violence on behalf of women's free agency. In the wake of extended reflections on the figures of the mystic, witch, and mother, Part II elucidates the questions and themes that generate this project's initial considerations of women and violence. It clarifies paralyzing investments in violence, as well as substitutionary patterns and protracted expressions of violence common to a sacrificial economy.

As this project closes, the subject of inquiry turns from sacrifice to the topics of agency and the unconscious first addressed in Chapter 3. Under interrogation, the sacrificial economy finally reveals its limits. Analysis oriented toward the unconscious discloses a space in which women who are victims of a sacrificial economy may acquire agency to survive and challenge it, becoming freed of the constraints of its sacrificial bonds.

The affirming note on which this project ends marks my faithful regard for humans, a regard that is central also to Kristeva's work. It stands as testimony also to my feminist commitments, which preclude me from accepting that an economy of sacrifice definitively and finally shapes human experience. The promise of the unconscious keeps ever present before us reasonable grounds for maintaining hope that the culture of violence in which women live might be otherwise.

Part I

2

KRISTEVA IN CONTEXT

PSYCHOANALYSIS, FEMINISM, AND BEYOND

> But through the efforts of thought in language, or precisely through the excess of the languages whose very multitude is the only sign of life, one can attempt to bring about multiple sublations of the unnameable, the unrepresentable, the void. This is the real cutting edge of dissidence.
>
> —Julia Kristeva, "A New Type of Intellectual: The Dissident"

Kristeva's sacrificial theory emerges in a context critically informed by contemporary currents in Continental thought: Lacanian psychoanalysis, poststructuralism, Marxism, and feminist theory. Readers of her work sometimes find that distinguishing Kristeva's own, unique voice from among those with whom she converses is challenging. Kristeva usually presumes familiarity among her readers with her partners in dialogue, regularly invoking her cohorts' ideas without citing them by name. This tendency, contributing to a certain opaqueness in Kristeva's writing, sometimes proves disconcerting to readers who only recently have discovered her work.

In order to facilitate enhanced encounters with Kristeva's work, this chapter brings to view key figures on whom Kristeva draws in her work and illuminates the larger intellectual context out of which Kristeva's views emerge. This chapter focuses, in particular, on Jacques Lacan. Kristeva's affinity for Lacan's work as well as her critical engagement with it are cited. Noted also are Kristeva's differences with Lacan, which have inspired her to offer a psychoanalytic theory of subjectivity, sexual difference, and sacrificial violence that is distinctly her own.

Moves Kristeva makes in claiming her own, unique voice are outlined, and her work is placed within a feminist context. Aspects of her thought which have proved insightful for feminist theorists as well as those which have appeared problematic are clarified. Kristeva's affinity for key tenets of feminism as well as points of critical difference between her and some feminist theorists are cited. This chapter emphasizes the utility of Kristeva's project for feminism's emancipatory aims, even as it frankly acknowledges that the challenge Kristeva poses to violence against women and the approach she takes to emancipatory politics set her at a distance from some feminist theorists.

Throughout, this chapter seeks to enhance readers' capacity to appreciate Kristeva and view her work as a vital resource for reflections on women and violence. Above all, this chapter aims to have Kristeva's sacrificial theory emerge as it surfaces in her actual work: by way of her conversation with others. As moments of this conversation are brought into view, the founding assumptions that shape Kristeva's work and ultimately inspire her original, constructive vision are illuminated.

I. The Lacanian Context: Human Existence as a Practice of Absence

Kristeva's work is very much indebted to the influence of Jacques Lacan. She draws on Lacan's reflections concerning human subjectivity, the cultural work of signification, and sexual difference. As points of similarity and difference between Lacan and Kristeva in these three areas are traced, Kristeva's own voice emerges, culminating in her theory of sacrifice.

Kristeva concurs with Lacan when he asserts that words—marks on a page or sounds—do not function as instruments of representation; rather, they produce a social, signifying space. Signs have meaning not because they attach themselves like labels to things, but because they relate systemically to one another. Linked with one another, words articulate a history, a politics, a world.

Moreover, Kristeva supports Lacan's efforts to differentiate between the Imaginary and Symbolic orders in the world of signification. What is the Imaginary? When tracing the history of the subject, Lacan discovers that human infants experience only fragments of being. Only gradually does a sense of "I" emerge out of a chaotic field of sensory experience. Lacan refers to this fragmented nexus of early experience as the Imaginary and notes that it is defined by an absence of clear differentiation between an "I" and an "Other" (1985, 163).[1]

What is the Symbolic? As the human infant matures, Lacan asserts that it develops the capacity to take a position in the world. He refers to this world as the Symbolic order: a field of exchange, language, and law. Within this world, the "I" that all of us use in our conversations with one another and from which we derive our commonsense experience of identity, finds its home. However, for Lacan, the transition to the Symbolic cannot truly be said to confer a self-possessed unity of being on humans. To the contrary, Lacan advances a radicalized notion of subjectivity. He claims that human existence is shaped by paradox: in its signifying practices, the human subject achieves identity only in difference and asserts a unity of being only in the context of alienation (1981, 205–206).

Lacan relies on a notion of the "mirror stage" to document this founding alienation of the human subject. When confronted with an idealized and unified image (in a mirror or through another's mirroring gaze) of an other, the human subject establishes itself *at the site* of that image. Significantly, the subject does not bring to the mirror a coalescing identity whose emerging self-sufficiency the mirror confirms. Instead, the mirror produces this effect. Whatever identity the human subject constructs therefore always is established elsewhere: out of the fragments of a wanting-to-be, the subject comes to be in a "place" where "it" is not. Split, the subject is posited as a space of difference bounded by the unity that is its founding pretense (its mirror image) and a disunity that is irrecoverable as the source of its being (the chaotic field of initial experience, sometimes identified as a maternal matrix). From this moment, the Law of the Symbolic order under which the subject lives becomes a Law of absence for the subject.[2] Moreover, the subject must abide faithfully by this Law if it is to secure its altogether fragile position in the world, for its self-possessed status is essentially a facade. The subject's carefully bounded identity is actually *mé-connaissance,* and the security it finds in the world rests on its capacity and willingness to invest in that *mé-connaissance,* to mistake its image for the thing itself (1981, 74). The subject's source of security, wholly unacknowledged, rests with its being beholden to that which has mirrored it. As Richard Kearney reminds us, for Lacan, "the I is Other" (1986, 274).

When Kristeva describes human subjects as *intertextual practices* (1990, 175), her words have clear precedent in Lacan. With this phrase, Kristeva not only concurs with Lacan that humans are creatures of language, she emphasizes as well that subjectivity is fundamentally enacted, by way of language, as intersubjective process. Humans do not establish position and identity in the world by claiming specific life-scripts as their own: humans always *are* between and among texts. Never the completed outcomes of the texts they enact, they establish subject-status on a signifying field where they are always mutually implicated in each other's speech acts. However, because they share a founding estrangement in being, subjects cannot claim by way of such acts to secure identities in or through each other against alienation. As Lacan has claimed, Kristeva asserts as well: because humans come to be in places where they are not, any desire they might express for definitive claims on identity must forever be deferred. Moreover, Kristeva concurs with Lacan concerning the fragility of subjects. Indeed, recognizing the intensity of subjects' commitment to self-deception, she emphasizes the costs that can accrue to other subjects when one or more are confronted with testimony to *mé-connaissance.* Subjects can become angry and fearful, for vitally invested in that which is not, they risk everything if their investments are exposed as ruse.

Lacan's portrait of processes by which human subjects take up positions in the world has profound consequences for his theory of the construction of sexual difference, on which Kristeva also draws. Lacan does not believe that the sexual differentiation of human subjects is based on differences in the bodies of males and females; rather, when language places subjects in the Symbolic order, it also positions them there as men and women. Lacan asserts that boys and girls are situated in relation to a placeholder Freud has previously defined with reference to the Oedipal scene: the phallus. Not the biological penis, the phallus is instead a point of fundamental division in the signifying field along which sexual difference is deployed. As a consequence, sexual difference is an arbitrary construction, set forth on a shifting ground of meaning.[3]

According to Lacan, subjects historically have challenged the caprice of sexual difference. Investing in the signifying chain's key reference point (the phallus) in order to differentially deploy and encode the lack that they are and accede to the Law of absence in the Symbolic order, they have attained a strong sense of security. As they have assumed differential positions in language in relation to an oppositional structure (a, not-a), which is fixed (knotted) by the phallus (1985a, 75), men have purported to "have" the phallus, women to "be it."[4] Nevertheless, under the legislation of the Symbolic order (the Law of absence, division, and disunity in being), their respective desires never actually have realized their goal. Because no one can stand outside the chain of signification to "have" being, no one has been able to "have" or "be" the phallus that would make possible the subversion of human subjects' founding estrangement.

Kristeva agrees with Lacan concerning the construction of sexual difference. She accepts as nonproblematic the generation of meaning along a signifying chain in which human subjects are differentially located and sexed in relation to the phallus as a master signifier and in accord with a Law of absence, the Father's Law. She concurs with him that, although subjects rely heavily on signs of sexual difference to buttress their fragile stance in the world, the differences they invoke have no firm base. However, even though Kristeva and Lacan share a basic theory of subjectivity and a common approach to the construction of sexual difference, distinct emphases in Kristeva's theory readily distinguish it from Lacan's. Where Lacan stresses that sexual difference functions to *secure* the subject in the world, Kristeva notes that it plays a role when subjects *contest* the circumstances of their existence in the Symbolic order. Discerning that subjects regularly perceive their positions in the world as hard-won, Kristeva observes that, when subjects feel threatened, they register along sexually differentiated lines their efforts to resecure their position. Kristeva's special attentiveness to subjects' fears and to their forceful efforts to lay these fears to rest shape her distinct perspective on subjectivity and sexual difference.

According to Kristeva, Lacan appears to suggest that, in the course of development, the human child emerges from the Imaginary into the Symbolic order largely reconciled to the circumstances of its life as a creature of language (1984c, 131). But for Kristeva, the Lacanian subject's separation from the sensory chaos of its origins appears all too neatly accomplished. Kristeva persists in seeing in the subject's "condemnation" to the Symbolic a threat which precludes its sanguine accommodation to loss: something remains hidden, as it were, in the lining of the curtain that rises on the Symbolic order. Kristeva wagers that, in staying with the process of signification at its point of cleavage, at the borders of speech through which are glimpsed the boundaries of being *and* signification, the Imaginary and the Symbolic, she can expose the persistence of the heterogeneous in the signifying process which Lacan has bypassed in his haste to raise the curtain on the subject of the Symbolic order. Kristeva can illuminate that which Lacan has left in darkness: echolalias, rhythms, and silences that comprise material aspects of language and their maternal markings.

Attentive to these borders, Kristeva can observe that, when speech breaks apart, the gaps and awkward rhythms of speech reveal something Lacan has tended to dismiss in his own observations of human existence in the Symbolic order. Kristeva recognizes that, on humans' accession to the world of language, their capacity to take a position in the world is not dictated only by their use of signs and syntax. Other forces are at work also, establishing subjects as effects of linguistic processes which, if law-governed, are also material and heterogeneous. Kristeva's theory of the unconscious focuses on these forces, the subject of Section II below. Most significantly, observing humans' responses to perceived threats to their positions in the sociosymbolic order, Kristeva documents their invocation of material labor she has previously associated with the unconscious and notes also the differential impact on men's and women's lives of their efforts to bolster and resecure these positions. Kristeva's account of the violence that shadows such struggles, its sexually differentiated aspects, and its deployment in an economy of sacrifice is the subject of Section III.

II. The Lacanian Context Subverted: Kristeva's Theory of the Unconscious

Attentive to a heterogeneity that remains hidden in the folds of the curtain of signification, Kristeva chooses to link the material aspects of language to which her attention is drawn with the *region of the unconscious.* She appeals to a cluster of terms in order to identify key nuances of this province which otherwise might be overlooked: *abject, semiotic, maternal matrix, negativity, death-drive,* and *death-work.* Kristeva's multifaceted discussion of the unconscious attests to the persistent legacy of Lacan in her own work even as it demonstrates genuinely novel aspects in her reflection.

Kristeva uncovers the *abject* at the point of cleavage between the Imaginary and the Symbolic. *Want* itself, the abject attests to ambiguity, an inassimilable nonunity experienced by one who, neither in the Symbolic order nor outside of it, is neither a subject nor object of being. The category of the abject enables Kristeva to recognize, as Lacan does not, that the rising of the curtain on the Symbolic, the bounding of the Imaginary, is not easily accomplished: the curtain threatens to suffocate. For the subject who is yet an abject, "it is a violent, clumsy breaking away, with the constant risk of falling back under the sway of a power as securing as it is stifling" (1982, 13). Indeed, the abject is a primary mark of the not-yetness of a subject who is embattled in its ascent to the Symbolic.

Although the drama of the abject suggests an incident that has transpired in the subject's early childhood, Kristeva does not restrict the abject to that time. At any juncture in the life of the subject, the abject can emerge to mark as untenable the identity of the subject in its objective worth. In particular, it materializes on those occasions when the subject of the Symbolic drifts toward self-deception regarding the lack that it is. If the subject seeks in objects an external support for being which eludes it because it is condemned to dwell in being-at-a-loss, the subject may find that the abject emerges, giving the lie to any identity-securing arrangement with objects (including sexual objects) that the subject attempts to engineer. Shadowing the subject, the abject is experienced as the uncanny; it creates a fading or instability in the arrangements undertaken by the subject in an attempt to secure its being, showing them as ruse.

The visceral connotations of the French *"l'abjection,"* cited by Kristeva, entail an aspect of nausea (1982, 3). Evocations of discomfort, linked with the abject, testify to the abject's disconcerting dynamism: would-be subjects of the Symbolic do rest easy in their roles. Like the thought or image on which we gag, the abject is experienced as garbage: it is the unwelcome waste, filth, and blood that litters the stage of the Symbolic. More succinctly, the abject is *refused refuse:* it is that which exceeds the subject who, attempting to disavow its life-sentence and seeking to practice presence rather than absence, would ask that the object fully fill and define it. As Elizabeth Grosz rightly observes, the abject is "the place of the genesis *and* the obliteration of the subject" (1989, 73). A symptom of object-failure, the abject, ever persistent, witnesses that the object does not and cannot fully fill the subject, anchoring it to the real (Grosz, 1990, 87).

In sum, the abject typifies the unconscious. The category of the abject enables Kristeva to emphasize that the unconscious does not so much suggest mysterious forces active in a hidden, interior province of the subject's mind as it does boundary-making practices of a world-creating subject. Attentive to this labor of the subject, Kristeva links the abject with the *semiotic.* Like the abject, the semiotic shows itself in breaks, nonsense, and puns that display a subversion of language by the imagination. Further, drawing on the somatic contours of the border between the Imaginary and the Symbolic, Kristeva associates the semiotic with the infant's perception of the world through the rhythms, melodies, and gestures of the maternal body:

> It is a matter of opening, in and beyond the scene of linguistic representations, pre- or trans-linguistic modalities of psychic inscription that one could call semiotic, in recovering thus the etymological meaning of the Greek *semeion*—trace, mark, idiosyncracy [*distinctivité*]. At the foundation of philosophy, before our mode of thinking was enclosed in the horizon of a language understood as a translation of the idea, Plato,

> recalling the atomists, spoke in the *Timaeus* of a *chora*—archaic receptacle, mobile, unstable, anterior to the One, to the father and even to the syllable, metaphorically identified as nourishing and maternal. (1985, 14)

However, for Kristeva, attentiveness to the semiotic uncovers no idyllic rendering of the chora, no sustaining and comforting configuration of maternal presence, no material object in which a subject finds itself and secures its being against threat. After all, although the curtain that rises on the Symbolic order may still bear the impression of a maternal body and retain its scent, the train of the signifier marks that body as irreducibly Other. Consequently, the semiotic legacy on which the subject seeks to draw as it emerges from the maternal container is not marked by nostalgia. Rather, should the subject attempt to contest being-at-a-loss and seek solace in the maternal matrix, an abject nausea, rather than an idyllic commerce with the semiotic, will serve to remind the subject of its orphan status within the Symbolic.

Notwithstanding Kristeva's acknowledgment of the subject's estrangement from its origins, among the terms Kristeva summons to mark the border work of the unconscious are multiple references to the *maternal matrix or body* (1975a, 247; 1981a, 205; 1984c, 27, 241 n. 21). If the child of the Symbolic order is an orphan, forever estranged from the maternal continent, to what does Kristeva refer with maternally referenced language that appears to attest to those origins? In a benchmark contribution to the new Kristeva criticism, Ewa Ziarek addresses this question with great clarity. She notes that the maternal body is "resistant both to symbolic inscription and to the 'presence' of the signifying subject" (1992, 99). For Kristeva, as Ziarek reads her, the maternal matrix cannot be summoned as an object in the practice of a subject, for Kristeva understands that *all* occupants of the maternal space are absent; there is no "one" positioned "there" to signify what is going on (1992, 99). Not productive of a coherent signifying position proper to the Symbolic, the maternal body is a "nonsite." Therefore, when Kristeva speaks of the maternal body, she does not have in mind our mothers, the specific parental figures of our childhood. Kristeva perceives that, however nuanced are our memories of infancy and childhood, we cannot cross the bar of the signifier to name the maternal body as we do our mothers. We cannot establish a direct link between the two, for we know our mothers in the Symbolic order.

However, this does not mean that humans have no commerce with the maternal body. Of course, as Ziarek rightly perceives, on one count, for Kristeva, the maternal body is irrecoverable. Even more radically than the subject, the maternal body *is not:* at most a thoroughfare, a threshold, a filter, the maternal body is no "someone" whom the subject encounters in the space of its difference (Kristeva, 1975a, 238). But, on another count, the subject experiences the maternal matrix as a space of difference that mirrors its own estrangement: the maternal matrix is semiotic chora *and* abject reject, witness to life *and* death, estrangement and fulfillment. However, mirroring the signifying practice of the wanting-to-be of a subject who never is, the maternal matrix necessarily is experienced only as paradox, difference, separation, and division.

Significantly, Kristeva's notion of the maternal body is distinct from Lacan's, who acknowledges the work of maternity almost exclusively in terms of its contribution to the production of the mirror stage that announces the Symbolic order. By contrast, although the maternal matrix about which Kristeva writes does evoke a mirroring function, as Ziarek perspicaciously observes, the maternal body to which Kristeva attests is best understood as the "tain" in the Lacanian mirror: the silver lining at the back of the mirror that produces the specular representation without appearing in it (1992, 100).

Or, to cite a linguistic analogy, the maternal body in Kristeva's work can be likened to the Derridean "trace": just as a silver lining makes possible the mirroring of the mirror, but is not represented directly in the mirror-function, so also is the mark of difference within the evocation of maternal identity "a trace that retains the other *as other* in the same" (1992, 98). It is known by the subject only *at* the limit of the Symbolic order, *at* the bar of the signifier, *at* the unmasterable breach in the Imaginary and the Symbolic (Kristeva, 1975a, 247–49). The subject does not master that breach in being to possess it.

Kristeva's notions of the maternal matrix, abject, and semiotic demonstrate the centrality of alterity to all configurations of the unconscious, establishing a link between these border-marks of the unconscious and *negativity* (1984c, 107). By way of negativity, Kristeva focuses most directly on alterity as process definitive of emergent subjectivity. She demonstrates also the material dynamics of that process and the centrality of labor to it. Encompassing the work of a subject in an economy of signification, negativity attests to the unconscious as a dynamic, fully integrated aspect of subjects' lives within that economy.

With negativity, Kristeva asserts that the practice of absence she has identified previously as definitive of the human condition is an activity of productive dissolution, a living toward death which is characterized by jouissance and rejection (1984c, 145–47).[5] By *jouissance,* Kristeva refers to an excess and surplus of being—inassimilable alterity—that establishes for humans the possibility of creation, communion, newness, pleasure, and transgression. By *rejection,* she refers to other qualities of human living at a loss in language: order, limit, finitude, separation, and expenditure unto death also characterize the lives of those who come to be in a place where they are not. Both processes of negativity are located on a dynamic, economic continuum. Indeed, Kristeva emphasizes that living-at-a-loss is pleasurable (witness a child who in separation from the maternal body takes pleasure in its own excess) even as, in the absence of limit or frame, jouissance gives way to rejection (1984c, 149–51). Both processes are productive and affirming of agency when, through cultural creations (e.g., literature, art) and institutional elaboration, humans establish meaning and value in the space of their absence. Both processes evoke death, for they are necessarily aligned with somatic processes of a human who lives always in the shadow of certain mortality.

Psychoanalytic theory often refers to the dynamics Kristeva observes in her exploration of negativity in terms of the *death-drive.* When Kristeva speaks of the drives, she does not have in mind a mute energetics undertaken by the body in a mysterious, interior space. To the contrary, under her purview, references to the death-drive echo her comments on negativity. Kristeva notes that the drives are material; however, they should not be understood as "solely biological" because they are a function of a "signifying body invested in a practice" (1984c, 167). Perceived rightly as neither "inside" nor "outside" the body, the drives generate meaning as they contribute to a dialectic "where an always absent subject is produced" (1984c, 167).

For Kristeva, terms that attest to the unconscious (abject, semiotic, maternal matrix) and define its work (negativity, death-drive) are very much implicated in the subject's life praxis. Yet, for the novice reader of Kristeva, these terms may not immediately bring to mind a context of active engagement by the subject in its world. For this reason, taking my cue from Kristeva's 1983 essay, "Within the Microcosm of the 'Talking Cure,'" I prefer the term *death-work. Death-work,* unlike other words that Kristeva summons to define the labor of the unconscious, emphatically evokes the social and cultural landscape crucial to the functions of negativity. The term *death-work* serves as a reminder that the human practice of absence, a worldly elaboration by the subject of alterity, estrangement, and lack, is oriented toward mortality. In the face of the subject's desire for the fullness of being, which humans historically have linked with immortality, the subject finds that full presence forever eludes it.

Although Kristeva affirms that the most basic stance of the subject in the world orients it toward death, her work is not ensnared by nihilism. Indeed, Kristeva is committed to the agency of the human subject and seeks, as a practicing psychoanalyst and theorist of the human condition, to enhance the subject's capacity for autonomy and active engagement in its world, notwithstanding its unavoidable mortality. Her advocacy of the subject's agency is evident in her reflections on the unconscious, for Kristeva asserts that the transgressive aspects of negativity—the inassimilable alterity of jouissance—are the prime locus for the subject's assertion of that agency. Although negativity can be conscripted for destructive purposes, as Kristeva demonstrates with her theory of sacrifice, the labor of negativity on behalf of creativity and productive excess also constitutes humanity's best hope for advancing forms of agency and community not built upon a foundation of sacrifice.[6]

That sacrifice is *not* part of the cluster of terms which share a common point of reference in Kristeva's theory of the unconscious should be most carefully noted. To the contrary, death-work is expressly distinguished from sacrifice. Death-work (negativity, death-drive), and its attendant constellation of images (abject, semiotic, maternal matrix) refer to a logic of loss and founding estrangement or alterity which, shaping all human subjects, requires that, in acceding to the Law, they come to be in a place where they are not.

By contrast, sacrifice speaks of problematic instances of death-work that belie such agency. When humans negotiate the terms of their existence according to specific rates of exchange dictated by a sacrificial economy, their death-work is conscripted to hostile forces. Although Kristeva observes nothing in the human condition that mandates this occurrence, under such circumstances death-work—the loss-management that is necessary for all humans to undertake—becomes murderous.

III. The Lacanian Context Enfleshed: Kristeva's Theory of Sacrifice

In observing the work of the unconscious, Kristeva's attention is drawn to that which is material and heterogeneous in signifying systems. Staying with that work as Lacan does not, Kristeva not only uncovers roots of human agency in the unconscious (jouissance of negativity) but also explores further than does Lacan a fragility of the human subject associated with its death-work: the abject image, the paradox of the maternal matrix, and the semiotic trace witness to a persistent fading and instability in the subject's life. For the subject faces immense challenges in its efforts to accede to the Symbolic order. As Kristeva continues to investigate this phenomenon, she begins to perceive the uneasy labor of the unconscious anew. Not only does it become clear to her that the material processes of negativity account for the human vulnerability to violence, but also she sees that these processes are deeply embroiled in the work of a sacrificial economy. Moreover, on close examination, Kristeva finds that sexual difference is wholly implicated in the transformation of death-work into sacrifice, with historically onerous consequences for women.

Where does Kristeva observe circumstances that lead her to these conclusions? Kristeva sees a sacrificial thesis emerge when she observes maternally marked contours of our linguistic and cultural codes. Attending to these codes, she traces the work of the unconscious in culture, at a bridge, as it were, that spans psyche and culture. There, she locates patterns of violence, detects the ongoing transformation of death-work, and establishes connections between death-work and sacrifice. Questions abound for Kristeva as she departs from a strict Lacanian context of inquiry to claim her original voice as a preeminent theorist of sacrifice. How and why do humans turn living-at-a-loss into living sacrificially? What steps do subjects take in their death-work which transform their labor into murderous acts, producing a sacrificial economy? And how and why do they so often make women their victims? As answers to these questions emerge from the Kristevan corpus, they form a thesis with compelling implications for feminist theorists.

That humans adjudicate the terms of their existence on the base of a sacrificial contract (1981a, 200) is revealed, Kristeva suggests, on those occasions when subjects experience boundary failure, a *thetic crisis* which poses a radical threat to subjectivity. What is the thetic crisis or boundary failure? We recall that for Kristeva, as for Lacan, the subjects of the Symbolic order are divided. They achieve a sense of inner coherence and secure for themselves a pretence of unity, on the one hand, by investing in mirror images at whose sites they establish themselves and, on the other hand, by bounding (repressing) anything that would pose a challenge to these investments. Boundary failure ensues when subjects' carefully crafted images fail, threatening to return the subjects to the inchoate chaos of their origins. All kinds of situations may precipitate boundary failure. Kristeva asserts that not only intimate and familial relationships may initiate this failure, as psychoanalysis regularly has observed, but global factors as well: economic and political disarray, cultural and social conflict also set the stage for boundary failure.[7]

Whatever the precipitating factors, according to Kristeva, boundary failure or the impending threat of failure leads humans to reenact the moments when the most archaic markers of identity are drawn at the somatic hinge of being. In repetition of a primordial conflict, they return to primary narcissism: a fluctuation of inside/outside, pleasure/pain, word/deed. In turmoil, they prepare to engage forces of abjection, which they perceive no longer as neatly bounded. Their conflict has *mimetic* overtones. Further, it has *maternal marks,*[8] recalling clashes of a nascent subject who struggles for position in the world when the stakes are "me or mommy." The mimetic aspects of the confrontation explain the escalation of violence in the wake of boundary failure. The maternal markings account for the introduction of sexual difference into that struggle. Both are crucial to Kristeva's discovery of how death-work becomes sacrificial.

Kristeva observes that the nascent subject's initial ascent to the Symbolic is not neatly or harmoniously accomplished. Rather, in the uncertain space of primary narcissism, a *mimetic crisis* precipitates the differentiation of the subject from the maternal continent (1987a, 23). The battle is characterized by mimesis because the maternal body mirrors for the subject, in a dynamic and wholly threatening fashion, its own division. The maternal body—threshold, paradox, division—and its abject marks (diverse material debris) are contested by the subject who struggles for differentiation from a matrix that threatens to subsume it. For a subject who is not yet one, the maternal space displays multiple marks of mimetic terror: it threatens as abyss, dividing wall, or suffocating vise. Only one can emerge victorious from this conflict. And the not-yet-a-subject seeks, by repressing difference, to be that one. Accession to language will mark its victory, for signs will enable the subject to incorporate and subsume difference—which, after all, is its own—throttle the threat posed by mimesis, and emerge victorious before its newly minted image.

With this scenario, Kristeva recognizes logical connections between experiences of the subject on two planes: language and space. On one level, the resolution of mimetic conflict is witnessed in the subject's use of language (the abject gives way to the object). But, on another level, the subject acquires space in the world because it successfully represses the space of another.

Kristeva asserts that the maternal body dies in order that the subject might live (1989, 27). Indeed, death-work oriented toward matricide is the founding defensive strategy of the subject, an initial bounding practice by means of which the subject emerges from the chaos of its origins to assert squatter's rights in the Symbolic order. But, if, with language, the embattled subject achieves high ground, establishing itself at the site of its image and vanquishing the mimetic demons of its past, the subject does not necessarily close forever its account with the past. Kristeva contends that boundary failure places the subject once again in the throes of mimetic conflict. Moreover, on such occasions, the subject's death-work historically is linked to sacrifice.

How does boundary failure place subjects in the grip of a mimetic crisis? When subjects confront a thetic crisis or fear its imminent announcement, do they set out to survey a scene in which they find themselves in order to reestablish control over their circumstances? No. This scenario distorts matters because it presupposes the existence of subjects. But a thetic crisis is problematic precisely because no subjects of crisis are to be found who could act to resolve it. Boundary failure means that, failing to find themselves, subjects suddenly are confronted with their own *mé-connaissance.* Lacking place, their estrangement in being threatens now to become radical loss. What are these veritable nonsubjects to do? The mimetic demon that first mirrored for them their difference must be engaged again. The abject markers of this demon must be exposed, challenged, and, if the subjects are to reclaim their boundaries, defeated.

How do subjects of the Symbolic order labor against death, when their claim on that order has been made tenuous by circumstances of boundary failure? Kristeva understands that, just as the universal extremities of human subjectivity are mitigated by the Symbolic, invoking order in the oppositional differentiation of names and roles, so also are they mitigated at the edges of the Symbolic order, when subjects find investments they have made in this order threatened. As a consequence, their activities on behalf of order attest not only to secondary repression, represented by accomplishments of the mirror stage which they seek to sustain, but also to ongoing commerce with primary repression (the tain in the mirror). Under circumstances of radical threat, subjects act not only to reassert positions in language. In the shadow of primary repression once again, they call forth also the world-creating gesture which first made their self-possession possible: their death-work invokes the maternal body.

How is maternally oriented death-work, which is associated with a thetic crisis and mimetic conflict, transformed into sacrifice? For the tiny, nascent subject, death-work most likely is a measured act of violence. Invoking its alimentary powers, summoning the resources of its bowels and digestive tract, the human infant wrests from the maternal matrix the control necessary for its survival. By contrast, under circumstances of boundary failure, death-work is more often an immoderate violence. Historically within human experience, it literally evokes sacrifice. Under threat of a radical loss of place, subjects turn to soma in order to reinscribe, resecure, and commit to memory the border-securing work of negativity that first saw them emerge out of the mimetic violence of a primordial difference into the world of the sign. That a mimetic crisis has precipitated the differentiation of the nascent subject from the maternal continent and has occasioned language, appears to make possible the immediate, and global, expansion of discursive claims on the maternal body. A violence that attended the crisis of infant individuation is "writ large" in culture: phylogeny recapitulates ontogeny. Death-work becomes sacrifice (1984c, 70).

When subjects in the throes of boundary failure invoke a sacrificial strategy, on whom do they visit their boundary-securing violence, and what are its effects? Kristeva links primary patterns of sacrifice with patriarchy.[9] As viewed by Kristeva, sacrifice is the unhappy result of a converging set of circumstances. She cites the basic social contract under which humans live. This contract bears not only the imprint of the Law of the Symbolic order (the Law of absence, which, in the Name of the Father, positions subjects in the world under conditions of estrangement), but also the persistent residue of an abject maternal matrix, notwithstanding subjects' efforts to bound it (repress it) in the course of their accession to the Symbolic order. When these two factors are forged in the crucible of patriarchy, the social contract becomes a sacrificial contract with very different consequences for women than for men. Fusion of a patriarchal code of sacrifice with a Symbolic Law of absence places women at absolute risk of violence when they are made to bear abject marks of the maternal body. So pervasive is the patriarchal influence on the social contract that Kristeva believes we truly do not know what men's and women's roles might be if the logic of separation legislated by the Law of the Symbolic order were to be inscribed in society nonsacrificially (1981a, 199).[10] We do know, at this sociohistorical conjuncture, that a sacrificial code frames contestations of maternal loss. Any woman is at risk when subjects under siege enact again the subject-securing work of negativity that first saw them emerge out of the shadow of the maternal matrix into language. Any woman may be marked for murder when subjects who struggle to resecure their roles in the Symbolic invest her body with the effects of that abject struggle and train or force it under the edict of patriarchy and the laws of a sacrificial economy to emit evidence of the abject matrix of origins.

At first, Kristeva's assertion that the mimetic conflict she associates with nascent subjects' emergence in the world and separation from the maternal matrix is writ large in the world appears problematic. For earlier, this chapter has stated that Kristeva grants subjects no access to the maternal body. In detecting a common pattern in mimetic conflict at two junctures—that immediately preceding subjects' accession to language and that emerging with subjects' boundary failure in the Symbolic—Kristeva appears prepared to allow subjects access to the maternal body through resources of the Symbolic order, notwithstanding her earlier refusal of that option. But, on closer examination, we note that Kristeva remains committed to her initial position. She does not conflate the maternal body with signs of maternity in the Symbolic order. Although embattled subjects desire to bring death-work under the force of signs, becoming creators rather than creatures of language, because they are shaped by an unalterable *mé-connaissance,* their desire remains unfulfilled. Their death-work is not transformed into immortal play with a mother they have captured with their signs. Instead, their violent gestures evoke only a maternal abject.

What are abject marks of maternity? Encountered in sacrificial movements so inconclusive and tentative that apparently they must be undertaken again and again, they emerge when subjects reach down into bodies to reenact their initial creation as subjects of language. With material, visceral gestures, subjects return to the bar of the signifier, "killing substance to make it signify" (1984c, 75). Marks such as blood, bodily fluids, and other refuse attest at the very edges of language to boundary failure and its contestation. Within a sacrificial economy, invocations of these abject marks are notably violent.

How do we know who is at risk of being marked for death? Biologically conferred potential for motherhood and historically and culturally specific traits of mothers are not reliable indicators in themselves. Moreover, the most common tools of psychoanalytic theory are largely ineffectual when employed to identify potential victims. Psychoanalytic theory, most often fixed on the drama of sexual difference in the Symbolic order, has theorized familial relations and patterns of sexual objectification. It has concentrated on language codes that position "boys" and "girls," "men" and "women" in the world. By contrast, the realm of the abject comes into view when subjects lose their grip on the Symbolic order. Because signs fade when the focus is abjection, those who would track the abject's lethal aspects learn little if they highlight only the Symbolic order and its sign-work; they need also to bring the margins of that order into view. There, sacrificial currents can be observed. Even though the abject contours of these currents must be read through signs, they are not captured by signs. They recall a more archaic script: a story of subjects beset by boundary failure who cast their net of violence and set out to capture that which threatens them. In patriarchy, sacrificial currents swirl most often around women. They become victims of sacrifice when, found to bear abject marks, they are made hostage to others' dramatic efforts to repeat individuation from the maternal matrix.

Kristeva does acknowledge that she always already arrives too late at the scene to directly witness such events, which replicate the birth and death of signification. Any evidence of maternal sacrifice is always circumstantial. For the maternal "body," naysayer of the Symbolic, which the subject seeks to capture, is glimpsed only for an instant, at a point of rupture in the Symbolic order made possible by a certain frailty in the Law of absence. Apart from a phantasy of maternal return that evokes in the subject nausea, an anxious cry, a perilous rage, no evidence persists of one whose sacrifice makes being possible. No access to that one is granted by the Law of the Symbolic order, for she necessarily is its hidden support: she *is* the very space of struggle that brings the cultural order into existence (1984c, 27).

Because Kristeva is denied access to the scene of sacrifice, which could offer direct proof of matricide, that Kristeva persists in linking abject conflict with a *maternal* matrix may, at first glance, appear problematic. Should Kristeva elect a neutral term such as *matrix of origin* or *presubject matrix* to describe the site revisited by subjects under siege? When Kristeva refers to the maternal matrix, does she not drag a sign of sexually differentiated existence across the bar of the signifier, notwithstanding her claims to treat the subject's space of origin as inaccessible by way of signs? After all, when Kristeva has described inaugural boundary work undertaken by nascent subjects, she has emphasized that the characterizing marks of the matrix in which this labor is undertaken do not belong to a mother. This matrix is not yet sign and object; it is not a mother's body. Instead, the identifying marks of the maternal matrix belong to the bounding mechanism of emergent subjectivity itself: in its labor, that which is not-yet-a-mother and not-yet-a-subject are differentiated, establishing necessary preconditions for sign creation. Movements within this matrix initiate patterns or styles of difference, but they are not yet patterns of sexual difference. Only on entry into the Symbolic order will these styles be articulated in sexually differentiated ways. Should not Kristeva observe the same limits on signification when discussing subjects' return visits to their field of origin, as she does when describing their earliest sojourn there?

If citizens of the Symbolic order who have attained proficiency in their associations with others were seen to rest comfortably in their citizenship, Kristeva would probably not be at pains to describe the matrix as she does. But the force of Kristeva's argument, which the term *maternal matrix* well captures, is directed toward showing us that subjects are not on holiday when they return to the site of their earliest boundary work. Instead, they are frantically mobilizing defensive resources under threat of dispossession of their stance in the Symbolic order. Their gestures, not Kristeva's, preferentially invoke maternally marked entities at the very bar of the signifier. Kristeva cannot be said to break any rules of language that subjects have not already set out to break in responding to threats to their being. She invokes the notion of the maternal matrix because she understands that, when subjects find reason to engage in border work, *their* initial movements transpire within an economy of signs in which sexual difference does figure prominently. *Their* actions are not neutral. As a consequence, when Kristeva refers to the maternal matrix she highlights a link others regularly forge between the Imaginary and the Symbolic when, losing their hold on the Symbolic, they revisit nascent efforts at sign formation. At the very bar of the signifier, when subjects grasp for meaning as signs fade, their gestures accord maternity a central point of place. Perceiving that the bodies of women attest to their continent of origin, they prepare to wrest from them new possibilities for being. Kristeva wants to examine and explain these gestures and the marks they invoke, not obscure them with misleading terminology.[11]

Following Kristeva, this project emphasizes that when death-work is placed in service to a sacrificial economy, abject marks accrue to women. Therefore, when marks of the abject are referenced in this project, they are often associated with the term *Mother,* which is capitalized in order to distinguish it from other signs of mothers. The Mother is a key effect of sexual differentiation within a patriarchal system that secures its boundaries (intimate, social, global) against threat when some bodies are invested with marks of sacrifice. Because the vanquished abject of subjects' struggles against boundary failure is described here as Mother, a vital point is underscored: sacrificial violence is close to home. Mothers, sisters, daughters, and friends are among those who are violated when death-work is drawn on sacrificially in patriarchy to maintain order.

Because Kristeva demonstrates that tales of subject formation not only summon images of subjects who resolutely assume roles in the Symbolic order, but also invoke images of refuse they encounter in their perilous journeys along the edges of that order, she shows that the abject is worthy of sustained attention. Precisely because the maternal matrix is not definitively set aside by humans in the course of their development but remains the hidden, economic support of the Law, Kristeva shows that images of abjection must be examined whenever, in a subject's struggle to be in a cultural order, they frame the bounding of order from disorder. If the cultural sites and intertextual practices created by these acts testify to "the other facet of religious, moral, and ideological codes on which rest the sleep of individuals and the breathing spells of societies" (1982, 209), they witness also to humankind's persistent failure to come to terms, however indirectly, with the death-work that is that order's secret cause. In all our refusals and contestations, those whose bodies are shaped by founding codes of abjection in sway to an economy of sacrifice—historically the bodies of women—are at risk.[12]

Kristeva's call to attend to the abject is heeded in the chapters that follow, sustaining the sacrificial thesis advanced here. Throughout, Kristeva's work illuminates key themes cited in the introduction to this project as decisive for productive analyses of the problem of violence against women. In establishing an economic point of reference for violence against women, she explains systematic aspects of violence as well as its intractability and global expansiveness. With the notion of boundary failure, she also thoughtfully addresses the problem of substitutionary violence: persons who perceive that familial, economic, or political problems pose a radical threat to their continued existence can exchange angry and fearful words for more powerful weapons of response, engaging in protracted acts of violence. Finally, because Kristeva explains how sexual difference figures in economic arrangements that produce patriarchy and its sacrificial traditions, her theory accounts for the predominance of women among the victims of violence. Therefore, in multiple respects, Kristeva offers a compelling account of violence which feminist critics of violence can ill afford to ignore.

IV. A Critical Context: Kristeva and Feminist Theory

Although this project is inspired by Kristeva's work, a number of feminist theorists do not find Kristeva's writings compelling. They contend that, in drawing on transhistorical structures of the unconscious in her analyses of violence, Kristeva necessarily represents women's oppression as inevitable and social change as impossible. Their criticisms fall into two camps. Each condemns Kristeva's appeal to the unconscious as the locus of human agency. Feminist theorists in one group read Kristeva as a social constructionist for whom the unconscious is a mechanism for the internalization of social norms. They have reservations about Kristeva because they perceive that Kristeva brings insufficient clarity to her accounts of agency-enhancing strategic interventions in social processes. They assert that Kristeva privileges men's agency in society and therefore is incapable of speaking adequately to feminism's concerns. Another group believes that when Kristeva turns to the unconscious in search of agency-enhancing resources, she turns wholly away from the social context. These critics assert that Kristeva links emancipatory agency with a prediscursive libidinal economy, home to the unconscious. Because it remains unclear to them how women might draw on this economy to enhance their agency in daily commerce with others, they too dismiss Kristeva's work as inadequate to feminism's interests.[13]

Elizabeth Grosz and Judith Butler are key representatives of these two schools of criticism. For Grosz, when Kristeva advocates a *cultural space of agency,* she empowers only the masculine subject to assert agency. For Butler, when Kristeva links emancipatory agency with a *prediscursive libidinal economy,* she bypasses the cultural arena in which are to be found the requisite tools of free agency. Both Grosz and Butler focus their attention on Kristeva's notion of the unconscious and find it problematic. Offering different criticisms, Grosz and Butler concur in their conclusions: in Kristeva's hands, one who would be an agent is incarcerated, confined to a prison of the unconscious located in the shadow of a sex/gender divide. Grosz places Kristeva on the side of gender, believing that she consigns agency exclusively to culture (an arena of socially constructed identities). Butler places her on the side of sex, believing that Kristeva assigns agency exclusively to nature (a realm of prediscursive sexual drives). Disagreeing concerning the appropriate placement of Kristeva on a polarized field of sex and gender, Grosz and Butler agree that, wherever she stands, her perspective excludes effective agency.

Even though Grosz and Butler rightly acknowledge the centrality of Kristeva's notion of the unconscious to her theorizing, they fail to appreciate that Kristeva offers a treatment of sexual difference and its deployment in a signifying economy that effectively subverts the paralyzing dichotomies about which Grosz and Butler express concern. Nor do they discern that Kristeva actually advances Grosz's and Butler's emancipatory objectives for feminist theory. Kristeva does not bifurcate the unconscious along a sex/gender divide. Rather, Kristeva traces the unconscious and its agency to subjects whose sexually differentiated identities emerge dynamically when boundary-making acts establish a signifying field: a site of shared intertextual practices. The work of these subjects—negativity—exhibits emancipatory and limiting, productive and constraining potential.

Noting possibilities in their labor for assertions of agency, Kristeva recognizes also constraints on agency. She observes that negativity is most seriously subverted when it is placed in service to a sacrificial economy. On those occasions, sexual difference does become implicated in violence. However, Kristeva does not construe sexually differentiated violence in terms of sex (a libidinous force of terror) or gender (a violent discourse). Instead, she understands that bodies which are sexually differentiated enact the signifying practices of the sacrificial economy. They are that economy's discursive product. Differentially producing its subjects, this economy brutally bounds bodies as it orders meaning and power. Thus, in the very act of coding bodies sacrificially, this economy functions to engender sexual difference, with onerous consequences for those who receive the abject mark of maternity.

Feminist theorists who draw on Kristeva's work need not fear entrapment on either side of a sex/gender divide. Kristeva enables feminist advocates of women's agency to recognize that they can promote nondichotomizing interventions when they analyze violence against women in terms of systemic connections among subjects. Falling on neither side of a sex/gender divide, these connections are forged by subjects who enact a signifying economy framed by sacrifice. Focusing on intertextual practices in that economy, supporters of women can challenge its violent aspects and promote strategies that advance women's agency when they free death-work from service to a sacrificial agenda. This thesis is explicated in further conversation with Grosz and Butler.

A. Kristeva and Social Constructionism

Writing in *Volatile Bodies: Toward a Corporeal Feminism,* Elizabeth Grosz treats Kristeva as a "social constructionist" (1994, 16). Grosz claims that social constructionists are committed to a "fixed and ahistorical notion of the body" (1994, 16). Grosz submits that, for them, "the mind is regarded as a social, cultural, and historical object" while the body remains "naturalistic" and "precultural" (1994, 17). Grosz finds this approach to bodies troublesome because it renders their histories invisible. Overlooked are bodies as sites of contestation as well as specificities of bodies which, in diverse ways, contribute to "the production of knowledge systems, regimes of representation, cultural production, and socioeconomic exchange" (1994, 19).

Problematic also for Grosz are social constructionists' strategies for enhancing women's agency. In making bodies mere "raw material" for the ideological work of culture, these theorists purportedly intend to "neutralize the sexually specific body" (1994, 17) through social reorganization (including child-raising). Dispensing with bodies by relegating them to an unexamined substructure of society, the proponents of social constructionism prepare to enact social change on a platform erected over that subfloor. This platform, imbued with a feminist ideology by these social constructionists, is newly hospitable to women's agency.

Significantly, Grosz believes that claimants to social constructionism, such as Kristeva, do not distinguish between the "'real' biological body" and its cultural representations in order to subvert or overturn the sex/gender divide. Rather, they summon these distinctions in order to assign to the body meanings and values that nullify its effects (1994, 17). Inclined to treat the biological body as a mute datum or base, social constructionists make social change dependent on a simple exchange: they would replace a cultural superstructure hostile to women with an emancipatory superstructure, "leaving the base more or less as is" (1994, 17). Grosz submits that the group of feminist theorists who are social constructionists, including Kristeva, treat the sexed body as a fixed, and essentially benign, category, either wholly irrelevant to the transforming work of culture or the neutral "vehicle for psychological change" (1994, 17).[14]

Grosz makes Kristeva's categories of the semiotic and Symbolic prime examples of a sex/gender dichotomy inhospitable to women's agency. On Grosz's reading of Kristeva, "the semiotic provides the energy for social and signifying upheavals which transgress the limits of the symbolic, reorganizing them into other, different forms" (1989, 98). Nevertheless, Grosz insists that the semiotic is only a vehicle, jazzed up, if you will, for the cultural work of the Symbolic order. But for the "possibilities of expression" (1989, 97) provided by the Symbolic, the semiotic vehicle valorized by Kristeva idles aimlessly, effecting no social change.

Grosz demonstrates this point by citing Kristeva's views toward motherhood. According to Grosz, Kristeva treats maternity as "organic, a-social, presignifying" (1989, 80). An aspect of the semiotic, maternity does not exist in the Symbolic order. Therefore, no agency accrues to women as bearers of children, for maternal actions are governed by the "species' requirement of reproduction" (1989, 81). If women assert agency in relation to their children, they do so only as architects of the social order.

However, Grosz does not believe that Kristeva places any confidence in women's capacity to assert leadership within that order. Of the cultural discourses that express the semiotic, Grosz would have Kristeva claim that only religion and art productively serve the social order. And religion and art do so only when in the hands of the men who guard the Symbolic (1989, 98). Maintaining that Kristeva cedes the task of cultural representation of semiotic value wholly to men, Grosz asserts that Kristeva believes "only men can transgress the symbolic because only they are subjects with a position to subvert" (1989, 68). The masculine subject of the Symbolic order serves as exclusive guide to social and cultural transformation (1989, 89). As a consequence, Grosz finds Kristeva's reflections on agency potentially antifeminist in their implications (1989, 95–96). According to Grosz, if Kristeva were to seek a new social order, more welcoming of women than is the current order, she would have women defer to men's directives: men would drive the vehicle of social change and women, seated beside them, would go along for the ride.

Grosz's exposition of Kristeva's theory is problematic. Most regrettable is Grosz's assignment of Kristeva and Nancy Chodorow to a common category of social constructionism. Because American readers of feminist theory often are well acquainted with Chodorow and are largely unfamiliar with Kristeva, when Grosz places Kristeva beside Chodorow, her gesture may prove especially misleading to them. Although the shared grouping suggests that the theories are similar, Kristeva's and Chodorow's theories are actually dissimilar. Moreover, in categorizing Kristeva as a social constructionist whose limited vision falls short of the emancipatory objectives of feminist theory, Grosz overlooks aspects of Kristeva's theory that not only support Grosz's own goals for feminist theory, but also advance them.

That Chodorow and Kristeva advance distinct claims about agency becomes readily apparent when their respective views of desire are analyzed. When Chodorow attends to processes whereby the social structure of parenting is reproduced, she identifies the construction of a set of needs that female children seek to meet through forging relationships with others and that male children seek to meet by detaching themselves from commitment to others (1989, 109–10). Chodorow finds that the production of such needs in processes of child development prepares females for a role of exclusive parenting (1978, 175–77) and males for socially independent roles that are well suited for the work place but not for parenting (1978, 186–89). For Chodorow, gendered personalities both reflect and recreate the gendered division of labor. A reconfiguration of the social structure of parenting, linked with the reconfiguration of needs, will free women and men from rigid gender-role expectations which traditionally have ascribed parenting exclusively to women. Changes in parenting roles will also create more balanced personalities in children (1978, 217–19).

The work of the unconscious for Chodorow is primarily a function of ideology critique: when children internalize norms of a feminist ideology, these norms replace ones which are less hospitable to women. By means of this housecleaning of the unconscious, space is found for new residents. Subsequently, when children internalize tenets of a feminist ideology, they act in ways that encourage the expansion of feminist politics in adult society.

By contrast, although Kristeva also focuses on processes by which a subject's needs are constructed, she does not believe that a reconfiguration of the social structure of parenting promises to meet the human subject's most basic desire. Precisely because identity-failure is constitutive in humans—to be human is to endlessly repeat and relive a history of coming to be, without ever wholly accomplishing it—Kristeva doubts whether any direct purchase on human identity is possible. Because the human subject is always already at a loss, efforts at social construction and reconstruction, such as Chodorow champions, cannot issue in a new human subject who basks in the light of conquered loss and fulfilled desire, even if the parenting received by the subject is wholly egalitarian. On Kristeva's terms, the human subject is not *deprived* by lack—of shared parenting, or enlightened education—but is *constituted* by lack (1981a, 198). The unconscious circles that lack and marks it as an intertextual practice. Consequently, Chodorow and Kristeva direct their attention differently. Chodorow identifies that which is wanting among humans as egalitarian family relations and recommends that such relations be promoted in feminist ideology. By contrast, Kristeva knows that the element lacking in human society, on which she focuses, is forever out of reach.

Kristeva's and Chodorow's distinct concepts of the unconscious highlight their differences. Chodorow finds testimony to the unconscious in male and female longings for a return to a state of oneness with the maternal body. Currently, these human longings are articulated in parent-child relations that divide rigidly along gender lines. Family configurations prepare men to enter adulthood deficient in their ability to forge relationships, whereas women enter adulthood deficient in their capacity for autonomy. Shared parenting should produce balance: a capacity for individuated connectedness or autonomous relationality in both genders that recapitulates their origins at an appropriate distance. Oedipal asymmetries, defensive reactions, fears, and repressions will weaken dramatically, if not disappear altogether (1978, 218).

By contrast, Kristeva does not attribute to the unconscious processes of socialization to adulthood that produce some persons who need others too much and some persons who need others not enough. Rather, as Teresa Brennan notes, Kristeva observes in the work of the unconscious a process of becoming that must occur if there is to be for a subject an other at all (1992, 69). Kristeva does not attend so much to a gendered subject's capacity for a balance of autonomy and dependence *in relations* with others as she does to the subject's capacity to hold the fragments of being together *in speech* (1987a, 26). Only to the extent that the subject is able to manage loss in language will there be a world for it. The coming to be of a subject in language becomes the necessary precondition of being in the world, for speech is essential to the boundary-creating enterprise whereby there comes to be an "other" for a "one" who attains a place in the world by virtue of the engendering of difference.

According to Kristeva, one who harbors a desire for a return to origins maintains a desire that, if fulfilled, would necessitate the dissolution of the subject itself. As a consequence of her belief, Kristeva must emphasize, as Chodorow does not, that the unconscious is fundamentally fractured. Identity of being is always already irretrievably elsewhere. When Kristeva refers to signifying processes that bound the semiotic and the Symbolic, she traces the contours—the linguistic space—of a lack that shapes human identity. Mappable by a psychoanalytic poetics or semiotics *only* on the fractured borders of a linguistic space, the *failure to be* (negativity) that haunts human identity—a desire torn between a longing to be oneself and a longing for a return to origins—is constitutive, not derivative, of human identity (1984c, 121).

That when these longings are thematized by the Symbolic they bear the mark of sexual difference—including representations of the maternal body which promise both life and death for the human subject—does not alter their phantasmatic nature. Although those who bear the sign of the lost body may conjure up for others a nostalgia for and threat of union with parental jouissance, human subject formation will not be altered if a subject's mother and father assume egalitarian roles as parents. The subject, in movement away from the ambiguity of abjection, will still ascend to the Symbolic always already at a loss, remaining "on trial" and "in process" (1984c, 101). Notwithstanding changes in parenting roles that are promoted by feminist ideology, the unalterable negativity of the unconscious will endure, shaped forever by a subject's longing for and ambivalence toward its body of origin. Kristeva's interest in the dangers that accompany any evocation of maternity rests with this persistent negativity, not with a trajectory that would link enhanced or depleted fortunes of women with the equitable or unequitable division of diaper duty.

This is not to say that a feminist theory modeled on Kristeva's work offers a fatalistic account of current relations among women and men. If Kristeva believes that the unalterable destiny of humankind is found in the division of being that creates a human subject as a being who lacks—who *is* in absence—she does not assume that the tactics humans have employed to manage loss are inevitable. Indeed, Kristeva deplores strategies that have advanced social order—institutional and intersubjective—by violently summoning tropes of maternal abjection, forcing women not only to live their own loss—the death-work that all humans must undertake—but also to bear the primary weight of others' death-work when contestations of loss are coded according to the dictates of a sacrificial economy. Kristeva maintains that patriarchy, the consequence of a loss-management strategy which ascribes to women the principal impact of the original separation that accompanies the human apprenticeship to language and culture, can be challenged. No longer should societies contest that loss by differentially employing sexual difference to secure their boundaries against threat. No longer should they force women to assume marks of sacrificial maternity. Means should be found to advance emancipatory agency among women and to make the feminist vision of a transformed society a reality (1981a, 207).

Even so, because Kristeva's theory places negativity at the heart of processes of human individuation, she does not advance a theory of agency which promotes new dynamics in family relations, as has Chodorow. She invites feminist theory to concentrate on a different dynamic when it considers questions of agency: negativity deployed as death-work or as sacrifice. Consequently, we should not be surprised that Kristeva, when asked in an interview about Dinnerstein's and Chodorow's resolutions of the problem of women's inaccessibility to agency within culture, maintains that the locus of her concern—the "fascinated rejection" of the maternal body and the forging of a sacrificial contract—lies at some distance from Chodorow's interests (1984d, 124).

Kristeva's comments on fascinated rejection render problematic Grosz's criticism of Kristeva's theory. Rather than confirming Kristeva's complicity with the polarizing tenets of social constructionism, these comments indicate that Kristeva actually contributes to principles for a nondichotomous vision of embodied subjectivity upheld by Grosz (1994, 22–24). Like Grosz, Kristeva does not believe that corporeality should be born as a burden by one sex (historically, woman). Like her, she understands that the body is a site of social, political, cultural, and geographical inscription. Like her, Kristeva advances a nonreductive articulation between the biological and the psychological that attests to a lived body while escaping binarisms of nature and culture, self and other, the psychic and the social. Most significant, Kristeva helpfully augments Grosz's own vision with her perspicacious reflections on the sexually differentiated violence which regularly ensnares the volatile bodies that Grosz would have us celebrate.

What does Kristeva mean by fascinated rejection? With this paradoxical term, Kristeva refers to intertextual practices of negativity—jouissance and rejection—undertaken by the subject. These practices attest to the work of the unconscious. A maternally marked metaphor, fascinated rejection marks the emergence in the world of a nascent subject in process and on trial. If fascinated rejection summons for the subject a notion of phantasmatic union with a maternally marked figure, it invokes also for the subject awareness of a threat which bounds its history. That menace is never wholly vanquished even though it is constantly, emphatically denied. In the shadow of that threat, historically, fascinated rejection has alluded to the stance of one who would become the master of its house by repressing all that is heterogeneous, wholly sacrificing to subjective and societal order all vestiges of the unbounded economy of the semiotic.

When fully explicated, Kristeva's notion of fascinated rejection supports a radically historical and nondichotomous reading of embodiment and sexual difference. Sexual difference emerges as a difference articulated by the subject in its intertextual practices. This subject does not experience its body as "inert, passive, noncultural, and ahistorical" (Grosz, 1994, 19). Rather, in its signifying practices, the subject is fully engaged in diverse struggles common to the Symbolic order. Most significantly, two terms that Kristeva uses, which Grosz would attribute to the sex side of the sex/gender divide—the semiotic and maternity—are displaced from that dichotomy by their implication in fascinated rejection.

The semiotic, on Kristeva's account, is *not* that which falls outside of language: a state of nature, an eternal feminine. Rather, the semiotic is the trace in language of the scission of being that brings the human subject into existence as the being who signifies (1984c, 40–41). The semiotic, a modality of language, is shaped necessarily by the Symbolic. Consequently, the unconscious, whose legacy the semiotic preserves, is not presented topographically by Kristeva as a wordless mother-land; for the unconscious emerges only in the space of words, in the gaps and fissures of language that mark the speech of the "I," belying its coherent, seamless self-representation as a subject fully in possession of itself. Therefore, notwithstanding the claims of her critics, when Kristeva focuses on the semiotic, she does not observe a feminine which has escaped language. Instead, as Jacqueline Rose reminds us, she articulates processes of negativity proper to the subject which language "normally glosses over *on this side* of meaning" (1989, 21).

Kristeva understands that circumstances of estrangement haunt the subject, precluding it from fulfilling its desires. Notwithstanding its quest for certainty, knowledge, and truth that could guarantee identity, the subject circles only loss in language. The moment of fascinated rejection to which Kristeva attends does not enable subjects to seek resolution of their desire outside the Symbolic in the maternal and women who bear her sign, as Grosz has claimed. To the contrary, fascinated rejection turns only on the Symbolic, on the division of being and Law of absence that bound the human subject (1984c, 27). Fixed on that moment, fascinated rejection marks the otherness of the maternal as a particular kind of relation of the Symbolic (Elliot, 1991, 202).

Therefore, Kristeva does not treat maternity as a precultural reality or the semiotic as the province of women, as Grosz has submitted. Rather, the maternity on which fascinated rejection turns, holds to the turn, subverting all dichotomies of sex and gender as it does so. Emblematic of processes in which all subjects participate—a coming to be in a place where they are not—maternity is not dichotomized along a sex/gender divide by Kristeva. Instead, as Kelly Oliver rightly observes, Kristeva treats the maternal function as a "material model of alterity within identity" (1993, 12). Invoking a negativity proper to all productive agency, the material dynamics of maternity—death-work—are a prime instance of the work that produces culture itself and a model of all other labor.

But why does the subject's fascinated rejection historically turn on the sacrifice of the maternal? Even as Kristeva asserts that the Symbolic order precludes humans from returning to the lost territory of the maternal body—that body is always, already a phantasmatic creation of culture—she recognizes specific patterns common to such phantasmatic work. Closely observing the work of negativity which bounds the subject in the world, she insists that, when the maternal body is marked *in* culture as *the* defining border of the intertextual practices that comprise social existence, the reproaches, threats, and fears which characterize this exercise make this body-border a site of contestation.

Kristeva's sacrificial theory is born of this observation. She sets out to bring further evidence of this contest to view so that we might glimpse in the wreckage of language that which has been lost so that the subject might speak and live. As Patricia Elliot eloquently reminds us, Kristeva wants us to more fully appreciate how forces of the Symbolic order have been "mobilized" to deny and hide that loss (1991, 207). Moreover, Kristeva wants those who traditionally have been made to display the sign of loss sacrificially to know something more than they have known before about that process. Kristeva wants to tell the story of a murder, of how the Mother is an effect of a process of sexual differentiation within a social order that secures its boundaries against further loss by violently marking some bodies with the sign of sacrificial maternity, as inspired by the signifying economy that structures that order.

Far from accepting as inevitable a societal order that secures itself against chaos by engaging in the sexually differentiated violation of bodies, Kristeva wants to challenge those processes by which a patriarchal law of sacrifice becomes fused with a Law of absence. Within the necessary constraints of the Symbolic—that system in which humans exist as beings who live always at a loss—Kristeva yet wants those who would refuse to be victims of patriarchy to be able to achieve some point of leverage against that order, "lifting what is sacrificial in the social contract from their shoulders" (1981a, 207). Litanies of loss—death-work—common to the subject should no longer be coded in ways that force women to bear loss sacrificially. Nor should women be constrained by the politics of patriarchal role play to assent to a masquerade of femininity promoted by a phallic economy as the condition for garnering a truce with the sacrificial order which might protect them from its most violent excesses.

Clearly distinguishable from social constructionism, Kristeva's theory is notable on several counts. She recognizes, by way of the category of the unconscious, the fictional status of a self-possessed, unified subject. She identifies, in the semiotic, indirect testimony to a subject who, articulated in the midst of multiple intertextual practices—at once linguistic and corporeal—is always already on trial. She unearths that disunity in being (negativity) which a sacrificial order (patriarchy) has denied as it has secured its own power by consolidating multiple discourses of death-work in a master-text. Escaping binarism in her account, she identifies processes by which, under the dictates of a sacrificial economy, the irrational moments, contradictions, and threats that shape human life have been explicated, coding women's bodies so that they function as a primary currency in that economy. She examines how the division of being that is humankind has, as a consequence, been managed and secured against threat within human society when violence has been directed against women. In all of these ways, Kristeva offers a succinct history of bodies and a compelling record of a crisis that still shapes human existence. Feminist theorists who advocate women's emancipatory agency can ill afford to ignore her words; indeed, Kristeva's theory can most helpfully inform their efforts.

B. Kristeva and a Libidinal Economy

If the previous commentary has set the terms for successfully negotiating Kristeva's release from the prison of dichotomous thinking to which Grosz has consigned her, viewed from a different perspective, Kristeva remains a captive. Citing other grounds for criticism, some feminist theorists assert that

Kristeva is hostage to polarities of sex and gender that prevent her from contributing to feminism's emancipatory goals. For example, Kristeva's theory remains problematic for Judith Butler. At issue is Kristeva's appeal to the unconscious as the subversive instrument of agency. Butler understands Kristeva to define the unconscious in terms of instinctual drives. As Butler reads Kristeva, an original, libidinal multiplicity of the semiotic, which she associates with a repressed maternal terrain and a prepaternal causality, can facilitate subversion of the Symbolic order (1990, 79–86).

Butler submits that Kristeva fails to perceive that the unconscious on which she focuses labors on behalf of the Symbolic order. Kristeva does not understand that the unconscious actually is produced by the paternal, social order as a tactic in its own self-amplification, which it conceals through convenient recourse to the notion of a prediscursive, libidinal economy oriented toward the maternal body. By virtue of that appeal, the paternal order extends and conceals its own investments, deploying the institutions of compulsory heterosexuality and motherhood to permanently legitimate its regime (1990, 92).[15] When Kristeva clings to a biological archaism, evoking a semiotic order of the unconscious (a law of the body) that, predating the Law and its power, serves as an extracultural base (maternal terrain) for its subversion, she actually promotes the paternal order (1990, 87). For that order has created the very notions of the body and maternity to which Kristeva appeals in seeking grounds outside of culture for emancipating initiatives. Instead of posing a feminist challenge to the sociosymbolic order, supportive of emancipating agency, Kristeva only strengthens it.

Butler's criticism of Kristeva is a powerful and nuanced account. However, Butler errs in her understanding of Kristeva's theory of the unconscious. Not perceiving it accurately, she too readily dismisses it. Butler's oversight is regrettable: were she to consider Kristeva's work more closely, she would see that it contributes to critical work supportive of emancipatory practices which Butler, among others, promotes. The dissent from Butler proffered here focuses on a key aspect of Kristeva's theory which Butler finds problematic: the abject.[16]

When Butler considers Kristeva's reflections on body-bounding and the compelling images of filth and pollution associated with its abject labor, Butler initially describes Kristeva's account quite sympathetically. Butler acknowledges that, in *Powers of Horror,* Kristeva describes the human body in nondichotomous terms. It is not a ready surface awaiting signification, but rather is a set of borders subject to signification (1990, 133–34). Absent from her initial account of Kristeva's treatment of abjection is any sense that the abject is problematically implicated in a precultural, ahistorical, libidinal economy that Butler finds suspect.

Nevertheless, Butler remains wary of Kristeva's body metaphors, for the nascent subject's efforts to emerge out of the inchoate chaos of its origins take a place in the signifying economy. Believing that notions of inner and outer boundaries of the subject on which the axes of differentiation turn unnecessarily invite binary literalism, Butler reminds her reader that when blood, excrement, and milk are invoked as markings of body boundaries they "remain linguistic terms" (1990, 134). Apparently apprehensive that signs which mediate the boundaries of the body will evoke a suspect material topos, Butler offers firm instruction in the appropriate reading of this body-work:

> The question is: from what strategic position in public discourse and for what reasons has the trope of interiority and the disjunctive binary of inner/outer taken hold? In what language is "inner space" figured? What kind of figuration is it, and through what figure of the body is it signified? How does a body figure on its surface the very invisibility of its hidden depth? (1990, 134)

According to Butler, as we reflect on these questions, we should be cautious in our assessment of key body-bounding exercises identified by Kristeva: "I expel *myself,* I spit *myself* out, I abject *myself"* (1982, 3). These exercises are significant not because they announce a subject who emerges out of chaos. Rather, they are noteworthy because they attest to the enormous success which the trope of interiority has enjoyed in our cultural order. That individual bodies and social bodies have been figured habitually in terms of inner/outer boundaries should hold our attention, but not because the bounding exercises themselves are compelling: they have no ontological status. Instead, we should be attentive to the illusions promoted by these exercises, which, in prosaic and culturally specific ways, promote set tropes of the body for the purpose of "regulating sexuality within the obligatory frame of reproductive heterosexuality" (1990, 136).

Butler, to her credit, does take the signifying labor of bodies seriously. However, her analysis ultimately proves disappointing. Flirting with what Susan Bordo calls "linguistic foundationalism" (1992, 169) and emphasizing "work" to the exclusion of "body" in the body-work she cites, under Butler's gaze, bodies are swallowed up (Bordo, 1992, 170). Having appropriately located signifying practices in culture, as does Kristeva also, Butler loses sight of bodies that enact them. The consequences of this oversight are particularly onerous for Butler's treatment of the abject, the primary mark of negativity. Contrasts between Kristeva's treatment of the abject and Butler's define their differences and show also that Butler has misunderstood Kristeva. In light of this comparison, the strengths of Kristeva's theory for feminist reflection are demonstrated. Indeed, because her treatment of the abject is more nuanced and inclusive than Butler's, it actually helpfully augments Butler's project.

For Kristeva, the abject is ambiguous and wholly incoherent in its very form, or non-form. An inassimilable nonunity, the abject is a primary mark of the not-yetness of a subject who is in process and on trial. By contrast, under Butler's purview, the abject becomes a mere species of the object. Functioning under the auspices of hegemonic discourses, the abject is placed, by Butler, in service to whatever master narratives these discourses advance. The abject confirms the subject-status of those who claim these discourses as their own. Formally juxtaposed by Butler with a subject so as to assume the position of a type of object, the abject is made party to Butler's own form of binarism. As a consequence, Butler's abject witnesses to a political geography of wholly linguistic boundary work authored by subjects who, in drawing on the powers of the abject, are fully in possession of themselves.

That Butler treats the abject expressly as a species of the object is most evident in *Bodies that Matter* (1993). According to Butler, homosexuality is abjected by a culture that assumes normative heterosexuality. Nonheterosexual identifications are deposited in "the domain of the culturally impossible," where they are rendered illegitimate through the force of the law (1993, 110). But this repudiation actually serves to entertain homosexuality. Indeed, heterosexuality persists only in the face of "an identification that institutes that abjection and sustains it" (1993, 112). Further, the subject position so attained is fragile: only repeated repudiation enables the subject to install its boundaries. Externalized figures of abjection are not abjected and buried in a forgotten past; rather, they must be "buried again and again" so that "the compulsive repudiation by which the subject incessantly sustains his/her boundary" holds that boundary in place (1993, 114).

But are the functions that Butler assigns to the abject appropriately inclusive of abject-work? Butler shortchanges the abject when she assigns to the abject a limited object-profile whose lineage can be traced from Hegel through Lacan. In accord with Hegel and Lacan, Butler argues that the subject and its other are correlates; indeed, the subject is dependent on that which it has made an other for its own identity. But this reading of the abject articulates some aspects and misses others.

That Butler reads the "abject" too narrowly is evident when her account of the abject is contrasted with Kristeva's. For Kristeva, the abject is that which marks as untenable the identity of the subject in its objective worth. The abject is a refuse of being that is doubly refused by the subject: it is that which exceeds the subject who would ask that the object fully fill and define it. In sum, if attestations of the object witness to the abject (e.g., in citations of disgust), the abject is not coterminous with them. Rather, the abject typifies boundary-making practices that retain a disturbing dynamism (productive of vertigo and nausea) which representation and its ready objects are unable to put out of play. Such material responses constitute the subject's categorical acknowledgment of the threat of inassimilable nonunity: the abject is the mud in the pool of Narcissus that gives the lie to the subject's claims to self-possession (1982, 14).

Kristeva's nuanced account of abjection can be embraced without fear of entrapment in binary representation. She does not deploy abjection in dichotomous fashion along a sex/gender divide, as Butler has charged. When an individual or members of a society, at a loss about absolute boundaries, engage in practices meant to secure their boundaries or borders, the abject they evoke in ritual and language on behalf of order is for Kristeva, as for Butler, an effect of culture. Here, as earlier, the semiotic recalls no idyllic precultural space of being; rather, if somatic images of abjection (blood, vomit, excrement) recall a body, they do so only in terms of marking a space from which a "body" that would predate language and culture has always, already been cleared away. Even so, the abject work that is executed in the shadow of the subject/object function calls for discrete analysis, especially when it is violent.

Noëlle McAfee rightly points out the direction of such an analysis when she observes that "the abject is the vandal *and* the policeman" (1993, 121) of the subject. Although Butler discerns the latter role (hence her assimilation of the abject's function to the symbiosis of subject/object play in a master narrative), she shortchanges the former. A nuanced portrait of the abject that brings to light its multiple dimensions is still needed, for we need to know what happens when object-work intended to produce a subject through the very sorts of cultural practices Butler describes, implodes. We must consider closely that moment, when, at the very point of maximum cohesiveness, the bridge to the real that the object is supposed to constitute for the subject collapses and an abyss opens up. Naming the refuse that marks the rim of that hole the abject, we need to consider it in its own right. Because the abject is a site of subject-creation and destruction, it is always symptomatic of object-failure. It always gives the lie to objects that purport to secure the subject in the world.

Kristeva's theory of the abject is a portrait of subject-formation evocative of human agency that extends and enriches, rather than thwarts, treatments such as Butler's. Drawing on that theory, we can assign the subject a history of discursive formation without identifying "subject position" solely with "power-plays among competing discourses." As Claire Pajaczkowska cogently observes, we can understand the formation of a unified and stable subjectivity in terms of "the movement between stability and crisis within discourse, and not simply as the articulation [of power] between different discourses" (1981, 151). Further, when we attend to a material dialectic summoned by the abject, we can affirm the discursive and institutional construction of bodies even as we recognize not only that the body is divided up among cultural discourses as Butler so brilliantly articulates, but also that the body is divided in the very process of its "apprenticeship to speech" (Pajaczkowska, 1981, 151).

Pajaczkowska's observations parallel McAfee's, who notes that Kristeva distinguishes primary from secondary repression (1993, 121). The first creates the possibility of difference that is a prerequisite for subject status; the second differentiates subjects from objects. Recognizing that objectification of others in secondary repression differs from encounters with uncanny alterity in primary repression, Kristeva traces the uncanny to the archaic bases of human being at a loss.

McAfee's comments demonstrate how Kristeva's insights concerning the abject can be reconciled with Butler's political concerns and even advance them. Articulations of difference that mark gender, sexuality, and race can be acknowledged, on precisely the terms Butler advances, as the objects that establish subject positions such as men, heterosexuals, and whites. However, terms Butler sets for the abject do not account for radically abject moments—a threatening vandalism—in the Symbolic order. Kristeva's more inclusive lexicon of the abject is needed. Employing it, we can track the abject in the breakdown of the subject's work, in visceral instances of fascination and repulsion, life and death, which, bypassing object-work, issue in the subject's dispossession from itself.[17]

Why should we join Kristeva on the trail of the abject that she tracks through a culture shaped by sacrifice when Butler would advise against it? What warrants a turn to Kristeva? We can make a decision to follow Kristeva when we observe a key difference between Butler and Kristeva's views about the Law of the Symbolic order and when we fully explore the implications of that difference for a theory of sexually differentiated violence.

Butler and Kristeva's analyses are distinguished from each other by their contrasting portrayals of the degree of honesty accorded by the Law of the Symbolic order to its activities and by their differing assessments of the extent to which humans can be in self-possession of the Law. Kristeva has recourse to the notion of the unconscious—the death-work of negativity—where Butler does not, because Kristeva explicitly wants to raise as an issue how and where one stands to see the dissembling of the Symbolic order. She wants to examine how emancipatory ideals can be advanced against an order that dissembles, not only when it is in full possession of its politics, but also when it is not at all in possession of itself, when it is engaged in the very exercise of *forging* self-possession. Because the Law presents itself as always already accomplished self-mastery, the paternal order needs to be challenged at those points where cracks in its facade recall the boundary-making enterprise: the unconscious, the point of repression of the order's own origins, constitutes the spot for such a political engagement. Although Butler remains wary of attending to the unconscious, Kristeva remains committed to inquiry attentive to the unconscious because she believes that, in focusing on its work, she is interrogating sources of agency: *the economic process by which bodies are invested with meaning.*

Kristeva directs her interest toward the diverse practices of death-work (jouissance and rejection) that confirm the subject in a signifying economy. She looks not only at constraints exerted on the subject, but also at the subject's potential for productive dissolution of bonds forged by the subject. The forward force of negativity is the key to emancipating agency. Its destructive currents are a check on that agency. Kristeva seeks to analyze these currents in order to theorize potential interventions.

Kristeva's interest in the seamy side of the signifying economy whose practices she investigates leads her to extend her analysis of violence beyond boundaries for inquiry set by Butler. Of course, Butler does describe subject formation in ways that suggest violence. Butler writes, for example, of "the forcible production and citation" of codes that govern behavior (1993, 1,

232), "the threatened exposure and violent erasure" of the subject (1993, 3, 44), and "the annihilating norms" in culture (1993, 124). But material references to violence are generally missing from Butler's work. As a consequence, Butler's language conceals and hides from view the agency of violence in a situation which veritably cries out for an examination of that agency.[18]

In view of Butler's reticence to look at violence face to face, we have reason to turn to Kristeva at this very juncture. In attending to the material referents of violence and to the abject subject, Kristeva sets out to follow the trail of violence to the place where meaning is born and dies, there to attend to a matter of feminist concern—the agency of sexually differentiated violence—about which Butler remains disquietingly reticent. Because Kristeva attends to the consummate stakes of human subjectivity, the forging and reforging of the subject in body-bounding exercises undertaken by one poised over an abyss, she helps us to understand the stance of agents who "lose it." She assists us in comprehending how rage, murder, and mutilation figure in the signifying practices of those who are lost. Directing our attention to the abyss of being, Kristeva aids us in understanding the erasure of being in ways Butler does not. Above all, Kristeva invites us to consider the work of the unconscious—negativity—in order to examine subject formation and destruction when the stakes are the highest.

Kristeva wants to inquire after investments made in specific signifying economies and to ask who pays the price when the investors, realizing that the roles others have performed have not purchased the security they have sought, second-guess their investments. She wants to know why subjects in the cultural order have regularly summoned the trope of sacrificial maternity and have forcibly deployed it, joining sexual differentiation with sacrifice, in the interests of managing and concealing the failures of their own investments.

For Butler, agents and their investment strategies, about which Kristeva would inquire, are inaccessible. In the signifying practices Butler monitors, there are no subjects of agency and no larger truths that, undergirding the field of cultural possibilities, guarantee investments made there: "there is only the taking up of tools where they lie, where the very 'taking up' is enabled by the tool lying there" (1990, 145). However, a feminist analysis of agency influenced by Kristeva would seek a stronger notion of agency. After all, in asking where they can stand in the social order to effect change and by what means they can advance permutations in its signifying economy, feminists inquire after a life-saving agency. They seek an emancipatory agenda that, countering death-dealing violence, can *underwrite* survival. Consequently, they must know how she who is marked with sacrificial maternity—and its attendant costs in violence—can refuse that deathly fiction. How can she whose being is rendered as a material site of struggle within a sacrificial economy gain leverage to resist it? Who is forging that violence? Why is their violence so often deadly?

That Kristeva would appeal to the unconscious in the wake of these questions does not mean, as Butler has charged, that Kristeva remains captive to a dichotomy-ridden precultural terrain. Rather, Kristeva reconnoiters the margins of language, seeking a site which, if not exempt from the Law, remains a site of absolute struggle with the Law: an abject site on the borders of language where *meaning is born and dies.* Butler, of course, remains apprehensive about emulating Kristeva because she is wary of linking any exposé of the fictional posturings of the Symbolic to a material dialectic, a maternal body, and a trope of sacrificial maternity, even though, on those occasions when, in the wake of feigned self-possession, the Symbolic is forced, under threat of loss, to reiterate its agency-evoking exercises in bounding and mastery, it regularly exercises that masterful reiteration on the bodies of women. By contrast, even though Kristeva, like Butler, recognizes that the maternal body is an effect of a signifying economy and, like Butler, displays considerable savvy concerning the fictive posturings of human subjects, Kristeva chooses as Butler does not a hermeneutic of suspicion that, oriented toward the labor of the unconscious, shadows abjection and sacrifice.

Contributing significantly to Kristeva's sustained attention to such a critical hermeneutic is her discovery of disguised and denied sacrificial interests in the signifying economy of the Symbolic. Because Kristeva believes that we do not easily and comfortably stand in a place where we can see exposed such dissembling, a radical politics of the unconscious is required if we are to expose and challenge the sacrificial dynamics of the signifying economy. In support of a radical politics, Kristeva insistently probes the abject. Seeing the abject as a primary point of rupture within the signifying economy, Kristeva gives it heed. Her reflections hone in on evil and horror that exist in the world, as the data of consciousness do not. At the same time, they give intimations of a space of agency that, if freed of its conscription to sacrifice, could empower women to lift the weight of the sacrificial contract from their shoulders.

Far from constituting a problematic contribution to discussions among feminist theorists about women's agency and the violence that constrains it, Kristeva's work helpfully augments their efforts. Having shown that Kristeva's work is useful to feminist theorists' emancipatory interests, this project can fully engage her writings. Chapter 3 focuses on death-work and general possibilities for subjects to assert agency. Chapter 4 attends to the displacement of agency, particularly women's agency, as death-work is placed in service to sacrifice.

3

THE SUBJECT OF PSYCHOANALYSIS

DEATH-WORK AND AGENCY

> The subject never *is*. The *subject* is only the *signifying process* and appears only as a *signifying practice*, that is, only when absent *within the position* out of which social, historical, and signifying activity unfolds.
>
> —Julia Kristeva, *Revolution in Poetic Language*

This chapter addresses subject formation as a signifying practice rooted in the material dynamics of the drives. It uses Kristeva's psychoanalytic theory to describe the most basic nexus for the emergence of a subject in the world: a being-at-a-loss that establishes the human subject as one who, lacking presence, abides in absence (1984c, 167). This chapter establishes that death-work identified by means of drive theory is distinct from, though necessarily related to, signifying practices shaped by dictates of a sacrificial economy in the Symbolic order. Although all subjects live at a loss, not all death-work is sacrificial.

When the origins of subjectivity in the movement of the drives are explored, we readily observe that negativity does not necessarily invoke sacrifice. Creative, formative, transgressive aspects of negativity—the inassimilable alterity of jouissance—position the subject in the world and enable it to entertain new expressions of agency. Ever open to resignification, the work that negativity does in language enables subjects to act in ways that actually resist ossification. At the same time, drive theory reveals that negativity does maintain a capacity to destroy as well as to contain subjectivity. When death-work is implicated in the work of a sacrificial economy, negativity is placed in service to violence-laden conflict. Subjects position themselves in the world by means of brutal assertions of presence that violate others.

This chapter sets forth necessary preconditions of the Symbolic order in the movement of negativity, establishes the foundations of human agency, and brings into focus the complex dynamics—constructive and destructive—that produce an always absent subject, in order to differentiate these functions of negativity from their more virulent counterparts in a sacrificial economy. Throughout, the subject's propensity for agency is addressed in a manner that neither relegates it to a province of culture nor to a mute, precultural strata. Instead, Kristeva's theory of negativity facilitates a nondichotomous understanding of the agency that belongs to subjects' intertextual, signifying practices.

Why is it important to attend to the work of negativity in subject formation and trace its movement, distinguishing death-work from labor performed in the name of negativity within a sacrificial economy? This distinction is critical for two reasons. First, this project intends to support feminism's emancipatory goals. Feminist theorists seek not only to understand constraints exerted on women in a sacrificial economy, but also to investigate prospects for women's release from those bonds. Therefore, this project needs to show that the signifying practices which shape and position subjects in the world can be ordered by an emancipating grammar, and not only by a murderous one. Because this chapter does demonstrate that death-work is not necessarily sacrificial, succeeding chapters can focus on circumstances that are exceedingly inhospitable to women even as they imagine more generous terms for women's economic engagements in society. Because grounds for hope are established in this chapter, this project can attend primarily to the work of a sacrificial economy, while maintaining its emancipatory goals. Indeed, the conclusion of this project comes full circle: it returns to themes first sketched in this chapter and entertains possibilities for nonsacrificial economic arrangements supportive of women's enhanced agency.

But there is a second reason to advance a clear account of negativity in this chapter. The pattern of death-work that drive theory reveals needs to be looked at closely because this pattern is precisely that which sacrificial labor attempts to replicate in order to secure its own fortunes. Of course, forces deployed by the sacrificial economy to manage death-work intend to impose their own order on death-work: they want to control and, if necessary, violently erase the threat it purportedly contains. Even so, in exposing pretenses of the sacrificial economy, drive theory suggests that the consuming intent of sacrificial theory is never fully realized. Because drive theory proffers a perspective on signifying practices that facilitates exposure of the sacrificial economy's spurious claims, drive theory can glimpse in the negativity of subject and societal formation forms of death-work that are not fully infused with a homicidal intent. As a consequence, when Chapter 4's theory of sacrifice is juxtaposed with this chapter's review of death-work, the limits of sacrifice are more readily perceived. Fair measure can be taken of sacrifice, and its power can be acknowledged even as its hegemony is challenged.

I. Drive Theory and Human Agency

A crucial element informing the work of negativity, as understood by Kristeva, is spelled out in Freud's theory of the drives. Drive theory enables Kristeva to see how processes of negativity produce a signifying position (1984c, 121). Notably, the drives have no fixed identity or specified content;

rather, they are that which makes possible a structural arrangement which produces positionedness. Assimilative and destructive aspects of their work render the subject as a permanent site of open division (1977, 137) and establish its motivation for the Symbolic: the roots of its agency.

In turning to drive theory, Kristeva disavows all notions of a body/subject that figures the body as a mute facticity, on which a transcendent consciousness imputes meaning or which nameless powers invest. She does not maintain a "body" and a "subject" prior to cultural inscription. Rather, Kristeva suggests that *the boundaries of the body are the first contours of the subject.* Moving beyond the impasse that attends notions of human agency which would juxtapose an ideational interior of a subject of understanding to an inarticulate material expression of force that is beyond all consciousness to possess, Kristeva deploys a materialist dialectic and directs her attention to "the repeated scission of matter that generates significance" (1984c, 167) at that place where a subject is produced as a practice of absence. Further, because the drive activity of expulsion and projection that bounds a subject is ongoing, the radical temporality ascribed to the human subject by drive theory leaves neither a biological nor an ideational "residue" which would condemn the subject of drive theory to reified status. Instead, in its capacity for the variable regulation of its boundaries, in its ongoing permeation and division, the subject who abides in temporal absence—in negativity—is capable of creative agency.

When processes of subject formation that establish it as a signifying practice are reviewed, the evidence confirms that the subject is not mired in the stasis of repetition, devoid of the difference that motivates change. Negativity is productive when it leads to the acquisition of the sign as the positivizing of the movement of negativity (projection) at the place of the Other. As the place for production of the sign, the process of negativity directed to the place of the Other halts or marks projection, replacing the mechanical repetition of identity with a state of newness. As Suzanne Guerlac (1993) rightly notes, this state is not properly contained by the Symbolic, as the possession of a subject. Rather, the very mechanism of transgression—the *rejet* of negativity—is the source of agency. Out of this heterogeneity, in which agency is enacted in the very dispossession of an agent from its positionedness, signifying acts broker revolution.

The speaking subject, as a practice of negativity, therefore establishes the space for rupture, renovation, revolution, and agency in the heart of the signifying economy. Because of this heterogeneous movement of significance, the subject—in process and on trial—collides with those practices in which it previously has recognized itself and produces new signs in order to continue communication. The practice of speech—material and signifying—is motivated by the heterogeneous contradiction that functions as its motor: the unity of consciousness is pulverized by a nonsymbolized exteriority (1984c, 203), setting out from objective contradictions out of which rejection will create the new object.

For Kristeva, the economy of signification that she uncovers in the drives—jouissance and rejection—promises "a new conception of social praxis, a renewal of the Hegelian-Marxist dialectic" (1985a, 218). Elaborating on this revolutionary economy, Kristeva describes the subject of this economy as an excess, always already divided. She asserts that excess harbors potential because, in the very heterogeneity of practice—the material contradictions of existence—the vicissitudes of the subject in its social context are joined in "an open system" (1986b, 8). Motivation for social change is rooted in the ongoing work of a subject who emerges and is positioned in the world through intertextual practices that simultaneously situate it and give it voice.

But Kristeva understands that drive theory demonstrates something else as well: if negativity is constructive, establishing the conditions for agency and societal transformation, it also can be destructive. The very economy of signification that ensures social communication and the subject's pleasure—jouissance—carries with it risk. The heterogeneous movement of signification can break down in mindless repetition, or processes of displacement can ossify in particular patterns, producing difference in a violent partitioning of subject-positions. Consequently, if productive possibilities in signification momentarily belie the association of negativity with "death-work," their destructive potential does not.

In the pages that follow, clues concerning the complex work of negativity are sought in a variety of images that cluster around the Freudian theory of drives and the work of negativity: the maternal body, the child's fort/da game, laughter, and the Freudian "sign."[1] These examples, which focus on the workings of language *and* the emergence of the subject within an intersubjective process, offer decisive testimony to the economic production of a positioned subjectivity that is capable also of free agency. What happens to the linguistic signifier by way of negativity, which makes meaning possible, happens also within the intersubjective practices that establish human society: in both instances are detected possibilities for agency and change as well as for violence and destruction.

II. Drive Theory and the Maternal Body

Kristeva's initial approach to the maternal body—a primary example of the marking of a bounded space that presages the birth of a subject—is made by way of a discussion of linguistic theory. In her essay on "The Speaking Subject" (1985a), Kristeva criticizes theories of signification that approach meaning as an act of a transcendental ego cut off from its body. For Kristeva, the relationship between a referent (as object and situation) and the signifiable is never one of identity; rather, it is a relation of contradiction. This space of contradiction is a space of emptiness. Unnameable and opaque, this space is, in other words, a body.

How does Kristeva locate a body in a space of unnamed opacity? Kristeva observes in language a plurality of signifiers that aim at and fail at being a signified. Although the apparent intent of the signifying process is to signify everything—to capture the referent exhaustively in the sign, so that there is no remainder—something is always left over, "a remnant, experienced as the body" (1985a, 215). Focusing her attention on this excess not yet captured by the sign, Kristeva surmises that theories of signification will account for the subject's acclimation to language and a world only as they are able to trace the path of the signifier through the body. But to whose body do we turn when seeking to trace the path of meaning?

According to Kristeva, we should turn our attention to two bodies: the infant body and the maternal body. Or, to state Kristeva's point more accurately, because one of these bodies is the mimetic pattern of the other, we should attend to the division of the one body that is the maternal matrix, inclusive of a not-yet subject and a not-yet object. An initial binding of space—that moment of turning that gives rise to a subject out of the material excess of the maternal matrix—hinges on mimesis. Consequently, to understand the origins of signification, we need to give close regard to mimesis. But how does the mimetic pattern that contains negativity move through the body to open onto the Symbolic, thereby joining the province of linguistic theory with that of emerging subjectivity?

Inspired by Freud's essay on "Identification," Kristeva employs traditional psychoanalytic language about the drives to describe the dynamics of mimesis. She focuses initially on orality. The breast of the maternal body,[2] both present and absent, given and taken away, is a paradigmatic mimetic "object." The breast is the infant's first other in whom its own being arises. However, not truly an "object," the breast is actually a model: it offers itself as a pattern—present and absent—which the infant itself assimilates when it incorporates the breast in its own body. And, introduced within the maternal matrix to the logic of mimesis—a pattern of presence and absence, fulfillment and rejection—the human infant receives its first lesson in the body bounding that presages its emergence by way of negativity as a subject.

Framing her discussion of orality in terms of a dialectic of negativity, Kristeva claims that the diverse dynamics of orality are misconstrued if orality is treated as an idyllic episode of infant unity with a maternal jouissance. Even as early as six months, the rotating movement of the infant's head indicates that a "fusing orality" is joined with a "devouring, refusing, negative orality" (1984c, 154). Anticipated by the bodily gesture proper to the buccal space—a gesture shaped by the disparate energies of fusion and separation—and long before the child acquires the language of refusal that is this gesture's later echo, the nascent subject learns its humanity as a practice of absence and division.

Subsequently, as Kristeva observes in *Tales of Love,* the practice of incorporation and introjection experienced in orality functions as the "substratum of what constitutes human being, namely, language" (1987a, 26). That for one there can be another thus hinges on the early model of mimesis, which, if displaced and deferred in language, nevertheless shares with language a common logic: in the potential for communion—in presence *and* absence, fusing *and* refusing—that the mimetic pattern sets forth are established also the grounds for the later assimilation, repetition, and reproduction of words. Because early vocalizations in children aim at a global pattern—appearing as conversational babble at odds with the "'phonematic austerity'" (1974c, 34) of later linguistic acquisition—Kristeva can sustain a claim that these early mimetic lessons in orality are retained in Symbolic language. These patterns of vocalization suggest that the Symbolic order is underwritten not only by linguistic processes that accommodate humans to loss and enable them to come to terms with the lack that they are, but also by a communicative ethos that hears in conversation the possibility for communion in difference.

Kristeva finds that negativity—the process of generation and negation that, moving through material being on its way to the Symbolic, constitutes a signifying economy and positions a subject within it—is illustrated not only by orality but also by anality. With orality, Kristeva has claimed that the subject receives foundational lessons in human agency: it duplicates with its body a pattern of presence and absence, learned in mimetic relation to the maternal body, that ascribes to its being a fundamental openness. As open, the subject would appear capable of agency: because the mimetic pattern that the subject harbors in its body contains lessons in both difference and sameness, the subject would appear destined neither to collapse in fusion with the other nor to break apart in mimetic conflict framed viscerally as alimentary threat. Likewise, with anality, Kristeva suggests that the subject's relation to the world is structured as an open system. For with rejection—the dynamic of the anal drive—the subject is introduced to possibilities of separation that entail not only pain and loss, but also pleasurable jouissance (1984c, 151).

When Kristeva discusses anality, she emphasizes that drives are always already part of a social space. An infant's access to this social order occurs when anality and orality acclimate it to a mimetic process, a process associated previously with the maternal matrix, which includes elements of dependence and of separation. However, the primary dynamic of anality places a heavier emphasis on the dangers that accompany rejection than has orality. The activity of expulsion, which the anal-aggressive drive marks, is a most significant lesson in difference which establishes the maternal body—incorporated previously in orality—in a position of alterity. Contrasting with the pleasures of dependency and notwithstanding its own moments of pleasure, the rejection of the anal drive is experienced also by the infant as the loss of a mimetic bond and ejection from the maternal matrix.

Kristeva places the motivation for this ejection within the context of the subject's own emerging agency. Consequently, she elaborates on the dynamics of ejection in terms of a theory of abjection. According to this theory, as the subject emerges out of undifferentiated existence, it becomes aware of fragmentation and disunity. Its awareness is marked not by language, but by bodily refuse: blood, excrement, and vomit. Suggested to the emerging subject by this refuse are borders and the violation of those borders.

If, earlier, Kristeva has acknowledged the element of pleasure (jouissance) proper to aspects of this nascent border phenomenon, she now underscores the threat it poses. Fundamentally insecure, this not-yet-subject, for whom a not-yet-object frames a tentatively bounded and not-yet-world, finds that ongoing mimetic processes within the maternal matrix from which it is emerging magnify a sense of instability. The nascent subject experiences the elaboration of mimetic forces within the maternal matrix as a crisis.

What motivates this crisis? According to Kristeva, the child who emerges from the maternal matrix experiences the doubling back and multiplication of mimesis. As the dynamics of presence and absence, fusing and refusing, shape life in the maternal matrix, they are, increasingly, subject to recognition. Made aware in this manner of the division that it is, the child experiences this division—and its mimetic pattern in the mother's own heterogeneous self-division—as ambiguity and threat. In response, it enters into mimetic combat, seeking to neutralize this threat. Drawing on its newly found capability to mark boundaries with bodily gestures and products, the child acts to contain all unity of being within its boundaries and to dispel all division and threat to being outside those boundaries.

Of course, the "it" of this process is not an initiator, but an outcome. Bodily gestures and products that are party to this conflict mark a set of boundaries that give rise to the subject. Indeed, mimetic conflict, which fluctuates between containment and eviction, unity in difference and unity in the absence of difference, is most radically creative: it produces a subject. The subject who is a product of this effort is literally spacialized into being.

However, in the wake of this effort and in the absence of an explicit engagement by the child with the management resources of the Symbolic, which are not yet firmly in hand, the child may experience spacialization as it might a horror film: if gaps, fissures, and holes do not threaten, slime, ooze, and blood do. Even though its boundary-creating venture appears to promise the fullness of being, the subject will experience only frustration, disappointment, and anger. For, when its boundary-making efforts verge on empire-building, they necessarily will be thwarted, based as they are on a false premise that the subject can counter the division in being that it is and incorporate all unity for itself. Consequently, because the subject is not yet able to summon a language of distance, disclaimer, and signification, which would educate it to loss and establish it within the orbit of the Symbolic, it becomes the abject, a creature of the border. There, in the grip of the violent currents of mimesis that offer neither the fullness of identification without difference nor the fullness of identification in difference (the creative possibility for mimesis glimpsed in orality), this not-yet-subject faces only difficult and mutually unsavory possibilities. Will it be the jettisoned object—the waste expelled from the maternal matrix—or will it be sucked into the matrix, which now horrifies rather than embraces? The stakes are of epochal significance to the abject who would be subject. If, with anality, the powers of mimesis are shadowed by pleasure—the nascent, agency-promoting jouissance of a subject—they are also characterized most emphatically by a destructive potential: the death in death-work.

Because Kristeva presents the subject's destructive capability in terms of a body-narrative of abjection, she approaches anality, as she has orality, in a manner that precludes any assignment of her views to a mute energetics of a death "instinct." As John Lechte emphasizes in his own discussion of the drives, the dynamics of the drives that Kristeva identifies in her discussion of orality and anality become part of—not language—but a *signifying process* (1990, 136). As a consequence, the drives should not be understood in terms of a vitalism that treats jouissance and rejection solely as biophysiological processes. Instead the drives should be analyzed in terms of their capacity, admittedly complex and varied in their signifying impact, to "'extract the body from its homogeneous expanse and turn it into a space bound to exterior space'" (Lechte, 1990, 136).

Again, that which Kristeva finds instructive in the instances she cites, of which the examples of orality and anality offer initial and most salient lessons, is not a specific content. Rather, these examples attest to the structuring of subjectivity in an economy of signification to which heterogeneity is central. The roots of language reach down into an always already divided maternal matrix. Language functions as a practice of absence because bodily engagements in the signifying process already have established an excess of difference—the inassimilable alterity of jouissance—that makes meaning possible. For orality and anality, processes of primary connection for a subject whose first acquaintance with structure is through them, are oriented around the maternal body. And that maternal body, in ordering the *chora,* is the first mediator for the subject of the Symbolic order and the Law (Weir, 1993, 90, n. 9). Moreover, because the dynamics of abjection associated with the maternal body entail a sometimes violent differentiation of the subject, these dynamics presage in significant ways connections between death-work and sacrifice in society.

III. Drive Theory and the Construction of a Social Space: The Fort/Da Game

Wishing to trace the signifier through the body and to reinscribe the body in language as a practice of absence, Kristeva observes that humans reconnoiter the boundaries of being in complex ways. That humans engage in rites of body-bounding that are both productive and potentially destructive of the subject and its agency is illustrated most dramatically in the fort/da game of Freud's grandson, Ernst. At play, Ernst picks up a reel on a string during his mother's absence. Throwing the reel away, the child says, "o-o-o-o [fort]."

Retrieving it, the child says, "da." Of course, Lacan has spoken eloquently about this game, emphasizing its paradigmatic quality as an instance of the mastery of the symbol (1977, 103–104). The child who plays at throwing a toy away in order to bring it back and send it away once more is, according to Lacan's interpretation of this story, acquiring by means of the toy a symbol of its mother. It likewise is mastering key rules that structure the signifying economy of the Symbolic order: the meaning of presence/absence, demand/lack.

Kristeva does not disagree altogether with Lacan's interpretation of the story. However, she insists that some aspects of the story do not receive appropriate emphasis in his account. If the child masters an ability to signify in this game, the child becomes proficient not only because (as Lacan claims) the child learns to use the toy as a symbol, "mastering his privation by assuming it . . . [and] raising his desire to the second power" (1977, 103; 1966, 319), but also because when the child plays with the toy, the child engages in a paradigmatic activity of spacial bounding. Consequently, Kristeva makes explicit and central to her account of the game what Lacan does not: the kinetic, vocal, and gestural components of the game (1984c, 170). Elaborating on Lacan's observation that the game is a lesson *in* the Symbolic, Kristeva emphasizes also that the game is a lesson in the visceral acclimation *to* the Symbolic. The materiality of rejection displayed in the movement of the game—the bodily act itself—is shown necessary to the child's transition to the Symbolic order.

Irigaray's essay, "The Gesture in Psychoanalysis" (1989), helpfully underscores Kristeva's own observations. Discussing the fort/da game, Irigaray emphasizes how the German economy of consonants and vowels elaborates the lesson of the reel. "O-o-o-o," Ernst's version of "fort," forms a triangle in the mouth. Inside the mouth, "o-o-o-o" nevertheless cannot be swallowed. "Da," also inside the mouth, is not sung as "o-o-o-o" is: "it stays in the mouth like a sweet difficult to suck, or else becomes a discontinuous signal, difficult to transform into a melody" (1989, 131). Irigaray rightly notes that Ernst is searching for mother, not with his legs, as would a toddler who has mastered walking, but with his arms, mouth, and ears. His world is bound by the gesture and by the sounds that vibrate in his mouth and resonate in his ears. These gestures and sounds frame a world, a space. Together, the movement of projection (literal in gesture and in sound) produces an outside and opens the possibility of signification.

Irigaray's account also lends emphasis to the most salient aspects of this bodily lesson in signification: the birth of the subject in the very *practice* of absence. Lacan, in stressing Ernst's visual play with absence, may appear to suggest a controlled intellection by a subject of the lesson of the reel. From that perspective, Ernst is a unified subject who gains control over "his" world by mastery over conditions of absence within it. Although Lacan notes the vocalizing elements of the game, the third-person pronoun—suggestive of a fully positioned consciousness—dominates his account: "his action destroys [*son action détruit*]," "he receives [*il reçoit*]," "he will seek [*il cherchera*]"

(1977, 103; 1966, 139). By contrast, Irigaray takes us into the mouth of Ernst. She describes vocalization in an extended narrative from which the third-person pronoun is wholly missing. In this way, Irigaray emphasizes the *emergence* of a subject for whom the lessons of absence are learned slowly and whose own unity is tentative, partial, and in flux. In depicting Ernst's embeddedness in the world—his legs are still rooted in the broad expanse of undifferentiated matter—Irigaray reminds us that the process of becoming an "I" proceeds slowly and awkwardly. Human subjects seek a world without a leg to stand on.

Moreover, when Irigaray describes the emergence of a world out of an undifferentiated buccal space, she highlights an economy in which mastery is discontinuous, tentative, and always hard-won. Where Lacan is tempted to treat the sounds of the game as a vocal accompaniment to a larger drama of words, Irigaray magnifies what happens "in the mouth, between the lips, the tongue, the palate, the teeth, the larynx" (1989, 131). When the child passes from undifferentiated buccal space—an intimate landscape that it has known at its mother's breast—to the bound and differentiated space of "fort" and "da," it learns a lesson of absence *in* the discontinuous signal, the awkward melody, and the syncopated rhythm. As it struggles to enter the Symbolic order, it fights with its mouth: it learns the division of being there, for the maternal body is now inside and outside, "already indefinitely divided by the teeth and by all the differences between the sounds" (1989, 131).

Because Irigaray stresses that becoming a subject turns not on a relation of knowledge, but on an economic relation of power, she glimpses the drives—those material dynamics of the Imaginary—that are the precondition for an emerging engagement of a subject in a world. Beautifully testifying to the material dynamics of signification with her account of Ernst's play, Irigaray hones in on the process of birth of the subject.[3] As Kristeva confirms, within the specific corporal and social space of Ernst's gestural and kinetic play—literally, the space of his mouth—operates a "nonsymbolized negativity that is neither arrested within the terms of judgment, nor predicated as negation in judgment. This negativity—jouissance and rejection—posits an object as separate from the body proper and, at the very moment of separation, fixes it in place as *absent:* as a *sign"* (1984c, 123).

Of course, Lacan has said that the child invests in the symbol, the stand-in (negation) of the object, in order to be able to demand a return of the object (mother). But Irigaray and Kristeva bring a magnifying glass to the process in order to look most particularly at what actually happens in the child's course of "investing" in the symbol. In the play of absences, the signifying act places *negativity* at the heart of its economy of expression. In the *very act of constituting the other*—an act played out in the movement and framing of space by the mouth, teeth, and tongue—signification becomes possible.

Although the child's lesson in absence is described as play, this scene should not be overly domesticated. To return to the world of the child with Ernst is to return to a world in which alimentary metaphors broker real violence. The mother who is divided—"fort" and "da"—is differentiated not only by sound, but also by the teeth. And teeth, for the child, are powerful, not only because they shape words, but also because they tear flesh. Consequently, in a child's play with absence, potential danger lurks. The practice of division in child's play that places the mother both inside and outside the mouth thus is doubly significant: for the child in its experience of loss and containment of that loss and for the mother who, in becoming party to a violent gesture, demonstrates a "productive dissolution" which brings forth the world.

In the fort/da game, a child's pastime lends itself to revealing that which generally remains hidden in the work of the signifying economy. For this reason, the fort/da game offers a most helpful summary of the lessons in negativity learned so far. As a model of the emergence of the subject into language and the world, the game shows that a child's desire for the presence of its mother is a gesture bent on appropriation. But it teaches also that, were desire to remain present in the gesture—contained solely in the movement of the gesture—it would not designate an object. It would not reach its aim, for the very notion of "aim" entails a distancing (sublation, *aufhebung*) that makes recognition possible. In playing with the reel, the child intends to evoke an other by means of a gesture, and the frustrated gesture is compensated for in words. The paradox of desire—the jouissance and rejection contained in it—is that the sign succeeds only because it fails. Were the gesture truly to produce assimilation to (fusion with) the maternal body, it would necessitate the dissolution of the subject whose desire has initiated the gesture. The game demonstrates that meaning evocative of a subject's agency transpires in the gaps, the absences, and the interstices of the gesture moving to expression.

In the fort/da game, the action that permits mastery of desire—the fulfillment of the gesture—works only because it negativizes the force of desire to make that force in its very absence an object. The subject is separated from one "source"—the maternal matrix of its origins—in order to be present at the creation of another: signification. At the axis of the signifier/signified, an axis that turns on death-work (negativity), a world of meaning and possibility arises. However, because this moment of creation reaches out over an abyss—in the absence of the maternal body that was its prior support—it is fraught with both possibilities and risks. In the section that follows, that risks as well as pleasures attend emergent subjectivity becomes even more evident.

IV. Drive Theory, Laughter, and the Sign

Kristeva cites laughter as an additional example of body bounding that serves as precursor and vehicle of productive subjectivity. Commenting first on infant laughter, Kristeva observes that, at three months, long before the mirror stage—chronologically as well as logically—"riant spaciousness" marks off an earlier period of indistinctness between infant and mother which has characterized the infant's first twelve weeks of life (1977a, 283). Framed by orality, a buccal space receives its first differentiation in the perception of infant motility and produces laughter.

The infant's laugh is born of the experience of spacialization. An infant will laugh when it is offered a distorted visualization (someone makes a "funny face") that is a displacement of the sensory flux (the breast, lamplight capturing a gaze, intermittent sounds of voices or music) of the infant's "world." Or the infant will laugh under the conditions of movement: if it is too rapidly set in motion by an adult; if the movement of the one who carries it or the object held before its face stops suddenly. Alterations and checks in movement are punctuations in the life of an infant that establish space, precursor of identity: producing movement, these incidents form an "archaic topos" (1977a, 284–85).

In recognizing this topos and calling attention to it, Kristeva cites laughter as initial testimony to the construction of the signifying economy in which the subject participates and to the process of negativity that governs that economy. Laughter demonstrates a linkage of expression between the body (out of which laughter wells, explodes, overflows, or bursts forth), the subject, and "a material outside." What previous epistemologies have divided now are joined in a single economy. As such, laughter offers preliminary lessons in understanding the development of an economy of signification and emerging subjectivity.

Kristeva cites the significance of laughter not only when she comments on emerging subjectivity in a child, but also when she discusses poetry and literature. In *Revolution in Poetic Language,* Kristeva observes that Baudelaire places laughter in the class of artistic phenomena that characteristically express "the power of being oneself and someone else at one and the same time" (1984c, 223). A principal witness to that process by which a subject abides as a practice of absence, laughter reveals the logic that governs this practice. Laughter is the primary symptom of rupture or breakdown in signification. As such, heard in laughter is the movement of heterogeneous contradiction within the signifying economy that makes possible both the bounding and re-bounding of a space that positions consciousness and produces an "I." Significantly, one who "observes and knows," who claims mastery of a scene, does not laugh. Laughter works only when, and because, the space of order that is the Symbolic is torn open by it (1984c, 224). But in the eruption of laughter, as laughter passes to expression, laughter binds one over to order once again, preserving only for an instant that fragile movement of negativity that gives birth to subjectivity.

Notwithstanding the benign portrait of laughter that emerges in a discussion of infant laughter or Baudelaire's discussion of laughter, there are very serious lessons in subjectivity to which laughter attests that should not be overlooked. Kristeva notes that the practice of absence, which laughter marks, takes on apocalyptic overtones in the work of Céline. In Céline, when laughter gushes forth, "it is neither jovial, nor trustful, nor sublime, nor enraptured by preexisting harmony" (1982, 206). Bare and anguished, Célinian laughter is caught in an interspace—abject and fascinated—that laughter generally only touches and from which it moves on. But for Céline, laughter is no harbinger of new meaning. No gesture moves toward expression, no loss toward hope. Instead, only a catastrophic exclamation, laughter drowns in a field of horror. In highlighting the abject, Kristeva draws on Céline's apocalyptic laughter to show that the space of emerging subjectivity is fraught with danger: in that space Céline has evoked all that is potentially deadly in death-work.

In "Within the Microcosm of the 'Talking Cure'" (1983), Kristeva makes her most concentrated effort to advance a perspective on the subject and its agency which is attuned to the materiality of signification as a condition of agency and to the death-work that is the necessary partner to this agency. Kristeva finds direction for her inquiry in Freud. Curiously, Freud enters her essay from the margins, in a dense footnote that interrupts an almost perfunctory recitation by Kristeva of familiar tenets of her theory of the semiotic. As Shuli Barzilai insightfully observes in her discussion of this essay (1991), the imaginative thrust of Kristeva's argument is literally relegated to the borders of the page.

The sign in Freud, Kristeva reminds her readers, is "*visual, tactile, acoustic and kinesthetic.*" As a consequence, although the Freudian "sign" accommodates Saussure's, Freud makes more far-reaching claims about signs than does Saussure. Because Freud links the *sound* and *visual* image, Freud does acknowledge the Saussurian point: the sign (signifier/signified) is always already *indebted* to that representability specific to language. Even so, attentive to kinesthetic impression, Freud takes hold of "the heterogeneous economy (body and discourse) of the speaking being" (Kristeva, 1982, 52). Working out the materiality of language, Freud understands that it constructs spacial boundaries: "topology," "territory," and "threshold" are leitmotifs of a Freudian theory of the sign. In view of these motifs, Kristeva's odd marginal inquiry now seems not at all strange: the spacial disruption of the Freudian sign—a disruption which will be confirmed by Kristeva's interrogation of borderline discourse—is enacted analogously as a spacial disruption of the written page.

Emboldened by her marginal inquiry, Kristeva advises her reader to study again Freud's essay on "Negation." Negation, echoing Hegelian negativity, ascribes to meaning a tension, an *interval,* an uncanniness, and an undecidability. Observing that analysis, rather than linguistics, seeks most often "to bring out" these elements, Kristeva ponders what, precisely, is "brought out" by analysis.

She suggests that analytic inquiry, directed toward the territorial and the uncanny, confirms that "language is the terrain of death work" (1983, 38). Alluding to Hegel in this evocation of the dialectic of negativity, Kristeva elaborates on the consequences of this instruction for analysis and, by extension, for linguistic theory: "the death instinct finds in language its master, but the analyst's task is to hear the slave behind the master, who, because of him, suffers and experiences pleasure: desire, death . . ." (1983, 38). Consequently, analytic inquiry "knows" what the Symbolic would obscure: the drives (processes) whereby in gesture, refusal, or laughter the body is extracted from its homogeneous expanse and, in the signifying practices of the emergent subject, bound within a space of expulsion/separation/loss.

In *Revolution in Poetic Language,* Kristeva identifies as "engrammatic" the stases that characterize this primarily vocalic, gestural, and holophrastic process of bounding. Prior to grammar and system, the "engram" is what rejection creates in marking, dividing, and immobilizing drives in order to place and displace boundaries. A step on the way to the signifier, the engram is a moment of stasis without which no symbolizing thesis could be established. If it did not generate heterogeneity under the precise conditions of the engrammatic function, rejection could not produce something new: the spacialization necessary for the establishment of the Symbolic would abort in "a mere mechanical repetition of an undifferentiated identity" (1984c, 170). Moreover, in *Revolution in Poetic Language,* Kristeva forges an initial connection between this necessary spatialization—the mark of the engram—and the economy of death-work. The tendency of the engram to reinscribe (*remarque*) rejection "thwarts rejection in order to reactivate it" and, as Hegel's discussion of negativity has promised previously, sets in place the thetic phase—the sign—"in the face of this murder" (1984c, 172). Kristeva identifies in poetic practice access to basic functions of the signifying economy. The engram—in rhythm, paragrams, and onomatopoeia—goes to the heart of a textual practice that is "that most intense struggle toward death" because the engram introduces and reintroduces the corporal and material elements of signification (1984c, 180).

In "Within the Microcosm of the 'Talking Cure,'" Kristeva observes also that aesthetic production has a most intimate acquaintance with the economy of rejection. It "knows how to deal with [*sait faire avec*]" its terms (1983, 39). Kristeva notes likewise that recent developments in linguistics suggest an increasingly astute attentiveness to the heterogeneous workings of language. Intonation, once believed to be the mere "carrier" of meaning, is now recognized as a vital, albeit archaic, component in language acquisition, a component that is essential to the very success of any act of communication. Indeed, Kristeva observes that, if linguistics teaches us that humans never enunciate without "stumbling up" against the horizons of meaning and form, theorists of linguistics are beginning to acknowledge that which Freud has taught previously: those horizons are "precisely, only *stumbling blocks,"* through which and against which operate heterogeneity: libido, desire, drive (1983, 40).

According to Kristeva, if the discourse that psychoanalysis describes as borderline is examined, inquiry about the origins of the sign and the processes of signification is decisively advanced. Because borderline discourse offers two distinct modes of "stumbling up" against the limits of language, it sheds light on death-work that goes on in all language: the topos of meaning and the economy of signification. Borderline discourse illuminates the workings of language because, in a variety of ways, language fails in borderline discourse. It is unsupported by the trajectory of the drive, the practice of rejection that generates the thetic heterogeneity which is the precondition of meaning. Language falters because both the mirror stage essential for subject formation and castration anxiety (which places the maternal matrix under prohibition) elude one who is borderline. A strayed subject, one who is borderline huddles outside the pathway to the Symbolic, beset by an abjection that resonates in speech.

This resonance tends to be registered in one of two modes. In some instances, borderline discourse fails or "gives up" when it retains the material specificity of language—the music of sound—but is unable to make the leap into representation: the necessary movement by which, following the Law of absence, a subject creates the sign in the absence of being. Desemantizing language, the speech of the borderline analysand breaks up to reverberate only as notes, echoing infantile discourse. In other instances, borderline discourse is characterized by well-constructed grammatical forms in which words fit, even though they seem empty of all affect: the bottom has dropped out of the sign.

Kristeva suggests that, as distinct experiences of an economy of signification gone haywire, these modes of borderline discourse serve as a reminder of the diverse work language must do if it is to successfully teach the lessons of absence: humans, coming to be in a place where they are not, use words to bridge the gap between the lack that they are and the fullness of being which they desire. Her reflections on the "talking cure" consequently function as a refresher course of interest to all who wish to recall the basic functions of the linguistic economy in which humans undertake death-work. On the one hand, the work of "construction," to which the analyst and analysand turn in seeking a way out of the borders of language, may enable them to build meaning anew and reintroduce the logic of the Symbolic. Psychoanalysis has functioned, traditionally, as such a constructive effort. On the other hand, for persons whose language suggests that the lessons of the Symbolic, although learned, have not "taken," analysis would seem to call for work in condensation. Condensation would introduce a "play" of signifiers which, in metaphor and pun, would reinforce an archaic mode of articulation and enable the analysand to return to the echolalia of infancy, from there to retrace the steps of its education to the Symbolic. On that basis, the "deconstructive" work of condensation would facilitate the binding of metaphor—the movement of desire in identification with the other—to the metonymic dimension of desire that constructs the space of the Symbolic.

Were analysts to attend more often to aspects of the talking cure that she has highlighted, Kristeva observes, they would focus not only on the content of speech—that of the analyst and that of the client—but on the dynamic of the sign in their speech: gaps, sounds, resonances, and vocalizations. They would view the sign more often in terms of economy, matrix, and system, substantively expanding the terrain of analysis to include new regions of death-work. Kristeva contributes to such an effort when she probes the dynamics of speech that her borderline clients frame with a maternal metaphor and when she follows the trail of that metaphor as it moves from the abject borders of speech into language and society.

Key themes in Kristeva's work cited here—the infant's differentiation from the maternal body, the fort/da game, laughter, and the sign—underscore her wager that drive theory has not outlived its usefulness. Indeed, in a world where issues of power and knowledge ever more intimately and violently intersect, drive theory is even more prescient. Kristeva's words suggest that those who dismiss drive theory, charging that it reifies an organic substratum of existence which purportedly functions as the subject's base, act precipitously. She counsels that a most careful consideration of drive theory be made a requirement for all investigations of human agency that would not occult the agency of the subject.[4]

In the chapters that follow, as the history of subjects whose agency is constrained by their submersion in a sacrificial economy is traced, there will be reason to recall possibilities for emancipating agency brought to light by drive theory. When sacrifice is read in light of the wager Kristeva makes here on behalf of agency, grounds remain to believe that, if all humans are assigned the task of death-work, not all death-work is sacrificial. In the space of that difference, women may find resources for emancipating agency.

4

IN SEARCH OF THE MOTHER IN MIMESIS

FROM DEATH-WORK TO SACRIFICE

> The symbol manifests itself first of all as the murder of the thing.
>
> —Jacques Lacan

The world is a space of material contradiction for human subjects, placing them in jeopardy. Because the boundaries of the body are the first boundaries of the subject, the subject remains vulnerable to all the vicissitudes of material existence: the ongoing division and permeability of the subject's body pose a persistent threat to the subject's discrete status and claim to autonomy and agency. What happens to an emerging subject when, in the face of threat, it draws on the resources of language and culture to stabilize and maintain boundaries? This chapter focuses on risks to a subject and its agency that arise in the wake of its acclimation, by way of language, to the social context.

This chapter demonstrates that the Symbolic order is home not only to subjects whose acquisition of language is an occasion to celebrate self-mastery, but also to subjects who are challenged and at peril. It explores the Symbolic order as a site of conflict and attends to subjects who are not only at a loss, but also under siege. As their situation is analyzed, practices of death-work that specifically serve a sacrificial agenda are glimpsed. This chapter culminates in a full theory of sacrifice.

I. From Heterogeneity to the Symbolic Order

When the subject moves beyond the rudiments of the signifying process associated with the drives and submits to the complex conditions of life in the Symbolic order, it raises to the next power (a Hegelian *aufhebung*) the mimetic drama of division in which it has participated previously. Out of the fragments of a wanting-to-be the subject now abides in and as a space of difference bounded by the unity that is its founding pretense (the mirror image-signified) and the disunity that is now, definitively, irrecoverable as the source of its being (the maternal matrix-signifier) (1984c, 47). But new lessons in loss await the subject. Functioning to preserve the subject against relapse and forgetfulness, castration puts the finishing touches on the subject's initial course-work in separation.

In appealing to the traditional psychoanalytic language of castration to describe the subject's education to the Symbolic, Kristeva recognizes that the emerging subject, who previously has experienced otherness in terms of orality and anality, now articulates negativity in signs. The language of castration dominates this narrative of difference, revealing the interpolation of an always already split subject in a family structure (1984c, 123). Kristeva observes nothing essential in this scripting mechanism. There are numerous articulations of social relations—multiple texts—which give shape and form to the subject's death-work. Even so, the "constancy and tenacity of the family structure" (1984c, 177) assures its historical dominance in the Symbolic order. As a consequence, when Kristeva describes what the subject does when it undertakes death-work within the world of language, she joins the psychoanalytic tradition in turning her attention to the castration complex.

Kristeva highlights two major consequences for the subject of this thetic phase. First, she stresses the crucial importance of the "work" of castration. When Kristeva says that the phallic function instituted by castration is *"the* Symbolic function" (1984c, 47), she claims that signification completes itself—becomes meaning—because it negativizes the force of desire to make that force in its absence an object. The phallic prohibition—the bar of the signifier in the linguistic register—radically and viscerally portrays the necessity that desire not reach its aim if the distance that makes recognition possible is to be achieved: "signification exists precisely because there is no subject in signification" (1984c, 48). And this gap—between the imaged ego and the dynamic of the drive, between the mother and desire—is the thetic break that "establishes the place of the Other as the place of the signifier" (1984c, 48).

Consequently, when Kristeva appeals to castration, she asserts that the dynamics of sameness and difference that have accrued previously to the mimetic functions of the maternal matrix are now overlain by the Symbolic. Experienced in a mode of detachment, the mother of language is present now only in phallic guise. This decisive moment in the history of subjectivity is fraught with consequences because it signals the end of the formation of the thetic phase and "totalizes the effects of signifieds as having been produced by the signifier" (1984c, 47). The phallus itself is now a signifier: it is not given in the utterance; rather, the phallus refers outside itself to the boundary-making enterprise that has made enunciation possible.

However, the second consequence of the thetic phase—a phase sealed by castration—is equally decisive for one who would be a subject: the signifier/signified break is synonymous with sanction. It is the first social censorship (1984c, 48). As a consequence, Kristeva treats the thetic phase as the boundary of the social rather than its base. Submitting that "language is a defensive construction," she emphasizes the fragility of the thetic accomplishment and the tremendous burden it poses to the subject (1984c, 49). Language may position the subject so as to preserve it from the vicissitudes of its early history. However, the process that has made possible the interpolation of the subject within the sociosymbolic order—the negativity of the drives—is not summarily and finally set aside. The heterogeneity of the drives, however much scripted, managed, and domesticated by the Symbolic order, maintains the potential for disruption that no mirror, no other, and no phallic mother ever can contain (1984c, 50).

Invoking the name of Melanie Klein, whose significant contributions to psychoanalytic theory have not been sufficiently acknowledged by her peers, Kristeva challenges those who would not take seriously enough the persistent force of the drives in the Symbolic. With Lacan clearly the intended recipient of her criticism, Kristeva disputes those who suggest that the force of the semiotic is vanquished by the work of castration. For Kristeva, those who acknowledge the import of negativity in analysis only in terms of an incidental "failure" of the thetic decisively misconstrue the history of the subject. All is not set aside when a subject emerges in the Symbolic: because the force of the semiotic is the very precondition for the Symbolic—the motor of its signifying economy—its power remains a factor in the life of the subject. In fact, processes of negativity in the semiotic (e.g., orality, anality) have been generated and continue to be produced so that an emergent subject may attain and persist in a signifying position within the Symbolic order. Indeed, the subject already is prepared for the thetic break by an experience of otherness in the semiotic body of the maternal matrix which prefigures lessons in castration. These prelessons in difference give the subject the means to enter the Symbolic and submit to the dictates of its economy, but they also infuse a certain fragility into its work.

II. An Orderly Death: Sacrifice and the Symbolic

Why does Kristeva insist that we join her in observing a trajectory of negativity in the movement from the semiotic to the Symbolic that produces a subject, a trajectory that would appear to risk crossing the bar that has been erected across the signifier by the thetic break? After all, she does acknowledge that a semiotic which "precedes symbolization is only a theoretical supposition" (1984c, 68). What then accounts for Kristeva's apparent preoccupation with that which precedes the Symbolic? And why does Kristeva seem transfixed by the legacy of the semiotic associated with the work of negativity within the Symbolic order?

The entire Kristevan corpus turns on these questions, for Kristeva claims that these questions are not only hers, but also ours. Indeed, Kristeva believes that when she expresses an interest in a subject-creating route to the thetic, she only highlights the lure that semiotic border-work regularly poses for humans. She maintains that she makes humans' fascination by the semiotic expressly and centrally her own, as a theorist and psychoanalyst, only because unquestionably humans already appear captivated by the course of the thetic whenever they attempt to reproduce for themselves the process of the Symbolic's production: the history of their death-work. Whenever persons attempt to grasp and replicate conditions and processes that attend the founding of the Symbolic code and what it represses, they enact an engagement with the semiotic on which Kristeva explicitly focuses.

Under what circumstances do persons attempt to replicate the founding of the Symbolic order? Kristeva notes that such movement regularly emerges when their ordered existence is under threat. Moreover, because Kristeva observes a preoccupation with the thetic break and its accomplishments or failures at multiple levels of the signifying economy, she observes that a fascination with origins pertains not only to individuals, but also to social aggregates. Indeed, Kristeva detects a common pattern in responses that individuals and communities make to potentially lethal threats. Just as a subject under siege may deploy defensive strategies modeled on the initial bounding-practices of emergent subjectivity, so also may a community under threat engage in boundary-building ventures based on those that first brought it into existence as a social order. Indeed, practices aimed at resecuring order—the border-bounding efforts of diverse entities—tend to be mimetic counterparts of each other.

What, in sum, justifies Kristeva's decision to speak of the legacy of the Imaginary and to allude to a drive register of negativity and the semiotic even though these are, strictly speaking, articulable only within the linguistic register of the Symbolic economy? That Kristeva elects to discuss the legacy of the semiotic in the Symbolic hinges on her assertion that she merely sets forth for our close observation a preoccupation with the boundary-work of the thetic—its origins, status, and accomplishments—that is readily discernible at diverse levels of the signifying economy in times of conflict.[1]

Kristeva observes a variety of border-bounding practices, most notably in art and religion, by which humans aim to master the thetic by submitting the conditions of the thetic break to reflective consciousness. Indeed, that such practices are a widespread social phenomenon she believes warrants her close attention to the persistence of the semiotic legacy within the Symbolic. Moreover, the patterns that these exercises in thetic mastery take—artistic, religious, sacrificial—are of decisive interest to Kristeva as a woman. For as far as she can gather, the female body is a favored site to which persons have turned throughout history to reproduce their origins. Whenever order is challenged and they wish to resecure their boundaries against threat, they turn to that body to reinscribe, reflect on, and commit to memory subject-creating forces of negativity (jouissance and rejection in death-work) that first secured them in the world. That women's bodies are privileged material sites for discursive struggle with the questions, fears, and threats that shadow the thetic crisis when it emerges in the intertextual practices of human society provides further cause for Kristeva's strong interest in the persistent legacy of the semiotic within the Symbolic order.[2]

How do these boundary-inscribing exercises work to reproduce a history of origins in which women figure so prominently? According to Kristeva, the thetic break ensures that, whenever humans make an effort to reflect on the history of how they came to be in order to replicate and consolidate the accomplishments of that history, they conceive of negativity in terms of a hard-won, positioned awareness, placing it in service to representation. However, because negativity is dynamic, eluding all efforts to grasp it in sign, the task they assign to representation is of Herculean proportions. How can they place under the sign of representation a process of the signifying economy that works by excess, absence, and division? How can they even grasp a negativity proper to an uncanny work of negation and regeneration? How, under the auspices of a signifying economy, can they divert, confine, and translate negativity into a Symbolic modality that fixes it in position?

Lacan advises us of his answers to these questions when, in summing up the lesson of the fort/da game, he observes that "the symbol manifests itself first of all as the murder of the thing" (1977, 104). Kristeva offers her own responses to these queries in *Revolution in Poetic Language,* drawing on the work of anthropologist René Girard to extend Lacan's observations about death-work and representation. According to Kristeva, sacrifice puts an end to the vicissitudes of the semiotic by focusing, confining, and translating forces of negativity—the jouissance and rejection in death-work that makes human society possible—onto the body of a victim. Circumscribing the trajectory of a violence initiated in archaic mimetic conflict, sacrifice focuses the violence of primary differentiation on a victim and "displaces it onto the Symbolic order *at the very moment* this order is being founded" (1984c, 75). Sacrifice confers position on the symbol *and* the Symbolic order when the sublating potential of a structured negativity, confined to a sign, enables an original victim to represent the founding of the Symbolic order. Kristeva writes of the work of sacrifice on behalf of the signifying economy:

> sacrifice sets up the symbol and the symbolic order at the same time, and this "first" symbol, the victim of a murder, merely represents the structural violence of language's irruption as the murder of soma, the transformation of the body, the captation of drives. (1984c, 75)

In asserting that the linguistic and social order is founded on sacrifice, Kristeva claims that when sacrifice simultaneously puts into play the symbol and the Symbolic order, it establishes an economic relation. The sacrificial economy follows the movement of negativity associated with the drives but transposes its dynamic in order to confine and control it.

That Kristeva describes as sacrificial the process by which humans come into self-conscious possession of processes that condition the thetic and establish them in the world may give us pause. Of course, her choice of terms does have precedent: after all, Lacan has described the site of Ernst's fort/da game as a murder scene. Even so, we may wonder if Kristeva reliably describes as sacrificial the cooptation of death-work by a specific economic agenda. Is Kristeva's invocation of the word *sacrifice* an instance of creative license on Kristeva's part, or can a compelling case be made for Kristeva's claim that, under the auspices of representation within the paternal order, death-work becomes sacrifice?

There are three reasons why sacrifice is a wholly appropriate descriptive term for exercises in representation that would place death-work under the sign in order to secure human experience against threat. First, sacrifice very well describes a defining aspect of acts that turn bodies into signs: sacrifice kills soma in order to create symbols. How so? As described by Kristeva, sacrifice halts the risk that negativity poses: the potential for destruction of a bounded subject in the uncontrolled violence of rejection. Using sacrifice to put mimetic violence associated with death-work (orality and anality) under the control of signs, subjects master and domesticate conflict. Making sacrifice the watershed on the basis of which they institute the social and the Symbolic (1984c, 75), subjects concatenate order, "killing substance to make it signify" (1984c, 75).

That sacrifice reliably depicts the efforts of a boundary-invested subject to capture the power of death-work that pervades negativity is demonstrated not only by the sign-producing aspects of sacrifice, but also by its capacity for material production. In making soma into a symbol, sacrifice localizes and materially concretizes that which is uncanny about death-work. Facilitating what Elisabeth Bronfen calls "the somatization of the idea" (1992, 196), sacrifice marks the thetic break even as it transgresses this break in order to sublate it. Enacted at the juncture of the real, sacrifice turns on it, even though subjects grasp signs in sacrifice, not soma. Nevertheless, Kristeva observes that, as an exercise in management of the unconscious that would intercept its work and exert control over it, sacrifice reproduces key elements in the economic process of the Symbolic's production: the foundation of that economy *and* what it represses (1984c, 78). Most significantly, sacrifice shadows symbolic functioning. It replicates it, but not as an already existing system. Rather, sacrifice reproduces the process of the Symbolic's production (1984c, 77).

There is a third reason why sacrifice is an appropriate term to use when describing subjects' efforts to come to terms with their archaic history and manage their current circumstances. Sacrifice highlights the persistence of the positive forces of negativity in the wake of the death-work summoned by sacrificial practice. For example, cultures practice ritual sacrifice not only because sacrifice is believed to destroy forces that pose a threat to their community, but also because, in the wake of sacrifice, an entire community is purified: sacrifice secures social order. Links between *pharmakos* (scapegoat) and *pharmakon* (poison and antidote) are forged in the uncanny work of sacrifice (1982, 84). Thus, when Kristeva observes that sacrifice mimes conflict in order to bring it under the sway of representation, she emphasizes that sacrifice *wholly* mimes conflict: "it repeats not a detached object but the movement of the symbolic economy" (1984c, 79). Sacrifice works because it crosses the border of the Symbolic to reenact the path taken by signification as it moves through the semiotic to the Symbolic. Ensuring that someone can emerge at and as a signifying practice, sacrifice reenacts an unfolding of the Symbolic, carrying with it the productive motility of the economy that has given it birth as well as its risk. Negativity as agency-creating jouissance—and not only death-dealing rejection—flows into language at the point of sacrifice as the productive limit of the social and Symbolic order (1984c, 79).

In sum, sacrifice describes key functions of negativity that are joined under the sign within the Symbolic order. On the one hand, sacrifice functions as a rite of closure on death-work. In sacrifice, the disruptive and destabilizing potential of negativity is mimed, placed under the control of the sign, and neutralized. On the other hand, sacrifice produces a localized violence: a focused and contained death-work. Associated with the body of a victim, the positive dynamic of negativity is maintained in sacrifice, which distributes broad-based renewal and order in its wake.

Of course, that sacrifice freezes death-work in place, capturing its risks as well as its benefits and displacing them onto a victim, may prove problematic for the victim, even as it functions to the advantage of a community. That the agency of the many is promoted at the expense of one—often a woman—is disquieting, to say the least. Part II of this project returns to this issue in order to address it more fully.

Compelling reasons exist for acceding to Kristeva's decision to describe as sacrifice ongoing exercises in boundary-work at the juncture of the thetic that produce and reproduce subjectivity within a signifying economy. Even so, concerns may persist. As highlighted by the reference above to the community-building function of sacrifice, the term *sacrifice* conjures up explicit and graphic images of death: a group gathers at a village square or on a mountain top to perform a ritual that culminates in the killing of an animal or a human. Because Kristeva's application of the term *sacrifice* in *Revolution in Poetic Language* focuses on linguistic functions (as exemplified in the fort/da game of a child) that lie at some distance from such broader cultural tableaux, her use of the term *sacrifice* may seem forced. One rightly may wonder whether a woman executed for the crime of witchcraft and Ernst's mother—the object of his game with a reel—are both victims of sacrifice.

Kristeva does attempt in a variety of ways to document the work in culture of a sacrificial economy. For instance, she dissents from strategies that would restrict sacrifice to the "beginning" of history. And Kristeva recognizes the prominence of murder in narratives of origin common to indigenous peoples. Anticipating an expansive field of inquiry into human efforts to secure the Symbolic order against threat, Kristeva does not restrict the sacrificial gesture to the individual psyche or script it solely as child's play within a familial drama. She does not adopt a chronological positivism, common to some forms of psychoanalytic theory, that would locate the sacrificial moment in any one level of a society's signifying edifice, present or past, individual or social (1984c, 70). As a consequence, Kristeva seeks signs of murder in diverse forms and at multiple levels of the signifying economy. In *Revolution in Poetic Language,* she highlights two: art and religion.

Art is a privileged discourse. It embodies in virtually complete form the sacrificial economy Kristeva has sketched: in performance, the dynamic of the drives "bursts, pierces, deforms, reforms, and transforms the boundaries the subject and society set for themselves" (1984c, 103). Art breaks through the sign, "tearing the veil of representation to find the material signifying process." Crossing the thetic break and taking on death, the artist approximates the "scapegoat" of the sacrificial ritual, differing from other victims of sacrifice only because she or he does not complete the thetic cycle. Remaining caught in the semiotic motility of the artistic gesture, the artist does not "harness the thetic" and complete sacrifice as sign. That task, Kristeva observes, is left to religions, which "set themselves up as specialists on the discourse concerning this radical, unique, thetic event": the murder of soma on behalf of the sign (1984c, 70).

Even as Kristeva recognizes that religion joins art as a favored site for the discourse and practice of sacrifice, in *Revolution in Poetic Language* Kristeva does not appeal to religion as a resource that might facilitate her explication of the workings of a sacrificial economy. Instead, she gives her full attention to art, asserting that religion's schematizing of the subject-bounding exercise of sacrifice is wholly "prohibitive" (1984c, 80).

Kristeva's outline of a sacrificial economy in *Revolution in Poetic Language* is provocative and enormously suggestive. However, on two counts it also is disappointing. First, Kristeva fails to give serious attention to the work of religion in a sacrificial order. Even though the language of sacrifice—ritual, victim, priest—finds its primary societal home not in art, but in religion, Kristeva mines no riches for her theory from the vast sacrificial quarries of religious practice. Kristeva misjudges the complex tasks performed by religions in the sociosymbolic order. As a consequence, Kristeva does not avail herself of the instructive and illuminating insights for her theory to be found in religion.

Kristeva's theory is problematic at this juncture for a second reason. The function of sexual difference within the sacrificial economy she has sketched remains ambiguous. On the one hand, Kristeva observes a wide diversity of sacrificial "objects": an animal, a crop, a slave, a warrior, or a god (1984c, 76). Their very diversity suggests that they have been selected for sacrifice based on criteria other than their sex. On the other hand, Kristeva muses in an endnote that even though she finds René Girard's sacrificial theory of societal formation compelling, she is puzzled when he "rejects the sexual nature" of the violence he documents (1984c, 250). Determining that Freud's work uncovers beneath the "ethnological heap" a sexually differentiated violence which Girard has not addressed, Kristeva credits Freud for opening the way to examine sexually differentiated violence among human subjects. Regrettably, Kristeva's observation, confined to a note, does not become an explicit theme in *Revolution in Poetic Language.*

Even so, that Kristeva draws insufficiently for documentation of her sacrificial theory on religions' testimony to the work of a sacrificial economy and that she thematizes inadequately the role of sexual difference in this economy are only momentary disappointments. After all, *Revolution in Poetic Language* is far from Kristeva's last word on sacrifice. In her later works, especially *Powers of Horror,* Kristeva subjects sexual difference in a sacrificial economy to rigorous scrutiny and fully explicates its function. Moreover, Kristeva's very reticence to explicate the operations of religious institutions in a sacrificial economy has served to inspire this project. This project makes the work of René Girard central to its theorizing about sacrifice, as Kristeva has not done, drawing on Kristeva as well as on Girard to set forth an expanded theory of sacrifice. It moves beyond the extant parameters of Girard and Kristeva's sacrificial theories in order to highlight the function of religion in a sacrificial economy and the significance of sexual difference to its work.[3]

Because Girard is included in this inquiry, the social text and context of Kristeva's sacrificial theory are augmented. Girard, the primary proponent of a sacrificial theory of societal formation, offers a sophisticated and nuanced account that amplifies Kristeva's own voice. Indeed, were a list to be compiled of the most significant works on the social ontology of violence, Girard's analyses of sacrificial practices (1977, 1986, 1987) would rank among the most important. As Kristeva's own account is bolstered by way of Girard, a framework for inquiry into the work of a sacrificial economy in cultural institutions, especially religion, is secured.

Even as Girard strengthens aspects of Kristeva's theory, Girard serves as a foil for Kristeva, who highlights the role of sexual difference within the work of a sacrificial economy. Girard's inattention to the role of sexual difference in the sacrificial economy is challenged, and sexual difference emerges as a central theme in the sacrificial theory advanced here. The full-blown theory of sacrifice that emerges from this conversation with Girard and Kristeva sustains this project's larger thesis: linguistic and cultural codes, especially religion, *are* structured by a sacrificial economy oriented toward matricide.

III. Girard: Mimesis and Murder

In *Violence and the Sacred* (1977), Girard places violence at the origins of human language and culture. All language and institutions are structured by that event, and rituals do but represent or reenact it. These linguistic and cultural structures do not expressly name the originating event; rather, we learn of that event indirectly when we note that language, institutions, and rituals seem to be shaped in a particular way and in service to a particular objective. They function to conceal something or someone. When we ask what or who is being concealed by the shaping, veiling function of language and culture, we uncover a murder. We arrive at the site of this murder when we attend to two mechanisms that found the linguistic code which shapes how we experience the world: mimetic desire and surrogate victimization.

A. Mimetic Desire

A mechanism of mimetic desire structures the human subject's most basic experience of the world. Desire arises in the subject because it *lacks being*. Looking to an other to inform it of what it should desire in order to be, the subject finds that its attention is not drawn toward the object that the other recommends but toward the other who "must surely be capable of conferring an even greater plenitude of being" (1977, 146). Desire is shaped in imitation of an other. Girard identifies this other not as the father of Freud's Oedipal theory but, in gender-neutral fashion, as the model (1977, 170). By contrast also to Freud, desire is not directed toward an object of the model's desire but is rooted simply in the quest to be like the other.

Desiring what the other desires because of the prior, and more basic, desire to be like the other, the human subject notes that the closer it comes to acquisition of the object of the model's desire and through that acquisition, to the model, the greater is the rejection or refusal of the subject by the model (1977, 146–47). Veneration and rejection, mimesis and difference structure the subject's experience of the world until, in a shocking denouement of the dynamics of rivalry that sees the difference between the subject and its model obliterated by their common desire, the model becomes the monstrous double by whom the subject is repulsed and from whom it seeks distance (1977, 160–61). Desire becomes death. So announced, the mimetic crisis ends in the violent resolution of the subject's quest for being. Having sought in the model the being it lacks, the subject finds that its quest culminates when sacrifice confers a plenitude of being (1977, 146; 1987, 29).[4]

Several aspects of Girard's theory of mimetic desire link it in significant ways with Kristeva's. Like Kristeva, Girard describes the founding drama of the subject in terms of mimesis framed by the subject's lack and its desire for being. Further, in focusing on this drama, both Kristeva and Girard retrieve primary identification from the shadow of the Oedipal complex and illuminate its contours. For his part, Girard notes that mimetic desire does prepare the way for the Oedipus complex, but the direction of desire is different. Identification, not desire for an object-mother, comes first. Criticizing Freud for underplaying the significance of the *mimetic triangle* and focusing primarily on the Oedipal drama, Girard vows to give identification its due. Kristeva would concur with Girard when he submits that only careful attention to the former can account for humans' entry into language and culture and for the violence that accompanies that entry (1977, 176). Indeed, Kristeva and Girard insist that, without such attention to the turbulent dynamics of identification, violence is mystified and removed from human culture and the arena of human responsibility.

Kristeva and Girard share too a common perception concerning the function of the unconscious. Admittedly, Girard is wary of the term *unconscious* and prefers not to use it. However, he acknowledges that, "supposing that there is still any point in keeping such a term" (1987, 359), the unconscious refers to mimetic processes of emergent subjectivity. Like Kristeva, Girard claims for the "real unconscious" a form of desire that draws on primary identification to issue in "non-representational mimesis" (1987, 359). In sway to mimesis, the imitator has no need to represent that which it is imitating; indeed, not yet an accomplished citizen of the social order whose desires revolve around its object-choices, the subject of mimetic desire actually is incapable of representation.

Where Freud and Lacan lavish their attention on the savvy inhabitant of the sociosymbolic order, Kristeva and Girard draw toward a less worldly creature: the nascent subject of mimetic desire. Although Freud, according to Girard, "saw the path of mimetic desire stretching out before him and deliberately turned aside" (1977, 171), Girard holds to the path. Along this path, he spies a subject who, before it pledges itself to object-desire, with which Freud and Lacan are preoccupied, commits itself to growing and being like the model and "taking [its] place everywhere" (1977, 170). Granted, the vocabulary Kristeva employs to describe this subject's labor differs from Girard's. Unlike Girard, she is quite comfortable with referring to the dynamics of mimetic desire in terms of the unconscious (negativity or death-work). Nevertheless, in the majority, Girard and Kristeva concur in their descriptions of formative mimesis.[5]

As a consequence, that Girard echoes Kristeva in his appraisal of Lacan is not surprising. Reproaching Lacan for neglecting the issue of violence, Girard asserts that only if violence is traced to its origins at the boundaries of human life and society will humans be able to come to grips with its ongoing presence in their lives. Girard finds Lacan's theory problematic because Lacan is preoccupied with signification in the Symbolic order and fails to account for the emergence of violence within that order. Because Lacan insists on an "over-absolute separation" between symbolic structures and mimetic relations that attend the Imaginary, his system is wholly static. It also lacks a temporal dimension, which would enable him to account for the emergence of conflict within it, were he to attend to it (1987, 402).

Just as Kristeva uses the fort/da game described by Freud in *Beyond the Pleasure Principle* as a basis for disagreeing with Lacan, so also does Girard draw on this game to criticize Lacan. Observing that the commentary on the fort/da game is a central text in Freud's corpus, Girard finds striking Freud's presentation of the game "from a perspective that is both mimetic and sacrificial" (1987, 404). The moment when the child throws the reel away is a "veritable sacrificial expulsion" whose motive originates in revenge directed against the absent mother (1987, 404). Moreover, Girard affirms Freud for noting that the child's pastime initiates it in culture by means of a kind of ritual expulsion. In contrast to Lacan's child, who plays a "coldly intellectual game," Freud's child has a "thirst for revenge." Its play constructs the social context when the reel functions as the first "sacrificial substitute" (1987, 406). Indeed, if Freud does not "actually uncover the scapegoat mechanism, he comes very close to it in this text" (1987, 407). By contrast, as Girard reads

Lacan, Lacan misses most of Freud's intuitions. He bypasses mimetic conflict, substitutionary violence, and sacrifice, subsuming all aspects of Freud's account under "an all-powerful principle of a differential structural order that is 'always already' given" (1987, 408).

In the wake of his discussion of Lacan, Girard suggests that two paths open for psychoanalysis after Freud. One, which Lacan takes, focuses on word-play and "sacralizes language." The other, which Girard elects, concentrates on acquisitive mimesis and forms of conflict that lead toward the scapegoat mechanism (1987, 408). Clearly, Girard's criticisms of Lacan, overlapping with Kristeva's, locate him on a common path with her. As Chapter 3 shows, Kristeva finds Lacan's perspective on the fort/da game unduly reductive. Because Lacan perceives in the game only the controlled intellectual labor of a subject, he fails to observe that the game highlights the emergence of the child in the world by means of a struggle. When the child spits out "fort" and "da," its teeth do bite off words; however, but for its substitutionary gesture, they also would tear flesh. Thus, Kristeva and Girard concur in their appreciation for the lessons of the fort/da game: the game paradigmatically renders the subject's introduction to mimetic conflict in boundary-creating processes of formative subjectivity.

Admittedly, although Kristeva and Girard share common perceptions about the struggles of emergent subjectivity, their paths do diverge. Girard eventually leaves the path of psychoanalysis altogether, believing that psychoanalysis never addresses the sacrificial mechanism on which he wants to focus (1987, 408–409). Kristeva stays with psychoanalysis, though she charts a way along it traveled only infrequently by others. The distinct trajectory of her thought proves instrumental to her recovery of the key role of the maternal figure in sacrificial theory. The larger implications of her discovery are discussed in Section IV.

B. Surrogate Victimization

For the moment, however, this project follows Girard along the path he has chosen. Girard turns toward the broad social context and locates there patterns of mimetic crisis he has traced previously in a familial drama. Mimetic crises are writ large in society when social conflict escalates into widespread violence, culminating in the sacrifice of a surrogate victim. How does this happen?

Girard submits that groups of persons within a given society often display symptoms of economic, social, and political discord crisscrossed by multiplying trajectories of mimetic conflict (1987, 13). These conflicts coalesce and reinforce each other until, wholly beset by violence, persons turn in acts of unified violence against a single victim. Girard identifies this channeling of violence, by which a mimetic free-for-all gives way to a focused attack on a single, arbitrarily chosen victim, as the *scapegoat mechanism* (1987, 24–25). When aggression and guilt are displaced onto a sacrificial victim—the scapegoat (1987a, 125–26)—a single entity serves as a mimetic substitute for the many who condemn it. But in death, the scapegoat also is an object of veneration (1977; 86, 161). Taking the community's violence with it, the scapegoat enables the community to return to stasis.

Previously, in discussing mimetic desire associated with processes of subject formation, Girard has observed the work of violence writ small: a resolution of mimetic conflict announces a conclusion to the subject's quest for being. In a violent culmination of its sacred quest, the subject who seeks in a model the being it lacks finds that sacrifice confers a plenitude of being (1977, 146). Now, Girard looks at conflict writ large in society and observes that, in a simultaneous and reciprocal manner, sacrifice confers being on the social order.

Girard's sacrificial theory, attuned to the social context, is indebted to his reading of Freud's *Totem and Taboo.* According to Girard, Freud's insights in *Totem and Taboo* never have been appreciated fully. A theoretical formulation that would link sacrificial practices—in all their richness and detail—to actual incidents of violence eludes Freud. Able to forge ties between sacrificial rites and societal conflict only at one point in time—a single act of murder committed in prehistory—Freud seeks more stable ground. He locates the dynamics of patricide and the incest prohibition in the psyche rather than in history and societal institutions.

Returning to a path abandoned by Freud, Girard notes the tension—unresolved in *Totem and Taboo*—between violent deeds and complexes. Freud, unable to place patricide securely at the origins of history, relinquishes his claim on the social roots of violence with one hand, only to reinstate that claim with the other. When Freud acknowledges that the prohibition on incest not only corresponds to a repressed desire of the Oedipus complex, but also has "'a powerful practical basis'" (1977, 211), he reinstates the social context of patricide. If the dead father resides only in wishes of those under the sway of the Oedipus complex, the prohibition on incest yet proscribes real deeds.

Because the brothers in the primitive horde who banded together to overcome the father were rivals of one another in regard to women, only a law against incest could make human society possible. That the brothers, in Freud's account, ultimately prepare to engage one another as if the father never existed suggests to Girard the most compelling insight of *Totem and Taboo.* When the threat of violence shifts to the brothers—each the other's rival and each indistinguishable from the other—a drama once confined to the familial stage moves into a larger arena (1977, 212). Read in terms of mimetic and sacrificial crises, the themes of *Totem and Taboo* take root in society: the incest taboo, writ large, signals society's birth and its operative conditions.

That the father as the signifier of violence explains nothing is, according to Girard, Freud's most significant insight in *Totem and Taboo.* Human community is brought into existence only as mimetic struggles of its members with each other are neutralized by a violence inflicted on a surrogate victim (1977, 217–18). Maintaining in his own theory only the structure of reciprocal violence highlighted by Freud, Girard sees mimetic and sacrificial crises played out repeatedly in culture. For Girard, these patterns of crisis—visible throughout history in our cultural institutions and social practices—and not the familial themes of patricide and the incest prohibition survive *Totem and Taboo* as its major insight.

Precisely because he believes that familial language is irrelevant to the key argument of *Totem and Taboo,* the structure of sacrifice uncovered in *Totem and Taboo* serves Girard as a paradigm of societal creation: all cultures are founded on the murder of a surrogate victim. Moreover, because the prohibition against incest marks the origin of all cultural interdictions that function to found and maintain the social order, *Totem and Taboo* is paradigmatic for the religious dimension of human life and its interdictory work as well. Indeed, myths and rituals are "the first fruits of an endeavor to think this miracle of a collective murder that restores peace" (1977, 235). They perpetuate and renew it. The contexts of prohibitions may differ—food, weapons, land, women—but their sacrificial structure remains the same. Interdictions, marked by ritual and attested to in myth, enable a community to sublate violence because they establish a pattern of substitution by means of which the community can set itself off forever from a maelstrom of violence which has snared it.

C. Ritual and Myth

Religious rituals empower every society to commemorate the crisis that signals its beginning and to manage future manifestations of this crisis in ways that do not put an entire community at risk. Thus, religion becomes the primary cultural institution for the enactment of a *double transference* associated with the sacrificial mechanism (1987, 49). Violence, widespread in the conflicted setting of the larger society, passes through and among the gathered community, centers on the victim, and returns to the group. "It leaves as violence and returns as hominization, religion, and culture" (Hamerton-Kelly, 1994, 13). As the victim bears the sacred so also does it generate principles of culture which, sheltering the sacred, enable persons to exist.

Religion facilitates this double transference because, throughout human history, religions have specialized in the management of intensely mimetic phenomena (1987, 34). In the ritual life of participants in religion, we may regularly observe an "accelerated reciprocity of mimetic reactions." As ritual engagements intensify, persons who previously have been able to distinguish themselves from one another and enact inter*in*dividual relations do so no longer. New rituals develop which express *interdividual* relations. Typically, in the absence of predicted patterns of order, the sacred emerges as "quintessentially *monstrous.*" Finally, from within the midst of a kind of "perceptual scrambling" (e.g., a trance), ritual is transfigured: conflictive mimesis becomes reconciliatory mimesis. At a decisive moment in ritual, the victim polarizes, signaling the arrest of hallucinatory phenomena (1987, 35). Sacralized, the victim is killed, and the movement of violence, transformed by that act, moves away from the group. The victim, now worshiped as the source of peace, is a reconciling scapegoat.

The dynamics of ritual are decisive for their culture-creating work. The monstrous god, attracting and repelling, marks the sacred as prohibited. Indeed, by means of the scapegoat mechanism, the first differentiation of the one from the many and the first prohibition are one (1987, 11–14). Mimetic conflict, bounded by ritual, is not remembered in terms of the violence that has driven it, but in terms of that which the society is able to set aside in the wake of its achievements. The Law marks this site. All other markers of sacrifice generally are repressed. Indeed, the only testimony remaining from the culture-creating work of violence literally is constrained to seep out of the Law, emerging solely in images of contamination and pollution (1987, 17).

Thus, according to Girard, religion "humanizes violence" (1977, 134). It purges from human memory the actual conditions under which humans, in the course of becoming creatures of sacred signs, establish the conditions for maintaining themselves in community. Equipping a community to acknowledge the forces of creation and recreation that elicit violent acts, religion also grants distance: because participants in ritual are but passive agents of powers that lie beyond them, violence that might pose an absolute threat to human community is domesticated and brought under control (1977, 134).[6]

Where rituals enable societies to replicate in a controlled environment the sacrificial violence that gives rise to human community, myth records the reconciling work of violence. In myth, the victim is presented as the passive instrument of its own transformation. Though violence is transfigured in myth, Girard dissents from Lévi-Strauss and Lacan, who he suggests present myth as the fictive representation of processes of cultural development (1987, 109). Girard does recognize that myth cleanses sacrifice of its raw violence: a sacralized victim presents the work of violence as always already accomplished. However, Girard insists that sacrifice does not fall solely in the orbit of representation. Its referent is a collective violence that culminates in the death of the scapegoat. Girard dissents, therefore, from Lévi-Strauss and Lacan, who note only that myth teaches humans to reason: differentially (Lévi-Strauss [Girard, 1987, 109]) or symbolically (Lacan [Girard, 1987, 122]). Girard asserts that violence shadows myth, belying Lévi-Strauss's and Lacan's view that myth encapsulates the "immaculate conception of human thought" (1987, 112).

Attending closely to myth, Girard notes the repetition of certain motifs. He acknowledges that Lévi-Strauss expresses an appreciation for these elements and affirms their *logical structure* (1987, 124); however, Girard questions the limits of Lévi-Strauss's vision. Observing that the patterns Lévi-Strauss notices attest to violence, Girard finds improbable the prospect that myth would exhibit a persistent preoccupation with these themes if violence were mere window-dressing on lessons in cultural linguistics. The constellation of elements which appears repeatedly in myth intimates of real violence. Heroes in myth are distinguished by physical peculiarities (infirmities, limps, blindness) or by odors emanating from them. Myth features conspicuous persons who are viewed with suspicion by their neighbors (strangers, latecomers, other marginal hangers-on). Finally, elements of contagion (evil, illness) are scattered through myth. In every respect, these classic victim-marks point not only to the structure of language, but also to a pattern of societal conflict that features collective murder and the reconciling work of the victim (1987, 122–23).

Girard conceives the work of sacrifice recorded in ritual and myth in terms of a signifying economy. Ritual attests to a mechanism of surrogate victimization that gives birth to language: it is the first object of language. Having established difference where once there were only doubles and having created stability of meaning where once there was only violent reciprocity, sacrifice is a divine epiphany. Violence becomes the signifier of being, the signifier of the sacred, that makes possible the founding of the social order (1977, 131; 1987, 103).[7]

But signification also records the labor of a reconciling victim through whom violence has already passed and accomplished its transforming work. The work of victimization is placed under the sign. Inherently reproducible, this sign regularly is invoked when a chain of substituting rituals attempts to maintain the miraculous peace that sacrifice has made possible. Nevertheless and notwithstanding long centuries of articulation and exchange, the world-accomplishing act of sacrifice never wholly is contained by the domesticated sign. Reconciliation remains dependent on ritual's capacity to preserve and reproduce "the screams and cries that accompany the mimetic crisis" (1987, 103). In this manner, ritual continues to acknowledge the visceral labor of an initial victim whose death makes society possible.

Girard's invocation of the transcendent work of the victim demonstrates that Kristeva and he share a common perspective about signification oriented toward sacrifice. Kristeva traces the sounds of sacrifice to death-work, which, even if transposed to a patriarchal economy, still witness to origins in the semiotic shadow of the Symbolic order. She highlights the acoustic and kinesthetic qualities of sound which attest to the world-creating labor of death-work. As a consequence, she would wholly concur with Girard, who observes that signs not only skim the surface of culture but also reach down into its depths and who asserts that "there is no culture on earth that does not hold its sacred vocables . . . to be primary and fundamental in the order of language" (1987, 103).

Accordingly, Girard and Kristeva agree that sacrifice emerges in a signifying economy. Indeed, the central motif within Girard's sacrificial theory—the sacred—is consistently defined by Girard in terms of an economic process. Recognizing in the sacred the same dynamic that Kristeva's signifying economy evokes, Girard observes that "the sacred concerns itself with the destruction of differences" even as "this nondifference cannot appear as such in the structure" but only in the "equivocation of difference" in the destructive movement itself (1977, 241). The sacred is proper to those cultural spaces where "order has not yet taken hold, has only begun to take hold, or has lost its hold entirely." The sacred is that movement that "engenders, organizes, observes, and perpetuates" that structure, even as it also "dissolves, transforms, and on a whim destroys it" (1977, 242). Girard also emphasizes the economic elements of the sacred when he describes it in terms of "the interplay of order and disorder, of difference lost and retired, as enacted in the immutable drama of the sacrifice" (1977, 257). Moreover, Girard observes, as Kristeva does also, that the movement of the sacred is marked not only by sacrifice, but also by a fluid imagery of contagion. Such imagery enables us to think of order-creating and order-destroying violence, not so much in terms of the work of an individual—the Cartesian subject of a Symbolic order—but in terms of an impersonal entity: "a sort of fluid substance that flows everywhere and impregnates on contact" (1977, 258).

Thus, economies of signification described by Girard and Kristeva are oriented toward the same phenomenon: the ongoing effort of humans to arrive at structured accord with each other in the face of a persistent threat of violence, which they never seem capable of placing wholly under the control of signs. Rather, both Kristeva and Girard find that violence as a process is generative. Violence is not something of which humans grasp hold; rather, it grasps hold of them. As Girard observes, human community is the product of a work of violence which produces social order in a space whose boundaries are etched within limits set by the oscillating movement of a polar sacred. If too close to the social order, the sacred may consume it; and, if too distant, the sacred may withhold nurture that is necessary for the social order to emerge as the product of its "fecund presence" (1977, 268).

IV. Kristeva: Mimesis, Mother, and Murder

Kristeva shares much with Girard. Like Girard, she claims that the human entry into language and society—in its fragility and propensity for violence—is decisively shaped by a founding drama of mimetic desire, which Kristeva refers to in terms of the legacy of the Imaginary. Similar also to Girard, Kristeva turns to *Totem and Taboo* in her efforts to understand language, violence, and the sacred. Moreover, Girard and Kristeva understand that violence, language, and society constitute an economic relation, which, always in process, eludes human efforts to define and understand it. Finally, both find that religion plays a decisive role in the sacrificial economy on which they focus. At the same time, Kristeva differs in significant ways from Girard. Steps taken with Girard toward a sacrificial theory are now retraced with Kristeva in order to uncover, as Girard has not, a sexually differentiated violence in sacrifice that is directed toward the abject figure of the Mother.

A. Mimetic Desire

In her discussion of drive theory, Kristeva previously has located the birth of the human subject in the creative and destructive possibilities of mimesis. As Kristeva elaborates on the circumstances of this birth in *Tales of Love,* the complex dynamics of mimesis receive a more nuanced reading. Emphasizing a founding experience of differentiation, which forms the subject and serves as precursor of the social, Kristeva directs her attention to a triad that shapes the dynamics of primary narcissism. Kristeva argues, as has Girard, that the narcissistic structure which first positions the subject in the world is a threesome. Held in place by twin magnets of attraction—a father of individual prehistory and an archaic mother—a fragile and unstable subject hangs suspended between them (1987a, 374). Who are these parents whose relation to the subject predates the Oedipal drama?[8]

Kristeva places these parents in a ternary structure which, in its first stage, reveals itself in "mimetic play" over emptiness. Viewed both in terms of the Saussurian sign that places one in front of a bar and in terms of Lacan's gaping hole, this narcissistic play screens emptiness, or lines it (1987a, 23–24). Thus, for Kristeva the twin parties to narcissism protect emptiness, causing it to exist, and guarantee that their child can bridge emptiness to enter language and society.

Kristeva describes this bridging in terms of primary identification focused on an Imaginary father. In language remarkably similar to Girard's, she argues that mimeticism is nonobjectal. She writes that one identifies "not with an object, but with what offers itself to me as a model" (1987a, 25–26). Processes aimed at incorporating the model and assuming its being as one's own recall processes of oral maternal assimilation. However, because the preobject is given in language, when the child assimilates the paternal model to itself it swallows words. In reproducing the other's words, having and being merge for the child: it becomes like the other.

Although Kristeva attributes primary identification to a father, because the mimetic process predates the Oedipal stage and sexual difference, the twin poles of the mimetic process do not pertain to parental roles in the empirical sense. As a consequence, her portrait of mimesis closely parallels that of Girard, who likewise dissents from the Oedipal thesis. Indeed, because the disposition under exploration is not marked by an awareness of sexual difference, the Imaginary Father of prehistory is the same as "both parents" (1987a, 26) or even "X and Y" (1984a, 23). Those who fixate on "daddy or mummy" risk missing the most significant site for inquiry concerning human origins: the *border* between the psychic and somatic, idealization and eroticism. Indeed, borderline *states*—the Imaginary—entail a differentiation in being which is not rigidly demarcated in terms of maternal and paternal positions. Kristeva makes reference to paternal and maternal modes only to the extent that this language supports her efforts to glimpse a ridge between connection and distance, fulfillment and emptiness. Detecting that site, she seeks to observe a process of displacement through which an embodied being becomes an expressive organism and finds itself constituted in the very opposition between presence and absence (1987a, 28).

Distinguished from a metonymic object of desire—Lacan's *petit autre*—the preobject of identification that Kristeva cites is metaphoric (1987a, 29).

Kristeva's notion of metaphoricity counters Lacan's, which says that the human, in its education to the Symbolic, necessarily is set adrift, never to be the all for another that promises unity and being. In distinction from Lacan, who tells his story for that sadder but wiser adult, Kristeva uncovers a playful tale of promise at the zero degree of subjectivity (1982, 24). In this love story, at the very splitting that establishes the psyche, the subject emerges in an open space and as an open system supported in being between the One and an Other. Because love promises that for the One there is an Other, love promises being in difference. Experienced only indirectly, as a logical possibility of language, the metaphoricity of being is testified to by sounds "on the fringe of my being that transfer me to the place of the Other" (1987a, 37). Apparent not in the words of the Symbolic that would seek to master space, but only in the sonorous quality of those words, this metaphoricity secures one in being. In this manner, the infant's anchors in the maternal matrix, which previously Kristeva has associated with the breast, move from the infant's mouth to its ears. The infant, rocked gently in a hammock of sound, is spacialized into being by One's words to an Other: "Isn't he beautiful?" (1987a, 34).

Moreover, and akin to the lessons in orality she has noted earlier, Kristeva observes that these lessons in metaphor acquaint the infant with division in being: just as a buccal space differentiated by the present and absent breast is, for the nascent subject of the maternal matrix, always already a world of difference, so also is the space of sound bound by difference (a voice directed toward the infant and away from it toward another). Where the Symbolic order will read this perceived difference as an interdiction—the mother's desire is directed elsewhere and I am not the phallus she seeks—the Imaginary suggests a metaphorical reading of the social space that balances the interdictory Law of desire with the gift of love (1984a, 22). Because the vocal chamber that is the world resonates for the child as triangulated space, the difference harbored by this space is offered to the child not only as interdiction but also as gift. As One's words to an Other immeasurably enlarge the world, they promise an alternative to the potentially implosive or explosive space of the mimetic dyad: a sound bridge to communion in difference.[9]

Nevertheless, if a sonorous anchor always already founds a subject, securing it in a world of possibility and shaping the inassimilable alterity of its agency-evoking jouissance, Kristeva emphasizes that the "narcissistic parry" reaches out over an abyss (1987a, 42). Like Girard, Kristeva understands that primary identification is fraught not only with possibility, but also with danger. Precisely because the parental poles are held in place within the Symbolic order only because of the maternal desire for the phallus, the quest for being that is to produce a subject is marked necessarily not only by metaphor, but also by the metonymy of desire. As a consequence, this quest is painful: the subject emerges in the world to learn that the other does not want it, but another. The nascent subject necessarily confronts the radical emptiness of being (1987a, 43).

Moreover, analogous to Girard, Kristeva perceives that violence shadows the subject who approaches the thetic break. Girard positions violence in the escalation of a mimetic struggle between model and disciple, in which the cancellation of difference between them leads the disciple to desperate measures in an effort to recover difference when challenged by a monstrous and threatening double. Interestingly, for Girard, the original triadic structure of mimesis becomes a dyad under the conditions of the thetic crisis. The object of desire fades from the view of the disciple and model who, mirroring an escalating violence for each other, are caught in a double bind—each a lethal threat to the other—until their violence can be visited on a scapegoat-sacrifice through whom thetic order is secured and difference, now domesticated, reinstated.

By contrast to Girard, Kristeva maintains the triadic form of primary identification in her analysis of the thetic break. The maternal abject does not fade from view in the thetic crisis. Moreover, Kristeva's analysis of the crisis of the thetic break enables her to offer a typology of violence whose nuances attend to sexual difference. Violence haunts a ternary structure whenever access to the subject-creating space promised by the play of the inassimilable alterity of Imaginary jouissance within an original triad eludes the child. Whenever the work of castration, remaining incomplete or ineffectual, precludes effective management of this space by the Symbolic, violence may erupt. Indeed, because of the essential fragility of bounding-work undertaken by the subject in its formative stages, strong potential for boundary failure exists. And when that boundary-failure occurs, invoking violence, that violence is likely to be enacted along sexually differentiated lines. Violence is enacted as matricide.

B. Victimization and Sexual Difference

Why do Kristeva and Girard part ways in their thinking about sacrifice? Clearly, they concur about formative subjectivity, as attested to in their similar criticisms of Lacan. They share also a notion of the origins of violence in mimetic conflict and its extension and elaboration, by way of sacrifice, in culture. Why then does Girard not join Kristeva in making sexual difference a key aspect of his treatment of sacrifice?

In Girard's recent work, he does not reject altogether the role of sexual violence in sacrificial conflicts, as Kristeva has claimed. He is open to considering ways in which sexual difference is associated with the victimage mechanism. He indicates that, were we to engage in an extensive empirical analysis of myth, we would be able to determine whether women are more often victims of scapegoating than are men (1993a, 141). However, if we were to investigate ritual and sacrifice as such, Girard doubts that we would obtain clear evidence concerning the privileged victimization of women. He does understand that women are mistreated in most human cultures. Nevertheless, he expresses reservations about efforts we might make to read sexual difference in sacrificial practices "in the broadest mimetic sense" because he believes that, in many instances, "it cannot be done" (1993a, 142).

Why is Girard skeptical of such a project? Why, to the contrary, is Kristeva strongly committed to this undertaking? Answers to these questions take shape when two key differences between Girard and Kristeva are observed. First, when Kristeva reflects on mimetic violence, she does examine the work of sexual difference in the broadest mimetic sense, following a route that implicates it in key operations of mimetic conflict. Second, when Kristeva examines visceral elements in mimetic violence, she focuses on a material dialectic of the unconscious. Girard does not join her in these pursuits. In the first place, Girard doubts that sexual difference and mimesis are closely linked in the *generation* of violence. He perceives that sexuality is oriented toward difference and mimetic desire toward sameness. All differences, including sexual difference, efface before mimetic desire, especially when that desire is transmuted in conflict (1993a, 139). Second, although Girard is cognizant of material indicators of mimetic violence (e.g., the sounds of sacrifice in ritual and victim-marks and smells in mythic citations), he remains wary of associating these factors in mimetic conflict with the unconscious.

Indeed, if the unconscious is a site dedicated to the repression of object-centered sexual desire, as Girard believes Freud to have claimed, Girard is prepared to dismiss it without qualification. Were he to make a foray into the hidden environs of the unconscious, Girard believes he would embark on a wholly unwarranted detour from his central mission of tracking violence in society. Girard, not unlike Butler, perceives the psychoanalytic appeal to the unconscious as a mystification of social prohibitions. From his perspective, sexuality is not the ultimate *concealed* force, but the ultimate *concealing* force (Schwager, 1987, 28). To the degree that humans invest their desire in sexuality, they remain ignorant of the actual locus of desire and the capacity it harbors for truly lethal forms of conflict (Girard, 1987, 220–21). Not disavowing that sexually oriented object-desire may constitute an occasion for conflict, Girard reaffirms that conflict attributable to sexual desire pales before violence that emerges with mimetic desire. Therefore, persons who seriously seek to come to grips with violence must focus on mimetic conflict. Sexual desire is of tangential interest only, especially since psychoanalysts have groundlessly magnified its powers by sequestering it in the so-called unconscious (1977, 177).

Not finding the psychoanalytic perspective persuasive, Girard attends closely neither to sexual difference in the fundamental work of mimetic violence nor to a material dialectic of the unconscious. Only Kristeva, on the trail of death-work, pursues sacrifice into and out of culture, tracking sexual difference all along her way. And only Kristeva, in focusing on death-work and its material markers, follows violence into the body and out of it again. Her distinctive mission, illuminating sexual difference and a material dialectic in the work of violence as Girard does not, speaks to weaknesses in his theory and usefully augments it. Simultaneously drawing her theory forward as well as his, Kristeva offers insights that enhance sacrificial theory in general.

Kristeva's efforts suggest that Girard's determination to subordinate sexual difference within sacrificial theory as a topic of secondary concern is not well founded. To be sure, Kristeva does concur with Girard that mimetic conflict is defined by a threatening sameness. Further, relations in the Symbolic order are framed by difference: coded by the phallus, sexuality is articulated in a system that oppositionally positions males and females within it. Agreeing with Girard, Kristeva avers that sexuality in this order is not the cause of mimetic violence. Nevertheless, Kristeva does not believe that sexual difference plays an ancillary role in a sacrificial economy, always subsequent to the generative work of violence. She intends to speak of sexual difference and not restrict her inquiry to sexuality within the Symbolic order, as have its masters (e.g., Lacan).

Demonstrating her point, Kristeva asserts that foundational violence is characterized by a material dialectic which bears marks of a maternal abject. The maternal body sets in place a scription, not yet a sign, that shapes iterative patterns of mimetic conflict. As a consequence, nascent human subjects receive from the abject their first lessons in violence. Detected in images of defilement and pollution, the abject offers information about violence that Kristeva finds crucial for a thorough assessment of mimetic violence. When humans mobilize the resources of the Symbolic order on behalf of sacrifice, Kristeva finds that they recall these maternally oriented markers. As they draw on these marks, they make sexually differentiated violence a privileged expression of sacrificial conflict.

Maintaining a psychoanalytic perspective, Kristeva glimpses in a material dialectic the ultimate concealed force of mimetic desire. This force is not the Father and his Law, the focus of prohibitions directed toward sexual objects. To the contrary, Kristeva associates it with the figure of the Mother, whom she detects at the borders of language in subjects' bounding work. Thus, for Kristeva, that which is ultimately concealed within mimetic conflict is not the patricidal sign that castrates, but the matricidal abject that threatens annihilation. When females predominate among victims in the sacrificial economy that we call patriarchy, those who violate them are acting to counter this abject menace on which sacrifice turns.

In sum, Kristeva would avow that, if Girard were to employ resources of psychoanalytic theory to address the material dialectic of the unconscious, he would not find his work on violence sidetracked. For Kristeva can concur with almost all of Girard's criticisms of psychoanalysis and still understand that, because the unconscious does not serve only the Symbolic order, legitimate grounds remain for maintaining an interest in it. Kristeva would invite Girard to adopt her own careful distinctions between primary and secondary repression, for she associates the broader, extra-Symbolic, mimetic investments of the unconscious with primary repression and the differentiation of subjects from objects with secondary repression. She associates primary repression with nascent subjects' visceral encounters with uncanny alterity. As these meetings create in the nascent subject the possibility of difference that is prerequisite for its attaining full status as a subject, primary repression harbors also a threatening mimeticism: a sameness that suggests a potential dissolution in being.

This uncanny alterity, tracked to the archaic bases of human being at a loss, does not fall solely in the orbit of the Symbolic. Witnessable at the very borders of language where meaning is born and dies, it attests to a material dialectic which signs never fully can possess. Marks of sacrifice—sounds, smells, fluids—confirm that encounters with the uncanny do not only accompany sacrifice, as Girard has thought. They also exercise a direct role in *shaping* for subjects the face of the mimetic threat they confront, a face Kristeva reads as maternal. They influence as well what subjects choose as weapons to counter this threat: material menaces call for *materially lethal* weapons.

Why should Kristeva's thesis be taken seriously? Why should Girard turn from analyses of the social context, which have enabled him to offer a powerful account of mimetic conflict, to join Kristeva in probing the margins of language, seeking evidence of subjects' hostile encounters with an all-but-invisible, abject, maternal entity? Reasons to do so emerge when we observe that, because Kristeva does attend to the border-work of subjects, she is able to bolster a weak link in Girard's theory. What is this link?

We can detect this link in the course of observing that a sacrificial theory has three major tasks: it should reveal why conflict emerges among humans; it should account for the elaboration of conflict; and it should explain why humans kill in order to bring an end to conflict. Girard skillfully addresses two of these charges. He explains how conflict emerges among humans when humans are caught up in processes of mimetic desire that attend emergent subjectivity. He describes how conflict is elaborated within a signifying economy when persons who are beset by multiplying trajectories of mimetic conflict invoke substitutionary violence or surrogate victimization to bring an end to conflict. But Girard is less successful in establishing why persons who are beset by escalating levels of violence kill each other. A full theory of *sacrifice* turns on this third point; in its absence, Girard has a theory only of cultural violence, not of sacrifice.

Girard postulates that ancestors of humans did experience conflict; however, they were not beset by a homicidal mimetic frenzy. They settled their quarrels, as animals usually do today, when one party to a display of force submitted to the other (1987, 90). But, at the threshold of hominization, violence-defusing animal instincts were apparently lost. Why? Girard cites the mental complexity of humans as a possible cause. As the evolving human brain became more powerful, humans became capable of intensified mimetic relations, aggravating "instinctual patterns" of acquisitive mimesis found among animals (1987, 95).[10] Further, humans used their enhanced intellectual powers to create artificial weapons, as animals do not, which were much more lethal than their animal peers' claws and teeth (1987, 87). But why could not enhanced intellectual powers have led humans, even more successfully than animals, to adjudicate their differences nonviolently (Webb, 1988, 198)? Would not gestures of submission that animals make to one another have been even more successful when, in the course of hominization, they were transposed into words?

Further, what led humans to believe that collectively killing a victim would garner them peace? Why did they imagine that it would create community? Did they arrive at this determination only after the fact, when an initial incident of collective violence was seen to generate peace? Girard is fairly much constrained to advance this argument (1987, 25–28) even though it requires him to treat the founding moment of his sacrificial theory as capricious. As a consequence, Girard cannot invest too heavily in ruminations on the origins of homicidal violence; instead, he must base the overall saliency of his theory on the preponderance of evidence that shows humans resorting to collective murder across the course of history.

What accounts for the vulnerability of Girard's theory before the question of collective and homicidal violence? We can trace to a common blind spot in his theory both his inadequate attention to the role of sexual difference in sacrificial violence and his inability to explain why mimeticism among humans escalates into murder: Girard does not attend adequately to soma. Assuredly, he does take note of it. In discussing victims, he observes that they bear common material marks: infirmities, odors, polluting fluids. He observes also that, under the repressive constraints of the Law, the only evidence to remain of the raw culture-creating work of violence is a contaminating refuse which, seeping from the Law, threatens to corrupt it. Even so, for Girard, material marks that regularly accompany mimetic conflict do not define its work. How might his sacrificial theory be advanced if he considered that they might?

Were Girard to make soma critical to the work of sacrifice, his sacrificial theory would be impacted in two ways. He would find that sexual difference has a privileged relation to the sacrificial enterprise, and he would be able to explain why the violence he tracks across culture reaches a murderous denouement. Because Kristeva already focuses on these two objectives in her work, the advantage for sacrificial theory of advancing along the path she blazes may be demonstrated readily.

Ever attentive to the roots of violence in subjects' semiotic ventures, Kristeva traces violence to the edges of hominization, analyzing, as Girard does not, the most archaic, prerepresentational forms of human signification. She observes in nascent subjects two factors relevant to their proclivity for murder: language has a very specific impact on their accession to a social world, and soma plays a distinct role in confirming for subjects their linguistic achievements. Drawing on these factors, Kristeva can demonstrate that violence escalates among humans to lethal levels more often than it does among animals, but not for reasons Girard has cited. Rather, it increases initially when humans, invoking and exercising their capacity for language, find that they literally *struggle* for the sign. It continues to escalate because they return repeatedly to the *somatic bridge* they have traversed in the course of hominization, seeking to secure themselves against loss by crossing it again and again.

To be sure, Girard shares with Kristeva an overall sense of the key role that language acquisition plays in intensified mimesis. Although animals share with humans a capacity to imitate, they are unable to stand outside their immediate circumstances (dominator or dominated) to apprehend the whole: they are incapable of representation (1987, 92). Therefore, Girard appears to concur with Kristeva that, in the absence of signs, animals do not perceive that circumstances of domination pose a radical threat: animals do not perform death-work. Although animals have quite useful gestures of threat and submission, their modes of communication do not divide them in being as does human language. They are not constrained, as are humans, by an alienation that causes them to be in places where they are not. When animals are beset by conflict, they are unlikely to perceive that they are radically threatened with oblivion and the total dissolution of being. By contrast, once in sway to the gravity of language, even if not wholly creatures of it, humans perceive conflict in reference to the lack that they are and experience it on a mimetic continuum that, even in the immediate absence of a lethal threat, always is perceived as potentially deadly.

But Girard misses an additional factor that is crucial to language and social world acquisition: the centrality of subjects' somatic work to their achievements. That Kristeva does take note of this activity is decisive for her differing treatment of mimetic violence and its causes. She is able to show that at the very threshold of hominization a material topos establishes a particular pattern for human conflict: humans attain social position when they *viscerally* extract themselves from a mimeticized morass of being which threatens them with a stifling safeness. This initial pattern of subject-creating conflict shapes future incidents of mimetic disorder among humans. Human violence is murderous because only humans, at the very borders of language, *linger over the flesh they tear* in their accession to a social space. These first lessons in violence teach them that, should they ever find themselves back at the very threshold of meaning because of life-threatening conflict, if they hold close to the flesh of a victim and probe it, they will be able to summon the very powers of life itself from within its somatic depths.[11]

Drawing on this insight, Kristeva does not trace sacrifice among humans to a blind fury that, if unchecked by social sanction, marches inexorably toward murder. To the contrary, she links sacrifice with the human propensity, under circumstances of threat, to engage in the extension and elaboration of violence. Sacrificial death is the final outcome of a violence that penetrates the body to its limits, seeking to wrest life itself from its hidden depths. Because only humans perform death-work, only humans desire by means of tortuous extensions of violence to surmount its limits and obtain that which eludes them as servants of signs. They return to the threshold of hominization in search of a life-giving and life-taking force, believing that, if they once again probe soma, retracing the steps they have previously taken in struggles of formative subjectivity, they may triumph over all current threats to being.

A cursory examination of sacrifice confirms the initial plausibility of Kristeva's thesis. After all, examples of sacrifice do not generally attest to frenzied killing where the enormity of force brought to bear on the victim culminates immediately in its death. To the contrary, the victim is made to gradually give up its life, as in instances of stoning or burning. Or the victim's body parts receive invasive magnification, as in instances of torture and mutilation, which culminates eventually in its death. These patterns suggest that, when violence is augmented in the face of escalating mimesis, blind rage is not an intrinsic element in that intensification. The fast and furious murder either is not an instance of mimetic violence or it is a permutation in its basic pattern. The basic pattern links lethal violence among humans with their labored attention to invasions of the flesh that are simultaneously deadly and life-giving.

Focusing on humans' somatic investments in violence, Kristeva accounts also for the emergence in human community of deadly surrogate victimization. Humans do not arrive at their confidence in the peace-generating potential of collective murder after the fact, as Girard suggests. Instead, they turn toward sacrifice when they draw on an internal logic of violence to which they have been introduced in the course of subject formation. Invoking this logic, humans believe that, if they kill, they create community. This logic is attested to in the work of soma: in the throes of formative subjectivity, humans call forth soma, crossing into and out of it, to create social space. They do this not because of mute biological instincts, but because, in sway to their emergent capacities for signs, they glimpse in that very process that the social world is created when soma is constrained by sign-making. And, ever after, they return to this process, painstakingly reiterating it, whenever the boundaries of their world appear threatened. Torturing and killing substance to make it signify, subjects master mimetic threat; conversely, somatizing signs, they cross through the thetic break, transgressing the limits of mimesis, in order to reestablish positions in the world.

Interpreted in this light, collective sacrificial violence constitutes a kind of shared reminiscence of origins, which, writ large, privileges the abject material markings that first grant subjects a place in the world. Not solely a feature of the signs that govern that world, these marks of death-work retain intimations of a divine or immortal labor. As a consequence, under absolute threat, subjects turn again to them, believing that, if they are able to draw on their power in rites of sacrifice, lingering over the flesh and evoking its powers, they will emerge from conflict no longer constrained by the mortality of labor which properly is theirs as residents of the Symbolic order.

Finally, because Kristeva focuses on work undertaken by humans at the very threshold of language, where they act to secure and subsequently resecure their existence in the world, she is able to trace here the privileging of maternally marked flesh. The initial pattern of sacrifice is a form of matricide. Writ large and repeated across the course of history, humans can be seen under circumstances of acute threat to preferentially invoke abject marks of maternity in acts of sacrifice. Images of contaminating fluids and other polluting substances serve ever after to recall the violent ejection/rejection of the nascent subject from the maternal matrix: the murder that has made possible its initial ascent into the Symbolic order.

In the next section, sacrifice as a coded, cultural response to the threatening maternal abject is discussed in detail. First, however, a nonsacrificial mode of encounter with the abject—melancholia—is examined, in order that victimization and sexual difference may be considered across the broadest expanse of a material dialectic. The comments that follow indicate that the sacrificial gesture, deployed along sexually differentiated lines, is more common to men than to women. They suggest also that mimetic violence among women, under circumstances of intense elaboration, is more likely to be implosive and suicidal.

This discussion of melancholia as a form of mimetic violence focuses initially on violence in the origins of subjectivity. However, multiple levels of the signifying economy are implicated in this analysis, as the discussion moves forward to address issues of sexual difference that emerge when the dynamics of violence are writ large. On those occasions, society may be read as a generalized text of an ongoing battle with abjection. In that conflict, the force of negativity—both promise and threat to structured order—is placed under the control of the sign and the institutions that support it.

What distinguishes the twin encounters—implosive and explosive, suicidal and sacrificial—with the abject by the subject of the thetic crisis? When the subject of the thetic crisis responds to the threat of the abject with implosive violence, as Kristeva recounts in *Black Sun,* the subject refuses the necessary Symbolic work of negativity (the castration complex) on behalf of the social order. When the subject reacts to the threat of the abject with explosive violence, as Kristeva delineates in *Powers of Horror,* the subject challenges the terms set by the Symbolic for brokering peace with the abject: the subject does not believe that the Symbolic has fully secured an object/order against threat. Although Kristeva insists that neither form of violence belongs exclusively to one sex,[12] ferment at the margins of the Symbolic order often bears the mark of sexual difference. As a consequence, in *Black Sun,* those whose violence is implosive are often women; in *Powers of Horror,* those whose violence is explosive are often men. How does Kristeva describe these diverse encounters with the abject?

According to Kristeva, when those who would be subjects are unable to cross the bridge to the Symbolic proffered by the Imaginary Father—there to inscribe a separation from the maternal matrix in sign—they may retreat from the Symbolic. "Melancholia" is the term given to this implosive gesture of withdrawal by Kristeva: to be melancholic is to persist in mourning for the maternal Thing. The Thing, only an ersatz object, is a light without representation: a black sun. The Thing is the center of attraction and repulsion from which subjects are disinherited, even though its fortunes are not yet secured by another dimension: the Symbolic. For those who are melancholic, the wound at the core of their being, which for others would summon the sign of castration, is unnameable, wholly archaic, submerged in sadness: the affect is their Thing (1989, 14).

Those who are melancholic refuse roles as initiates of language and act out the loss that language mandates without the protective distance that language willingly provides as compensation for loss. According to the rules of initiation, humans are required to leave the maternal body in order to be: matricide is mandated (1989, 27). But the Law decrees also that humans must agree to find Mother again in signs: in the work of negativity that makes of the Mother the very space of loss that brings the Symbolic order into being. But melancholics decline to accept the behest of the Symbolic. As Ewa Ziarek insightfully observes, in refusing loss, they absorb alterity within the structure of their own identity (1993, 71): they carry the maternal Thing inside. Writes Kristeva of the consequences of this submerged, imploded gesture, more common to women than to men:

> They have lost the meaning—the value—of their mother tongue for want of losing the mother. The dead language they speak, which foreshadows their suicide, conceals a Thing buried alive. The latter, however, will not be translated in order that it not be betrayed; it shall remain walled up within the *crypt* of inexpressible affect. . . . (1989, 53)

Those whose pact with the Mother precludes them from coming to terms with Mother-loss in the language of death-work may carry her inside; however, they risk a loss not only of words, but also of self.

Why do melancholics refuse the life-sentence of the Symbolic order (the Law of absence or the Father's Law)? On what basis do they find that their only options for dealing with abjection are suicide or matricide? And why do they embrace the former rather than the latter? For Kristeva, women fulfill the mandates of the thetic break—the castration complex—with much more difficulty than do men. Only by means of an "unbelievable symbolic effort, is the other (other sex, in the case of the heterosexual woman) eroticized" (1989, 28). That the Symbolic order does not pose the attraction for women that it does for men thus accounts for the unsettled prospects of women in the social order and for the seriousness with which they may consider other options.

Writing of Kristeva's comments on melancholia, Ziarek (1993) submits that Kristeva's perceptions of the motivation for melancholia differ substantively from Freud's. Freud sees in melancholia a violent cannibalism: a hidden, hostile attack on the other. By contrast, Kristeva emphasizes that, acutely aware of loss, those who are melancholic do not challenge loss by attacking its signs. Indeed, Ziarek observes, Kristeva is extraordinarily precise in her analysis of the gesture of melancholic refusal: melancholics do not so much refuse loss as they *refuse to accept that the Symbolic system compensates adequately for their loss* (1993, 73). Consequently, their atheism before the Symbolic order and its sacred Law does not hinge on sheer refusal of its tenets; rather, they disbelieve that the other can be appropriately mourned through processes of representation touted by the Symbolic. For those who live in its grip, melancholia is, Ziarek suggests, "a powerful critique of the desire to master alterity through the order of representation" (1993, 73). Ziarek suggests rightly that, when Kristeva discusses melancholics, she does highlight their political stance: when they resist an order that would master alterity in terms of linguistic proficiency, they criticize the arrogance of language and invite others to experience death-work in ways that honor the excess of a difference beyond all capacity of signs to subsume it.

If the Symbolic order and its Law are not welcomed by those who are melancholic as the means by which they might deal with abjection (and survive), so also is sacrifice an unpalatable alternative for them. Sacrifice—an explosive rather than implosive violence—works to abreact abjection through representing it in maternal hatred. But this tack is wholly problematic for most women: how can the Mother be that "bloodthirsty Fury" whose murder is warranted? After all, "I am She (sexually and narcissistically), and She is I" (1989, 29).

But what of those persons who do not disavow a strategy that would justify matricide on grounds of self-defense? How do they respond to the maternal abject found lurking in the ruins of the bridge to free and full agency, which, under the guidance of the parents of preindividual history, they were to have crossed? According to Kristeva, those who spy a murderous, maternal menace in these ruins summon every resource of the Symbolic in their struggle against her: the ruins become a battle turf of abject warfare with the Mother. And, when the terms of this struggle are subjected to the full force of the sign, the ensuing conflict is often subject to widespread institutional elaboration: death-work by sacrifice is writ large in culture. Historically, vast resources—most notably religion—have been mobilized on behalf of those forces that would do battle with the abject.

C. Coding Matricide: Abjection, Defilement, Ritual Sacrifice

Kristeva's typology of matricide, attentive to the historical legacy of matricide, is articulated most fully in *Powers of Horror.* Her typology is characterized by three moments. First is her account of the conflict that is associated with that most archaic aspect of emerging subjectivity: *abject violence.* Second is her description of a modality of death-work that, rooted in the movement of abjection, serves as precursor to sacrifice: *defilement.* With her account of defilement, Kristeva claims that, before sacrifice places death-work under the sign, defilement—a scription without sign—functions as a prologue to sacrifice. Pollution fears which focus on defilement identify the territory of death-work as an abject threat to be contained, and they map that threat so that steps can be taken to excise all corrupting powers and rebound order from disorder. Finally, Kristeva's typology culminates in a review of efforts the subject makes to submit death-work to the full force of the sign: *sacrifice.* An examination of each moment in this typology indicates that, because sexual difference plays a decisive role in the sacrificial economy, Kristeva's sacrificial theory is, above all, a theory of matricide.

In *Powers of Horror,* Kristeva writes of an abject violence that, illustrating the first moment in her typology, serves as preface to narratives of defilement and sacrifice: "I imagine a child who has swallowed up his parents too soon . . . and to save himself, rejects and throws up everything that is given to him. . . . Even before things for him are . . . he drives them out . . . and constitutes his own territory, edged by the abject. . . . What he has swallowed up instead of maternal love is an emptiness, or rather a maternal hatred without a word for the words of the father; that is what he tries to cleanse himself of, tirelessly" (1982, 5–6).

Kristeva observes that the child in exile from the psychic space promised by the Imaginary strays and does not get its bearings. Asking "Where am I?" instead of "Who am I?" the child who experiences abjection is no longer supported in being by the parental poles of possibility that bridge emptiness. Foundering, this child risks at every moment a fall into the abyss. Given that threat, the child who asserts a sacrificial strategy (in contrast to the implosive gesture of the melancholic) seeks to maintain itself in the Other in a manner similar to that employed by the twin protagonists of Girard's mimetic drama. Having been led astray on the bridge that was to lead to an open agency first promised in the Imaginative play with absence and presence at the juncture of the parental poles of possibility, the child explores the dark side of being. It seeks to incorporate a devouring maternal body in order to give birth to itself in that way. Falling back on the archaic possibilities of oral assimilation—now perceived in terms of reciprocal threat—the child will bite before being bitten (1982, 39).

In contrast to the child for whom the Imaginary constitutes a successful bridge to agency in the Symbolic, this child is beset by ambiguities. Of course, the imagery of abjection is inscribed symbolically, but the terror so inscribed always recalls a prior moment at the margins of order when outside and inside have threatened to merge and annihilate one who would climb free of the abyss. Without the ladder to the Symbolic offered to the child by the Imaginary father—the X and Y of preindividual history (1984a, 23)—the Mother is the primary site of abjection. Fluids from the maternal body evoke for the child its violent expulsion from the maternal interior in all of its risk. Her blood and milk—source of life and death, nourishment and threat—are first witness to the drama of archaic differentiation. They form an initial topos—not yet representation—for a subject who must vanquish the threat to its being that the abject is (1982, 54).

But what happens to abjection apart from this archaic drama that leads Kristeva to believe that other levels of signification display its legacy and maternal referent? Like Girard, Kristeva appeals to *Totem and Taboo* in order to establish a context of inquiry that can trace abject labor at multiple levels of the signifying economy and record the various ways in which resources at the very boundary of the Symbolic are summoned to diffuse the thetic crisis that arises in the absence of the father of individual prehistory. In *Totem and Taboo,* Kristeva observes a narrative structure of abject violence all but overlooked by Freud. Reflecting on the two taboos of totemism identified by Freud—murder and incest—Kristeva notes a slippage in the Freudian argument. Freud virtually sets aside the origins of incest dread to attend to murder, that keystone of the Oedipal structure. Kristeva aims to give incest its due, for she sees that reflection on incest is crucial to any theory that would analyze violence at multiple levels of the signifying economy.

In distinction from Girard, however, Kristeva maintains the centrality of sexual difference in the drama that engages the horde of brothers in violent struggle. Girard thinks that he can account for the societal context of violence only if sexual difference and the familial drama are ancillary to the founding pattern of mimetic violence that structures human community. By contrast, Kristeva reclaims the literal significance of the incest prohibition. She recognizes that, if she is to explain adequately the violence that accompanies the birth of human society, she must be attentive to *embodied* prohibitions. Accordingly, that the brothers fight over the bodies of *women* is not incidental. In fact, if *Totem and Taboo* tells in mythological form of the birth of society, the confrontation with women registered there is, above all, a confrontation with the abject Mother. *Totem and Taboo* captures in mythic form a truth that eludes direct confrontation in society: whenever border-bounding efforts of emergent subjectivity in the Symbolic order (i.e., the work of castration) prove ineffectual against the persistent threat posed by abjection, the trope of sacrificial maternity regularly is summoned and deployed as a weapon of choice against that ongoing threat.[13]

Kristeva's reflections on *Totem and Taboo* issue in three findings that are decisive for her sacrificial theory. First, she observes the shadow of the maternal body in processes of societal formation and reformation. Second, she notes the role of sexually differentiated violence within that process. Third, because she is attuned to the play of sexual difference, when she reads *Totem and Taboo,* she attends to the narrative of abjection she has traced in processes of emergent subjectivity and follows the trail of abjection back into the maternal matrix and out into society once again. To follow that trail with Kristeva is to move from abjection through defilement to sacrifice.

Kristeva's findings are indebted to her reading of a bipolar sacred in *Totem and Taboo.* Whereas the aspect of the sacred most familiar to a reader of Freud is that associated with the sacrificial exchange of the father for a totem animal, Kristeva reminds us that *Totem and Taboo* begins with an evocation of taboo: the dread of incest. Claiming that its pages are "haunted" by the maternal, Kristeva argues that *Totem and Taboo* speaks of another sacred "oriented toward those uncertain spaces of unstable identity, toward the fragility—both threatening and fusional—of the archaic dyad" (1982, 58). Focusing on this aspect of the sacred and linking it with body-work of emergent subjectivity, Kristeva arrives at the second moment in her typology of matricide: defilement.

Exploring the facet of the sacred evoked by taboo, Kristeva identifies it as the "true lining of the sacrificial" (1982, 64). She determines also that it is structured by spatial ambivalence. An ambiguity of perception—a confusion of inside and outside, pleasure and pain—attends the psychosomatic reality of this other side of the sacred. Tracing the contours of uncertainty, Kristeva claims that this aspect of the sacred is assigned the task of warding off the danger posed by the maternal body. Indeed, in sway to the Symbolic, when subjects seek to grasp that danger for themselves, rituals of interdiction mark and remark that which a nascent subject once experienced as its most basic threat: irreversible submersion in the maternal matrix. Evoking that most basic context of emergent subjectivity, these rituals also structure a protective space. They establish boundaries that, in repetition of the body-bounding practices of the emergent subject's proper self, also bind the social order. The incest prohibition, a paradigm of all interdictory processes, thus functions to throw a veil over primary narcissism, a veil that promises to block forever the abject menace found there: the fluctuation of inside/outside, pleasure/pain, word/deed (1982, 62–63).

Kristeva probes these processes which, inscribing boundaries, contain danger when they confine pollution to an outside from which society has set itself off. Surmising that such efforts preserve humans from an escalating violence that might demand a stronger measure—sacrifice—Kristeva borrows language from anthropologist Mary Douglas. From Douglas, she takes the notion of "the excluded" as the basis for religious prohibition. Kristeva notes that, in a number of societies, religious rites function to separate groups differentiated by class, gender, or age *by means of prohibiting a filthy, defiling element.* A rite of purification serves as a "ridge" separating that which is abominated (the abject) from that which is whole and clean. Indeed, defilement *is* that which has been jettisoned from the social system, for order (that which is clean) is inscribed on the social aggregate only as disorder (dirt) is proscribed (1982, 65).

Extending Douglas's insights, Kristeva establishes the logic of abjection within processes of emergent subjectivity *and* cultural practices while documenting their maternal cast. Although abjection may be variously coded in culture—defilement, food taboo, sin—its logic recalls the death-work of emergent subjectivity. In that most basic form, defilement enables the human subject to come into being as an expressive organism. Neither sign nor matter, defilement is a translinguistic spoor of the most archaic boundaries of one's clean and proper body (1982, 73). Belonging to "a scription without signs" (1982, 73), defilement constitutes the primal mapping of meaning at the somatic hinge of human being.

If Kristeva has shared with Girard an analysis of the logic of interdiction, her reflections on defilement distance Kristeva from Girard and advance understanding of acts of ritual prohibition that serve as precursor to the sign-work of sacrifice and, when effective, enable persons to manage conflict and disorder without recourse to sacrifice. Defilement functions as Kristeva's Rosetta stone, enabling her to read the signifying economy as Girard has not. With defilement, Kristeva also identifies basic processes of a sacrificial economy that link diverse narratives of death-work in a common text about the Mother. She demonstrates that our linguistic and cultural codes are structured around the murder of the Mother because defilement accounts for myriad substitutions which conceal the victim over whom society has arisen. These substitutions keep at bay the threat she represents, enabling society to persist without regular recourse to matricide.

Traversing the multileveled territory of the abject, Kristeva employs the category of defilement to further analyze an abject history that shadows death-work. Kristeva observes that the opposition between the pure and impure is "a coding of the differentiation of the speaking subject as such" (1982, 82). More basic than the coding of difference by the Law of the Symbolic and less violent than sacrifice, scripts of purity and impurity mark the subject's most archaic repulsion from the maternal matrix. Although the oppositional structure of defilement mimics the logic of the Symbolic—subject/thing/meaning—(1982, 82) the object of violence is displaced or denied in defilement. Not bound by a signifying dimension, defilement and purification demarcate materially, actively, translinguistically (1982, 74). A binary logic of borders is impressed initially on the human subject in the maternal matrix, before the human subject accedes to the Father's Law: blood speaks to the subject of life and death; sphincteral training evokes for the subject a struggle with Mother for a clean and proper self.

Persisting in texts of common life—for example, pollution rituals aimed at countering defilement—humans may invoke this most basic logic of the sacrificial economy whenever, in responding to threats against the social order, they find that they must summon material resources. Parceling bodies and creating borders, humans then invoke the most archaic images: those that engage them at the visceral depths of their being. Kristeva notes also that, as they render schematically border-threatening pollution, excrement and its equivalents (decay, infection, disease) stand for the danger to identity from without; menstrual and birthing blood represent the danger from within (1982, 71). Both form the pretext for pollution-countering ritual and myth: rites focused on the former bound society against threats from without;[14] those focused on the latter protect society from dangers issuing from within.

That this semiotic rendering of the body is regularly elaborated in culture may be attributed to the fact that the boundary-practices of the semiotic are a precondition of language itself. They participate in a common economy of death-work. Language may repress the corporeal mapping of maternal authority, but the prohibition enacted by the castration complex is weak. Neither the abject nor the demoniacal potential of the maternal body are banned sufficiently within the Symbolic economy. Speaking being, hoping to augment the management resources of Symbolic language that seem forever inadequate to the enormity of the threats which it confronts, attempts to express in body-invoking ritual its abject advent into an ever fragile, ever threatened order.

When the order threatened is that of a community, and abjection is magnified as diverse representations of the Other threaten, body-bounding rituals may play even more important roles in securing a community against threat. We think, for example, of early Israel's encounter with its gentile neighbors, an encounter preserved in the purity codes of Leviticus. Or we recall medieval Christendom's relation to Jews and the motifs of Christian ritual—particularly those focused on the power of the Eucharist to make the body of Christendom inviolable—that promised to protect Christians from the defiling presence of Jews.

Why do humans, under siege, so often turn to body-invoking rituals? Ritual practices that engage the body are experienced as more vigorous agents of border and body-bounding than is language proper. When humans graphically and viscerally engage the body in ritual, reimpressing order and securing boundaries against threat, the force of their actions outweighs that exhibited by Symbolic edicts generated by the castration complex and replicated in institutions bound by the Father's Law. When contrasted with the potency of body-inscribing ritual, these Symbolic edicts' capacity to effect order appears feeble.

But why do humans find that their visceral, bodily engagements with outlying threats create such powerful experiences? Why do they not treat their bodies as mute and neutral vehicles, useful for getting around in the world but irrelevant to its generative work? Answers to these questions emerge when Kristeva's typology of sacrifice is joined with her theory of negativity. The trajectory of death-work that she has traced serves as a reminder that the signifying economy draws on the maternal matrix of origins for its agency. In the negativity of the drives—jouissance and rejection—are found vital sources and resources for subjects' later work. Thus, not surprisingly, in rituals of defilement alimentary motifs—material witnesses to that most archaic struggle of nascent subjects within the maternal matrix—often predominate. That within the Symbolic order food is both pure (a source of life, sustenance, and community) and a polluting threat (when corrupted or poisonous) suggests also the centrality of food to the border-bounding work of defilement. Moreover, because food (chewed, spat out, swallowed) is literally implicated in embodied death-work, it is linked at multiple levels of the signifying economy to the territory of abjection.

Having outlined her notion of defilement, Kristeva traces this second moment of her typology of matricide in paganism, Judaism, and Christianity. In each case, she observes the success and failure of ritual practices which seek to deter and neutralize a threat that, in the absence of effective ritual, would mandate stronger medicine: sacrifice.

Paganism wards off the Mother through elaborate rituals that separate the pure from the impure. Whether the impure be food or fire touched by a woman's hands or her blood, always, in its generative power, it is potentially deadly. The fire that cooks food does not necessarily purify it; in fact, fire may pollute food, necessitating ritual cleansing. Because fire and food point to boundaries—social and somatic—which the act of cooking violates, cooked foods function as oral abjects, marking also the ambiguous boundary between the human and its first other: Mother. Similarly, food remainders threaten. In their incompleteness, they are "residues of something, but especially of someone" (1982, 76).

Judaism cuts off the Mother. Judaism inscribes impurity in an abstract moral register as potential for abomination, but not before it pays its last debt to the maternal matrix. The rite of circumcision carves definitive protection against pollution onto every male body. In repetition of the knife that cuts the umbilical cord, the knife that cuts the flesh of the foreskin "displaces through ritual the preeminent separation, which is that from the mother" (1982, 100). That pains are taken in Leviticus to condemn all other cuttings and marks on the human body (Leviticus 19:27–28) as abominations before God underscores the point: the ambiguity of human corporeality is countered by an act that offers decisive protection against maternal impurity. All traces of life in the maternal matrix are lost to a new identity. Circumcision bonds speaking being to God.

Judaism moves away from the maternal register and its attendant sacrifices even as it radicalizes separation. Judaism thus "throttles murder": matricide is forestalled because the maternal body is a threat to be contained, not destroyed. The borders of Symbolic order are transposed from the body to the temple. Food, death, and women are dangerous, not because they are occasions for impurity, but because they are occasions for idolatry. Rejection of food or of other maternally marked objects are mere pre-texts for a symbolic relation between Israel and God (1982, 111). The pre-texts secure the existence of the One, but are without sacredness themselves. That circumcision separates Israelite men from the impurity of women is then significant only as a sign of alliance with Yahweh.

In its notion of sin, Christianity interiorizes Jewish abomination, absorbing abjection in speech through subjection to God of a speaking being who is divided within and who precisely through speech does not cease to purge himself or herself of impurities (1982, 113). Evil, displaced into the subject, torments but not as polluting substance. Instead, evil is met as an "ineradicable repulsion of divided and contradictory being" (1982, 116): Christianity binges on and purges the Mother. By that token, Christianity is a revenge of paganism, a "reconciliation with the maternal principle" (1982, 116), except that the Mother, swallowed up, is not for that matter revalorized or rehabilitated by Christianity. Of the nourishing and threatening heterogeneity of the maternal matrix, Christianity keeps only the idea of sinning flesh (1982, 117).

The division of Christian consciousness finds its catharsis in the Eucharist. Identifying abjection as a fantasy of devouring, Christianity effects its abreaction. "This is my body" mingles themes of devouring with those of satiating. Removing guilt from the archaic relation to the abject of need—the Mother—the Eucharistic narrative "tames cannibalism" (1982, 118). The body of Christ, both body and spirit, nature and speech, promises reconciliation. Absorbed in the Symbolic and no longer a being of abjection, the Christian is a lapsing subject (1982, 119).

Even so, the account with the archaic Mother, which the Symbolic would hold in trust, is not yet settled, as the discussion of sacrifice in the history of Western Christianity in Part II demonstrates. There, the third moment in Kristeva's typology of matricide—sacrifice—is explored through constructive analyses of three paradigmatic cases: holy women in late medieval Christianity, victims of the witch hunts (1450–1750), and representations of the mother in the cultural archives of the West. We may observe, in each situation, that the linguistic code of the Symbolic order (the Law of absence or of the Father) bounds the forces of negativity, enforcing the lessons of death-work, managing the potential excesses of jouissance, and containing an abject threat, but only with great difficulty. When paroxysms of violence shatter the social order, explosions of terror reveal that the abject threat experienced in the maternal matrix again menaces. Actions taken to suppress this threat confirm decisively that, when death-work is subject to the full force of the sign, under the dictates of the sacrificial economy, sacrifice is enacted as matricide.[15]

Chapter 5 offers an analysis of the lives of late medieval women mystics which demonstrates that "bulimic Christianity" pays a price for interiorizing the terror of the abject as self-error (Kristeva, 1982, 127). Exhibiting in large numbers the symptoms of self-starvation (Bell, 1985), these women identify with a Mother-Christ both as victims of abjection and as aggressors in struggle against it. With their bodies they share the guilt of lapsing—the torment of the murderous subject. With their souls they share in the sacrifice of self that lays anger to rest. Murdering and murdered, they fight an archaic battle—in all its abjection—to the edge of death.

Chapter 5 emphasizes the larger social significance of the struggle enacted on the fractured bodies of the mystics. Because late medieval Christendom is itself in the throes of a thetic crisis—a crisis precipitated by social disorder that is perceived to pose an absolute threat to its continued existence—abject threats issued against late medieval society are registered in highly focused form on the mystics' bodies. In turn, the power claimed over their bodies is a power asserted in the social sphere to effect social order: efforts to bound the bodies of the mystics to Christ are, in reciprocal and mimetic form, exertions aimed at bounding the walls of Christendom against a menace that lurks outside. When rituals aimed at protecting Christendom from polluting disorder fail, a more emphatic gesture—sacrifice—is made. The deaths of the mystics—as instances of sacrifice—structure a protective space which, in ritual elaboration, binds the community to God and secures social order.

According to Kristeva, that the mystics' struggles with the forces of abjection on behalf of the body of Christendom are overseen by confessors introduces a troubling new dynamic of abjection in Western culture. The confessors take on the task of determining whether the sacrificial gesture embodied by the mystics has come from God or the devil. In confession persons disgorge sin in words. This is freedom, but it also delivers them over to death because it permits conscription of archaic powers by a priestly authority who determines the true source of their words (1982, 129).

The legacy of this new dynamic of abjection is visible in the witchcraft craze, the subject of Chapter 6. During the witch hunts, the dynamics of an ongoing struggle with abjection are rendered most dramatically in the practice of confession. Whether women accused of witchcraft are forced to confess to a priest or to his secular counterpart in the bureaucracy of the newly developing nation-states, confession plays a decisive role in the witch hunts: it authorizes the trials of witches, their bodily mutilation, and their executions. Confession, instrumental in this most widespread and public of battles with abjection, is fully exposed when held under the light of an analysis inspired by Kristeva. When the torturous trail of the confessional rites is followed, the confessors are shown to pursue the sign back into the maternal body in order to move out of that matrix once again, purged of the abject menace that previously has posed a lethal threat.

As is the case for the mystics of earlier centuries, so also do the witches bear on their bodies vital signs of social crisis. The abject threat inscribed on their bodies is a threat registered against the social body itself, in the face of widespread political and economic unrest. Again, because a fragile social order is at risk of destruction and nonlethal weapons prove insufficient protection against the menace that society confronts, a most ancient rite—the sacrifice of a scapegoat—is invoked to reinstate order. As torture and confession—simultaneously death and rebirth—delineate a space of matricide, women's bodies become, for their persecutors, expressive instruments which, at the very bar of silence, return others to speech.

But what may be said of discourses common to the cultural archives of Western Christianity that purport to valorize women's roles as mothers? Chapter 7 argues that the denial of the Mother in such phallic discourses of maternity—often focused on the mother of Christ—attests to the most deeply rooted violence against women and lies at the heart of the sacrificial economy in Western, patriarchal culture. Representative works of literature and art are discussed, which, according to Kristeva, display the conjunction of the antimaternal dynamic of patriarchy and the "a-maternal" logic of the Law of the Symbolic order in a single economy. Nowhere does safe space exist for the Mother. Any truce with her to which the Law is a party is momentary, for the dynamics of a sacrificial economy which permeate the Law portend continued violence and matricide.

V. Conclusion

This project began with a series of musings about women and violence. An initial interrogative agenda has been followed to conclusions that are striking and unsettling. As Kristeva has been read against Girard and Girard against Kristeva, key aspects of a sacrificial theory have emerged. An economic reading of patterns of mimetic violence has brought to the fore *a paralyzing continuum* of violence. The scapegoat mechanism has shed light on widespread *substitutionary patterns of violence* in society. A careful investigation of violent acts has shown that *soma* is the key currency within the sacrificial economy. Finally, the centrality of *sexual difference* to the work of sacrifice has been confirmed: the female body is a favored trope in discourses of sacrifice that create and secure the social order.

In Part II, as key figures in a sacrificial economy—the mystic, the witch, and the phallic mother—are discussed, the interrogative agenda of this project is sustained. The pervasiveness of mimetic violence in history and its differential effects on women are documented. Episodes cited in Part II confirm that women not only have been immobilized by sacrificial bonds—life-sentences—but also, under circumstances of crisis, have been victimized by lethal violence.

René Girard remains a conversational partner in Part II because the continued juxtaposition of Girard's and Kristeva's perspectives lends strength to this project. Every critic who accepts Kristeva's view of a human subject but doubts whether "sacrifice" conveys the true nature of the struggle in which subjects who are always in process and on trial engage should hear Girard's emphatic voice. Responding to those who say, "Yes, humans live at a loss, but is their death-work ever really *sacrifice?*" Girard asserts its reality: sacrifice is no mere literary trope or historical relic, for the economic investment that humans make in sacrifice has deep roots in our cultural institutions. And those who accept Girard's broad context of inquiry and acknowledge that the social order is founded and maintained by sacrifice but doubt that the violence which ensures social order is sexually differentiated should attend to Kristeva's strong voice. Responding to those who say, "Yes, humans live by sacrifice, but is this violence visited more often on *women* than on men?" Kristeva confirms that death-work in sacrifice is directed toward the Mother and those who bear her sign.

In Part II, Mary Douglas and Bryan Turner are featured also. Their insights position sacrificial theory ever more firmly in a social context. The work of all four theorists serves to secure a framework for inquiry about violence that is particularly suggestive for a feminist theory which seeks, through a study of violence, to position women's agency—and threats made against it—not only in the body but also in our social codes. Above all, Part II seeks to offer feminist theorists insights about violence against women that will sustain feminism's efforts to transform the codes by which humans live so that they may engage in the death-work that is necessary to their species, but may do so less violently.

Part II

5

"THIS IS MY BODY"

ABJECTION, ANOREXIA, AND MEDIEVAL WOMEN MYSTICS

In the anguish or the repose or the madness of Love . . .
The heart of each devours the other's heart,
One soul assaults the other and invades it completely,
As he who is Love itself showed us
When he gave us himself to eat. . . .

—Hadewijch (1980, 353)

Mary Douglas, Bryan Turner, and Julia Kristeva offer instructive insights into the formation and maintenance of social order. Likewise, they cite the centrality of religion to this enterprise and the key role the human body plays in religious practices focused on creating and preserving social order. So too do they forge links between conflict and self-contradiction that beset a society, threatening its order, and modes of crisis management offered by religion. According to them, because religion proscribes disorder and inscribes order in sacrificial ritual and myth, it takes up social conflict and resolves it.

The work of Douglas, Turner, and Kristeva illuminates church and society in Europe in the thirteenth and fourteenth centuries and, in particular, the lives of women mystics of that age. Viewed through the eyes of these theorists, the bodies of the mystics—fractured by self-imposed starvation and other practices of extreme asceticism—mirrored society at large as it responded to dangers that threatened it. Indeed, because threats issued against the social body of late medieval Christendom were registered in highly focused form by the mystics, power claimed over their bodies was, in turn, a power asserted in the social sphere to effect order.

In Section I of this chapter, Douglas and Turner provide direction for a preliminary inquiry into the formation of social order. In Section II, they are a focal point for an argument which suggests that the mystics dramatized with their bodies and especially in their devotion to the Eucharist the social strife that beset late medieval Christendom. A quest for social order was enacted on the bodies of the mystics. In Section III, as Kristeva's critical insights concerning sacrificial theory are joined with a perspective on medieval society indebted to Douglas and Turner, a previously hidden subtext of late medieval life is revealed. When Kristeva's theory is applied to the signifying practices of the mystics, the meaning of their asceticism is clarified: the mystics were victims of a sacrificial economy.

I. Drawing the Line Somewhere: The Construction of Social Order

Kristeva's theory of emergent subjectivity that emphasizes the boundary-making investments of humankind has much in common with principles that govern Mary Douglas's work. According to Douglas, that there is meaning at all depends on the human capacity to create boundaries, draw lines, affirm differences and, in so doing, both create and maintain order. Aside from bricks and stones out of which actual fences and walls are constructed, the order we create elsewhere in the world we owe to the capacity of the human mind to make mental fences and walls. According to Douglas, testimonies to our attempts to humanize ourselves by creating boundaries lie everywhere. We order our days with clocks and calendars, our relations with each other by complicated patterns of etiquette, and our surroundings by banishing disorder, which we call dirt, from our midst.

Underlying this fence-making activity, by which order is demarcated from disorder, Douglas asserts, we find ambiguity. Gray marks the border between black and white; good cannot clearly be distinguished from evil. Thus, at the boundaries separating order from disorder lie power and danger. Power lies there because those parts of existence which are set aside—the irregular, anomalous, or unnatural—are not simply dismissed. Because order results from restricted selection of acceptable human experiences from among the broad materials for existence, we can always see potential for regularity in the irregular. Lurking always in the margins of any ordered experience are claims of disorder to pattern and meaning (1966, 94).

But in potential for order lies danger. What if, in erecting fences and fortifying borders, we err and include in our midst elements that threaten order? Significantly, Douglas believes that, wherever in premodern societies we locate attempts to answer the difficult questions about the boundaries between order and disorder and to determine the dangers lurking in the margins, we find religion. While in modern societies medicine has inherited this sentry duty, traditionally, religion, more than any other institution, has patrolled the borders that separate order from disorder, dispensing information, protection, and judgments. Religion has told us that certain persons are our kin and that we must not sleep with them. It has determined who should live and how we should die. It has acknowledged those with legitimate claims to power and has prophesied against those with no right to power. Interestingly, when religion has attended to meaning and pattern, chaos and confusion, the human body has been among its most common reference points. Why the body?

Douglas notes that "the more personal and intimate the source of ritual symbolism, the more telling its message. The more the symbol is drawn from a common fund of human experience, the more wide and certain its reception" (1966, 114). Religion, engaged in mental fence-building, has appealed to the human body, rather than to actual doorposts, fence rows, and stone walls for images of order and meaning because the body is the most intimate and certain of boundaries. The body, a complex structure, is an ideal source of symbols for other complex structures. As the body is circumscribed by lines and patterns, the social structure is "reproduced in small" on it (1966, 115).

Moreover, the body is a paradigmatic reference to danger. While all social structures are vulnerable at their margins, bodily orifices are especially invested with the symbolism of power and danger (1966, 121). Bodily margins are exposed to disease, assault, and aging. In many cultures, matter that issues from body orifices—spittle, blood, milk, urine, or feces—attests to that vulnerability. Imbued with symbolism, this matter marks the threat of pollution.

Douglas's imagery of symbol creation as fence-building and of religion as the institution chiefly responsible in premodern societies for building such fences and for manning the sentry posts that fortify them is continued and elaborated by Bryan Turner. Turner offers an organic metaphor for the regulating processes of society. For him, a society is an organism bounded by an outer membrane. Within the outer membrane are protective clusters—cellular groupings—that embody the organism's values, beliefs, and identity and protect it against attack by hostile forces. These forces—experienced as evil in premodern societies and as disease in modern society—threaten the organism as a whole. The organism responds through actions concentrated in the protective clusters of the outer membrane. These actions—rituals in premodern societies and their medicinal alternatives in modern society—fend off the attack and maintain the internal purity and health of the system (1984, 212).

Turner's organic metaphor for societal creation and maintenance is telling. In his materialist critique, imagery of the social organism must in some ways be understood literally: a power claimed over a body is a power asserted in the social sphere; a threat issued against the social body is a threat registered by a human body. Moreover, the organic metaphor underscores the fact that power does not seize human minds and consciousnesses. Rather, as Foucault has claimed, power seizes bodies. Institutions embed cultural meanings and political legitimations on individual bodies that line the outer membrane of the social body. Power relations have an immediate hold on any body located there: "they invest it, mark it, train it, torture it, force it to carry out tasks, to perform ceremonies, to emit signs" (1979, 25).

Symbolic systems that forge relations of power between the social body and its individual members vary as do cultural attitudes toward body orifices and their refuse: menstrual blood may pose a lethal hazard for one society, excreta for another. To which bodily margins and their attendant refuse a culture will attribute power and danger depends on the nature of the social situation that the body is mirroring (1966, 121). Cultural differences notwithstanding, common patterns of symbolism are detectable.

A. Eating Order: Food and the Social Body

Food imagery often predominates in the symbolic and ritual clusters that bound a cultural system. In both modern and premodern societies, food links the social body with its individual members. Food signifies the dynamics of order and disorder: life and death, sin and sanctity, health and disease. Douglas detects a particular pattern in body-texts associated with external threats to a society: a society's preoccupation with social exits and entrances often issues in food symbolism (1966, 126–27). When a society is under attack or threat, that society's concerns are matched by fears that the bodies of its members also risk attack. Both interests coalesce around food symbolism. As illustrated by the purity ethic of Leviticus, ancient Israel's attention to the dangers of food pollution mirrored that nation's concern to maintain its borders—geographical, cultural, religious—against attack.

Turner emphasizes the intimate and graphic connection forged between social order and body order by food symbolism. Several examples underscore his claims. The multivalence of two words—*diet* and *regime*—links food with social order. A diet refers to both the regulation of individual bodies and the body politic: a political assembly. A regime refers to both a bodily regimen, usually involving diet, and a government regime (1984, 165). The development of table etiquette in the late Middle Ages and Renaissance further illustrates Turner's point. Eating with one's fingers, drinking soup directly from one's bowl, spitting on the floor, placing one's knife on the table, cleaning one's teeth with the knife or brandishing it at one's neighbor—all common occurrences at the communal table of the Middle Ages—became unacceptable for all social classes during the Renaissance. An unregulated appetite signified an unregulated society. A new cultural order was produced, not only because the populace was offered new images of civilized behavior on which to reflect, but also because their bodies were actively engaged: the population of Europe did not just think the Renaissance, they swallowed it (1984, 171).

B. Out of Order: Women and the Social Body

Douglas and Turner observe that women's bodies also predominate in symbolic and ritual clusters of a cultural system. Concurring with the assessment of religion that is offered also by Kristeva, they suggest that religions do not account for order and proscribe disorder in the world by appeal to generic human bodies. Rather, religions often demarcate order from disorder, sin from sanctity, by appeal to women's bodies. Their bodies, sites of processes men have perceived historically as mysterious and potentially dangerous, offer a most graphic symbolism of issues of ultimate concern. Women carry potential for order and meaning and for disorder and chaos in their very bodies. Menstruation, reproduction, and aging all testify to the triumphs and tragedies of existence. Moreover, because religions choose symbols not only to distinguish order from disorder, but also to effect order and control disorder, the female body often has been religions' symbol of choice. Because women's bodies are associated most closely with life and death processes, authority asserted over their bodies is power asserted over the very forces of creation.

Turner clarifies why women predominate among those beings who populate the outer membrane of the social body, bearing the brunt of attacks on the larger social body and appearing as objects of religious rituals that protect the integrity of the social body, proscribing disorder. Women, those humans most likely to be perceived as embodied, also lack the power to protest against the literal inscription on their bodies of societal meaning or to distance themselves from the ritual body-work which is enacted on behalf of the social body. But following Foucault, Turner also makes a stronger claim: women are found in the social margins because they are precisely those beings the social organism produces in its development to fill its outer wall. Affirming the absolute historicity of human embodiment, Turner defines women as the creation in history of the system that oppresses them (1984, 3–5).

Turner's assertion is significant because he dissents from a perspective on the body that would ascribe the social inscription of meaning on bodies to an imprinting process on blank and ready surfaces. For Turner, the body is established *in the very marking* of its contours, divisions, and boundaries. Drawing on Turner, the discussion that follows does not presuppose that the mystics' bodies predated their inscription with an ascetic and sacrificial narrative. Rather, the discussion affirms Douglas's own insights: "separating, purifying, demarcating, and punishing transgressions have as their main function to impose system on an inherently untidy experience" (1966, 4). Consequently, when sacrificial discursive practices were engraved on the bodies of the mystics, they did not transpire on what, before that moment, had constituted neutral body surfaces. Rather, the boundaries of the mystics' bodies and the boundaries of the social were one: the ascetic text they lived was demarcated materially, viscerally, *in its very practice.*

Douglas and Turner's theories, as attentive to the female body in its historical specificity as they are cognizant of structural commonalities that pervade history to affect women in a variety of contexts, are suggestive on two further counts. First, they make possible addressing the sexually differentiated specificity of power relations without reducing these relations to variations on a long-standing male conspiracy against women. As Foucault has argued, a clear logic may pervade power relations—a logic with aims so decipherable that we believe not only that it has been invented by someone, but also that it is available to us like a "game plan"—without that logic actually being self-consciously possessed by anyone. To the contrary, if we believe that humans do consciously pursue goals and advance their positions, we cannot conclude that prescience characterizes power relations as a whole. The play of power relations in a society will involve domination of particular groups—prisoners by guards, students by teachers, amateurs by experts, and women by men—without the participants in the play being wholly in command of their performances. This is the case not only for those who dominate, but also for those who are dominated (Foucault, 1979, 95; Bordo, 1985, 73–104).

Second, and more significantly, Turner and Douglas's theories account for the prominence of women's bodies in conflicts over social order. Noting the contradictions that plague the social construction of women, Turner locates the source of these contradictions within the wider society. Citing anorexia nervosa in the modern era as a key example, he claims that the anorectic's body is the product of a particular classifying system of knowledge and power.

Rather than see in anorexia a young woman's private and misplaced struggle for freedom from an overprotective family, Turner perceives that her starvation behavior is overdetermined by culture. Before a young woman ever begins to starve herself free, only to find herself constrained by processes that spiral out of control toward death, she is already caught within the contradictions of late capitalism. The dilemma of the victim of anorexia—she dies to live free—is possible only because her body has already been fractured by dichotomies—reason and desire, public and private, body and mind—that characterize Western culture itself (1984; 5, 201–202).

For her part, Douglas forges a link between the rending of a society by structural instability and the fear of female sexual pollution. According to Douglas, fears of sexual pollution run rampant when a cultural system is at war with itself. Citing the Lele as an example of such a self-contradiction which splits a cultural system, Douglas notes that, among the Lele, women are the currency of male transactions with each other. But because women, unlike other forms of currency, can take an active role in the transactions made with their bodies, the Lele are beset by conflicts. Not coincidentally, they have a great fear of female pollution, which Douglas relates to their attempt to treat women simultaneously as persons and as currency (1966, 149–52).

Because Douglas has argued that individual bodies mirror larger social bodies, so also does it appear that contradictory expectations for men and women in a society mirror contradictions in the social system as a whole. The destructive power, which Douglas highlights as characteristic of the former, seems but a contained version of the explosive potential rooted in the latter. The social order masks a founding disorder—a contradiction rooted in the depths of a society itself—and the struggle to maintain the mask of order in the face of underlying instability issues in dramatic efforts to control the risk to a society as a whole by controlling female pollution. Such efforts have two aims. They seek to address dangers posed for society by women whose lives conflict with gender-role expectations. They also focus on a larger threat to societal order that is visible only as refracted onto the individual bodies of women.

Douglas and Turner's theories highlight the centrality of the body to the play of power in history and religious life and call attention to the link between conflicts that beset a society and the inscription of those conflicts on women's bodies. Their theories contribute to an analysis of salient factors in late medieval Christendom and, in particular, the women mystics of that time. Their work establishes a helpful context on which to build in Section II, which looks more closely at the mystics' lives.

II. Holy Women, Holy Food, and Holy Order[1]

Cultural order in Europe during the thirteenth and fourteenth centuries can be seen as dictated by the regulation of the intake and outtake of food from human bodies. At one extreme, recorded in folk literature, were images of magic vessels brimming over with food and drink. Such tales symbolized, according to Caroline Walker Bynum, unbridled sensual pleasure and, when combined with imagery of gorging and vomiting, presaged cultural ambivalence associated with food (1985, 2). At the other extreme were ascetic behaviors centered on renunciation of food and drink. Food, in all its comings and goings, mirrored at a microlevel of the society processes of order and disorder that were writ large. In a time when famine was on the increase, as indicated by stories of food hoarding, cannibalism, and infanticide (1985, 1), those who could enact control of individual bodies through regulation of food could control order and resist forces of disorder in the larger social body as well. Food structured the culture, dividing rich from poor, and informed its ethic: overeating was a mark of privilege, and sharing food with the hungry was a primary symbol of benevolence (1985, 2). Moreover, Bynum reminds us that the cultural ethic, focused on food, was instantiated as a religious ethic: those who luxuriated in food paid the penalty for the sin of sensual pleasure; those who renounced food obtained salvation (1987, 45).

Standing guard over the cultural order in the thirteenth and fourteenth centuries, policing its margins, was the church. For its sentries, food was *the* sign that marked the borders of Christendom. The body that ate or refused food, so imbued with religious meaning, was the primary vehicle by which—through feast or fast—the tasks of Christendom were carried out. Throughout the Middle Ages, Christians were defined by their eating behavior: a Christian was someone who fasted. For example, Bynum observes that, of the four behaviors required of one who professed to be a Christian—receiving yearly communion, fasting on Fridays and in Lent, paying tithes, and having one's children baptized—the fast was the most regular and most visible sign of one's faith or apostasy (1987, 40).

According to Bynum, food was also at the center of religious ceremonies: in the Eucharist, Christians ate their God and obtained their salvation (1985, 1). Late medieval piety emphasized the individual reception of God in the Eucharist: one tasted, saw, and met God. The God whom one encountered appeared to humans as broken flesh. Eating that God, one became one with the suffering flesh crucified on the cross (1987; 53, 65). Although the salvific powers of the Eucharist centered on the individual who received that suffering flesh, the Eucharist also had a corporate meaning: when Christians ate God together, it was the church and humankind who were saved (1987, 62).

Notable among those for whom the Eucharist was central to faith were women who, in saintly asceticism, deliberately abstained from all food but God's food: the Eucharist. Most significant for our purposes here is the fact that food—as practice and as symbol—featured more prominently in women's lives than in men's suggests that the church in the thirteenth and fourteenth centuries did mark the boundaries of Christendom with women's bodies. In particular, as its ethic valorized food asceticism, the church made women primary bearers of this sign.

Bynum's research amply demonstrates this point. According to Bynum, although women were only 18 percent of those canonized as saints between 1000 and 1700, they comprised 23 percent of those who died from asceticism and 53 percent of those for whom illness was central to their sanctity (1987, 76). Moreover, the majority of eucharistic visions and miracles were attributed to women: of the twenty types identified, only two were performed exclusively by men and those were linked to consecration of the Eucharist, which was a male prerogative in any case. Eight other types of miracles featured women primarily, and four were associated exclusively with women's spirituality (1987, 78–79). Women also predominated among those whose miracles consisted of exuding from their bodies wondrous fluids—food—that healed others (1987, 273).

Bynum's research is augmented by Rudolph Bell (1985), who also documents the high number of cases of women for whom self-starvation was central to their asceticism. Bell narrows his focus to the Italian peninsula and to those 261 women recognized by the Roman Catholic church as saints, blesseds, venerables, or servants of God. Excluding 90 women about whom the historical record remains virtually silent, of the remaining 170, half engaged in severe ascetic practices (1985, x). Using J. P. Feigner's criteria for anorexia nervosa,[2] Bell demonstrates that for 39 percent of these women, a pattern of anorexia is evident (1985, 135). The percentage is lower among the Franciscans (32 percent of women for whom Bell has strong documentation; 52 percent for whom he has moderate or strong documentation) and highest among the Dominicans (56 percent of the women for whom Bell has strong documentation; 65 percent for whom he has moderate or strong documentation) (1985, 135).

The centrality of food asceticism to women does not rest, however, with the quantitative evidence. As Bynum observes, female hagiography is not entirely reliable in the reconstruction of history. Hagiographers may valorize fasting that actually did not occur or, in the case of obsessive fasting, may downplay its features. Partly because women's lives were less diverse than men's and less open to nuanced treatment on the part of hagiographers, evidence from those sources needs supplementation (1987, 82–85). Bynum provides such evidence by appealing to the lives and writings of men.

Bynum can locate food asceticism and eucharistic devotion in the vitae of men; however, in contrast to the holy women of the late medieval age, for whom references to food and the Eucharist constitute the "leitmotif," references to food—both human and holy—are not at the center of men's lives (1987, 94–95). Documenting her case with reference to Suso, Rolle, Tauler, and Ruysbroeck, Bynum demonstrates that the spirituality of these men, although characterized by an affective and lyrical form more typically associated with women than with men, differs from women's on two counts. Unlike the holy women of the day, these men do not make hunger the basic synonym for desire of God. Nor do they, as do the women mystics, make eating the central metaphor for uniting with Christ's suffering, experiencing mystical union with Christ, or saving souls (1987; 93, 105–106).

That bodies and body-work are signs that create cultural order and serve as harbingers of cultural disorder, that women in the late medieval age were principal sign bearers in a crucial area, which was associated with food symbolism in general and with the Eucharist in particular, calls into question women's status on the boundaries of Christendom and the multivalence of the signs women lived. That multivalence is nowhere more dramatically evident than in the endpoint of extreme asceticism: death from self-imposed starvation. Were women's deaths from starvation indicative of asceticism run amok, or did they highlight an ambiguity, a tear in the cultural membrane, a structural break at the borders of late medieval Christendom, which came to expression in women's bodies but did not originate with them?

The medieval women mystics who engaged in self-imposed starvation, sometimes to the point of death, were living with their bodies a contradiction of the larger social body. They embodied—literally, socially, and politically—what Turner would describe as a structural crisis within the society (1984, 113). The medieval mystics' starvation was a "psychosemantic fallacy"[3] (1984, 185): living the discourse of medieval society, they found their bodies rent by its contradictions. Moreover, as the boundary situation signified by their fractured bodies led toward death through self-starvation, the crisis of the social body as a whole reached its logical denouement.

The contradictions that the women mystics embodied were shaped by struggle: a struggle to control the social body against threats to its unity and to control the individual body against the risk of fracture. Self-imposed starvation, linked to women's devotional focus on the Eucharist and refusal of all other food, marked the parameters of the conflict. Bodily control through self-starvation was inscribed in two contradictory discourses: in one, the body was left behind; in the other, the experience of the body was intensified.

That the body was left behind in the mystics' self-imposed starvation is the notion more familiar to contemporary scholars, for whom asceticism is generally associated with a practical dualism that issues in various forms of world-rejection. Bynum concurs that misogynistic views of the body and a dualistic concept of a body opposed to spirit were expressed in holy women's asceticism. For these women, to cease to eat was to discipline and defeat the body (1987, 212–13). Fearing that any food would lead them madly into gluttony or lust from which there would be no escape, these women embraced an asceticism focused on the Eucharist. When they ate only the Eucharist, only God's body, they acquired a discipline of self that denied to their bodily members any power. That starving holy women ceased to menstruate was interpreted, Bynum acknowledges, as freedom from the bodily curse of Eve which had led women and, through them, all humanity into sin (1985, 11). Moreover, she recognizes that abstinence from food was linked with sexual abstinence, which enhanced the spirit and defied sexual desire (1987, 214–15).

Miracles associated with holy women of the time underscore that bodily control signified a salvific defeat of the powers of the body and its sinning members at two levels: that of the individual woman and that of the social body for whom she was a sign. For instance, Bynum notes, a corpse that failed to decay and which had belonged to a holy woman who had died from starvation became a valued relic: a symbol of the ascendance of the spirit in victory over the corrupting and corruptible body (1987, 211). Further, Weinstein and Bell indicate that, just as some preliterate societies are known to mark their borders with the corpses or skulls of sacrificial victims in order to protect themselves from invasions, so also did the incorruptible body parts of a holy woman, dispersed as relics in churches—an arm here and a leg there—mark the borders of Christendom (1982, 53). In signifying the victory of a woman's body over the forces of death and decay, these relics also symbolized the victory of society over disorders that threatened the social body.[4]

Even as the salvific potential—social and individual—of world-denial through asceticism is affirmed by Bynum, she observes that fasting could be "flight not so much from as into physicality" (1987, 250). The social text of late medieval Christendom was shaped not only by a discourse of denial, but also by a discourse in which the body was intimately and intensely experienced. Within this discourse, the body was not an obstacle to salvation; rather, the body was the primary vehicle of saving grace. Late medieval theology, emphasizing the crucifixion of Christ, not his resurrection, accorded to Christ's humanity a positive value: God saved the world through physical, human agony. Vividly evoking the visceral elements of the piety that appropriated this theological belief, Bynum writes that "to eat was to consume, to take in, to become God. And to eat was also to rend and tear God. Eating was a horribly audacious act. Yet it was only by bleeding, by being torn and rent, by dying, that God's body redeemed humanity. To become that body by eating was therefore to bleed and to save—to lift one's own physicality into suffering and into glory" (1987, 251). In piety, theological text was made body text: when one ate God in the Eucharist, one incorporated his suffering body. One became the suffering flesh that saved.

Bynum argues most persuasively that holy women embraced this theology of *imitatio Christi.* Their quest to conform themselves to Christ was facilitated by widely held beliefs of the day. First, medieval theology believed that Christ took his physicality from his mother. Aristotelian physiological doctrine suggested that the mother provided the "stuff of the foetus" and the father provided the form or animating principle. Galenic interpretation claimed that both male and female seeds together produced a child. However, since Christ had no human father, on both Aristotelian and Galenic grounds, Christ was seen as taking his flesh from Mary (1987, 265). Thus, when one received the Eucharist, one partook of a body that was, in essence, female. Second, because medieval natural philosophers understood that breast milk was transmuted blood, the Eucharist was prominently associated with mother's milk. Late medieval portraits of a Christ who feeds humanity with blood that streams from his nipple tell the story: that Christ took his humanity from his mother means that Christ, like a mother, nourishes humanity from his breast.[5]

Bynum cites the miracles of holy women that, for these women and for those who knew them, confirmed their literal embrace of Christ's humanity. Finding redemption in the shared agony of the crucifixion, like Christ, their bodies bore stigmata (1987; 200, 255–56). Or, eating and drinking only the body of Christ, they incorporated him into themselves. With their own bodies merged with Christ's, from the mystics' breasts or mouths also streamed healing, saving fluids (1987, 273–74). In their mystical ecstasy, these "women ate and became a God who was food and flesh. And in eating a God whose body was meat and drink, women both transfigured and became more fully the flesh and the food that their own bodies were" (1987, 275). Claiming the redemptive possibilities of their embodiment, becoming one with Christ's suffering, crucified body, the holy women effected others' salvation.

The mystics' privileged relation to the Eucharist in late medieval piety—demonstrated most graphically by their miracles—placed them on the "front line" of late medieval Christendom to do battle against forces that threatened it. That their suffering on behalf of others' redemption could provide the church with a highly focused response to outside dangers was facilitated by the church's preoccupation with the host as a symbol of its mystical body. Bynum reminds us that the host in late medieval Christendom came to express "an almost frantic sense of wholeness, the inviolability, of Christ's body and a tremendous fear of rending and breaking" (1987, 63). Miracles of consecrated wafers that oozed blood or of wafers that turned to stinking flesh and accused those who had desecrated them underlined a dual threat: just as the host could be defiled, so also could the society. Indeed, persecutions of the Jews, who signified a threat on the borders of late medieval Christendom, focused often on alleged Jewish desecrations of the host (1987, 64).

Precisely because the host which the holy women consumed signified both Christ's saving flesh and blood and his church, when these women united with Christ's body by means of extreme asceticism they signified both the specific body of Christ, marked by stigmata, and his larger body, the Church. For this reason, when the mystics drew down onto their bodies the crises of a society racked by conflict, their actions could effect Christendom's salvation as well as their own.

The host that signified social crisis and the women who, in eating the host, embodied crisis, were linked in a common symbolic universe. Women were both the first line of defense against outside dangers which threatened Christendom and, in the fragility of their embodiment, those who would succumb first to corruption. Because these holy women represented powers and dangers, order and disorder, that which was to be condemned and that which, through salvific transformation, was to be venerated, the battle of the church against external threats to societal order and unity could be waged on their bodies. Thus, as they embodied, through the eucharistic drama, the society's struggle for control and unity, these women produced and reproduced on their bodies all the ambiguities of a society under siege. When, in their devotion to the Eucharist, they fled *from* their bodies through self-imposed starvation, they signified the defeat and destruction of the dangers that threatened the church. When, in their suffering and at the risk of death from the same ascetic practices, they fled *to* physicality so that their bodies merged with Christ's, they enacted Christendom's salvation.

The medieval mystics bore the crises of Christendom on their own bodies and were a two-edged weapon with which the church confronted power and danger. But a further ambiguity also characterized their lives. If the women who ate only the Eucharist were controlled by Christendom, which marked their bodies and forced them to emit signs and carry out its tasks, they also could control Christendom. As Bynum observes, they could use their ascetic behaviors to manipulate parents into acceding to their wishes not to marry (1987, 222). Were they to vomit up the host, as some did on occasion, testifying that it had not been consecrated and was yet human food, they could successfully challenge the authority and integrity of the priest who had offered it (1987, 228). Many were drawn to the charismatic authority of the women who suffered and who saved (1987, 234).

Bynum attends, in particular, to the subversive aspects of the mystics' asceticism. Notwithstanding constraints placed on these holy women by their environment, they maneuvered within those limits in order to triumph over them: their asceticism aimed at freedom. These women "by their very extravagance, audacity, and majesty . . . rejected the success of the late medieval church, rejected—for a wider, more soaring vision—an institution that made a tidy, moderate, decent, second-rate place for women and for the laity" (Bynum, 1987, 243). French philosopher Luce Irigaray also has written that the medieval women mystics occupied the only space in Western history where women spoke and acted free from the shaping, controlling powers of patriarchy (1985a, 191).

Nevertheless, Bynum and Irigaray's valorization of the mystics' soaring vision is necessarily tempered by a grim reality: the compulsive rituals associated with the mystics' asceticism. They suffered deeply from the stigmata, nails, and thorns that accompanied their dramatic reenactments of Christ's crucifixion. Caught in a contradiction, the women who embodied the opposing discourses of flight *from* the body and flight *to* the body embraced Christ-likeness but risked death from their efforts. In death, the bodies that bore the sufferings of Christ in sometimes extraordinary mimetic forms ceased to take up space. Crucified in the contradictions they embodied, the faith of these holy women joined utter darkness and blinding light, total fulfillment and absolute emptiness.

Such self-inflicted violence, even when interpreted as the rebellion—cultural, political, and spiritual—of women who quested after salvation was not an emancipating gesture. Instead, it was always, already the rebellion of bodies colonized by the larger culture. The mystics' bodies were not so much free as they were fractured by the conditions of their production within the larger social body of late medieval Christendom. Because the mystics' bodies could not, at the end of self-imposed starvation, withstand the assaults made on them, because, at that point, the mystics were consumed, rather than freed, by the "psychosemantic fallacy" they embodied, their emancipating vision was not encountered as a vista toward which the mystics soared. They failed to gain a foothold on such a space of freedom; rather, the freedom to which they aspired was glimpsed only on the margins of the social body, at the point of bodily fracture, at the moment the mystics plummeted into the abyss of being.

III. Crossing the Line: Abjection and the Abyss

The mystics' encounter with this abyss can be assessed best when a Douglas-and-Turner–inspired portrait of the mystics is joined with a theory of sacrifice articulated by Kristeva and influenced by Girard. Because all four thinkers link body-work and sign-work in the linguistic practices of humankind, the psychosemantic fallacy which the medieval women mystics embodied can be investigated from a common base of inquiry. When this fallacy is traced to the sacrificial economy of late medieval Christendom, key issues that remain unresolved so far in this chapter are addressed.

For instance, a treatment of the mystics' lives indebted primarily to Douglas might indicate that bodily orifices doubtlessly intend power, danger, and vulnerability. But do they? Moreover, does food self-evidently predominate in symbolic and ritual clusters that bound a cultural system? Further, why do women figure prominently in symbolism of danger? Turner, of course, has claimed that women's bodies bear the brunt of attacks on the larger social body because women, more than others, are perceived as fitting agents for boundary-creating work and because women lack the power to refuse the conscription of their bodies in service to that objective. But what are the sources for these common perceptions of women? Are women privileged performers of boundary-creating work in society because, in the face of their physical and social vulnerability, they are unable to refuse the signifying practices they are assigned? Are the dynamics of power-plays enacted on the bodies of women informed primarily by the tactical disadvantage of women in combat, as Turner seems to suggest, or is there a more complex rationale?

Turner's own notion of the social body suggests a more nuanced reading of women's roles. When he analyzes the status of women, he does not presume that women who reside in the outer membrane of the social organism are deported there from elsewhere, against their will and in the wake of their defeat by stronger powers, to do boundary-work from which persons of greater physical strength and higher status are exempt. To the contrary, Turner indicates that women materialize in the protective dermis of the social organism at the moment of that membrane's creation. Indeed, that they do so makes Turner's organic metaphor for the formation of social order more telling than Douglas's fence-building imagery. For Turner, the boundary-work that margin-residers do and the boundary that they are are one.

In view of Turner's own metaphor of societal creation, accounts which Douglas and Turner give of body-conscripting work appear inadequate, though evocative. If holy women were located on the margins of Christendom, as its "front-line" defense against outlying threats, why were they found there? Why and by means of what apparatus were the walls of Christendom constructed so as to fracture while they were being built, as the boundary-securing work of the mystics was divisively disrupted by their deaths? Perhaps the mystics were not placed in the margins of the social organism of late medieval Christendom; rather, emerging in and as the margins, they were the outcome of Christendom's border-work. But why did the organism that was late medieval Christendom produce as its protective outer membrane bodies that were rent in their very production?

For medieval holy women did express conflict with their bodies. On the one hand, when they intensified their bodily experience, mirroring Christ's body in their rigorous asceticism, their signifying labor secured the inviolable power, order, and borders of Christendom. On the other hand, when they rejected their bodies, witnessing to sinful flesh, their signifying gestures freed late medieval Christendom of life-threatening pollution. Concentrated in the mystics' bodies, a threatening menace did not spread from the dermis of the social organism to other cells. However, when wholly divided against themselves, in simultaneous flight to *and* from their bodies, the mystics died. What possible work of a social organism could mandate the joining of lethal processes in a single cellular configuration?

In discussing anorexia today, Turner offers one explanation. He suggests that contemporary women who suffer from anorexia embody a psychosemantic fallacy that manifests a dualism proper to late capitalism. Ideological conflicts of modern life—public and private spheres, body and mind, reason and desire—are inscribed, albeit fatally, on anorectics' bodies (1984, 202). Thus, in dealing with a deadly conjunction of discourses, Turner sets aside his commitment to treat body-work as generative of meaning. Instead, he describes practices that reflect and bear diverse social interests produced elsewhere.

Did the mystics share a like experience? Were their bodies also under siege as proponents of competing ideologies vied with each other to inscribe their tenets on their neutral body-surfaces? No, the mystics' *somatic* investments suggest another direction of inquiry. Their ascetic practices, producing fractured and starving bodies, indicate that holy women's signifying ventures were comprised of *contradictory* rather than *competing* discourses. Moreover, because many of the mystics who simultaneously embraced *and* refused soma died, the materiality of their asceticism and their starvation-induced demise mandates an analysis that examines ways in which holy women were divided not only *among* cultural discourses, but also *within* speech. In the absence of an analysis that attends to the very sundering of signification in the silence of death, the radically abject moment in the mystics' practices which is central to any adequate assessment of their lives is bypassed.

The collapse of meaning and boundaries in the mystics' bodily dissolution invites the kind of rich analysis that Kristeva offers. For she looks at signification not only as reflective of social agendas and meanings, but also as productive. As a consequence, she observes an *economic* process that links jouissance and rejection in human society and in emergent subjectivity within a common nexus of negativity. In particular, because Kristeva attends to the abject, she illuminates forms of signifying that, reconnoitering the borders of language, subjects, and society, linger over the abyss of being. She highlights the larger implications of the term "psychosemantic fallacy" that Turner has coined in order to describe the contradictions of women's self-starving practices.

That Kristeva views signification in economic terms is suggestive on several counts. As a kind of systems analysis, an economic approach indebted to her envisions organic connections among various aspects of medieval society and imagines that common patterns (value, order, meaning, interests) ran through it at multiple and integrated levels. These patterns produced lived social and somatic investments; they did not only reflect persons' deliberate and intentional engagements from which they were exempt in the absence of their explicit consent. Moreover, a Kristeva-influenced approach submits social roles in medieval Christendom (e.g., a peasant, a guild merchant, a cleric, a holy woman) to a principle of immersion: persons within medieval society accepted tasks "assigned" to them as their own and did not think to consent or dissent to them. Indeed, the very meaning and value of the medieval system lay *within* the interrelations its members effected: they authorized these relations in their very doing. The products of a complex web of social and somatic investments that comprised the medieval economy, medieval subjects never were in a position to perceive or advocate an alternative cultural system.

Acclimated by Kristeva to an economic perspective on the lives of the medieval mystics, the contradictions that the mystics lived—their desire to be rid of their bodies *and* to live their bodies more intensely—can be examined from a new perspective. Their asceticism exhibited a founding contradiction of a signifying economy: humans come to be in places where they are not. Human *life* is *death*-work. It *is* a practice of *absence.* The mystics lived this practice literally, viscerally, to the last breath. But if this psychosemantic fallacy of human life is common to all human experience, why was the take on this contradiction among medieval mystics lethal, transforming their death-work into sacrifice?

A response to this question invokes the three themes of a sacrificial theory set forth in Chapter 4: a sacrificial theory explains the origins of conflict in mimetic violence, accounts for its elaboration in surrogate victimization, and demonstrates why killing a victim brings conflict to an end. This three-part scenario suggests that when a conflict-ridden, late medieval Christendom set out to reestablish the truth of its social codes and assert control over its boundaries, it adopted a sacrificial stance. Drawing on key institutional resources, it submitted mimetic processes of creation and destruction—the death-work of negativity—to the full force of signs. Grasping at the contradictions of life and subjecting an unruly process of societal formation and reformation to border-securing work by means of surrogate victimization, Christendom enacted a supreme gesture of control in the sacrifice of the mystics.

Each element of this scenario can be analyzed, beginning with mimetic violence. In a society beset by crisis, the mystics manifested mimetic conflict in two ways. Because the mystics' female bodies were seen to pollute and corrupt, the mystics were perceived to embody an invading menace. But when the mystics ate God and merged their flesh with God, their threatening mimesis was transformed into a saving mimesis. Multiple instances of abjection and defilement count as key evidence of mimetic conflict. When late medieval Christendom worshiped a lactating Christ and ate Christ's maternally identified body in the Eucharist, it returned to an archaic drama of abjection. Its struggle for unity and control was, at its most basic level, a conflict modeled on early lessons in emergent subjectivity when a subject secures its boundaries only by surviving and triumphing over a mimetic threat: it will eat or be eaten. This battle—enacted in concentrated form by holy women—exhibited all the ambivalence that characterizes mimetic desire. For as they alternately embraced and refused their bodies and Christ's, the mystics reenacted on the stage of late medieval Christendom the ambivalence that characterizes the archaic movement of identification with and differentiation from the maternal matrix.

The mystics' abject death-work held to the borders of being—boundaries of subjects and society—there to take measure of an inassimilable nonunity of existence that was absolute promise and absolute threat. The miracles of these holy women—bodies that did not decay in death, healing blood of stigmata, virginal lactation, Eucharistic visions—tracked the founding journey of subjects in the world. To their miracles seemed to cling residue drawn from the nether regions of being: spaces where meaning is born and dies. Invoking the maternal container, material marks of their saving work were embraced by others as sacred signs of excess, for they appeared to promise salvation at the very limit of human existence.

The mystics' actions touched the absolute danger that shadows the cultural work of mimesis—submersion and death in undifferentiated being—even as they revealed the immortal promise of salvation. As a consequence, in the ambiguities and contradictions of their ascetic practices—by means of which they alternately embraced their bodies and denied them—others could directly observe matters of life and death. Sheltering the abject, the mystics invoked boundary-work that drew on the most archaic expressions of difference: fluctuations of inside/outside, word/deed, pleasure/pain. Because the topos on which the mystics drew was not one of representation but of *spacial interdiction,* in the sacred excess of the mystics' acts others could directly and immediately experience their saving powers. Because the abject moment in the holy women's labors demarcated meaning in its very movement, at the thetic break, those who shadowed the mystics' death-work could grasp life itself from the mystics' dying bodies.

Of course, that a distance proper to the sign was absent from the mystics' miracles did heighten the risks that attended their work. The abject as an abyss of being always threatened. Nevertheless, that for at least two centuries the mystics' efforts were believed to circumscribe this threat rather than succumb to it suggests that the drama of the medieval holy women can be read most insightfully as a mimetic moment in the work of a sacrificial economy. When the mystics ate only God and died, their bodies made manifest sacred powers and secured Christendom against threat.

The lives of the medieval mystics lend themselves to the sacrificial thesis in respect to its second theme as well: surrogate victimization. At a moment of crisis in a medieval community, a mimetic free-for-all did focus on a single person: a scapegoat. Within a late medieval town or village that role was filled by a holy woman who bore the extraordinary consequences of radical asceticism on her starving body. On the one hand, she embodied the intrinsic culpability of a victim: her public abnegation of her sinful and polluting body stood as proof. On the other hand, near death or in the wake of her death, she became a venerated object: her healing fluids and protective body parts attested to her saving role. Bearing the community's violence, the mystic was a scapegoat: in the wake of her sacrificial gift, the community returned to stasis.

The key role that ritual plays in sacrificial violence also warrants labeling the medieval mystics as surrogate victims. Of course, even apart from holy women's special investments in eucharistic devotion, a double transference of sacrifice is manifest in the medieval ritual of the Eucharist.[6] When medieval Christians accentuated the physical elements of the eucharistic rite, emphasizing that they partook of the body and blood of Christ, they dramatized the explicitly sacrificial components of their experience. Violence passed among those gathered for the rite and centered on the body of the victim (Christ). In partaking of the victim, those gathered found that violence was transformed into peace. The intensification of double transference in the eucharistic devotion of a holy woman could only have made the sacrificial act and its receipt by the community more immediate and more powerful: when a holy woman performed eucharistic miracles and mirrored Christ with her body (e.g., received the stigmata), she magnified Christ's saving work for all who observed her labors. As a consequence, the testimony a holy woman offered to her unification with Christ summoned an uncanny awe among persons. Initially, they wondered if she polluted or harmed others: was she a witch? was she possessed? However, in the wake of a holy woman's death, miracles associated with her body augmented the community's capacity to believe that violence enacted on her body had been transfigured into peace. Did not her body, transformed now into relics, protect them from contagion, pollution, and other outlying threats? Suspicions about her were wholly set aside; hagiographies would recall only her saving sacrifice.

But why were the powers of sacrifice attributed especially to women, making them a favored currency in the sacrificial economy of medieval Christendom? Because the mystics rendered the abject with a particular intensity and evocative power, they functioned as ideal tropes of the sacrificial economy. The mystics registered with their bodies in especially dramatic ways not only the defiling and polluting forces that were believed to threaten medieval Christendom, but also the saving powers that would protect it. When holy women ceased to emit polluting fluids (e.g., menstrual blood) and began to produce saving fluids (blood of the stigmata, or healing milk), they directly enacted the healing and transforming work of purifying rituals from which not only they, but also the entire society could benefit.

Of course, men were not excluded from performing salvific work on behalf of others: the ascetic life was chosen by some men. But Bynum reminds us that women predominated among those whose asceticism was *somatically productive:* women, more than men, received the stigmata (1987, 25), emitted healing fluids (1987, 273–74), or received visions whose lactation motifs anticipated and came to reflect the mystics' own healing powers. Further, because women, more than men, could enact forms of radical asceticism that, spanning years and even decades, veritably constituted a living-death, their lingering sacrifice may have accentuated the community's ability to experience their labors as transforming. Certainly, an ever more vigorous asceticism that did culminate in death from self-starvation was found almost exclusively among holy women.[7]

So far, the lives of the medieval mystics have been assessed in terms of two elements of sacrificial theory: mimetic violence and surrogate victimization. Is the third element also present? When the holy women's ascetic sufferings culminated in death, were their deaths a rite of sacrifice? Perhaps the mystics who died simply confronted an inescapable physiological mandate associated with the final stages of starvation. That holy women's ascetic suffering, associated with mimetic violence and surrogate victimization, had social significance seems clear. But did the deathly extension of this suffering speak to a larger social mandate: a sacrificial agenda?

Kristeva provides support for a sacrificial thesis.[8] If medieval holy women frequently exhibited marks of pollution and purification that enabled them to play an especially vital role within the medieval signifying economy, when they fasted to the point of death, they moved to the center of that economy. When rituals directed toward pollution and defilement proved incapable of fully purifying a community of disorder and unrest, the community summoned more drastic measures. In responding to this call, the mystics accelerated their asceticism, acting primarily to affirm a social mandate. For in its quest to reestablish communal boundaries and reinforce its borders against threat, Christendom did deploy the ultimate weapon: sacrifice. There were three ways in which the deaths of the medieval mystics were sacrifices.

First, the holy women of late medieval Christendom enacted sacrifice when, in their eucharistic devotion, they killed soma in order to create saving signs. The body and blood of Christ—the only food that passed the mouths of these holy women—was a sacrifice. In partaking of the Eucharist, the holy women perceived that they ate God. But, of course, so did medieval Christians in general. What then distinguished the mystics' sacrificial observance of the Eucharist from that of their neighbors? The mystics' gesture entailed a decisive intensification in the signifying economy of late medieval Christendom. For the Eucharist within that economy was a sacrifice for most persons only in an attenuated sense: its raw cannibalism was domesticated by its containment within the Symbolic orbit of the Church. By contrast, the mystics' multivalenced receipt of its benefits cast the Eucharist into a different orbit. In their ascetic devotion to the Eucharist, they created a sign anew: when their flesh became Christ's flesh (as attested to by the stigmata and the mystics' ability to heal), the mystics literally became the crucified flesh that saved.

That the endpoint of mystics' asceticism—their deaths from self-starvation—constituted a sacrifice is demonstrated also by the manner in which the uncanny—the sacred—was localized and concretized in their bodies. As holy women approached death through self-starvation, they enacted the somatization of the symbol. Their ascetic devotion approached the thetic break in order to mark and even transgress it. The importance of these transgressive aspects of the mystics' sacrificial devotion can be appreciated if the kinds of restrictions under which signification operates are recalled. Humans are barred from assuming control of the signifying economy. They cannot subject its founding dynamic to the forces of representation, for were they to display that kind of power, they would become the source of the Law and creators of the Word. But under siege and at a loss, such power is exactly what medieval Christendom desperately sought.

How did the mystics contribute to this daring quest? In the ritual of sacrifice, medieval Christendom could approach the bar in the signifying process because the work of the thetic is actually breached in sacrifice. Although it was sign, and not soma, which these supplicants of sacred power grasped, the productive function of sacrifice shadowed the thetic so closely that it was able to replicate the *process* of the Symbolic's production even though it remained unable to capture and grasp for its own the full power of the symbol.

Even so, when medieval Christendom drew on the third sacrificial aspect of holy women's asceticism, it did come close to achieving this feat. These holy women's collective death-work compellingly reenacted work done by humans when they follow the signifying path through the abject chaos of mimesis to the order of the Symbolic. In miming that movement in all its nuances, its creative and destructive aspects, the mystics facilitated a community's effort to retrace steps made by humans in the earliest journey of emergent subjectivity in order that the community might position itself again safely and securely on the high ground of the Symbolic. Because their thetic-transgressing acts appeared capable of all the dynamics of negativity—creation and destruction, jouissance and death—holy women embodied a sacrifice that was *pharmakos* as well as *pharmakon.* Poison and antidote, pollution and cleansing power, their labors most powerfully evoked the sacred.

In sum, the sacrifice of the mystics was a border-securing rite which was intended to thwart a destabilizing and potentially lethal disorder located on the margins of Christendom. Sacrifice and its attendant rituals of purification from pollution resecured the social order because they served as a vehicle by which disrupting forces could be placed under the control of the sign and neutralized. Sacrifice tapped also a dynamic of localized violence which, restricted to the bodies of select victims, drew on the powers of negativity to distribute broad-based renewal within the restored order.

How compelling is an analysis of asceticism among medieval mystics which is rooted in sacrificial theory? Because this analysis highlights the complex interplay of holy women's asceticism with boundary-work of late medieval Christendom, it stands at a distance from a psychological analysis that, bypassing the social context, would trace a mystic's motives to individual neuroses. A typical psychological analysis of what Bell has called "holy anorexia" would describe a mystic's behavior in terms of her struggle for control in her interactions with her family or community. Or it might focus on her ambivalent feelings about her developing adult female body. On both counts, the psychological portrait is problematic: made a fixture in a bourgeois family drama, a holy woman's struggles attest only to dysfunctional processes in adolescent development.

Several factors differentiate a sacrificial analysis of the mystics' lives from a typical psychological treatment of their ascetic practices. Most obviously, in a sacrificial theory, if a conflict with the Mother is registered on the bodies of the mystics, she is not the mother of a contemporary psychodrama whose impossible standards of perfection make her daughter feel hopelessly inadequate and cause her to seek self-mastery in food denial. If that mother is not wholly unknown to medieval Christendom, as Rudolph Bell suggests (1985, 17–20), telling only her story accounts inadequately for medieval holy women's lives. As Bynum demonstrates so compellingly, if the mystics' lives are construed in terms of anorexia, practices of medieval asceticism that had complex, widely acknowledged, and socially significant meanings are treated reductionistically. Much more was going on in the holy women's asceticism than can be gathered if it is viewed primarily in terms of its instrumental role in young women's struggles to escape from troubling familial relationships. By contrast, if the significance of the social context to the lives of medieval holy women is affirmed, a wider dynamic of conflict in the lives of medieval holy women can also be observed. Writ large in medieval society, this conflict is directed toward the maternal matrix and places the mystics squarely in the midst of a sacrificial economy.

Indeed, the Symbolic order and its Law are constructed to conceal the maternal matrix: the Mother. In the work of negativity that makes the Mother the very space of loss that brings the social order into being, the Law provides for the Mother only in her absence. However, this process is fraught with danger. Vestiges of the Mother-quest may haunt multiple levels of a signifying economy and especially its somatic investments (e.g., milk, saliva, blood). The death-work of medieval holy women indicates most strongly that medieval Christendom was in the grip of such a Mother-quest.

What accounts for the implication of diverse sectors of the signifying economy of late medieval Christendom in death-work directed toward the Mother? When persons employ language in order to bring negativity (jouissance and rejection) under the force of the sign, that which counts as a sign and, therefore, as a successful instrument of boundary building, is preferentially coded with markers of the maternal which can resonate at multiple levels of the economy in diverse linguistic and cultural codes. Thus, for medieval society, alimentary motifs marked a currency that was distributed broadly across multiple sectors of Christendom. Not surprisingly, these motifs were subject to a common exchange rate within the sacrificial economy as medieval society was beset by conflict and threats to its bounded order. When this happened, and in mimicry of the abject, preindividuated body of an infant who experienced a fluctuation of boundaries (inside/outside, pleasure/pain, fascination by the maternal matrix/and fear of sinking irretrievably into it), medieval Christendom framed its border-battle with the abject threat of disorder in terms reminiscent of this early struggle. Imagery of abjection in ascetic practices—blood, vomit, milk—testified to the persistence in medieval society of boundary issues. Because margin-challenging matters shaped individual bodies only because they also created social bodies, diverse intertextual practices which resided at multiple levels of a signifying economy were joined: in sway to a sacrificial economy, late medieval Christendom engaged in a common struggle to recreate and sustain the sociosymbolic order.

Because sacrificial theory recognizes diverse social tasks performed by holy women on behalf of that economy, it clearly commends itself over readings of "holy anorexia" offered from a psychological perspective. However, it is still possible to inquire from a position friendly to Kristeva whether the mystics' lives are accounted for adequately by the space allotted them in this sacrificial theory. Was the mystics' death-work an instance of sacrifice, or was it suicide? Should not their encounters with the abject be viewed as symptomatic of an implosive rather than an explosive violence? After all, the unnameable Otherness, toward which the mystics' spirituality drifted, was less a murderous maternal entity than it was a "solid rock of *jouissance*" (Kristeva, 1982, 59).

Perhaps, the jouissance of the mystics is best understood as a rock of freedom against which they brushed but to which they could not effectively cling as they fell into the abyss of death. Of course, the battle they fought on behalf of freedom rooted in jouissance was the most archaic one. Because the Law barred the Mother/sacred, the linguistic crisis the mystics embodied was twofold. First, the Mother/sacred could be encountered only in her absence—as the Law decreed—or in abjection. And, as abject, the paternal order dictated that she could be embraced in the implosive violence of melancholia or challenged in the repetition of the original sacrifice that had brought that order into being. Which of these scenarios is most compelling?

On the one hand, the mystics' power to heal others and to function as charismatic leaders within late medieval Christendom does suggest what Irigaray and Bynum have highlighted: the mystics carved out a space of freedom from the Symbolic order and Father's Law, creating lives for themselves that exemplified open and free subjectivity. Even so, that the holy women's freedom culminated in lives of acute physical suffering and, to a significant degree, in early deaths from self-starvation suggests that their freedom was measured. But by what measure were their lives constrained? Did their rejection of the Law constitute an abject refusal of the Law (melancholia) or an abject challenge to it (sacrifice)?

Because the mystics were able to unite with the Mother-Christ in fulfillment of extreme asceticism, one could argue that the vision toward which they soared was a black sun: in dying they dissolved into the maternal Thing. Embodying the founding contradictions of human existence, the mystics absorbed alterity into their own identity. The mystics were not so much submerged in the sadness of unmediated maternal loss as they were ecstatically transported by their response to that loss. On each of these counts, Ewa Ziarek's analysis of melancholia is salient (1993, 73). Drawing on that analysis, one could propose that the mystics' reality-subverting miracles displayed their refusal to accept that the Symbolic system compensated adequately for maternal loss. Perhaps, in that respect, the mystics' lives were a powerful critique of desire within the paternal order. Exposing that order's arrogance and claim to control the vicissitudes of human existence by constraining them within narrowly specified modes of linguistic proficiency, the mystics assumed a radically subversive stance that honored an excess of difference—an abject sacred—beyond all capacity of paternally sanctioned signs to subsume.

Notwithstanding the suggestive power of an assessment of the mystics' lives oriented toward melancholia, it is not wholly persuasive. The mystics' multifaceted labor suggests more powerfully a sacrificial narrative of abjection, defilement, and ritual sacrifice. In their replay of the mimetic and sacrificial crises, the mystics were both sacrificers and the ones sacrificed. In their death-work, the mimetic play of the sacred turned back on itself. And, as the rock of jouissance necessarily eluded these holy women who were also daughters of the Law, the mystics fell into the abyss of self-and-Mother-murder.

Admittedly, they ate the Mother-Christ to save her and to save themselves. Unlike the Fathers, they did not have murder in their hearts. One consequently does not wholly err if one observes in their death-work a shadow cast by a black sun. However, because the bodies of the mystics had already been colonized by the forces of a sacrificial economy, which not only barred them forever from the jouissance they sought, but also restricted their freedom to write the story of that loss in ways not dictated by tenets of representation mandated by the paternal order, their asceticism attests to sacrifice rather than to melancholia.[9]

Although a sacrificial scenario for the mystics' lives is more compelling than either a typical psychological explanation such as Bell's or a rationale focused on melancholia, perhaps a Turner-inspired argument that joins self-starving practices among contemporary women with those of the medieval mystics will prove the most salient. Conceivably, medieval holy women's bodies were conscripted by competing cultural ideologies. But the strength of the sacrificial over the ideological scenario lies with the claim that the mystics' signifying practices not only reflected cultural codes, but also created them. These practices occurred within the *generative* processes of a signifying economy. That bodies and discursive meaning were joined in the very rending of the bodies that served as the productive limit of this economy is demonstrated in the three previously cited works of sacrifice performed by the mystics: soma (the body of ascetic practice) was killed to create the sign (of a saved community); the symbol (a community infused with the saving power of Christ) was somatized (in a sacrificial transgression of the flesh which touched the sacred on the far side of the thetic order); and the power of the sacrificial economy to destroy *and* create was demonstrated as a dying mystic—both poison and antidote—sacrificially cleansed the community and secured it from threat.

Even as this analysis brings to the fore the mystics' sacrifice, some ambiguities persist. The complex experiences of these holy women invite no pat conclusions; they lead only to a welter of possibilities. Perhaps in no other time did Western culture come so close to unveiling the truth of its origins. Perhaps in no other time were the fractures at the foundations of the sacrificial economy deeper or the possibilities for women's subversion of the Law greater than during the late medieval age. Even so, if decisive testimony to the truth of that time is available, it is located in subsequent centuries. The late medieval age, site of the struggle to resurrect the sacrificed Mother and to retrieve her daughters from the grip of the sacrificial economy, ended in paroxysms of violence. In the sixteenth and seventeenth centuries, the witch craze claimed the lives of more than 100,000 women (Barstow, 1988, 7) and reasserted the hegemonic power of the sacrificial economy, in which women's bodies unambiguously were a favored currency. The mystics' stigmata became devil's marks and milk from their breasts no longer healed the sick but nursed incubi (Bynum, 1987, 270, 273).

Indeed, women victimized by the witch hunts occupied a position within society which had been filled by the mystics in preceding centuries. They too performed death-work on behalf of a sacrificial economy even as they sought to subvert its mandates. However, when their persecutors read the sign of the Mother on the bodies of women they suspected of witchcraft and attacked them, their violence was more direct and more devastating than was that of those persons who read the sign of the Mother on the mystics' bodies. The raw immediacy and intensity of the witch hunters' violence pose a challenge for interpreters of the witch craze and call for extended reflection.

6

"THE DEVILS ARE COME DOWN UPON US"

MYTH, HISTORY, AND THE WITCH AS SCAPEGOAT[1]

If our ancestors had thought in the same mode
as do today's masters, they would never
have put an end to the witch trials.

—René Girard

This project is at a critical juncture. When a sacrificial theory is brought to bear on the witch hunts, a dialogue with historians is initiated that is fraught with risk and possibility. On the one hand, a sacrificial theory may appear all the more compelling in the wake of this dialogue. But, equally, the issues at stake in this conversation suggest that an examination of the witch hunts may show that a sacrificial theory does not contribute to feminist reflections on violence against women.

That the witch hunts place a sacrificial theory in jeopardy is unexpected. After all, even on cursory examination, images of sacrifice proliferate in narratives of the witch hunts. Moreover, historians feature the scapegoating phenomenon in their accounts of the craze. Little distance need be traveled, we might imagine, from references to scapegoats to a full sacrificial theory. Finally, many of the ambiguities that were associated with medieval holy women's lives appear absent from the lives of women accused of witchcraft. That women accused of witchcraft can be more easily situated within a sacrificial economy than were the mystics appears plausible.

After all, considerable groundwork had to be laid in order to establish that medieval holy women performed a sacrificial role in the signifying economy of late medieval Christendom. The larger social significance of their suffering and deaths was not immediately obvious. It seemed that their behavior might be accounted for most credibly if it was attributed to a familial psychodrama or to the vagaries of adolescent development. By contrast, that the signifying practices of women accused of witchcraft had social import appears obvious. Although historians do argue about precipitating factors for the witch craze, they concur that witch hunting calls for a broad-based social analysis. Scholars who turn a critical eye on witch hunting do not inquire, "What was wrong with *those women?*" They ask, "What was wrong with *that society?*"

Thus, as scapegoats and as murdered victims, the witches fall more neatly within the orbit of a sacrificial economy than did the mystics.

However, such an optimistic assessment is wholly unfounded. For ironically, the very aspect of the study of the mystics that made a sacrificial analysis of their lives seem most plausible is absent from most discussions of the witch hunts. What is this missing factor? Under Bynum's encouragement, our examination of the medieval mystics' lives emphasized their distance from the contemporary world. Sacrificial metaphors in the mystics' lives were accepted at face value; they were not translated into other terms. Encouraged by Bynum to perceive the mystics' world as a vital religious culture profoundly alien to our own, we found credible the notion that such a world was structured by sacrifice.

By contrast, the vast literature on the witch hunts does not offer such maneuvering room. Historians of the witch craze tend to adopt a stance that collapses the distance between that time and our own at precisely those places where the structure of sacrifice is most prominent: in the mythic language of the hunts. They use tools of analysis that often render invisible or epiphenomenal to the hunts the reality intended by witch hunters' words. Whereas witch hunters spoke of devils, incubi, monstrous births, and bestial encounters with demonic familiars, when historians take up the hunters' narratives, they regularly bypass a sacrificial enclosure, an abject and polluted space, to which we might have thought that the hunters' words attested. Historians relocate the signifying work of witch hunting on a plain of economic and political interests. Because they make mythic language tangential to the economic, political, and social functions of the witch craze and treat it as a coded instance of these other functions, witch hunting does not appear to be a sacrificial phenomenon.

That historical inquiry seems to place out of the reach of direct analysis those aspects of the witch hunts which would lend themselves most obviously to sacrificial analysis is all the more disquieting because, on first acquaintance, the ethos of contemporary historical inquiry is highly compatible with a key goal of feminist scholarship. As Adrienne Rich rightly observes, feminists desire to recover the lost memories of women in ways that do not perpetuate the structures of history-making that first relegated women to invisibility (Rich, 1996, 146). Feminist scholars are wary of explanations of the witch hunts that might mute victims' voices. On behalf of the witch hunters' victims, feminist scholars seek to challenge those who charged women with witchcraft; they do not want to strengthen or affirm the accusers' voices. The historians would appear to support that goal because they do not take into serious account the accusers' own justification for witch hunting, which was expressed in a demonological discourse. Instead, they focus on the accusers' economic and political interests. When the historians free the victims of the witch hunts of the labels their accusers assigned them—devil, nurser of incubi, poisoner—feminist scholars feel empowered to proclaim the innocence of the accused.

Should feminist scholars make common cause with those who cite economic and political factors behind the hunts and downplay the significance of myth in the society that hunted witches? Should they welcome social-scientific analyses that promise to give voice to the victims of the witch craze by silencing their persecutors? Girard's *The Scapegoat* renders problematic affirmative responses to these questions. In that work, Girard suggests that if today's historians and sociologists had weighed in on the witch craze in its time and brought their expert testimony to bear on it, their analyses would have sustained, rather than brought to an end, the trials. On what grounds does Girard offer this assessment?

Girard issues a challenge to social scientists when he submits that only a sacrificial theory which engages directly the demonological narratives of the witch hunts can break open and contest the structure of victimization that sustained them. Any other approach to the hunts, especially one that treats demonological themes as tangential to the craze or as mere coded narratives of political, social, or economic unrest, leaves intact the dynamics of violence that created the witch craze then and could do so again.

Most serious consideration needs to be given to Girard's argument that contemporary research on the witch hunts is fatally flawed, notwithstanding its many strengths. Indubitably, the stakes involved in accepting and rejecting his thesis are high. If Girard is right, and current historical analyses of the witch hunts account inadequately for the victimizing process because they leave its sacrificial structure unaltered and uncontested, the emancipatory commitments of feminist scholars may be at risk.

Further, if witch hunts cannot be shown to fall in the orbit of a sacrificial economy—despite the markers of scapegoating that suggest they do—then serious doubts are raised about the relevance of a sacrificial theory to issues of sexually differentiated violence. If women accused of witchcraft—who appear on multiple grounds to paradigmatically embody the figure of the scapegoat—were not victims of sacrifice, then perhaps no woman ever has been such a victim. If the work of a sacrificial economy cannot be detected and analyzed in a context in which the mythic narratives of the Christian religion spoke of sacrifice directly and without apology, then efforts to detect and analyze the work of a sacrificial economy in other times and places are seriously compromised. In an era when functions of that economy previously ceded to the Christian religion have been dispersed among other institutions, which dissemble and disguise their sacrificial agenda, exposing sacrifice becomes immeasurably more difficult.

Notwithstanding risks associated with taking Girard's claims to heart, this chapter advances an interrogative thesis sympathetic to Girard: current studies of the witch hunts, attentive as they are to tracing the demographic, economic, political, and sociological factors of the witch hunts in ever more sophisticated ways, are inadequate to the emancipatory goals of feminist scholarship. The complaint is twofold: scholars treat violence in witch hunting in problematic ways and they make religion an extrinsic factor in the hunts without proper justification.

The people who accused women of witchcraft, who put them on trial, tortured, banished, or executed them, offered a rationale grounded in religious beliefs. But, according to many current theories, those beliefs were but external trappings for social, political, and economic agendas. Chosen for its efficacy and by historical accident, religion and its sacrificial narratives accompanied the witch hunts but did not form or define them. Moreover, while wisely avoiding a detailed analysis of the violence that attended the witch hunts which might verge on voyeurism, current scholarship meets this violence with virtual silence. It does not adequately explain either the torture of the accused or the brutal deaths of the convicted. Because analyses of witch hunting bypass the issue of the intrinsic relation of religion to the hunts and do not attend systematically to their violence, they are seriously flawed. Specifically, because researchers misread the dynamics of persecution, their explorations leave unchallenged the persecutors and the sacrificial economy in which they operated. In sustaining an uncritical perspective on the work of a sacrificial economy, they perpetuate the victimization of the women charged and convicted by those persecutors and place future generations of women at risk. Thus, despite their attention to detail and evidence, scholars of the witch craze share an amnesia which they ignore at their peril.

Feminist scholars should find the problem of amnesia particularly acute. For Girard inspires us to believe that if feminists are to speak adequately of the witch craze and remember all that they must remember if they are to contribute to efforts to free their foresisters and future sisters from a history of victimization, feminists must treat sacrifice and its discursive practices as essential to the witch craze and its violence.

In this chapter, a sacrificial theory of the witch hunts is advanced in four sections. Current theories of the witch craze are summarized in Sections I and II. In Section III, extant explanations are challenged as inadequate and scholars are called to refocus current strategies of analysis in the direction of a sacrificial theory. In Section IV, a theory of the witch hunts informed by Kristeva is set forth. Witch hunting and its sexually differentiated violence are placed within a sacrificial economy.

I. The Witch in Historical Perspective

During three hundred years from 1450 to 1750, women throughout Europe and in the American colonies were accused of witchcraft, tried, convicted, and executed. Witches—persons who practiced magical arts, sorcery, and healing—had always been part of the European cultural landscape, but it was not until the fifteenth century that prosecution of them began to reach panic proportions. Prior to that time, legal charges were brought against individuals only if their sorcery caused personal or property damages. Recent scholarship cites a variety of factors that contributed to the development of a witch craze. These factors locate women accused of witchcraft at points of flux in the society where changes in the legal system, the pattern of marriage, the economy, the dominant social ethic, and the primary ideology of gender were most dramatic and unsettling.

Christina Larner cites a changed legal system as an essential precondition of the witch craze. Interpersonal, restorative justice was in transition in the sixteenth century to a system of retributive justice. Where formerly an individual took the initiative to bring charges of sorcery against a neighbor who had harmed him or his family and also assumed the risk of reverse charges should the case be proved frivolous or unsound, now centralized systems came into existence which functioned on the premise that the whole society was the potential victim of witchcraft. For example, in Scotland, statutes against witchcraft, formerly linked with sexual and religious offenses, were abstracted from their traditional ecclesiastical context. The Scottish Witchcraft Act of 1563, like that of the Holy Roman Empire in 1532 (*Constitutio Criminalis Carolina*), made witchcraft a civil offense (1981, 193). As centralized and secularized processes of control replaced the mode of individual prosecution of neighbor against neighbor, religious beliefs functioned in service to a secular system.

According to Erik Midelfort, preconditions for the witch craze in southwestern Germany during the latter half of the sixteenth century were founded similarly in a new legal possibility: the inquisitorial trial (1972, 67). The court took over traditional functions of an accuser. A single panel included as one body the accuser, the prosecutor, and the judge. The examiners' skill resulted in increasing numbers of charges, trials, and convictions (1972, 104–106). The court needed only two items of proof to find a person guilty. First, the court required three independent denunciations. Under torture, women were called to denounce other women. Since the court mandated independent denunciations, that three different persons would name the same suspects tended to limit suspects to two groups: women notorious in the community for eccentric or unusual behavior, and well-known women (e.g., midwives, wives of village innkeepers or of well-known merchants) (1972, 187–88). The second item of proof was a devil's mark, a sign of one's relationship to the devil. A devil's mark was any spot on the body that was insensitive to pricking with a pin or needle or which failed to bleed if pricked. The court authorized their representatives to strip and search for devil's marks the women suspected of witchcraft. Klaits observes also that, in some areas of Europe, professional prickers made an occupation of the search for these marks (1985, 56–57). This new legal system set in motion a remarkably efficient machinery for witch hunting.

Why did witch hunters, in utilizing this new legal system, find their victims almost exclusively among women?[2] Midelfort offers two explanations. First, the women's accusers believed that women were prone to the devil's seduction. They were both more lustful and weaker than men. Thus, women as a group were vulnerable to the suspicions of witchcraft (1972, 182). Second, a change in marriage patterns in the sixteenth century created widespread social instability and uncertainty. An excess of women of marriageable age, a high number of spinsters and widows, and a late age for marriage increased women's vulnerability in a society beset by social unrest (1972, 184).

John Hajnal traces the specific rationale for the late marriage pattern to the high standard of living in western Europe. Late marriage brought about wealth, because one could conserve resources over many years; wealth, or the insistence on it, brought about late marriage. The standard of wealth was property, and in the sixteenth century men had to wait for land to become available, generally until their father's deaths. The stem-family pattern, according to which the oldest son inherited his father's property, contributed to the economic incentive for late marriage (1965, 101–47).

Midelfort argues that the changed marriage pattern threatened patriarchal control and caused a fundamental disturbance in the family unit (1972, 184). When men made efforts to consolidate patriarchal control, they viewed with increasing suspicion unmarried women. Moreover, on a practical level, unmarried women were outside the key institution—the family—that would offer them protection. Widows and spinsters number high among the initial victims of witchcraft charges. Once in court, the sophisticated process of condemnation, founded on the principle of three independent denunciations, would extend as well to less-suspect members of the society.

For Carol Karlsen, historian of the witch hunts in New England, that women accused of witchcraft were women who threatened the economic order is of decisive significance. Daughters of families without sons, mothers of only female children, and women with no children predominated among the women charged with witchcraft. Women in these categories "were aberrations in an inheritance system designed to keep property in the hands of men" (1987, 101). In New England, women without male heirs comprised 64 percent of the females prosecuted for witchcraft, 76 percent of those found guilty, and 89 percent of those executed (1987, 102).

Like Midelfort, Karlsen traces tension in the social order to the intersection of familial and economic pressures. The new European marriage pattern occurred in New England in the late seventeenth century. Moreover, at that late date, changes in the family unit coincided with disruptions associated with the society's transition from a land-based to a mercantile economy. Sons who wanted their inheritance but faced a shortage of land experienced frustration and resentment. So also did the religious and landed elites and a newly risen, religiously diverse mercantile elite who competed with each other. Because the basic economic unit in the late seventeenth century was the family, to whom one owed respect, not complaints, and because there were few institutional avenues available to all alike to deal with economic conflict, witch hunting became the vehicle of stress release, according to Karlsen. That frustration and resentment was then visited on the witch who, in Puritan belief, had come to symbolize all that was disorderly and evil in the society. The Salem witch trials were the clearest indication that, in an economic war, competitors vied for control by using women as pawns in their struggle. Accusers tended to come from the old farm economy and those accused of witchcraft from the new mercantile economy that was threatening the old order (1987, 214–18).

Klaits joins Keith Thomas and Alan Macfarlane in suggesting that, in addition to familial and economic disruptions to the social order, insecurities about social mores contributed to a climate of suspicion conducive to witch hunting (1985, 87–94). Villages and developing towns throughout Europe were experiencing a transition from a communal ethic to an ethic of individualism: a tradition of mutual help was being challenged by a new economic order (Macfarlane and Thomas). That change exacted its highest cost from those persons who had depended most on the older order of charity: widows, the poor, the elderly. In transition from old to new ethic, residents of a community were more likely to resent a neighbor's appeal for help, yet to feel guilty about their refusal of help. Notably, the accuser in the witch trial was nearly always more prosperous than the accused. Moreover, the poorest of the poor generally escaped charges of witchcraft. Instead, the borderline case—the moderately poor woman who thought she ought to receive her neighbor's help but whose overtures were rejected—was most likely to be linked to witchcraft (1985, 90). With the decline of a social ethic, which had been firmly articulated by the church in previous times, the individual bore sole responsibility for adjudicating the parameters of charity. Not until the state, in the next century, made charity the province of a government bureaucracy would a social ethic be articulated clearly again. In the transition period, the guilt feelings of an individual uncertain about his or her responsibility to a neighbor became "fertile ground" for witchcraft accusations. Misfortunes might be a witch's retaliation against her neighbor (1985, 91).

John Demos argues that this scenario is particularly applicable to witch hunting among the Puritans in New England. Although the Puritans brought with them to the New World the traditional ethic of Christian charity, court records of struggles over land, money, and inheritances demonstrate that these fragile communities were fed increasingly on an ethic of individualism. Marginalized women, at greater risk in communities populated by people maneuvering for "personal advantage," bore the brunt of communal insecurity about the new ways (1982, 298–300).

Insecurity about new social mores characterizes another factor contributing to the witch hunts: new gender ideologies offered by the Church created unrest similar to that unrest associated with the new ethic of individualism. Both Karlsen and Larner note the ambiguous status of women during the sixteenth and seventeenth centuries in respect to expectations for their gender. On the one hand, the pre-Reformation view that women, morally inferior to men, were weak-willed and susceptible both to lusts of the flesh and to enticements to greed, still functioned. On the other hand, and more explicitly, voices of the Reformation espoused a new gender ideology. According to Larner, women, granted a greater autonomy and capacity for virtuous behavior, were responsible for the state of their souls (1981, 101).[3] These twin religious ideologies of gender, appropriated by the state, had major consequences in women's lives. On the basis of the *pre-Reformation* theology that still formed the background to cultural perceptions of women, the witch hunters could justify a position that made witch hunting synonymous with woman hunting. On the basis of *Reformation* theology, the witch hunters could make women responsible, as pre-Reformation governments had not, for the crime of witchcraft.

Prior to the Scottish Witchcraft Act, women were invisible in the courts. Their behavior, notes Larner, was the responsibility of their husbands and fathers, and the punishment for any crimes they had committed was that thought appropriate for children, whipping (1981, 102). With the Witchcraft Act in force, the state began to explore the parameters of women's responsibility for their own behavior.

Indeed, Larner argues that the contrasting theologies of gender were introduced into the court in order for the state to educate women to their new roles (1981, 102). Women who misjudged the limits of their responsibility and saw a license for equality in the Reformation's affirmation of their capacity for responsible behavior were instructed by the witch trials to the error of their views. The witchcraft trials were therefore pedagogical: by means of the trials, lines of appropriate female behavior were drawn, and overly independent women had the new theory of female responsibility turned back on themselves.

Karlsen's study of accusations of witchcraft directed against radical Puritan women, such as Ann Hutchinson and Mary Dyer, who believed that the mandate for spiritual equality before God justified equality in the church, closely parallels Larner's. Basing their views on the notion that gender arrangements were not only divinely ordained by God but mandated by nature, the Puritan male leadership strove to disabuse women such as Hutchinson and Dyer of their views (1987, 120–25). That women accused of witchcraft were linked with the crimes of bearing illegitimate children, having abortions, or committing infanticide (1987, 141) served to confirm, for that leadership, witches' sinful interference with divinely ordained gender roles. So also did imagery associated with witches—they hatched, bred, or suckled either heretical ideas and/or actual monsters—exemplify the Puritan male leadership's view of witches' sinful challenge of divine mandate (1987, 144). Unmarried women, childless women, midwives, and women in business—all aberrations in the divinely ordained system that defined women by their role in procreation—were particularly vulnerable to charges of witchcraft.

Again, like Larner, Karlsen traces the preoccupation with gender roles in colonial New England to the ambiguity of those roles in Puritan society. As was the case in Scotland, Puritan views of gender maintained an implicit reference to the pre-Reformation suspicions about women while externally advocating a more optimistic portrait of women. Karlsen argues that the witch trials ensued during the time in which both views were still held. The trials were, in some ways, the very occasion for adjudicating the truth about women (1987, 154–55). The witch was the negative model by which the virtuous Puritan woman was defined. She set off in stark relief the values of Puritan society and the borders of its moral and cultural universe (1987, 181).

II. The Witch as Scapegoat

For each scholar of the witch hunts, contributing factors, such as those discussed above, form the background for analyses of essential aspects of the craze. The figure of the scapegoat appears in three typologies that frame the witch craze: the witch as scapegoat served the ideological interests of the ruling class; she was chosen to bear the brunt of the fears of the peasant class; or, standing at the juncture of popular and learned cultures, needed by each, she was the one torn apart in their struggles with each other. For none of these typologies was religious belief—myth and practice—central to the witch craze. Religious discourse was located at the periphery; other factors constituted the core dynamic of witch hunting.

Erik Midelfort's work is representative of those which locate the impetus for the witch craze at the low end of European society. Arguing that, even at its worst moments, the churches in southwestern Germany—both Catholic and Protestant—supported the craze only ambivalently, Midelfort claims that the witch primarily served the needs of peasant culture. The call for witch hunting issued from popular pressures: the peasant majority needed to locate scapegoats for the pain and suffering of plague, famine, or other disasters. His model example is Balingen in Württemberg where, in response to the town's devastation by fire in 1672, the search for a scapegoat led the townspeople to take matters into their own hands and stone a suspected witch when the Oberrat (the Superior Council in Stuttgart) would not act (1972, 190).

Contrasting with Midelfort's "bottom-up" theory of witch hunting is Christina Larner's work. Representative of "top-down" theories of the craze, Larner's analysis indicates that witch hunting was a ruling-class activity aimed at social control (1981, 64). Specifically, witches were pawns in the struggle between secular and church authorities for control of the Scottish countryside. In a game of "who is the godliest of them all," the church and state struggled for authority (1981, 73), tossing the bodies of witches between them and blurring the lines between sin and crime.

Larner's thesis echoes those of Peter Brown and R. I. Moore. Brown argues that "sorcery beliefs may be used like radio-active traces in an X-ray: where they assemble, we have a hint of pockets of uncertainty and competition in a society increasingly committed to a vested hierarchy in church and state" (Moore, 1972, 128). Moore, who focuses on the development of a persecuting society in the Middle Ages, claims that European society defined itself and established its borders by engaging in persecution of Jews and lepers (1987, 146–48). Larner's analysis extends Brown and Moore's theses to the Reformation: it was not the masses who found a voice for their protests against societal uncertainties and cruelties in the courts; rather, it was the courts who found their voice and reason for existing in hunting the masses for witches.

Larner notes that, in the battle for control of the geographical, cultural, and moral borders of Scotland, the state increasingly had the upper hand. Indeed, while it was possible to prosecute a witch under the old machinery of the church, that witch prosecution in Scotland was "conducted throughout under those parts of the machinery of social control which were entirely new" is notable. The statute of 1563 centralized the administration of the Witchcraft Act and extended the authority of the Privy Council in witchcraft cases (1981, 58). The new machinery, once in place, moved only slowly at first. In 1583 the General Assembly of the Church complained to the King that incest, adultery, and witchcraft were not being punished. In 1591, however, the Privy Council rocketed into action and appointed commissions to examine witches. The Privy Council's license to hunt witches lasted until 1597, when the relegated powers were restored to the King (James VI), and witch hunting entered into a period of decline (1981, 71). Despite the efforts of the church to proceed with witch hunting, it was not until the 1620s that the Privy Council interested itself in witchcraft cases again, as part of a general reassertion of its authority (1981, 72). There was a brief lull in the 1630s, a time of plague and famine.[4] But witch hunting entered into a new panic phase in the 1640s, a period which coincided with tension between church and state over their respective boundaries. Again, as in 1583, the General Assembly of the church chastised Parliament for its inaction against witches. The Privy Council established commissions to hunt witches, and witch hunting moved forward on a rising tide until the witch hunting machinery of the state ground to a halt under Cromwell (1981, 73–75).

Crucial to Larner's thesis that witch hunting was a ruling-class activity among institutions competing for social control is her analysis of the role landowners played in the witch hunts. Landowners, rather than ministers, requested most of the commissions and conducted most of the witch trials (1981, 40). Clergy participated in this structure in two ancillary ways. First, the Kirk session functioned as a policing force for local landowners. Appointed and paid by the landowners, the ministers—though nominally of the landed class themselves—stood midway in social structure as a mediating force between landowners and peasants (1981, 56). Second, the ministers facilitated preliminary searches for witches and served as witnesses at their trials (1981, 106–107). But, in each case, the power lay with the landowners and not with the church. Thus, the rise and fall of witch hunting in Scotland is traced by Larner, first, to the structure of centralized authority—the Privy Council—and to its inclination in any particular time to prosecute witches and, second, to the authority of the landowners who, through commissions, carried out the work of the Privy Council (1981, 88). These two groups—council and landowners—hunted witches in order to establish and reinforce their jurisdiction over the countryside. By contrast, the moral and religious fervor which the church directed against witches expressed itself in ways that, though visible, were largely inefficacious. Religion may have accompanied witch hunting, but other social and economic agenda defined it.

Larner's discussion of the dynamics of power played out between the Privy Council, the landowners, and the church offers intriguing prospects for understanding the integration of theologies of gender in the discourse of the witch trials. Suggested by her work is the possibility that, in their struggle to be the primary institution of social control, both the church and state exploited the ambiguity about gender roles expressed in the differences between pre-Reformation and Reformation theologies. The power of the church and state to impose a particular ideology on women was not just the power to impose that ideology on women's minds. Rather, they forced women to embody the ruling ideology. Applied to the witch trial, the metaphor of "writing the body" well describes this power: in the course of the craze, an underlying fifteenth-century text—engraved on women's bodies in terms of lust, weakness, and greed—was covered over with a new sixteenth-century text, that of responsibility and adulthood. Throughout the craze, old and new texts were inscribed and reinscribed on women's bodies as church and state vied to scratch out a final and definitive sentence that would confirm their sovereign control over the society. Through torture and trial, ideological conformity, which allowed female responsibility only within the context of a patriarchal system of female submission, was engraved on women's very bodies.

Representative of a centrist position, falling between theories advanced by Midelfort and Larner, is Joseph Klaits's work. Klaits argues that interpretive frameworks that emphasize the role of popular pressures in the witch craze and those that highlight the interests of the educated elites in the craze are not mutually exclusive. Klaits blends interpretive models and suggests that witch hunting impulses both "trickled down from the society's leaders" and "rose upward on a tide of popular anxieties" (1985, 150). The witch, as scapegoat, served both groups.

For Klaits, the decisive factor in the witch craze, from the side of the educated and politically powerful, was an atmosphere of spiritual reform. That the masses of Europe were being Christianized for the first time is demonstrated by the preoccupation of the clergy with the values and habits of the peasant folk in the countryside (1985, 60). As religious evangelism became increasingly preoccupied with issues of sexuality, the witch appeared as the figure of deviant sexuality on whom evangelistic fervor focused.

Klaits's thesis is influenced by the research of Richard Kieckhefer. Kieckhefer, whose work focuses on preconditions of the witch craze established during the late medieval period, has argued that a conjunction of popular belief in sorcery with a demonology created by a learned culture laid a foundation for the worst excesses of witch hunting. The superimposing of the language of diabolism on that of sorcery "added fuel to an already blazing fire" (1976, 105). Specifically, because charges of diabolism embellished charges of sorcery, the discourse of the elite was directly responsible for the craze of spiraling accusations and increasingly harsh punishments. Sorcery—the weapon of the socially powerless when illness, love affairs, quarrels, and communal inhospitality placed them at odds with their neighbors—was elevated in diabolism. Diabolism was used by the devil and his legions in the battle for the souls and bodies of an entire people. Where sorcery called for reparations—the lifting of curses, the return of "borrowed" property, reciprocal apologies and protestations of forgiveness—diabolism summoned forth all the powers of the state to do battle with evil. At stake was not the harmony of a single community or clan, but the survival of human society itself.

Moreover, if at first demonology served primarily to "translate" popular belief into the language of the educated, it was not without its own popular appeal. With a theory of demonology in place and a legal system prepared to bring all its powers to bear against the devil, when demonological theory "trickled down" to the masses, after gestating among the elite in the fourteenth and fifteenth centuries, the zeal to exterminate devil worshipers knew no limits. Thus, for Kieckhefer, beliefs in sorcery and in demonological witchcraft mingled to form one virulent world view. With their fears joined, popular and learned cultures required and hunted down a virtually endless supply of victims (1976, 73–92).

Extending Kieckhefer's analysis of the links between popular sorcery and demonological theory, Klaits attributes the reformers' preoccupation with issues of deviant sexuality—as expressed in their demonological theory—to the association of sexuality with the core of human identity. The decisive proof of successful inculcation of Christian values and habits required by the reformers issued upon one's ability to demonstrate one's liberation from the wiles of Satan, specifically one's freedom from the perverse sexuality of Satan's servants (1985, 76–77). Moreover, because the reformers believed that women were weak and particularly prone to the devil's seduction, clerical suspicions rested more and more on them, feeding an increasingly virulent hatred of women among the clergy (1985, 72).

At the same time as spiritual reform was advancing across the countryside, the ordinary masses upon whom the clergy turned their attention had their own problems, according to Klaits. Social unrest created great insecurities. The search for scapegoats came to rest upon lonely, poor women who "touched the subconscious anxieties of the villagers who saw in their isolation the worst fears they had for themselves" (1985, 102). Fed by the misogynistic suspicions of the reformers, these frustrations precipitated the witch craze.

Thus, for Klaits, witch hunting served a dual purpose. For the masses, it focused anxieties, provided an explanation for their miseries, and "took the people's minds off their troubles" (1985, 103). For the clerical elite, it served to validate the authority structure of society and to give vent to their misogynistic feelings about women. Moreover, because an "unanticipated side effect" of legal reform was the creation of a judicial apparatus conducive to witch hunting, both the masses and the elites found their search for scapegoats efficaciously channeled (1985; 132, 176). With their fears and hopes joined in the courts, the clergy and lay peasantry could accomplish their objectives: the witch trials both publicly demonstrated the truth of the reformers' vision and power—bringing the battle with the devil to a decisive conclusion—and provided the cathartic release the masses had been seeking.

Klaits can be applauded for attempting to honor the complexity of the witch craze by meshing "top-down" and "bottom-up" interpretive frameworks into a single theory of reciprocal influence. Moreover, he can be commended for wanting to accord religion a more central role in the witch craze than have Midelfort and Larner. Nevertheless, his own efforts remain marred by oversimplifications. When Klaits identifies the religious reformers as the vehicle by which the sentiments of the masses and the machinery of a judicial elite were brought together in one place, with explosive results, he misreads key factors in that sequence of events. First, mitigating Klaits's notion of misogyny as the driving ideological force behind the witch hunts are Larner and Karlsen's demonstrations that misogyny characterized the dominant, pre-Reformation ideology of gender, but not that of the Reformation. Second, notwithstanding the fact that the Reformation did Christianize the European countryside, Klaits errs in imputing vast power to the church. Because Klaits fails to integrate the rise of the nation state into his portrait of the Reformation, he ascribes to the clergy more power than they actually had. He makes religion central to the witch hunts, but only because he oversimplifies the notion of religious power, reducing it to clerical politics and mistakenly designating the clerical vision as the dominant ideology. If religion did have a decisive impact on witch hunting, it cannot be for the reasons Klaits cites.

If Klaits overestimates the power of the church, he underestimates the power—ideological and practical—of the courts. Larner's analysis of the conflict between the lay courts and the clergy suggests that Klaits's vision of the role of the courts in the witch hunts is naive. Her thesis is both more specific in its documentation and more comprehensive in its scope than Klaits's: witch hunting was not the "unanticipated side effect" of the new judicial system but was, in fact, integral to the development of that system.

Finally, even if Klaits's portrait of the elite is amended to include judicial as well as clerical elites, his portrait of the peasant masses is problematic. If Klaits's interpretive framework is to stand, we need to know not only the discourse of the elite which trickled down to the masses, but also the discourse of the masses which rose up as a tide toward the elite. Klaits identifies the frustrations of the masses without giving those frustrations voice. Cited only as "primordial fears," the anxieties of the peasant folk remain amorphous (1985, 176). If the language of fear expressed by the peasants was more than or other than the language of the elite that had trickled down to them, Klaits must show his readers this language, but he does not. Thus, in a variety of ways, Klaits fails to meet his own challenge to honor the complex dynamics of witch hunting by setting them in a single, integrative framework.

III. The Witch in Mythic Perspective

Current analyses of the witch craze, reflecting broader trends in historical scholarship dealing with religion, make a laudable advance over earlier treatments. None, in discussing the religious backdrop to the craze, argue that belief in witchcraft was a superstition held by the masses of which they were finally freed by the great wisdom of eighteenth-century humanism. Not only have scholars realized that such an interpretation betrays a kind of ethnocentrism that distorts our understanding of the sixteenth and seventeenth centuries, but, more to the point, research on the witch craze has shown that the witch craze ended with beliefs about demonology still intact among both the educated elite and the peasant masses. According to recent scholarship, witch hunting did not end because persons ceased to believe in witches. Instead, the state and church machinery that was needed to hunt witches fell into disarray, no longer able to discriminate reliably between real witches and those falsely accused (Midelfort, 1972, 196; Larner, 1981, 73–75). Nor did the state and church need to use this machinery. The eighteenth century would see each employ different strategies of legitimation. Moreover, the eighteenth century saw the resolution of earlier ambiguities about gender roles. Freed from the borderline status women had had in the flux of pre-Reformation and Reformation times, women were secured within and "as" the walls of a newly created domestic sphere. As Karlsen observes (1987; 180–81, 255–56), defined by and confined safely to that moral preserve, women in the eighteenth century did not pose a substantive threat to the social order, and reason to suspect them of witchcraft declined dramatically.

Despite their advances over earlier scholarship, analyses summarized here, which have replaced earlier theories about religious superstition with theories that attend to the social, political, and economic function of religious discourse in the witch craze, are not substantively more adequate than those which preceded them. The strength and weakness of each theory hinges on its notion of the witch as scapegoat.

The common thread linking all of the typologies of the witchcraft craze is the figure of the scapegoat. According to Midelfort, a changing court system played into the hands of those bent on finding a scapegoat for various natural and social disasters. For Larner, the witch, a scapegoat for various natural and social disasters, played into the hands of a political institution bent on legitimating itself. Finally, opting for a centrist position, Klaits locates the scapegoat at the juncture of new institutional structures where peasant anxieties were channeled into mass panic.

For the most part, each account does advance knowledge about the witch craze. Moreover, of the lot, Larner offers the most persuasive analysis. After all, Midelfort and Klaits must see the court's change to the inquisitorial trial, so advantageous to the prosecution of witches, as serendipitous. How convenient that, just when the peasants and/or the clergy needed a scapegoat, court procedure changed to accommodate them. By contrast, Larner describes a straightforward convergence which acknowledges the changing political forces of Europe: that the court changed is precisely why witches were hunted. Witches were what the court generated in the state's process of self-legitimation.

Nevertheless, the theories cited here remain problematic. The category of the scapegoat does eventually betray the adequacy of these accounts to the phenomenon of witch hunting. In seeking to understand the scapegoat phenomenon, current research, for the most part, treats these women as cogs in the machinery of a persecuting society without examining thoroughly why they, rather than others, perform that role. Reasons cited—the social, political, and economic vulnerability of the women charged with witchcraft—are reminiscent of Bryan Turner's view of socially marginalized women discussed in the previous chapter. There, Turner was asked whether women are deported to the margins of a social organism because they lack the power necessary to refuse the assignment. Here, a different metaphor invites a similar question: are women forced to do the dirty work of the machine of a persecuting society because they lack the strength and social status to refuse that assignment? Current historical accounts do not answer this question; they do not establish an intrinsic connection between women and cog-work. Recent analyses are problematic also because they reduce religious language about witches to a coded language of politics and protest without explaining why economic and politic interests did their work under the cover of that particular code. Neither tack does justice to the scapegoat. Instead, these modes of analysis continue to participate in an historical amnesia that perpetuates the victimization of the women condemned as witches and leaves their persecutors unchallenged. They are inadequate to the goals of feminist scholarship.

By contrast, René Girard's *The Scapegoat* offers direct testimony to the structure and modus operandi of a sacrificial economy. In that work, Girard closely examines key narratives, often described as myths, that are located in the religious and literary archives of Western culture. These narratives attest to sacrifice.

With Girard's study in mind, let's consider one possible record of a witch trial and execution, written by an accuser, which states that "a woman was executed because she caused the plague."[5] From the vantage point of current witch craze scholarship, we make two judgments about such a record of an historical event: we are sure that the woman did not cause the plague, and we believe she really was executed. On what basis do we confidently and blithely disregard an account of a day that recorded the execution of a woman for witchcraft? The author/accuser says both that the woman caused the plague *and* that she was executed. Why do we want to split in two a text that records an execution, affirming one half and denying the other? Apparently, Girard surmises, the frame of contemporary analysis is one in which we feel that we must either do such violence to the text or let the text continue to do violence to the victim of persecution, thereby affirming the accuser's charge and justifying his murderous actions (1986, 8).

Our intentions are honorable, but we may not achieve our aims. Why? Our current efforts to vindicate the woman accused of witchcraft deny her access to a truth that is crucial to condemning her persecutor: the persecutor's own belief in the witch's guilt. That belief cannot be challenged if we, on behalf of the victim, rend the unity of the persecutor's text. Instead, we must go back inside the text, inside the mind of the persecutor, if we are to expose and break the pattern of violence they exhibit.

According to Girard, the cause of the innocent victims of persecution can be advanced only if we ourselves set out on the trail of persecution that the prosecutors were too naive to cover (1986, 8). Because traces of that truthful trail are left in the mythic language that the persecutors used to justify their acts, analyses which bypass that language or replace it with codes of political and ideological intrigue may make sense of the witchcraft craze, but only at the price of leaving the victims of the witchcraft craze where their persecutors left them—unvindicated—and the way of persecution still open for future use.

When we ask of a woman accused of witchcraft, "Was she who her accuser said she was?" and, by appeal to analyses such as those reviewed in this chapter, gather evidence, put her on trial again, and pronounce her innocent, we play a strange game with truth. We say that the accuser, speaking as he did about demons, diabolic contagion, and the witch's pact, was unaware of what he was doing: he was frustrated by changing marriage patterns, confused by economic instability, angered by plague and famine, and embattled over claims to political turf. Angered, frustrated, confused, and embattled, he picked out an innocent woman and killed her. What we do not say in all of this language is that this man was a persecutor. The reason we do not say this, Girard claims, is that the language of witch *persecution* had only one home: sacred myth (1986, 38). If we alter the language of witch persecution, severing it from its roots in myth in order to render its meaning in other terms, we will never unpack the meaning of the word *scapegoat.*

That epithet *scapegoat,* which so often characterizes our gut-level reaction to the witch craze, needs more careful analysis if it is to become a well-grounded claim. Ungrounded, the category of scapegoat is highly vulnerable to expropriation to the interests of ideological analysis, where its meaning, impoverished and malnourished, will always be under threat of complete extinction. To properly ground the notion of the scapegoat, Girard submits that we must locate its place within a persecutory structure and locate the roots of that structure in those practices that constitute a sacred or sacrificial economy. Only then may it be possible to overthrow the persecutor rather than to overthrow only the persecutor's texts, as has current witch craze scholarship (1986, 10).

What then is the structure of persecution? Girard cites four stereotypes of persecution. In referring to these characteristics as stereotypes, he leads us away from the pejorative connotations which attend the use of that word. He reminds us that a "stereotype" is a metal cast used in printing that enables the unvarying and fixed reproduction of an original image or pattern. Hence, stereotypes of persecution are persecutory patterns advanced by the type in fixed and unvaried reproduction across cultures and centuries.

The first stereotype of persecution locates it only in times of crisis. Plague, famine, floods, institutional collapse, all qualify as crises. Such crises announce the obliteration or collapse of hierarchical or functional differences between persons (1986, 12–13). Violence attends this eclipse of culture: persons at both ends of the social scale—kings and women or children—are the most vulnerable to violence. Sexual and religious crimes abound: rape, incest, bestiality. Ultimately, a small number of persons are determined to be extremely harmful to the whole of the society (1986, 15).

A second stereotypic accusation is needed to bridge the gap between this very small group, sometimes a sole individual, and the social body. What is at stake is order: of the community and even of the cosmos (1986, 15). How could one small group or individual carry the powers that could destroy a much larger whole? Images of contagion provide the answer and fuel the stereotype: the individual's capacity to cause illness or to use poison augments his or her powers to destroy and closes the gap between the individual and the society as a whole (1986, 16).

The crowd's choice of victims points to the third stereotype: the victim is generally characterized by a lack of difference from his or her accusers (1986, 22). This stereotype seems at first counterintuitive. Aren't persons persecuted because they are different—a Jew is not Christian, a woman is not a man, a spinster is not married? Certainly, the many feminists who have understood the problem of woman's oppression in terms of her role as the "Other," using a typology of "dualism," have identified the "woman-problem" as an issue of difference. But Girard's claim is not as surprising as it might seem. He offers the example of the physically disabled person. Disability is disturbing to others, not because of its difference, but because of its impression of disturbing dynamism (1986, 21). Life goes on, in difference, giving the lie to the exclusive truth of our own lives. What bothers heterosexuals, ethnic and religious majorities, and the able-bodied about those who are different—gays and lesbians, the ethnically and religiously diverse, the disabled—is the potential they see in those persons "for the system to differ from its own difference, in other words not to be different at all, to cease to exist as a system" (1986, 21). The relativity, fragility, and mortality of one's own small world is put into relief by the one who is different. Different persons are reproached not for their difference, but for being not as different as expected, and in the end for differing not at all (1986, 22).

In failing to respect "real" differences, those who are "not-different-enough" incur others' anger and bring down upon themselves the fourth stereotype of persecution: the violence that would defend difference by inscribing that difference on the bodies of the indifferent and, in so doing, would create the expiatory sacrifice which could return the whole community to order. Torture and death complete the persecutory structure (1986, 45–57).

Two stories highlight Girard's analysis of these stereotypes of persecution. In one story, a Jewish woman is depicted contemplating two pigs to whom she has just given birth. In another story, a woman has intercourse with a dog and gives birth to six puppies. Her tribe banishes her, and she is forced to hunt for her own food. The first story is from a 1575 German text describing the Jewish proclivity for witchcraft. The second is from a myth of the Dogrib people. Each story bears the marks of the stereotypes of persecution. The background for each, explicit in the former and implicit in the latter, is crisis. The women flaunt cultural distinctions, engaging in bestiality. Because they are women, they bear essential victim marks. Moreover, they fail to differ as they should from others, inviting the scapegoat mechanism. That lack of difference is implicit in the former story of the Jewish woman[6] and explicit in the Dogrib myth, which states that the puppy children are really human, having the ability to remove their fur coats at will and reenter the world of human society (1986, 48–49).

With these examples, we begin to see that lines separating history and myth are arbitrary in stories of persecution (1986, 47). The structure of persecution is indifferent to such categorical distinctions, for the Dogrib and the author of the 1575 German text are telling the same story. Yet we want to read them differently. We want to deny the mythic meaning of the story from Germany and translate its meaning into an ideological code of competing political, economic, and social interests, following rules of witchcraft interpretation represented by scholars such as Midelfort, Klaits, and Larner.

Why do we refuse myth? For those who are not scholars of religious myth, that question is easily answered. We live in a society that has a highly impoverished view of myth. That myths found and shape a people's common life—their memories, their hopes and dreams, their fears, their ultimate concerns—is virtually forgotten. But how do those of us who are scholars of the mythic narratives that are fixtures in our cultural archives answer this question? An approach to myth located in the disciplines of religious studies or literature allows for a far greater appreciation of myth. We know that the standard of truth in myth is not empirical correctness, but its life-founding and life-shaping potential: a myth is true if persons live by it and find their hopes, fears, memories, and values carried forth by it. Thus, for scholars of mythic narratives, the question of myth-refusal in analyses of witch persecution is not so easily answered. In the earnestness of our quest to recover the memories of the victims of the witch craze, have we shied from an embrace of myth that would bring us too close to the accuser? Is that why we have forgotten the lessons in myth offered by our disciplines? Perhaps another of Girard's stories will jolt our memory:

> Harvests are bad, the cows give birth to dead calves; no one is on good terms with anyone else. Clearly, it is the cripple who is the cause. He arrived one morning, no one knows from where, and made himself at home. He married the most obvious heiress in the village and had two children by her. All sorts of things seemed to take place in their house. The stranger was suspected of having killed his wife's former husband, who disappeared under mysterious circumstances and was rather too quickly replaced by the newcomer. One day the village had had enough. They took their pitchforks and forced the disturbing character to clear out. (1986, 29)

Girard places his tale in the Christian Middle Ages: it is a tale of persecution if ever there was one. But others may recognize another, much older story: the myth of Oedipus. Again the lines between myth and history blur.

What can be made of Girard's play with the boundaries of myth and history? His comments suggest that scholars of the witch hunts need to grant to the stories of the witches the respect ethnologists grant the Dogrib (1986; 53, 96). We need to listen to those stories the way we listen to the myth of Oedipus. To listen to them in that way is to understand persecution in a way that only myth preserves because only myth carries forth the stereotypic structures of persecution intact. Only myth reveals persecution as the dark lining of religious beliefs and practices. Only myth holds together in one frame, for better or worse, both violence and creation in death-work: a sacred, sacrificial economy.

Thus, if we are really to listen to a witch's story, Girard would have us return to the rite of sacrifice of the scapegoat (1986, 40). But when we think of the ceremony, the priest, and the expiation of sins, we must go further with our reflection on the scapegoat than does current scholarship. If we are to enter the mythic world of the witch craze, we have to enter a persecutory, sacrificial structure in which the victim—the chosen scapegoat—was not only responsible for public disasters but also *was capable of restoring, symbolizing, and even incarnating order* (1986, 42). We have to honor the power of the victim to do what scapegoats do (1986, 44).

But that we will not allow. In attempting to enter the sixteenth-century mind, we find it extraordinarily difficult to suspend our disbelief in order to see that, for her accuser, the witch was responsible for public disasters: plagues, famine, and civil unrest. We balk at giving to the witch the power her persecutor gave her. We cannot see that so great a power did the witch have that, for her accuser, extraordinary measures were required to capture and channel it for the good. We do not understand that, in accord with that belief, her accuser had to torture a woman accused of witchcraft in order to gain her confession, which was the required proof of her power, and that he had to execute her in order to demonstrate that her powers had been successfully foiled. Not understanding, we fail to listen to the accuser's tale of violence and overlook the clues he gives us about the place to which he has taken his victim. Not heeding his words, we leave the scapegoat where her accuser has left her—unvindicated—and do not seize the opportunity to wrest from his hands the key that would unlock the persecutory structure of a sacrificial economy so that the scapegoat could be freed.

Our resistance to according to the scapegoat the power her persecutor granted her, nowhere more evident than in recent scholarship's silence and puzzlement before the protracted violence which announced the witch's power and marked the struggle against it, highlights our incapacity to read the mythic elements of the witch craze. Challenged by the need to integrate accounts of violence into its theoretical perspective on the witch craze and denied the old "superstition" argument by its advocacy of nonethnocentric analyses, current scholarship uses two strategies in order to make sense of torture and execution. Neither strategy acknowledges adequately the sacred: a persecutory structure of a sacrificial economy to which myth attests.

Scholarship informed by the first strategy documents the elements of persecution—descriptions of torture and transcripts of confessions—recorded by the witches' accusers. Observations count as explanations. Thus, Larner, Midelfort, and Klaits dutifully record the importance of the witch's confession for the accusers and those accusers' stated opinion that torture alone would free the witch from her enslavement to the devil. Repeatedly, each scholar also notes the persecutors' oft-stated claim that the witches told the truth under torture. Midelfort highlights it (1972, 142). Trevor-Roper documents it, observing that the accusers' confidence in the mechanism of torture to extract the truth from the accused outlived their confidence in the existence of witches (1967, 122). Klaits also comments about the "genuine concern" the accusers had for the accused. He underlines the sense of integrity he reads in their statements: they truly believed in the guilt of the women they prosecuted and were absolutely confident that those women, confessing under torture, told the truth (1985, 150).

The inadequacy of this strategy of analysis to the violence of the witch hunts becomes apparent when the surprise of the historians before their recorded observations is noted. Midelfort is not the only one to be confounded by the persecutors' repeated claims that the witches told the truth under torture. Others seem equally bemused (Midelfort, 1972, 142; Trevor-Roper, 1967, 121; Klaits, 1985, 149). The absolute confidence of the accusers in the truthfulness of the accused appears irrational to the contemporary mind. That witchcraft suspects would lie under torture to save their lives is as comprehensible today as it was apparently incomprehensible to the accusers of the witches. Seeking to better explain the beliefs they have observed in the accounts of the witch hunters, scholars turn to a second strategy.

Observing no rationale in the external discourse of the witch persecutors, they appeal to masters of unstated discourse: the psychologists. Aware they are testing the limits of their methodologies, each is circumspect in his or her conclusions. Noting that her views are "just speculation," Larner muses about the "psychological cleansing effect on a community" of the witnessed execution of witches (1981, 115). She also describes the witch's confession as "the triumph of the state in the battle for minds." Confession demonstrated the accused's sentience: correct ideological commitment (to the state) was accompanying ideological reeducation (in the interrogation and trial) (1981, 184). In a similar vein, Klaits compares the interrogators of witches with the interrogators in the Stalinist purge trials. He suggests that, immersed in an ideology and committed to a higher good, each looked to confession as a necessary step in "ideological reeducation" (1985, 84). Further, comparing the judicial application of torture in the sixteenth and seventeenth centuries with the use of the lie detector in today's judicial system, Klaits suggests that, in each case, absolute confidence in the ability of the machinery to extract the truth leads to the willing confession of the accused. In the earlier time, accusers believed the women they tortured were telling the truth because the women themselves came to believe they had been rightfully accused. Providing a contemporary parallel is the case of Peter Reilly, a Connecticut teenager who was accused of murdering his mother in 1973. Repeatedly interrogated by lie detector, Reilly came to believe in his guilt. He confessed to the murder, even though subsequent investigations established his innocence. Such "brainwashing" or "thought reform," according to Klaits, whether located in the witch hunts or in contemporary judicial practices, appeals to the same "psychological dynamics" (1985, 155–58).

Although these explanations need not be wholly disavowed, the theorists considered here would do well to entertain a greater variety of interpretations. An appeal to psychology may once again entail a distorted "translation" of the witch-hunting dynamic. Is Peter Reilly's lie detector ordeal the closest parallel to the witch's ordeal by torture on the rack? The persecutory structure of myth suggests not. The witch's closest kin is not Reilly, but the sacrificial victim of an earlier time. The key dynamic of her ordeal is not "brainwashing," but "ritual." And the end to be achieved is not psychological catharsis or successful thought reform, but the cleansing of a polluted community, the expiation of sin and the restoration of cosmic order.[7]

The mythic model accounts best for an accuser's confidence in the truthfulness of his victim's confession. How could he believe that the witch had real power, that all initiative came from her, that she alone was as responsible for the cure as she was for the sickness in the society (1986, 43)? Proper neither to political ideology nor to psychological thought control, the logic of his discourse expressed the sacred and appealed to a pattern of causality proper to it: expiatory powers had to cross the threshold of death, and only that which was transcendent and supernatural could cross that line. The witch had to be made to appeal to powers beyond herself if, at her death, those powers were to live on after her. The woman accused of witchcraft had to be tortured and killed because only those actions followed the trail of death back into the body, there to summon the very powers of creation against the forces of darkness in order that polluting evil could be vanquished and godly order reign again (1986; 44, 94).

Scholars' resistance to a mythic reading of the witch craze is well intentioned. We think that if we acknowledge any power in the women charged as witches—which in myth we must acknowledge—they will cease to be victims unjustly accused. We think that, if we listen to their stories as their persecutors did, even for a moment, we will bloody our own hands. But if we resist the mythic reading of the witch craze, the persecutors cease to be persecutors. If the persecutors were not persecutors, then the women whose innocence we wish to proclaim were not victims. We must read the tales of persecution through the eyes of the persecutors because in their eyes alone lies the full persecutory structure of the sacrificial economy undisguised. And we must seize the key to the witch hunts offered by the protracted violence that circles myth if we are to unlock its secrets.

We will not save the victims of the witch craze by snatching them from the grip of the violent economy to put them on trial again and to declare them the innocent victims of economic unrest, political change, or psychological manipulation. Rather, we will save them by putting their persecutors on trial. Such a trial will lead us back to a mythology of sacrifice in order that we might plumb the complex nuances of human violence. To truly challenge the persecutors we must confront them there, on their own turf. Only then will we be able to name the myth that has fueled their violence and to free the victims from the place of their incarceration. Only then will we know enough about the persecutor—his motives and his weapons—to condemn him. We must turn to sacrificial myth if we are to grasp the persecutory structure at its roots and break its power.

If we are to protect victims of scapegoating, we must examine why Christianity has functioned as a religion of sacrifice. We must find out why humans live by myths of persecution, and we must seek alternate myths to live by that enable us to address crisis, anomie, and angst in human life without recourse to expiatory sacrifice. Vigilance is required to protect victims: past and potential. But we practice vigilance on behalf of victims only by turning toward the persecutors and the myths by which they live, seeking them out wherever they may be. Ironically, faithfulness to history is possible only if we embrace myth.

Can we do this? The forces of amnesia which make impossible our reading the mythic elements in our own past history are very strong. Indeed, Girard's further examples of our confusion before the arbitrary distinctions between myth and history must give us pause. Girard notes that, in the Middle Ages, physicians first resisted the notion that the plague could be spread through physical contact with the disease. They opposed quarantines of plague victims. Did they harbor naive superstitions about the workings of disease? Were they stubbornly clinging to current theories of the plague because they had some ideological investment in the status quo? No; Girard applauds their enlightenment. The theory of contagion smacked too much of a persecutor's prejudice not to be suspect. The physicians saw in the contagion theory of the plague the structure of persecution. For the idea of contagion to be accepted by physicians, it had to be freed from the persecutory structure. And that, Girard notes, did not happen until the nineteenth century (1986, 19).

With this example, the lines between myth and history blur once again. The physicians, we would say, misjudged the parameters of myth. They made a mistake. But are mistakes always made in the same direction? Consider the witch trials. In a movement directly opposed to that taken by the physicians who viewed the new theory of the plague as part of a persecutory myth, and sought real causes elsewhere, we deny to the witch craze its mythic elements, confident in the truths offered by the social sciences. Both we and the medieval physicians have denied myth in order to make room for truth. The medieval physicians got it backwards. Have we?

Girard's verdict on the present poses a profound challenge to the social sciences and to the adequacy of their discourse about witch hunting to the phenomenon. That today's masters could have acted on their current scholarly insights to offer testimony about the witch trials that would have put an end to them (1986, 99) is doubtful. Indeed, it appears that, only if scholars look anew at the mythic investments humans have in the scapegoat, will they be able to come to terms with the terrors of persecution and advance emancipatory efforts on behalf of victims. A sacrificial theory indebted to Kristeva and Girard offers scholars the most insightful analysis of these mythic investments, the mark of sexual difference on them, and the economy which gives them life.

IV. Witch Hunts and the Work of a Sacrificial Economy

A sacrificial analysis of the witch hunts is mandated because Girard brings to light two weaknesses in historical inquiry: in bypassing the myth-shaped confessional discourse of the witch trials, current research on the witch hunts accounts neither for the role of religion in the hunts nor for their violence. As these weaknesses are considered, this analysis invokes three goals of sacrificial theory: to explain the origins of conflict, account for its elaboration, and demonstrate why humans kill, terminating conflict. Two of these goals are addressed while discussing the emergence and spread of the witch hunting phenomenon, clarifying its persecutory structure, and subjecting to serious analysis the language of diabolism and pollution in the persecutors' narratives. As the violence of the witch craze is considered, attention is given to the third goal in order to explain why the hunts became murderous and why their lethal violence was visited preferentially on women.

Historians have argued rightly that the witch as scapegoat emerged in a time of crisis: society was eclipsed by destabilizing violence associated with economic, political, and social unrest. However, the lens of sacrificial theory generates an interpretive nexus that does not address only economic, political, and social factors in witch hunting. Instead, sacrificial theory understands that, if unrest precipitated the violence that culminated in the witch craze, the structure of violence which emerged mandates distinct analysis. Specifically, the conflict which beset society was characterized by *mimetic violence,* to which Girard's four stereotypes attest.

Mimetic violence, signaling the failure of personal and social boundaries, is indicated by the proliferation of contagion in communities beset by unrest. Markers of pollution—illness, poison, body fluids—enabled persons to discover among themselves some women who posed a destabilizing threat. Mimeticism associated with contagion served also to infinitely augment and amplify the power of individual suspects. A single individual, once identified as the source of pollution, would constitute an absolute threat to all others. Mimetic violence is indicated too because someone who was accused of witchcraft was dangerous precisely because the menace she was presumed to embody did not clearly differentiate her from others: indeed, her body was all the more frighteningly diabolic to the degree that her accusers remained unable to ascribe to it a monstrous difference from other bodies. The vigilance with which the persecutors sought marks of the devil on the bodies of the accused—even when they were invisible—attests to their preoccupation with the issue of difference.

Mimetic violence accounts for the emergence of a sacrificial structure in a society. Specific facets of mimeticism, particularly elements of contagion, account for its expansion. But sacrificial theory asserts also that mimetic violence, once summoned by humans, regularly intensifies. Escalating violence is associated with the mechanism of *surrogate victimization:* a mimetic free-for-all accelerates and comes to rest on a single victim. When communities invoke scapegoating, they demonstrate a key sacrificial belief: the victim they select not only is responsible for disasters, but also is capable of restoring order.

Narratives of the witch hunts confirm that victims of the craze functioned as surrogate victims. Violence, widespread in the conflicted setting of the larger society, passed through and among those gathered to observe a trial, to hear a confession, and to witness an execution. Centering eventually on a victim, violence rested with her until, at the moment of her death, it could return to the community, miraculously transformed into peace. The community's violence polarized on the victim: in the course of her confession, which was extracted under torture, she was sacralized. Indeed, as the victim ceased to utter evil and began to speak words of God, she bore immediate witness to the reemergence of a sacred order in the community. Made a direct conduit of saving powers in her act of confessing, the victim was transformed from a monster into an instrument of God. As a consequence, those who killed witches did not perceive themselves as agents of death; rather, they believed that they were passive recipients of God's grace. At the witch trials, God visited them and rooted out devils; God worked among them to reestablish social order.

Most significant for a sacrificial theory of mimetic violence is the rationale that ultimately founds its murderous components. Why did surrogate victimization conclude with the death of the one who was believed to incarnate order? Why did cultural violence become a rite of *sacrifice?* Could not those who engaged in a ritual of scapegoating that reestablished social order have experienced the same unrest, heard the same confessions and anguished appeals, but left their victims to live another day? As indicated above, current scholarship in the social sciences is at a loss to explain why witch hunting culminated so often in murder. Most scholars dutifully record the deaths, but maintain silence concerning a rationale. If they do write of lethal violence, they tend to remove the most extreme moments of the hunts from a context of social analysis. Tiptoeing around deadly torture, they speak of processes visible only to a trained psychologist: internal catharsis, brain-washing, thought-reform.[8]

By contrast, sacrificial theory attests that those who hunted witches treated violence as a common, visible, and public value. Violence was defined by its *socially productive elements.* For example, Girard asserts that, over the long expanse of their history, humans have learned that the death of a surrogate victim does end cycles of violence: they have tested the scapegoat mechanism and have found that it works. To be sure, when Girard speaks of humans' propensity for *lethal* violence, he only is moderately successful in maintaining a social analysis. He has difficulties asserting that the murderous part of deadly violence has social meaning. Instead, when Girard discusses lethal aspects of mimetic conflict, he speaks of an unabated mimetic frenzy among humans. He attributes this frenzy to an inopportune release of high levels of adrenaline or to an accelerated mimeticism associated with humans' enhanced intellectual powers. When he focuses on the very core of the sacrificial mechanism, Girard does not keep its social context in clear view.

By contrast, a sacrificial theory of the hunts influenced by Kristeva promises to round out a sacrificial theory of the witch hunts, for she brings a sustained focus to the sacrificial moment in cultural violence. Kristeva is successful in this endeavor because she traces the productivity of violence to work done by humans at the borders of the Symbolic order and language. Never disavowing the socially productive elements of violence, Kristeva insists that violence is structured by patterns that emerge at the very threshold of social existence. Specifically, an assessment of the witch craze which draws on Kristeva asserts that, when persons who were beset by social conflict and entrapped by mimetic violence turned on women, accused them of witchcraft, and made them scapegoats, their actions exhibited the still persistent influence of iterative patterns established in formative subjectivity. Associated with subjects' first lessons in signification, these patterns influenced the manner in which the persons who hunted witches interpreted the nature of the threat they confronted. These patterns also shaped their responses to that threat. This account explains why the violence of the witch hunts became deadly and why it was directed preferentially against women.

In the comments that follow, one of the lessons in signification whose impact is visible in the witch hunts is identified with *the truth of torture.* Why did persons perceive that they were called to invade the body of a woman accused of witchcraft if they were to respond decisively to the threat posed by the mimetic contagion that she harbored? Their incursions into soma attested to the fact that those caught in a mimetic morass were, under the most trying of circumstances, led to recall early lessons in world-creation. Under threat, a nascent subject is able to take a position in the world and secure its boundaries against radical loss when it viscerally extracts itself from a material matrix which has exhibited a threatening mimesis. Applying instruments to flesh that opened and broke it, those who hunted witches summoned once again the divine and sacred powers of order-producing sacrifice which they first had experienced in the throes of formative subjectivity: they tortured substance to make it signify. In doing so, they expressed an archaic wisdom. If initially they had garnered and secured a place in the world by means of a somatic contestation, so also should they do so again in order to recreate their position in the world.

A second lesson in the nascent subject's education in signification on which the witch hunters drew is identified with *the truth of sacrifice.* Under circumstances of social conflict and threat that recalled their initial ascent to the Symbolic order, when they summoned order-creating strategies of somatic incursion, they turned preferentially toward women's bodies. For the material dialectic—the scription without sign—that shapes mimetic conflict for nascent subjects had previously established the maternal matrix (Mother) as the prime threatening abject. When social unrest returned the persecutors of the witches to the throes of mimesis, presenting them once again with a threatening abject (pollution, contagion), they found that the most threatening of abject marks were those that recalled their initial confrontations with a maternal abject, before whom they had risked an absolute loss of being. As a consequence, the witch hunters primarily victimized women. Because female bodies were perceived to bear abject maternal marks, they most immediately and powerfully conveyed to others threats to the Symbolic order, including all ultimate menaces. In attacking women and vanquishing the evil which came to expression in their bodies, the witch hunters made all the more sure their victory over lesser threats as well.

That these two moments in a sacrificial theory are associated with truth is significant. Whereas contemporary scholars look askance at weapons of torture and disavow testimony to misdeeds garnered by such means, believing that testimony offered under torture is wholly unreliable, Girard encourages us to believe that, if we are to listen to the persecutors and actually hear their words, we must take seriously their belief that those they tortured spoke the truth. We must do so if we hope to break the persecutors' hold on their victims. As this analysis of the witch hunts concludes, the truths of which it speaks are shown to belong to a sacrificial economy.

A. The Truth of Torture

What can be said of the persecutory pattern of confession and torture common to the witch trials if an accuser's words are taken seriously? Why did he believe that the abused and broken body of a woman accused of witchcraft spoke its own truth? Was it significant for his understanding that a woman spoke that truth? And what was the truth that her body spoke?

Page duBois's extraordinary book, *Torture and Truth* (1991), suggests a fruitful strategy for answering these questions. In that work, duBois examines ancient Greek literary, philosophical, and legal texts in order to determine the role torture played in trials. Learning that the torture of slaves in the judicial processes of ancient Greece was routine, duBois discovers also that the evidence obtained from the slave was considered more reliable by the courts than was the unconstrained testimony of free men. DuBois suggests that the legacy of the Greek world has long persisted in the West, where truth and torture have been joined by a common logic. Indeed, truth consistently has been perceived as requiring violence for its production, for its purported distance from us and difficulty of access eludes our immediate vision and grasp.

DuBois likewise observes that, for the ancient Greeks, when the body was engaged in the productive work of violence, the truth that emerged from torture arose from a secret space whose contours regularly bore marks of the female sex. Although not every slave tortured was a female, duBois notes that the truth born by the slave's body consistently evoked images associated with Greek perceptions of woman. Tracing key elements of duBois's argument and applying them to an examination of the role of torture in the witch hunts, the powerful association between torture and truth—an association the persecutors of the witches exploited—can be confirmed and the mark of sexual difference in that relationship can be established. Insights extrapolated from duBois make a notable contribution to our efforts to understand why the persecutor of a woman accused of witchcraft believed that the body he tortured spoke a truth that was its own and why it was significant for his efforts that a woman's body offered up that truth.

As duBois offers documentation drawn from the judicial archives of ancient Greece, she demonstrates that, for the Greeks, bodies of the earth, women, and slaves were linked in a common construct of buried truth. One attained knowledge of this truth only through acts that violated another. In the courts, for example, the master who possessed the capacity for reason could choose to tell the truth or to lie. But the slave, incapable of reason, was incapable also of choice. When the torturer reached into the body of the slave, he could extract only truth: the slave could "only produce truth under coercion, could produce only truth under coercion" (1991, 68). Significantly, the courts were at pains to distinguish the evidence offered by the slave from all others: the court records duBois has examined speak again and again of the special veracity of slave testimony. They attribute the testimony of the tortured slave to "a higher order of truth" (1991, 49). Where the master may use reason to dissemble, legal annals recount that the tortured body of the slave does not and cannot lie.[9]

DuBois does acknowledge that torture in Athens delineated the boundaries of the polis. Torture functioned to produce Greek democracy in the course of generating distinctions between slave and free, between the untouchable bodies of citizens and the torturable bodies of all others. However, because the archives of the ancient Greeks—legal, philosophical, mythic—so often speak of torture as a search for a truth that lies elsewhere, duBois makes a special effort to understand that distinct narrative claim (1991, 75). Although duBois does not use the phrase *sacrificial economy* to describe the locus of her investigation, on all other counts her analysis points to such an economy.

Seeking to understand the logic which governed the aspect of the judicial process in ancient Greece that asserted the absolute reliability of the testimony of the slave—the truth-evoking nature of torture—duBois observes that the Greeks speak of truth as *alêtheia*. The mark of sexual difference on this word is clear. The interior space of earth, like that of woman, represents darkness and oblivion, that which is unseen and unseeable. Indeed, to obtain the truth, one must journey to it. One must move between light and dark, interior and exterior space, enclosed and open terrain in order to gain access to the truth that is unforgetting (1991, 82). Significantly, earth, women, and slaves are bodies privy to this space, but they do not know it.[10]

For duBois, the spatial metaphors that attend discussions of truth are essential rather than incidental to her efforts to understand the ancient Greek concept of truth. When the Greeks characterize truth in terms of a journey or descent into the earth, their invocations of truth do not merely echo political interests and powers. Preserved in the narratives of ancient Greece are reflections that, linking earth, women, and slaves with truth, expose a distinct logic and set of powers. When we attend to them, we embark on a journey that takes us beyond the plain of political and economic interests. Where do we go?

DuBois indicates that myth offers one answer.[11] Figures such as Odysseus, Teiresias, and Amphiaraos penetrate an invisible world by means of a journey marked by descent, symbolic death, and rebirth with uncommon knowledge (1991, 77). Moreover, the land of the dead which is their destination invokes abject images of return to a maternal matrix: images of woman as receptacle or container, origin of life and receiver of the dead, are common to these mythic narratives. For instance, when Odysseus dwells in the lower world, he is subject to *lêthe,* a forgetfulness that the drinking of blood only temporarily remedies. Death, an interior space of the earth, evokes diverse images focused on the interiority of the female body: we meet the mother of Odysseus, against whom he must use his sword to defend the pit of blood; Kalypso, the veiler and concealer; Circe, who would bury him in the unconsciousness of an animal body; the Cyclops, who would devour him; and the Phaiakains, who desire to retain him (1991, 82). If Odysseus is to endure, he must have *nous* and *alêtheia:* intelligence and unforgetting. But that which permits Odysseus access to the truth of unforgetting is the journey itself: the crossing from life to death, from open to enclosed space. Indeed, the passage itself and the dialectic it enjoins demonstrates why, if the threats to Odysseus are so often attributed to women, the truth he seeks is a goddess. Although *Alêtheia* does not know the truth, she *is* truth. Not an object of representation, but representation itself, the *Alêtheia* that the hero encounters, duBois suggests, bears "the fruits of the passage between light and dark without having access to those fruits herself" (1991, 82).

The mythic narratives duBois cites explain why, when the logic of myth was joined with the logic of torture in the Greek courts, the terrain of a body-politic retained remnant markers of a journey to truth undertaken in a different register. Truth met on a mythic journey through the earth was an allegory of force and pain—of truth given up only when mined or forcibly drawn from the depths—which also shaped judicial truth in ancient Greece. The logic of myth and the logic of torture were joined in the sacrificial body of truth, and this body belonged to a woman. Indeed, *Alêtheia*—goddess of unconcealment—was akin to a slave under torture (1991, 83). One who wished to know was required to pass through her space in order to acquire truth. Moreover, just as the body of the slave bore a message the slave was unable to see or read, so also did the body of *Alêtheia* bear a sign that belonged only to those who possessed her. Taken by the hero of myth and law, the abject figure of truth—earth, woman, slave—was made to deliver up from the space of forgetting a sought-after prize. From *Alêtheia* were forced secrets which she herself did not possess.

DuBois's exploration of the history of torture in ancient Greece facilitates a nuanced understanding of the work of torture in the witch trials. Illuminated by her study is that which the witch hunter sought to name with his violent gestures and the truth he believed he discovered in the body of his victim. Although the signifying practices that characterized the quest for truth in the courts of Christian Europe are not identical with those of ancient Greece, the myths and judicial codes of each time point toward a common material labor. Parties to this effort believed that they could grasp truth only if they wrested it from a secret space. Only when they viscerally extracted order from a threatening morass could they reliably draw on its powers in their efforts to create or recreate the world. Moreover, in the mythic and judicial contexts of ancient Greece as well as Christian Europe, attestations to or actual incidents of torture—slowly and deliberately advanced—conveyed a shared confidence by persons in each time that substance had to be tortured to make it signify. As journeys and exercises in force, the truth of myth and the truth of torture in each time conjoined presence and absence in the very movement of the signification, by means of a gesture whose limit was earth and death. Meaning and order that created or recreated an orderly world were not advanced in this economy by a logic of representation, but by a logic of spatial interdiction. Finally, that myths and judicial accounts of torture in each time record that one who sets out in search of that truth regularly encounters a threatening or saving woman on his way, helps to explain why the slave torturers of ancient Greece and the witch hunters of Christian Europe who sought the truth so often summoned a woman to accompany them on their journey.

Even so, questions remain at this juncture. To which trope of truth is travel intrinsic? To which is spatial metaphor endemic? In what practices of truth is a woman—both threatening and saving—regularly invoked? If truth is a woman who gives up her secrets only after a long course of trial and yet does not know the truth herself, what truth is it that woman holds to which myth attests and after which judicial truth quests? As answers to these queries emerge, the truth of torture is shown to belong to a sacrificial economy.

B. The Truth of Sacrifice

As the journey to truth espied in Greek myth, Greek traditions of torture, diabolism, and the witch trials of Christian Europe are linked with processes of negativity that shape human agency as a practice of divided being, sacrifice comes into focus. Efforts to forge this link are facilitated when we recall that a thetic break announces humans' emergence in the world as creatures of language. To be human is to be in a place where one is not, bound by a pretense of unity (the signified/sign) and a matrix of origin that is irrecoverable: the true/real, the signifier, an other, an elsewhere, a maternal body. Ambiguities attend the phallic prohibition whose task is to initiate humans into the world of language in a manner that enables them to come to terms with living at a loss. Historically, despite all efforts by the phallic gatekeeper of the thetic order to dissuade humans from their persistent fascination with their origins, humans remain captivated—particularly under conditions of threat—by the forces of negativity that initiate their journey to the Symbolic order and maintain them there. When imperiled, humans regularly embark on a voyage to the borders of the Symbolic, there to seek the creative force of their origins—the jouissance and rejection of death-work—in order that they might grasp it in sign and claim its power as their own. But condemned by the economy of negativity and the strictures of the thetic break to be unsuccessful in their efforts to grasp in sign the divided truth that they are, humans sometimes make the most desperate of gestures: they attempt to localize and constrain the dynamic of negativity—its destructive and creative power—by grasping hold of particular bodies. They undertake to wrest from them, through acts of torture or other visceral forms of body-work, the jouissance and rejection that is the truth of negativity. By means of violence they would possess the truth that they are.

Can such a pattern of sacrifice be detected in Christian Europe? Once again, duBois is a helpful guide: her comments on ancient Greece suggest analogies between it and Christian Europe that sustain a sacrificial thesis. DuBois indicates that myths paradigmatically render the sacrificial efforts of humans. Of course, myth has no direct access to work undertaken at the boundaries of the Symbolic. Instead, myth records an overdetermination in Symbolic discourse in which may be discerned a sacrificial agenda. Thus, when we reflect on one mythic narrative—the tale of Odysseus—we observe that challenges Odysseus faces are reminiscent of an archaic battle. He engages the forces of negativity in all their abject menace and promise at the thetic bar. Journeying there, he confronts pits of blood, monsters, and multiple devouring threats. Only after vanquishing a plethora of threats—which regularly bear the mark of the maternal—does Odysseus emerge from abject waters and return to the bounded and ordered existence of the Symbolic. In turn, the place which Odysseus will call home is tended, not by the maternal presence of his origins, but by a phallic mother, Athena.[12]

Just as myth attests to the dynamic of negativity that governs the human journey to language and societal order so also is this dynamic visible in the Greek courts. Myth suggests to the ancient Greeks that truth is possessable only at the conclusion of a journey marked by death and rebirth. So also did the Greeks perceive that a like journey toward death was necessary if they were to secure their polis against threat. Just as the heros of Greek myth are obliged to overcome a visceral, bodily threat in the course of their travels, so also did the guardians of justice in their truth-seeking ventures anticipate that truth could emerge only when wrested from a material signifying process. Therefore, in the Greek courts torture was a counterpart to the bodily trials of Greek heroes. Moreover, that mythic characters so often encounter maternally marked menaces, which they are forced to vanquish if they are to survive and conquer, helps to explain also the preferential violation of the female body on behalf of truth in the courts of ancient Greece.

Analogously, those who hunted witches in Christian Europe summoned a truth they believed that they encountered when viscerally engaging the human body. They too read in the bodies of the accused a truth born of the earliest struggle of humans to exist in the world. Aiming to possess the secrets of the thetic order, the witch hunters sought to submit the truth of negativity to the full force of the sign: women who were believed to be the bearers of the truth of the maternal matrix—the Mother—were sacrificed to that objective.

Precisely because the stakes were high—a fragile social order was at risk of destruction—the most ancient and powerful of rites was invoked to reinstate order. During the course of the trial and especially in their torture, the accused were made to journey to the threshold of death—the absolute boundaries of language and existence—because the chaos that menaced the borders of Christian Europe constituted the most radical of threats. And, because the maternal body marked that boundary, when those accused of witchcraft were tortured and killed, the persecutors who exacted that sacrifice from female bodies were able to follow the trail of death across the bar of language to that place where transcendent powers of creation and destruction could be summoned. As torture and confession—simultaneously death and rebirth—delineated a space of matricide, women's bodies became expressive instruments which, at the very bar of silence, made others' speech possible. Women died when the Mother was made a sign, but the law and patriarchy survived.

The sacrifice of women secured the thetic order in three ways. Each moment shows that the truth of difference expressed in the signifying practices of women accused of witchcraft is the truth of negativity. First, a woman accused of witchcraft could express that truth because in her torture and death, soma was destroyed and the sign created. Thus, the threat that negativity poses—the potential for destruction of a bounded subject in subsumption by the raw indifference of an encompassing, devouring maternal matrix—was halted when sacrifice contained that menace under the sign of a violated body. Likewise was the death-work that pervades negativity—a power that causes humans to be in difference from each other and a power that, if insufficiently delineated, may threaten to consume them—submitted by the sacrifice of the women accused of witchcraft to a protective sign: dissatisfied with the capacity of pollution-work alone to contain the political, economic, and social threats they experienced, the hunters of witches exchanged nonlethal rituals of cleansing (e.g., banishment of the witches, a communal fast among the faithful remnant) for stronger medicine. Thus, in making polluting soma—especially flesh evocative of the maternal matrix—into a symbol, the sacrifice of the witches localized and concretized a disturbing uncanny. In that act, the threatening aspects of death-work which the witch hunters observed in society were sublated and their constructive potential—evidenced in the purified sign—exploited. Finally, the sacrifice of women who had been accused of the crime of witchcraft enacted the truth of difference as the truth of negativity because the entire movement of the symbolic economy—jouissance and rejection—was drawn up in the suffering and death of the accused: in the body of the witch were joined both a society-destroying poison and an antidote to that polluting threat. For the truth that was bled from the body of the witch in the course of her confession under torture was drawn from a place that promised life and not only death. Summoned by means of material production, through torture and death, a sacred truth that comprised the productive limit of the Symbolic order was made to emerge from the body of the accused. In all these ways and by replication over three centuries across Europe and in the American colonies, external threats to societal order were neutralized. The death-work necessary for the practice of truth was confined to select bodies, in order that by their sacrifice Christian Europe would experience broad-based salvation and renewal.

The truth of a difference born of a woman accused of witchcraft and articulated in the myths and rituals of the Christian religion represented one of the last direct engagements by this primary cultural institution in the West in the work of a sacrificial economy. For with the rise of the nation-state, religion ceased to dominate the cultural landscape of Europe: although myths and rituals of the Christian religion would continue to exhibit sacrificial themes,[13] management of human hopes, dreams, threats, and fears traditionally ceded to religion would be done by other institutions, which did not represent themselves, as had the Christian religion, as specialists in the discourse of sacrifice. Did the decline of the Christian religion as a primary cultural institution mean that Europe was no longer in thrall to a sacrificial economy? As Girard's chilling words echo again, we are well advised to inquire of today's masters: if we are no longer attentive to the mythic narratives of old, can we recognize a scapegoat when we see one?

We must ponder whether, in our own time, if humans have not lost the capacity to create scapegoats, humans may have lost the capacity to recognize that a scapegoat who has no expiatory powers is no scapegoat. Unless we can confront that problem directly and take its lessons to heart, the risk of new witch hunts remains high, for the violence that we confront daily suggests that we continue to live in a society that searches for scapegoats and lives by the scapegoat myth, even as its capacity to recognize myth fades from memory (Girard, 1986, 50). The tragedy of our cultural amnesia may be not only that our society can recognize everyone's scapegoats but its own (1986, 41), but also that we who no longer are at home in a mythic universe but still are in need of scapegoats may seek them in ever more virulent ways.

No easy insights into women's present circumstances are located in this examination of the witch hunts; rather, this analysis counsels vigilance before dangers which do not necessarily present themselves as such. If we are to remain watchful in the face of the continued risk of sacrificial violence, we need ever more sophisticated analyses of cultural codes that harbor the scapegoat mechanism. Feminist scholars who have particular concerns about the implication of sexual difference in the work of a sacrificial economy need to keep vigil on another count as well: because women are made to bear with their bodies not only aspects of a sacrificial economy that generate the rawest and most brutal forms of violence, but also those that dissemble and displace that violence, feminist scholars should remain wary before even the most benign forms of sexual differentiation, for they too may express the trope of sacrificial maternity. Indeed, Chapter 7 suggests that, if women are to find means to break free of a sacrificial economy, a thoroughgoing hermeneutics of suspicion is warranted, lest they discover in the very valorization of women evidence of their ultimate incarceration: life-sentences from which women are freed only in their death.

7

LIFE-SENTENCES

THE MOTHER IN THE CULTURAL ARCHIVES OF THE WEST

> There have to be ways of relating that are completely different from the tradition ordained by the masculine economy. So, urgently and anxiously, I look for a kind of desire that wouldn't be in collusion with the old story of death. This love would not be trapped in contradictions and ambivalences entailing the murder of the other indefinitely. On the contrary, each would take the risk of *other,* of difference, without feeling threatened by the existence of an otherness.
>
> —Hélène Cixous and Catherine Clément, *The Newly Born Woman*

Feminist scholars who are committed to promoting women's autonomy and capacity for free agency should give careful consideration to the work of a sacrificial economy, lest, in misjudging the dynamics of oppression, they fail to strategize adequately a way to a liberating future. Moreover, in pursuing their emancipatory objectives, feminist scholars should not assume that sacrificial discourse always functions with the raw brutality displayed in the witch hunts. In fact, when Kristeva engages in an extended exploration of a sacrificial economy—focusing on testimony to its work in the cultural archives of the West—she demonstrates that the signifying practices of this economy are all the more troublesome to the extent that their deadly work is deployed in ways that actually appear to champion women. Surrogate victimization is quite capable of presenting itself as surrogate valorization. Indeed, the matricidal aims of the signifying process are encountered at full strength when the figure of the phallic mother overlays the maternal body of origins, disguising sacrifice. That the sacrificial economy operates with an apparently boundless capacity to mask its matricidal aims mandates that feminists employ a thoroughgoing skepticism before every emancipatory claim lest their efforts to free women from the grip this economy secure women ever more forcefully within its bonds.

Heeding Kristeva's warning, this chapter advances the primary goal of this project: to address and counter a paralyzing continuum of violence, widespread substitutionary patterns of violence, and the protracted nature of violence, which exhibits a propensity to draw ever deeper into the human body. Section I employs a feminist hermeneutics of suspicion to expose the trope of the phallic mother in patriarchy and criticize the work she performs on behalf of a sacrificial economy. Sections II and III examine this trope for evidence of the trace—a difference or otherness—that, portending the subversion of patriarchy, could release women from its paralyzing grip. Two aspects of nonsacrificial creativity that are associated with an economy of difference are highlighted. One, a signifying practice of somatic productivity, is an alternative to hostile invasions of the flesh associated with deadly mimetic violence. The other, a practiced regard for the stranger, is an alternative to perspectives on the other informed by patterns of substitutionary violence which threaten to cast every stranger in the role of scapegoat. Section IV focuses on these nonsacrificial marks of difference while addressing signifying options in religion and feminism which women might summon in order to write the sentences of their lives in new, nonlethal terms.

I. Time's Truth

The sacrificial economy's awesome capacity for multiple disguises is most rivetingly attested to in a painting by Giovanni Battista Tiepolo (1696–1770) titled "Time Unveiling Truth." The representation of woman in this painting is a cautionary motif for all feminists who seek emancipation. Tiepolo's painting depicts Father Time—muscular, sunburned, gnarled with age—grasping the figure of Truth, who is a beautiful young woman. As this painting is described by Perry Townsend Rathbone (1969), Truth sits serenely on the lap of Time, yielding to a "ceremonious disrobing." Regally dominating the composition, Truth's foot rests on the globe below her; her symbol, the sun, flies high in the sky above. For his part, Time's giant wings spell "irresistible strength" and his lowered head "speaks of determination." At the feet of Time are his customary attributes: a chariot, a scythe representing death, an infant symbolizing birth, and a parrot attesting to the vanity of human life. Rathbone's appreciation for the painting is clear: applauding the "sumptuous color, mastery of drawing, and brilliant brush work," he indicates that Tiepolo "surpasses almost every eighteenth-century artist" (127).

In Tiepolo's fantasy, as Rathbone reports it, Truth conquers all: does she not have the world at her feet? And her elegance, which Rathbone classifies as "triumphant," makes Time a rough-hewn servant to Truth's sacred authority. Even so, Rathbone's gushing commentary is curious; for, to an observant eye, something is terribly amiss in the painting. Notwithstanding Tiepolo's mastery of the art of drawing, Truth's right leg is positioned in relation to her body where her left leg should be. What is the meaning of this apparent dismembering and re-membering of Truth? Does Time hold her in coitus or, to the contrary, has Truth been the victim of a brutal rape (Kristeva, 1974, 154)?

Kristeva submits that Tiepolo's painting attests to a scene of conflict which, but for the telling leg, would be unknown. Only Truth's misplaced limb confirms the work of sacrifice: Truth is not the solar priestess of the Symbolic order, for she is one whose violation has caused Time and the sign to be. For Kristeva, the dis-ease of Truth's body suggests that heterosexual coitus is not the subject of Tiepolo's portrait, as Rathbone claims. For a difference which the love-making of Time and Truth might celebrate has been supplanted in the wake of a violent erasure of that difference by Time. Thus, in the homologous logic of the painting, Truth is a phallus (1974, 155).[1]

What is the lesson of Tiepolo's painting for feminism? According to Kristeva, if feminists applaud that moment when woman becomes the truth of the temporal order through surrogate valorization, they fall prey to a crude but enormously effective trap (1974, 155). This trap is all the more lethal to the degree that the seductive beauty of a phallic Truth appears to attest to a feminine difference—a salutary trope of woman—which promises to elevate women's position in the world. Kristeva asks that feminists not overlook the dismembering of Truth's body by Time: her awkwardly placed limb gives the lie to the phallic fantasy of Tiepolo and shows that emancipation does not follow a dream of a goddess. To the contrary, within the sacrificial economy which bonds Time's Truth, the difference she bears—an alterity paradigmatically represented by sexual difference—always already has been throttled. Its force—jouissance and rejection—always already has been subjected to a matricidal sign. Thus, for Kristeva, the emergence of a nonsacrificial Truth awaits a change in the signifying economy. Only then could sexual difference, now structured by sacrifice, be expressed on other terms. Only then could genuine alterity and difference among persons be affirmed.

If Kristeva's discussion of Tiepolo's painting warns feminists of difficulties they may encounter when they try to augment women's agency, what emancipatory strategies does she recommend? What can feminists do to counter the compelled performance of Truth under the constraints of a sacrificial economy? Discussing the tactics of two generations of feminists, Kristeva makes recommendations for strategic interventions in the work of a sacrificial economy.[2]

The first generation of feminists which Kristeva identifies all but disregard the difference-erasing sacrificial dialectic that links surrogate victimization and valorization. Primarily white, heterosexual, and middle-class, they model their emancipatory strategy on the politics of the nation-state: they advocate equal pay, professional recognition, and reproductive rights (1981a, 194; 1995, 207). For these feminists, who are called liberal feminists in the United States, emancipation mandates assimilation to the logic of identification. That they are blind to crucial issues of difference is most evident when we note that they do not seriously engage differences among women. Although they are willing to listen to the distinct concerns of women who did not sit at the table with them when they first crafted their political agenda (e.g., women of color and poor women), first-generation feminists do not perceive that these new voices truly are novel. When first-generation feminists amend their original agenda, adding ideas and values expressed by diverse women, they always treat these additions as mere elaborations of ideas that have always been inherent in their program (1981a, 194; 1995, 208). Constrained by a logic of identification, first-generation feminists are unlikely to effect social change. Their disregard for others, attesting to a deep-seated suspicion of difference, demonstrates that first-generation feminists assume a sacrificial stance.[3]

For second-generation feminists, whose commitments American feminists would associate with radical or cultural feminism, the liberating agenda of the first generation is suspect. Explicitly refusing the first generation's posture of assimilation, the second generation celebrates irreducible differences in and among women. Valorizing difference, second-generation feminists locate emancipating practices outside the signifying economy of men. Kristeva cites the aims of a second-generation feminism as a clear advance on those of the first generation. Where the first generation seeks equal access to a terrain whose emancipatory contours it perceives as given, the second generation self-consciously calls into question the entire social order. Not promoting women's claim to privileges already granted to men, the second generation criticizes privilege itself. Not demanding women's rightful access to a level playing field, it asks instead what counts as a "game" and a "playing field." Perceiving that sexual difference is socially mediated and that negotiations which distribute difference do so by means of varied relations to power, language, and meaning, second-generation feminists understand that they must make inquiry into the most basic elements of the social order—their driving force—if they are to effect change (1981a, 196; 1995, 208).

Kristeva embraces the questions, if not the emancipating strategies, of second-generation feminists. She applauds them for leaving open, rather than seeking closure on, the dialectic of difference among women. They rightly recognize that all negotiations of difference among women and between women and men can be challenged and reconfigured (1981a, 196; 1995, 208–209). Above all, Kristeva commends second-generation feminists for pressing the most basic issue affecting women's agency—the place of women in the Symbolic contract—in ways that enable them to observe in that contract an "essentially (ultimately) sacrificial relationship of separation and articulation of difference" (1981a, 199; 1995, 212).

Nevertheless, Kristeva questions the strategies by which second-generation feminists seek access to nonsacrificial signifying practices. When they valorize women's difference, they risk succumbing to the matricidal aims of Time, for "the very logic of counterpower and of countersociety necessarily generates, by its very structure, its essence as a simulacrum of the combated society or of power" (1981a, 203; 1995, 216). Kristeva claims that second-generation feminists encounter difficulties because of the overdetermination of the signifying economy. After all, the Symbolic order needs transgressions in order to sustain itself. As a consequence, the violence about which second-generation feminists have become aware is "the implacable violence (of separation and castration) that underlies *any* symbolic contract" (1995, 216). Indeed, an economy of disorder and order are inextricably bound one with the other. Women are caught in this economy, whose own mimetic logic, turning on a sacrificial ethos oriented toward matricide, makes highly problematic the exit from it that second-generation feminists seek. Therefore, Kristeva dreams of a third generation of feminists who can advance innovative signifying practices which, unlike those of second-generation feminists, are not constrained by the gravitational forces of the sacrificial economy (1981a, 209; 1995, 222). These new arrangements would allow for the recognition of difference—plural and multiform discourses—which the paternal order has not permitted.

How does Kristeva imagine that the goals of third-generation feminists can be realized? In Chapter 3 of this project Kristeva has been shown to express confidence that humans are capable of nonsacrificial ventures. She does identify forms of death-work associated with the emergence of the subject in the Symbolic order that portend such practices. Here, however, that Kristeva envisions no easy access to a nonsacrificial economy must be emphasized. Kristeva ascribes to a third-generation feminism a position that puts it at odds with all cultural or radical feminisms. She asserts that, as subjects of Time, women's only access to the linguistic order goes through the paternal order. Subject to it, women's options are clear-cut and limited: either they can make a melancholic identification with the Mother, rejecting the Law's mandate for the representation of alterity, or they can repress the maternal body and identify with the Law. Whichever tack they choose, they cannot evade the constraints of a matricidal economy: violence, implosive or explosive, surrounds them.

The cultural archives of the West display the truth of Kristeva's critical vision: this phallic culture, intoxicated with the possibilities of mastery, always alternates between a vision of woman as angel or whore, holy woman or witch, goddess of light or of darkness, guardian of order or chaos (Moi, 1985, 167). Therefore, Kristeva well demonstrates that patriarchy's daughters cannot easily evade the grasp of Father Time. Because she observes no route for an immediate escape from the sacrificial configurations of the Symbolic order, Kristeva calls for the subversion of the Symbolic order from within.

How would this work? Observing that women are effects of a phantasy of sexual difference, Kristeva notes that the real work of difference which phantasy seeks to broker is always elsewhere (Elliot, 1991, 191). Indeed, if the economy that anchors Imaginary investments in phallic women—lending them the weight of the real—were undermined, phantasmatic claims made on women would grasp only an empty space. Women would not be in the space assigned to them by the economists of sacrifice. Were women to pursue a strategy of disengagement with work they conduct for others in the Symbolic order, they no longer would serve as repositories for what others reject as threatening to their own identity and power.

But how can women advance such a disinvestment strategy and promote insurrection if, in the sacrificial economy in which they are immersed, they are unable to elude Time and his penchant for a phallic Truth? Kristeva suggests that, if women are to take on the fictional posturings of identity and successfully subvert them, they need *to make the process by which they have come to be an event of their own subjectivity.* Describing the stance they should assume as analytic, Kristeva emphasizes that, in opting for it, women will recover subject-forming negativity in process. Although they will not return to an original space of becoming—a presacrificial Eden—if women take up an analytic stance toward death-work, they will be able to more freely negotiate subject-status, succumbing neither to phallic mastery nor to abject victimization. Granted crucial maneuvering room, they will be able to engage an order of difference that will not force them to conform to the sacrificial sign. Working back to and through the phantasy of sexual difference harbored in discourse—the Symbolic idealization of the human relationship to the maternal matrix (1976, 161)—they will be able to approach *the generative work that produces the relation itself.*

The analytic method that Kristeva commends to a third-generation feminism elaborates a distinct signifying practice that obviates the work of sacrifice. In her early work, Kristeva experiments with this method when she interrogates phantasies of the maternal body in the cultural archives of the West. Seditiously intervening in maternal death-work, reclaiming it from its sacrificial masters, Kristeva brings to expression its productive logic: a nonsacrificial alterity oriented toward agency and transformation. In her more recent work, Kristeva identifies nonsacrificial alterity in signifying practices oriented toward the stranger. As Sections II and III examine these experimental ventures, a politics supportive of a third-generation feminism and its vision of a nonviolent world comes into view.

II. *La Femme Enceinte:* Pregnant Body-Politics

Kristeva arrives at a radical maternal politics in the course of examining narratives of Christianity preserved in the cultural archives of the West. For Kristeva believes that, if Christianity is a discourse of sacrifice par exemplar, in its overdetermined sign of maternity, it also harbors options for women to disinvest from that economy. Kristeva finds the figure of Mary particularly instructive. On the one hand, the Virgin Mary, impregnated by the Word, is a paradigm of the violent erasure of difference in patriarchy and the ascent of phallic Truth. Yet representations of Mary in the cultural archives of the West suggest also that Mary's virginal discourse, which imprisons her in the homologous grip of a paternal Law, can be subverted. In gaps, breaks, and paradoxes of Mary's archival legacy are glimpsed new opportunities for women: attesting neither to phallic idealization nor to mimetic abjection, they portend a nonsacrificial economy of signification. Kristeva registers these diverse possibilities for critically engaging maternal discourse with particular clarity in two essays: "Motherhood According to Giovanni Bellini" (1975a) and "Stabat Mater" (1976).

Kristeva studies the paintings of the Madonna by Giovanni Bellini in an effort to locate subversive potential in the overdetermined signs of maternity within a sacrificial economy. Holding to a point of rupture in the Symbolic order, she wants to make it visible without overturning it, reversing it, or subjecting it to the embrace of phallic Time. Kristeva gains entree to the text of Bellini's paintings through a series of preliminary musings on becoming-a-mother, the process of gestation by which, "within the body, growing as a graft, indomitable, there is an other" (1975a, 237). Initially she attends to two discourses that attempt to account for this process: science, which remains silent about the mother as the site of these proceedings, and Christian theology, for which motherhood remains an impossible elsewhere: "a spiritual tie with the ineffable godhead, and transcendence's ultimate support—necessarily virginal and committed to assumption" (1975a, 237). Why do the masters of Symbolic discourse either fall incoherent before a mother who would be the subject of gestation or make a mother but the thoroughfare for the imposition of the Word? Possibly, Kristeva suggests, they do so because the maternal body is the *place* of the splitting of social reality, a point of revelation.

Of course, at the limit of imagining *someone*—Mother—guardians of the paternal order always fall back on the phantasy of the phallic mother. After all, beyond that is chaos:

> . . . if the mother were not phallic, then every speaker would be led to conceive of its Being in relation to some void, a nothingness asymmetrically opposed to this Being, a permanent threat against, first, its mastery, and ultimately, its stability. (1975a, 238)

Therefore, in the sphere of the Symbolic, the sphere of survival, becoming-a-mother is invariably read in accord with the Law of the Father: as the desire of a woman to bear the child of her own father. A phantasy summoned only to accomplish his function, it guarantees peace "to those who firmly adhere to the paternal symbolic axis." Even so, at the limit of the Law, Kristeva suggests that a woman experiences becoming-a-mother as a reunion with the body of her mother. She is her own mother, creator. This homological-maternal facet is "a whirl of words, a complete absence of meaning and seeing. It is feeling, displacement, rhythm, sound, flashes, and fantasied clinging to the maternal body as a screen against the plunge" (1975a, 238–39). In this moment, Kristeva observes that what women see as resurrection, society as a whole understands as murder (1981a, 200). After all, one who becomes-a-mother on such terms must be a most radical atheist, a killer of the Lawgiver and Father-God. The price of her knowledge surely must be madness. Or must it?

Kristeva wants to hold to this moment of *la femme enceinte:* woman at the limit, woman pregnant.[4] She who stands at the threshold of becoming-a-mother harbors no illusions: Symbolic destiny seals off *la femme enceinte* and censures her in order to preserve the homology of the group. Thus, maternity is *understood,* can be understood *rightly,* only as the demand for a penis. As long as "there is language-symbolism-paternity, there will never be any other way to represent, to objectify, and to explain this unsettling of the symbolic stratum . . . this event called motherhood" (1975a, 241–42). Naming the masters—legislators, grammarians, psychoanalysts—Kristeva acknowledges their indubitable power to prescribe the stance that women must take in the sacrificial economy that is their paternal heritage. According to the dictates of this economy, "every body is made homologous to a male speaking body." As a consequence, motherhood can be nothing more than "a phallic attempt to reach the Mother who is presumed to exist at the very place where (social and biological) identity recedes" (1975a, 242).

Cognizant of the Law, Kristeva nevertheless moves on to subvert it, discovering in the artist's work intimations of a nonsacrificial economy in images drawn "at the intersection of sign and rhythm, of representation and light, of the Symbolic and the semiotic" (1975a, 242). The artist does not objectify or represent becoming-a-mother, for his art transpires "from a place where she is not, where she knows not." The artist *delineates* what, in a woman, "is a body rejoicing [*jouissant*]" (1975a, 242). The artist, "bearing witness," touches on primal repression, the founding of Law. As a consequence, in Bellini's brush strokes, Kristeva finds "traces of a marginal experience, through and across which a maternal body might recognize its own, otherwise inexpressible in our culture" (1975a, 243).

Kristeva is struck by his work, perhaps because it contrasts with that of Leonardo da Vinci, his contemporary. For Kristeva, Leonardo is a master artist of homology. His fetishistic paintings of the Madonna tell the Father's story: the maternal figure is absorbed in her child. Her body turns toward him, who remains the real focus. A phallic mother, da Vinci's Madonna testifies to the cult of the masculine body. Indeed, the very economy of representation of which Leonardo partakes is that of Desire, first, for the forbidden Mother and then for objects, as Leonardo becomes a servant of the maternal phallus (1975a, 244–48). By contrast, the Madonnas of Bellini show distance, if not hostility, between infant and mother. The faces of his Madonnas turn away, never centering on the baby. Their eyes flee the paintings to an elsewhere to which we have no access.

Bellini's own story illumines the economy of his painting: history does not record the identity of his mother. Clearly the son of a father, bearer of his father's name, worker in his father's studio, artist son of an artist, Bellini claims no mother. Was he illegitimate? We know only that his father's wife does not claim him in a will she wrote three years after his birth or in the will recorded shortly before her death. Bellini then had reason to paint his own biography: mother dead, absent and lost, mother elsewhere (1975a, 246–47).

More than this, Kristeva sees in Bellini's painting an aspiration to "become the very space where father and mother meet," to recover in painting *la femme enceinte,* and to witness thereby to a heterological expanse unknown to the Law (1975a, 249). Strikingly, even though Bellini accords symbolic status to his aspirations, he does not search for the phallic mother but for her silent predecessor: "Bellini penetrates through the being and language of the father to position himself in the place where the mother could have been reached" (1975a, 249). In that aesthetic gesture Kristeva observes that Bellini hopes to gain access to the space where Father and Mother meet—an Imaginary bridge to the Symbolic constituted by the parents of prehistory—that if unrepresentable, nevertheless is shown in art to inform the phallic economy which, in history, is always already its successor (1975a, 249). Thus, even as Bellini's paintings portray an inevitable fetishized image, they reach the threshold of maternal jouissance. In the luminous work of color and the "architectonic" of volume and contrast and apart from all representations of woman as "body" or "object," Bellini invests in the very *function* of jouissance (1975a, 248).

As such, Bellini's art, even when not representing religious themes, opens on to the sacred and witnesses to a positive mimesis. He summons with his art a negativity that does not wholly serve a sacrificial agenda (1975a, 250). For in the space of difference toward which Bellini reaches, he glimpses, without aiming to possess, a distinct alterity. In that moment, he confronts neither a threatening maternal abject nor a fetishized image of maternal loss; instead, Bellini evokes alterity as "a pleasurable excess" (Oliver, 1993, 80) suggestive of a nonsacrificial, signifying practice.

Studying Bellini's paintings, Kristeva charts moments of his sacred search. His earliest Madonnas (1450–60) are distant figures. Their hands barely touch their son. Thereafter follow Madonnas (*Madonna and Child,* Amsterdam, Venice, and Bergamo; 1460–64) who bear witness to a maternal appropriation of the child. A possessive Madonna grips her child, holding him tightly. The child struggles against her as she prods his stomach and penis. At the same time, separated by folds of fabric, the Madonna's face remains at peace—elsewhere. Struggling with the Law of the Father, Bellini still paints the split character of the maternal body. Following this period, Bellini begins a long series of experimentations with space: triptychs, altar pieces, and collective scenes. Kristeva writes:

> It seems as if Bellini had to experience, but especially to surpass, the trauma of maternal seduction in order to insert space into his organization of chromatic markings, and thereby, better to approach the ineffable jouissance transcending the mother. (1975a, 259)

Bellini, unlike his contemporary, Leonardo, travels the route of the Father but does not end his journey with him. Instead, the split in the maternal body portrays the persistent elsewhereness of the Mother, the subversion of the Father's Law (1975a, 253–59).

In the next series of paintings (1480–90), Bellini emphasizes distance, and for the moment the maternal psychology in his paintings changes: the child grabs his mother by the neck as if to strangle her: the guilty mother (*Madonna and Child,* Sao Paulo, 1487) (1975a, 260). But as this theme emerges, Bellini also emphasizes landscapes: eventually, they occupy two-thirds of the surface of each painting. Color accentuates the split between figure and background within the paintings as Bellini transposes the elsewhereness of the mother to a safe distance, for the moment. During these years, Bellini's own history provides confirming landmarks for his journey. He marries and has a son; then he loses his wife and son to death.

In the last of his motherhood paintings (1500–1509), light inundates Bellini's canvases, landscapes abound, splits in perspective identify divergent spaces. The Madonna appears "only to justify this cleaved space" (1975a, 264). What then becomes of Bellini's efforts to approach the maternal body in the gesture of artistic expression if the imprint, object, and figure of woman are all but absent from the glorious expanse of color and space his art celebrates?

A final group of paintings records the limits of Bellini's journey. The first is *Venus* (1515), in which a play of light falls upon the face of a young woman who bears the features of 1509 and 1490 Madonnas. Her gaze is an elsewhere that turns in upon itself. Face to face with primary narcissism, Bellini exercises restraint even as he makes "a statement of insurmountable limits." But in *Woman and Mirror* and other paintings completed near the end of his life, Bellini "enters easily into the sex shop of his age" (1975a, 266). The equal of a Giorgione or Titian, Bellini is a connoisseur of the objectified female body. Only his use of color belies the assimilation of the female form to fetishistic object (1975a, 265–66).

Even so and despite such ambiguities in his vision, Kristeva notes that *The Sacred Allegory* (1490–1500) confirms the persistent direction of Bellini's journey over a lifetime. In this work, form gives way to space and creates pure luminosity. Color functions to direct the eye beyond the painting and the limits of representation: in a shattering of figure and form in a space of graphic lines and color, signs are differentiated until they disappear in pure light (1975a, 269). Thus, Bellini remains faithful to a sacred that attests to a nonsacrificial economy even when, and perhaps especially when, no female figure is present in his work. In the final analysis, for Bellini "motherhood is nothing more than such a luminous spatialization, the ultimate language of a jouissance at the far limits of repression, whence bodies, identities, and signs are begotten" (1975a, 269).

Even as Kristeva perceives that Bellini unsettles the Symbolic stratum and witnesses to nonsacrificial death-work, delineating a positive mimesis, she locates analogous processes of subversion in her own life as an artist and mother. In a remarkable essay, "Stabat Mater," whose title refers to the Latin hymn on the agony of the Virgin Mary at the Crucifixion, Kristeva issues a call to women to risk a postvirginal discourse, a heretical ethics, an "herethics" that will crack the symbolic shell of patriarchy and its sacrificial codes (1976, 185). Focusing on death-work that transpires at the bar that separates the signifier from the signified, "Stabat Mater" anticipates a new signifying practice that can witness the *aufhebung* of a sacrificial economy. For Kristeva locates in the pregnant body an experience of subjectivity that honors difference and does not violently assimilate it to itself.

The express subject of Kristeva's essay is the Madonna; however, her specific interest is in women's experience of pregnancy and childbirth.[5] She begins the essay with a question, "If it is not possible to say of a *woman* what she is, would it perhaps be different concerning the *mother,* since that is the only function of the 'other sex' to which we can definitely attribute existence?" (1976, 161). Kristeva wagers that the mother's concern is different; in fact, a mother's discourse on mothering bears witness to and delineates what in a woman "is a body rejoicing."

Ewa Ziarek describes this maternal joy as a practice of othering that is "resistant both to symbolic inscription and to the 'presence' of the signifying subject" (1992, 99). It is not the practice of a subject. After all, there is no "one" positioned in the maternal "space" to signify what is going on (1992, 99). The maternal body, doubling, dividing, and separating, is a nonsite. So also is the child met in maternal joy not an object, a phallus, the focus of an unquenchable desire, for its mother encounters it only in the form of a somatic, or bodily, proof, not a transcendent one. Not yet armored for a battle of recognition which it will wage before the mirror, this child remains part of its mother's flesh: it is known at the limit of the paternal prohibition, at the bar of the signifier.

Describing Kristeva's musings on a maternity that dwells at the thetic break, Kelly Oliver insightfully elucidates key nuances in a mother's reading of this division in being (1993, 67–68). A mother knows that she meets neither God nor the phallus in her child: working out her maternity in a sacred topography of inevitable loss, in the gaps, discontinuities, and absences of life, her love must be for the impossible. But in a mother's love for that which is of herself but yet not herself, she experiences something that is not without meaning. Positioned at the limit of the thetic order, she responds to the masters of the Symbolic who would, in guarding the thetic break, reduce her to silence before the phallus or place her labor under the sign of matricide. Kristeva imagines, from a motherly peace of mind, thoughts that assert a **"just the same"** and ever after **"gnaw . . . at the symbolic's almightiness"** (1976, [the bold typeface is Kristeva's]). Thus, a mother's **"just the same"** reverses the dialectic of the sacrificial economy which authorizes mimetic violence when it constitutes the social bond through force. In the maternally marked transformation of that logic, a mother's gesture is directed toward a social bond forged of love, not of sacrifice. It attests to an alterity that can presage the productive jouissance of free agency.

In "Stabat Mater," the vehicle for Kristeva's subversive invocation of such a nonsacrificial economy is a parallel discourse. Kristeva begins her essay with a critical study of the treatment of maternity by theologians in the Christian tradition. Midway through the first paragraph, her writing splits, and the page divides in two. In bold face, the left-hand column introduces a mother's dreams and fears, initiating a series of poetic reflections on the birth and development of Kristeva's own son. Asserting itself, persisting, the Father's discourse continues, interrupted again and again by the words of Kristeva the mother.

Kristeva's writing evades the reader's grasp—attuned as the reader is to the analytic demands of scholarly thought. The more the unity of the essay is probed, the more signification leads the reader elsewhere. The reader's experience of Kristeva's essay is akin to Kristeva's experience of Bellini's art. Just as she found that an economy of light and color led her away from the objective images Bellini painted, so also does the reader find that an economy of difference in Kristeva's parallel writing leads her away from the grasping logic of a phallic code. The reader cannot say that Kristeva's boldface poetry distills a Mother's voice and that her prose belongs to the Father. Nor can the reader join these two discourses and find "a point" that leads her to subsume each to a unifying, master discourse. Carried away by Kristeva's writing, the reader knows only that she is drawn toward an unnameable space at the limits of the two discourses.

Speaking of "Stabat Mater" with Rosalind Coward, Kristeva confirms that it "is not a coherent text." She states that when she juxtaposed two kinds of texts and two typefaces, she "wanted to give an impression of a sort of wound, a scar" (Kristeva, 1984a, 24). She asserts that the place of the scar is precisely the space that readers would expect the theorist, "the one who is supposed to know," to occupy. Certainly, feminist critics of Kristeva have suggested that Kristeva takes on a role of mastery and writes as if she has conquered this space as a mother "in the know" (Edelstein, 1992, 40). But Kristeva distances herself from the space of authorial control as a psychoanalyst and as a mother. She states that she intends that her scarred text exhibit only the contradiction and pain of a wound.

As such, Kristeva's evocation in "Stabat Mater" of "one who is supposed to know" is reminiscent of the psychoanalytic scene. In conversation with each other, the analyst and the analysand circle a scar: the phallic prohibition or castration. As David Crownfield suggests, when the analysand addresses the analyst—"one who is supposed to know"—the ensuing conversation is worked out in the Imaginary: the analysand's Imaginary is constituted by the reflection given in the gaze and address of the other and, through transference, the analyst's Imaginary is located also by this reflection (1992, 55). Ultimately fictitious, the discourse they enact responds to a disturbance in the thetic function which must be brought forward in order to be resolved. If a reader's conversation with "Stabat Mater" is analogous to the psychoanalytic scene, as Crownfield proposes, the reader is not drawn to the site of authorial mastery, which she or he would presumably accept or reject; rather, in the systematic incoherence of a divided text, the reader migrates toward "the Imaginary place in which the reader locates him/herself by identifying with the text as a mirror" (1992, 56).

Despite the similarities between the psychoanalytic encounter and the reader's engagement with the text of "Stabat Mater," there are importance differences. Whereas the psychoanalytic scene is constructed around a conversation driven by the question of the phallic scar, Kristeva's scarred text attests to labor done at the thetic break which is not identical with the action of castration. For Kristeva believes that preceding the pain of the phallic prohibition, in the death-work of emerging subjectivity, the would-be subject encounters another loss: a rupture within the maternal body that presages the sign. This splitting causes a child to lose its mother and a mother to lose her child in order that both can be. Of course, the Symbolic order will summon every resource to ensure that those who read the text of a mother's body observe only a phallic scar. In a sacrificial economy, a mother's tears—to which the Latin hymn on Mary's suffering attests—must always be tears of a phallic mother confronted by her own castration before the Law (1976, 175–77).

Even so, as Oliver thoughtfully argues, "Stabat Mater" is not, for Kristeva, ultimately a tale of phallic mothers: the Virgin Mary or Kristeva. For "rather than occupy the phallic position from which she has evacuated the Virgin Mary, Kristeva claims to occupy the position of the scar that results from that evacuation" (1993, 55). And even if this scar can be read as the castration of Kristeva, the phallic mother, the pain to which Kristeva's text attests is not only that which afflicts those forced to submit to the prohibitory Law. "Stabat Mater" turns on another pain: before the child learns of a scar that marks sexual difference, the child experiences the maternal body as abject: marked by a tear. Felt as an "inverted castration," the abject threatens as a "lack of separation" (1993, 55). Not wanting to be sucked back into the mother through the space of the scar—the source of its birth—the child fears "a lack of lack" (1993, 54). Thus, Oliver traces the scar to which "Stabat Mater" refers to the Imaginative structure of the abject, which castration and *its* scar will attempt to hide altogether in the virginal robes of Mary (1993, 55). And if that repressive function fails, a more lethal violence will ensue: maternal labor in its difference will be submitted to the sign of matricide.

Oliver's comments suggest that Kristeva's encounter with Bellini's art and the reader's encounter with "Stabat Mater" are a common Imaginative endeavor which contributes to the sedition of the Symbolic order in both its phallic and sacrificial modes. However, the venture that is joined in these two readings does not turn on any effort to submit "mother" and "child" in these texts to signs. Bellini's painting is about a child without a mother. Kristeva's writing is about a mother without a child. And even as they record the phallic censorship that opens up a void in language, they dwell in that void. As Kristeva notes:

> **Then there is this other abyss that opens up between the body and what had been its inside: there is the abyss between the mother and the child. What connection is there between myself, or even more unassumingly between my body and this internal graft and fold, which, once the**

> **umbilical cord has been severed, is an inaccessible other? My body and . . . him. No connection. . . . The child, whether *he* or *she*, is irremediably an other. . . . Trying to think through that abyss: staggering vertigo.** (1976, 179, emphasis Kristeva's)

Kristeva experiences intimately the break in being, the division of soma, that is mothering. A trace of nonsacrificial death-work, which emerges at the boundary of speaking and the spoken, at the very limits of signification, this difference is a kind of death of identity. At the edges of the Father's Law—his lack-drama—Kristeva explores the limits of his Limit. At the edge of death, the void in being, she detects the scar of inverted castration, which gives the lie to that which the Symbolic order has sought always to represent, absent the repressive force of phallic oblivion, with the sign of matricide.

How can such an experience even be described in words? Ziarek suggests that the theme of "catastrophic infolding" in "Stabat Mater" (1976: 173, 182, 183) best portrays the limit experience of vertiginous mothering. Distinct from the clear separation and noncoincidence of the signifier and the signified—marked by a scar—which the Symbolic monitors of the thetic break have advanced as exclusive terms for ordering human experience, an infolding maternity models alterity "as the imprint of the other *within* the same" (1992, 102).[6] On that ground, notions of identity and difference proper to the categories of the Symbolic prove strikingly insufficient; indeed, they no longer hold up (Kristeva, 1976, 182). After all, as Ziarek suggests, citing Rodolphe Gasché, infolding suggests a mode of heterological thinking which can articulate otherness "prior to the principle of contradiction" and "independently from the process of self-definition" (1992, 102). Heterologically speaking, otherness is understood to "always already inhabit every identity and interrupt every principle of thought" (1992, 102).

Thus, in the somatic discourse of maternity, thematized as an exercise in catastrophic infolding, is glimpsed a positive mimesis that emphasizes a "plenitude of difference in the field of historical existence" rather than a Law of absence (Prosser MacDonald, 1995, 128). Not oriented toward sacrifice, as is the conflict that transpires before the mirror, this mimesis is a fecund movement of persistent negativity that, if wholly archaic, serves also to forever demystify the Symbolic order. Its labor suggests that just as the maternal body is infolded, interrupted, and increased, so also is the negativity that transpires as a practice of absence within the Symbolic order, always, already shaped creatively within the somatic register by an archaic elaboration of difference associated with a catastrophe of being.

Nevertheless, Kristeva's evocation of a maternal economy does not claim to grant direct access to an archaic mother—a lost presence—to whom humans might return and through whom they might know themselves. The very infolding of Kristeva's narrative along its margins subverts the Father's story of such an immortal and virgin mother. When that mother is encountered, as in religious narratives on the cult of the Virgin, Kristeva submits that she remains within a phallic orbit. Kristeva's words—scarring the sacred text of holy virginity—lend no support to its phallic fantasy of "me-and-mommy." Neither John Chrysostom—"For where there is death there is also sexual copulation, and where there is no death there is no sexual copulation either"—nor Jerome—"Death came through Eve but life came through Mary"—would want to hear Kristeva's message (1976, 165). Knowing that otherness is born of her body, Kristeva knows also that a mother can offer no primal shelter against death, even though man will try to overcome death by postulating a deathless maternal love (1976, 176) or vanquishing a death-bearing maternal body. Not offering an ode to the Virgin, Kristeva proclaims the anarchy and atheism of a real mother: **"between myself, or even more unassumingly between my body and this internal graft or fold. . . . No connection. . . . Nothing to do with it"** (1976, 178–79). Whereas the Symbolic order would wrest from the Mother phallic signs that promise immortal being and immunity from the perils of history, the somatic particularities of maternity that Kristeva experiences constitute a "catastrophe of being that the dialectics of the trinity and its supplements [are] unable to subsume" (1976, 183).

After all, if maternity summons a trinity, it is not the triad of the Father's law. Rather, in a sound-space evoked by the parents of prehistory in conversation with each other—"Isn't he beautiful"—a new option emerges. A third party attests to a possibility for sociality that engages genuine otherness (1987a, 34). Thus, in Imaginary labor undertaken by the parents of prehistory, work to which the heterological dynamics of maternal infolding always, already attest, a child is not subsumed or consumed by the Mother's desires nor shaped solely by the prohibitory logic of the Father's Law. To the contrary, conceived in the drifting of a possible metaphor (1987a,37), a child is born to write its life on terms other than those dictated by a sacrificial economy. A sentence, a phrase formed in the gestural dialogue of love, a child can affirm the sacred work of language and live out a heretical ethic oriented toward the productive potential of jouissance: enfleshed, infolded, and free.

Notwithstanding the attractions of Kristeva's nonsacrificial vision, the promise of "Stabat Mater," hinging on a model of open subjectivity that honors alterity while still allowing for connection, is slim comfort to those who, no longer children, are already well established in a sacrificial economy. Of course, Kristeva does argue compellingly in the two essays examined here—"Motherhood According to Giovanni Bellini" and "Stabat Mater"—that the very overdetermination of the trope of sacrificial maternity does, in fact, make room for a seditious encounter with it. If this trope is engaged critically, it can be undermined. Moreover, when Kristeva does link revolutionary interrogations of a sacrificial economy explicitly with feminism, she firmly contends that, if feminists are to locate what is "irreducible and even deadly in the social contract" and "lift what is sacrificial in the social contract from their shoulders," they rightly should focus on the work of sexual difference in a sacrificial economy (1981a; 207, 209).

However, even as Kristeva suggests that a feminist articulation of a heretical signifying practice modeled on the alterity of the maternal body may be a necessary intervention in the social order, she submits that it should not be the only intervention. Distancing herself from an exclusive commitment to a feminist politics focused on issues of sexual difference, Kristeva indicates that a third generation of feminists should opt for diverse engagements with politics and multiple strategies of intervention in the sacrificial economy. Not focusing their concerns solely on the scapegoating of women, they should attend instead to the "victim/executioner which characterize each identity, each subject, each sex" (1981a, 210).

What is the impact of Kristeva's move away from a direct interrogation of the work of sexual difference in the signifying economy for investigations of violence against women? Having drawn on Kristeva's insights in order to make the question of sexual difference of vital significance to the study of a sacrificial economy, must feminists now depart from Kristeva if they are to maintain their feminist commitments?

Feminists should not depart from Kristeva. Although this argument is grounded in a textual analysis of Kristeva's work, it originates with a personal reaction to Kristeva. When I first encountered Kristeva in the mid-1980s, I saw in her readiness to address the role of "victim/executioner in each of us" a disturbing willingness to accept the status quo. Notwithstanding Kristeva's own claim that her new direction of inquiry entailed a "radical process" (1981a, 210), I interpreted Kristeva's generalization of concerns about violence and oppression as an evasive tactic: in refusing to commit to a specific emancipatory agenda, Kristeva intended to avoid feminist politics. I was deeply disappointed. Having so profoundly analyzed women's oppression, why would Kristeva not take the next step and articulate political objectives of a third-generation feminism?

But I now realize that Kristeva did not fall silent. She did offer advice to feminists when she suggested that feminists need to consider multiple deployments of the scapegoating mechanism in and among us. But I did not want to hear that advice. Now, as I reassess my feelings of dissatisfaction at that time, I no longer believe that they arose because Kristeva gave up on feminism and ceased to address women's concerns, for I am unconvinced that she did.[7] Rather, I attribute them to my willingness to give up on the analytic method when Kristeva did not. In those years, I was attracted to Kristeva's writing because I could ascribe to her the role of master: Kristeva was "the one who was supposed to know" better than I the truth of the paternal order. But when Kristeva did not proffer solutions to the problem of women's oppression that I expected from her, she no longer was the master on whom I could rely. And I believed that her inaction exhibited a failure in her resolve, rather than in mine.

Now more appreciative of Kristeva's analytic method, in part because of insightful commentaries on that method by Elliot (1991, 192–200) and Oliver (1993, 147–52), I am prepared to view her work differently and to inquire most seriously of her concerning the analytic method. If we persist with Kristeva in the course of an analytic encounter and seek out the victim/executioner which characterize each identity, each subject, and each sex, where do we go? If we assume the analytic stance, neither professing mastery of our own visions nor expecting someone else to be the "one who is supposed to know," what do we learn?

Kristeva's recent work demonstrates that sustained attention to her method—even when she does not engage women's concerns directly—is most insightful for the work of feminist scholars who are concerned to address sexual difference and violence. Admittedly, the route of the stranger that she proposes does not promise feminists direct and immediate access to an alternative economy supportive of the free agency of women. But neither does it appear blocked: women are not forced to remain where they are, paralyzed by a patriarchal Law. Instead, the path of the stranger suggests a narrow course among the land mines and disorienting mirages of a sacrificial economy. There, along that very route, Kristeva suggests ways in which women may find the strength to speak and write the sentences of their lives anew.

III. The Scapegoat among Us and the Stranger within

Kristeva's commitment to multiple modes of intervention in a sacrificial economy is longstanding. Indeed, her writings attest to her persistent recognition that women are not alone in desiring nonsacrificial engagements even though, as often privileged bearers of violent death-work, they have a particularly strong investment in "lifting the weight of what is sacrificial in the social contract from their shoulders" (1981a, 207; 1995, 220). For Kristeva, that which is crucial to any viable mode of intervention in the work of a sacrificial economy is not the sex of those who would challenge its lethal investment strategies; rather, subversive mediation requires persons to commit to a specific ethic. No longer calling forth scapegoats in the face of mimetic violence, those who draw on this ethic direct the force of signification toward practices that neutralize violence-precipitating threats by engaging an other who is always already within. Those who claim this ethic assert that "instead of searching for a scapegoat in the foreigner, I must try to tame the demons in myself" (1990, 164).

Identifying ventures in signification that advance this ethic, Kristeva elaborates a discourse of the other that does not set out from a sexually differentiated Imaginary and its myths but from an Imaginary attentive to the stranger. For if Kristeva still affirms that woman is the prototypical other—the "irrecuperable stranger" (1990, 168)—she now contends that woman is not "the only can-opener [*le seul ouvre-boîte*]" (166) whose subversive labor can break the phallic seal on the Symbolic order. Space in a homologous social order for heterological options can be created by other means as well. Indeed, if sexual difference is the only force of differentiation on which persons draw to subvert phallic and sacrificial social codes, "we may arrive at a new form of homogeneity" (1990, 166). Seditious death-work requires a persistent overturning of *all* claims of signs to grasp the true/real. Therefore, Kristeva asserts that emancipatory interests are best served when persons "multiply differences" and draw on diverse "uncoded marginalities." When they do so, persons are less likely to treat as enemies those who differ from them. Nor are they as likely to cast strangers from their midst and make them scapegoats (1990, 164). Thus, a stance of subversion and ethical possibility emerges for Kristeva with the one who embodies sustained and irrecuperable difference: the stranger who sojourns among and within us.

Kristeva's notion of the truth of the stranger is suggestive on several counts. It intimates of a nonsacrificial process of signification that is open to creation and change. It attests also to the generation within that process of social relations not shaped by a mechanism of surrogate victimization. Most significantly, it claims that an effective subject position—a position oriented toward emancipatory agency—is a position of permanent strangeness. In the comments that follow, each of these themes is addressed in detail.

A. Analysis as a Practice of Strangeness

There are several ways in which analysis as a practice of strangeness distinguishes itself from sacrificial practices.[8] For example, the truth of the stranger is necessarily entertained *only* in process, in the course an analytic encounter with the work of negativity. In an analytic mode of inquiry, we do not inquire "Which truth?" (the stranger's truth?) nor "Whose truth?" (that of the stranger?). Instead, we ask, "What is it in me that wants the truth?" (Elliot, 1991, 195). Analysis names as the stranger "that in me which wants the truth." Analysis tells us that the stranger is the heterogeneity in our own death-work which fuels our desires and our fears and which we bound off from ourselves as alien. Thus, in returning the scapegoating mechanism and its accompanying mimetic demons to their place of origin, analysis initiates a critical intervention in a sacrificial economy.

Analysis sustains this critique because it advances a distinct mode of inquiry into death-work. Analysis interrogates the strange function of the subject-bounding mechanism, "that in me which wants the truth," in a manner that preserves its dynamic process and returns us to that from which we have become estranged: the negativity of our own life-process. When death-work is explored on such terms, it is not restored to us under the force of the sign with its perceived dangers domesticated and contained by the work of sacrifice. Instead, it is restored to us with its vital alterity, inevitably both promise and threat, intact.

Why is analysis a mode of inquiry that can accomplish this task? According to Kristeva, analysis is not a discourse possessive of the truth; rather, it is concerned at any particular moment to scrutinize death-work—"one should say a style" of speech utterance (1980, xi)—without censoring or confining that work to a sign. Analysis does not "make an interpretive summa in the name of a system of truths." Instead, it recognizes the erosion of meaning in discourse, around which the quest for truth circles. Not papering over difference, analysis acknowledges a crisis "inherent in the symbolic function itself" (1981, 319). Not itself a discourse of mastery, analysis advances an interpretive construct that establishes ever larger spaces for death-work in the face of crisis. Sustaining a stance of vigilant skepticism, analysis perceives "as symptoms all constructions, including totalizing interpretation, which try to deny this crisis" (1981, 319).[9]

Kristeva traces the specific utility of analytic discourse as a critical intervention in sacrificial codes to the fact that the subject who engages in death-work is not in possession of itself: in process and on trial, it always is to be found only in a place where it is not. Analytic discourse keys on the phantasies which attend the performance of absence undertaken by the subject who would yet possess the truth of its being. Where these phantasies promise to secure it in the truth and against threat, analysis holds before the subject the prospect that its Imaginative labor is never final, never reaches its goal. Analysis exposes the heterogeneity that is the only guarantee of the subject's free agency. Instead of locating the subject *in* the truth, analysis invites the subject to entertain a strangeness *before* the truth that offers it the distance necessary to entertain the truth of its difference. As a consequence, analysis acts on behalf of truth's best interests to subvert its work, not in order to claim the truth for itself or for another, but "only to lead the subject, faced with the erosion of meaning, to the economy of the subject's own speaking" (1981, 313) as an open system or process.

Can analytic inquiry truly promote nonsacrificial investments in death-work? For Kristeva, that which sustains analytic inquiry as an open discourse to which all claims of mastery are antithetical is the work of transference. In acts of transference—fictional posturings that displace every act of representation—no one is found to reside in the place assigned to "one who is supposed to know." Instead, as analyst and analysand circle that space—a space of unrepresentable alterity—they work out the dissolution of every identity and its other. But what prevents this process of dissolution from ossifying in an act of sacrifice? If signifying practices of subjects tend regularly toward sacrifice, what preserves the analytic encounter from that fate?

Of course, the subject who is formed in the wake of the thetic break is bounded always by exclusions: it is always absent from the place where it would *be.* But within the constraints of this given, the subject can undertake diverse economic ventures. No single economy need govern its investments in death-work. Indeed, a sacrificial economy and an analytic economy turn differently on negativity. A sacrificial economy intends that negativity submit signifying practices to signs that displace an other with the same, absence with presence, threat with control, and that which is uncanny with a certain object. Even so, the subject's work within a sacrificial economy is interminable: that which it wants to possess—the difference that is the necessary companion of negativity—always eludes it. It never vanquishes or definitively surmounts the threat that difference poses for it. Notwithstanding the persistent efforts of the masters of sacrifice on the subject's behalf, what it seeks to possess is always elsewhere.

By contrast, an economy shaped by analytic inquiry invites the subject to hold to the turn in negativity. Not denying the risks that negativity poses, the subject can elaborate those risks as promise rather than as threat. It can engage negativity while claiming the inevitable loss that transpires at the thetic break as a work of its own subjectivity. Analysis empowers the subject to articulate death-work so that there can be fewer deaths (1977, 296; Oliver, 1993, 147).

As a consequence, an ethics of analysis advances as a wager: if the subject can work through and articulate that which has been barred in the course of its own formation and division, the subject need not sacrifice that which has been excluded in order to secure its own being. Instead, it can enjoy an expansion of boundaries. Because analysis challenges all property claims made by a subject who would possess the truth of its being, it assists the subject in reconceiving the kind of space it needs to engage in the work of truth. Analysis prepares the subject to create truth in the very taking up of difference in discourse. Sustaining a broad deployment of the forces in humans which want the truth, analysis promotes the investment of those forces in emancipatory labor because it offers the subject space in which it can do death-work and not submit that labor to proprietary interests alien to free agency.

B. From Fascinated Rejection to Familiar Strangeness

In some respects, the work of analysis that Kristeva describes is not new. Kristeva previously has delineated an analytic logic in her writings on maternity when she has suggested that maternal death-work generates distinct linguistic practices which obviate the cultural work of matricide. In the logic of the maternal economy, Kristeva already has detected an ethical relation toward alterity that she now wishes to ascribe to analysis. In both instances, Kristeva speaks of a practice of strangeness that opens onto a nonsite, evoking heterogeneity and an infolding of being. This practice of strangeness retains the other as other in the same and, in so doing, frames mimesis and separation as fecund possibility rather than as threat.

Even so, an analytic discourse directed toward the stranger promises to be productive of a more effective social ethic than would be one oriented toward maternity. Because cultures for so long have invested in the notion that sex is *someone's* summa, anyone who seeks to release maternity from its traditional economic function in order to align it with an analytic discourse confronts an enormously difficult task: endemic in humanity's readings of sexual difference is a long, sedimented history of representation. As a consequence, parties to these signifying traditions veritably insist that someone must have the wherewithal to speak the truth of sexual difference. Despite Kristeva's own resistance to treating sexual difference as a discourse of truth, she finds that forging a heretical ethics of maternity is most challenging.[10] For this reason, in her recent work, Kristeva no longer emphasizes an ethics of alterity that emerges from maternal reflections; instead, she advances an ethics of analysis that emerges in reflection on the uncanny. For Kristeva, the uncanny is that by means of which humans are introduced to the "fascinated rejection of the other" (1991, 191). Although Kristeva previously has associated "fascinated rejection" with the maternal body (1984d, 124), she observes now a broad landscape "of borders and othernesses ceaselessly constructed and deconstructed" that appear to humans as strange and uncanny (1991, 191). Resistant to all notions of summa, the uncanny is not submitted easily to the grasping mastery of the sign. Indeed, the uncanny is the truth of negativity: a nonsite at which resides that which is not there. As such, the uncanny attests to the truth of death-work which humans have bounded wholly from themselves as alien and proper only to another: the stranger.

Kristeva's reflections, leading toward the stranger—woman, alien, other—whom the subject encounters on its life journey, point toward a nonsacrificial ethic, as have her musings on maternity. However, the route she takes now does not begin with the scapegoat or victim. Instead, she works forward from a subject's experience of the uncanny to the stranger in its midst, rather than backward from one who is different to the subject's own strangeness to itself. Not invoking initially the death-bearing other whom the subject encounters and ejects from its midst, Kristeva speaks first of pre-texts of death in a subject's own life. She writes:

> My discontent in living with the other—my strangeness, his strangeness—rest on the perturbed logic that governs this strange bundle of drive and language, of nature and symbolic, constituted by the unconscious, always already shaped by the other. It is through unraveling transference . . . that, on the basis of the other, I become reconciled with my own otherness-foreignness, that I play on it and live by it. (1991, 182)

She anticipates a sojourn with the uncanny that moves through strangeness—of analyst and analysand—to issue in "an ethics of respect for the irreconcilable" (1991, 182).

Kristeva indicates that a journey toward the stranger begins with careful attention to the uncanny, whose labor its premier analyst, Freud, carefully has preserved in a semantic study of *heimlich* and *unheimlich*. For *heimlich* intends both the familiar, friendly, and comfortable (*heim*) and that which signifies discomfort, concealment, secrecy, and deceit: *heimlich*. Harbored in *unheimlich* is an entire "psychoanalytic hypothesis": the uncanny (*unheimlich*), Freud tells us, "is that class of the frightening which leads back to what is known of old and long familiar" (1991, 183). That which *is* strangely uncanny *was* once familiar and this constitutes its uncanniness. The uncanny attests to a work of mimesis which is both doubly familiar and alien. Indeed, the negativity to which the uncanny attests marks emergent subjectivity. As a consequence, Kristeva asserts that the uncanny abject does not function as a side effect of secondary repression, bolstering a subject whose nascent borders already have been secured. Rather, the uncanny marks primary repression. Tagged by Kristeva as proper to the constitutive work of a subject, the uncanny belongs to a bounding function by means of which a subject emerges at the borders of being. Linking the uncanny and the abject in a common reference to space, Noëlle McAfee notes rightly that nausea threatens one who is overcome by the abject uncanny (1993, 123): "at the precipice, my self dissolves in vertigo" (1993, 119).

That uncanny encounters with strangers are symptomatic of abjection distinguishes these from confrontations with an objectified other. As McAfee advises, when Kristeva talks about the stranger, she emphasizes a *dread* rather than a *fear* of strangeness (1993, 122). Those who fear strangers encounter them within the Symbolic order. As the Hegelian dialectic of the master and slave establishes, the fear of the master/subject is generated by his vulnerability before the other/object, on whom he depends for his own bounded self-possession. But when one dreads the stranger, one's anxiety has no object. Dread is a border-phenomenon, an encounter with nothing, a glimpse of the abyss. Therefore, Kristeva would propose that strangeness ensues not only when humans project *objective* alterity onto the other, through whom they would secure their status as subjects, but also at the fringes of a radical mode of subject formation: an uncanny, *abjective* alterity shadows one who exists only by dwelling in and with strangeness, as a practice of absence.

A labor undertaken paradigmatically in emergent subjectivity, the uncanny shadows multiple practices of death-work, evoking Symbolic gestures intended to neutralize its disturbing force. Most significantly, under the organizing auspices of the Symbolic order, a sacrificial economy summons its resources to diffuse and repress an uncanny history: from the Symbolic is to be excluded all knowledge of the journey undertaken by a subject from *heim* to *heimlich* to *unheimlich*. Sundering that which has been held together—for better or worse—in the founding work of negativity, the sacrificing symbol bounds off the other and, in so doing, tries to preserve the subject from the uncanny. Even so, "pretexts" of the uncanny wander through Symbolic narratives: representations of death and the feminine persistently evoke feelings of familiar strangeness (1991, 185).

Likewise are persons occasionally unnerved by uncanny encounters with others. Meeting someone whose presence before cannot be framed immediately with a sign, we may momentarily feel at a loss, incoherent, out of touch, stupid, or disoriented. Confronting a stranger in the momentary absence of the usually predictable management resources that would ascribe to him or her a place—friend or foreigner, compatriot or alien, kin or outsider—we may even for a moment lose composure (Kristeva, 1991, 187). In a haze and at a loss, in such uncanny encounters we return again to that which representation, in the wake of the thetic break, was to have portrayed as completed work:

our most nascent efforts to situate ourselves in a world as beings evicted forever from our natal home, thanks to language.

What are our options before the uncanny and its effects? Remaining at a loss, we can dwell in its catastrophic aspects. Or we can suppress the symptom that the uncanny provokes, eliminating the strange by making it a scapegoat and exiling it elsewhere, according to the dictates of a sacrificial economy. Or *we can articulate its strangeness.* For Kristeva, the third option—an expressive strategy of analysis—has the most to offer, for it enables us to meet up with "the fascinated rejection of the other at the heart of that 'our self'" (1991, 191), not to throttle difference, but to live with it. In that encounter we can take up mimetic desire again. Not fleeing from our fears, we can acknowledge them at their source: as dreadful evocations of "the other in me that is an other in the same."

What is the ethical purchase on this analytic encounter with that which is strange in ourselves? Kristeva appreciates Freud's wisdom in not speaking of foreigners when he teaches us to detect foreignness in ourselves. That Freud does not explicate the connections that link strangeness and strangers, she believes, is not because Freud is oblivious to political capital that he might exploit were he to join the question of the uncanny with "the problem of the foreigner." For Kristeva surmises that Freud, a Jew who sojourned in Vienna, London, Paris, Rome, and New York, was intimately familiar with the discontent and ill-ease that mark encounters with the other (1991, 181). Instead, Kristeva attributes Freud's desire to focus on the other scene within to a cogent regard for an analytic politics of difference. Freud perceives wisely that only if we learn to detect strangeness in ourselves will we obtain the courage not to see it everywhere *but* in ourselves (1991, 191–92). The apparent Freudian distraction before the "problem of foreigners" Kristeva interprets as an invitation to approach the question of the stranger not as a truth to be known and placed outside our selves, but rather as a symptom of our desire. In question for Freud is that which in us calls up a demon—an apparition of the other—that must be hounded from us if we are to maintain our own, proper selves. Attentive to the symptom of the stranger, Freud's contribution to a social ethic that would envision a more generous and open society is consequently not presented as a truth. Not offering a treatise on the stranger, Freud proffers instead an interrogative space in which we may find the "courage to call ourselves disintegrated in order not to integrate foreigners and even less so to hunt them down, but rather to welcome them to that uncanny strangeness, which is as much theirs as it is ours" (1991, 192).

C. A Cautionary Tale of Hoffmann

Kristeva's desire to explore an ethics of alterity oriented toward the stranger in which musings on the maternal body do not figure prominently should be honored. Nevertheless, signifying traditions oriented toward the maternal body and those which attest to uncanny encounters with a stranger should not be rigidly distinguished. Because each becomes violent when it is implicated in a sacrificial economy, an inclusive approach to the uncanny abject is mandated. Indeed, were signifying practices oriented toward the stranger to become a sole focus, in exclusion of those marked expressly by sexual difference, the dynamics of the space of absence that Kristeva has identified as a site for the productive work of negativity might be misread. We might fail to note that, under force of threat, this site regularly becomes a scene of sexually differentiated sacrifice.

Persistent markings of the maternal body that can be located in the practice of strangeness—the *heim* in *unheimlich*—suggest that Freud's essay on the uncanny should be looked at again.[11] In doing so, Kristeva's appreciative reading of this essay is not to be disavowed; however, a hermeneutic of suspicion must be exercised. As Freud's thoughts on the uncanny are considered once again, we must emphasize the fragility of the analytic exercise in alterity that Kristeva proposes. The promise that Kristeva reads in Freud is matched by Freud's continued fascination by the Law of the paternal economy, which all but obscures the insights Kristeva finds so appealing in his work. Such words of caution, scarring this text and Freud's—serve as a reminder that the space which is supposed to be occupied by "one who is supposed to know" the truth of alterity always remains empty. They stand as evidence also that the analytic terrain still portends sacrifice and the route of the stranger still poses risks to potential scapegoats.

In writing about the uncanny, Freud insists on placing the uncanny neatly within a Symbolic orbit. Of course, he does acknowledge maternally marked instances of the uncanny: the fear of being buried alive, he suggests, is traceable to a maternal Imaginary (1955, 244). Female genitalia are uncannily reminiscent of beginnings: "the place where each one of us lived once upon a time and in the beginning" (1955, 245). Even so, Freud appears driven, for the most part, by a predilection for explanations of the uncanny oriented toward the Symbolic. What could he learn of the uncanny were he to set that insistence aside? Freud's primary example of the uncanny—Hoffmann's "The Sandman"—offers instructive insights that suggest an answer to this question.

In the story, a young man named Nathaniel leaves the woman to whom he has become engaged when he falls in love with Olympia. At the time, he does not know that Olympia is an automaton whose clock-work has been produced by a Professor Spalanzani and whose eyes have been constructed by a man named Coppola. In the course of the narration, Nathaniel becomes convinced that Coppola is Coppelius, a man who, in Nathaniel's childhood, customarily visited his father in the evenings and who is believed to have engineered an explosion that killed Nathaniel's father. As a child, Nathaniel regularly was sent off to bed by his nurse with the warning that the Sandman was coming. A gruesome figure who was said by Nathaniel's nurse to steal the eyes of children who refuse to go to sleep, the Sandman was readily associated by Nathaniel with Coppelius. In the denouement of the story, Nathaniel discovers that Olympia is only an automaton when he spies

Coppola (a.k.a. the Sandman and Coppelius) and Spalanzani quarreling over Olympia's dismembered body and observes Spalanzani throwing her bleeding eyes at Nathaniel.[12] Made mad by that which he has witnessed, Nathaniel rallies briefly from his illness to reunite with his fiancée. But he becomes deranged once again when, standing with his fiancée atop the tower of the town hall, he spies the Sandman (Coppola) approaching. Spinning wildly, he tries to throw his "wooden doll" fiancée over the edge only to fall to his own death from the parapet.

Citing Jentsch's 1906 essay, "Zur psychologie des Unheimlichen," Freud notes that Jentsch attributes the uncanny effect of Hoffmann's story to the uncertainty that surrounds Olympia: is she a living human or a mechanical doll? However, Freud disavows Olympia as the source of uncanniness in the story. Instead, Freud suggests that "the feeling of something uncanny is directly attached to the figure of the Sandman, that is, to the idea of being robbed of one's eyes" (1955, 230). Why does the eye-snatching Sandman produce anxiety for readers of this tale? Why is he one whom they find uncanny in the story? The Sandman (Coppelius/Coppola) has taken Nathaniel's father from him, has diverted him from his fiancée, has exposed him to the lifelessness of his second love, Olympia, by means of a brutally destructive act, and has driven him to his death. But, after all, Freud observes, characters in stories do all sorts of dastardly deeds without summoning feelings of the uncanny in the reader. Why do readers of Hoffmann's tale find the actions of the Sandman so disturbing?

Freud argues that the anxiety produced in readers by the Sandman belongs to the castration complex, whose lessons they receive from him. Dismissing the possibility that the lifeless doll Olympia fills them with dread, Freud claims that fears about eye-extraction are actually fears about castration (1955, 231). Indeed, the Sandman is a father-figure whose image has been split from Nathaniel's own "good father" by Nathaniel's ambivalence toward the Law (1955, 232, n. 1). So also is Olympia Nathaniel's double: the threat Coppelius/Coppola/the Sandman and Spalanzani (another "good father") pose for her is actually a threat posed to Nathaniel by the Law of the paternal order. That which readers experience as uncanny is their intimation that the chain of threats all issue in a single peril: the threat of castration.

But is the story of the Sandman as wholly vested in processes which secure the Symbolic order as Freud would have his readers believe? The uncanny moments in the story are not met in a confrontation with the Law, from whose consequences Nathaniel and the reader would rather hide; rather, the uncanny is encountered when they witness the failure of the Law. The uncanny emerges in the breakdown of social borders associated with a father's death, a lifeless love, and a vertigo-inducing encounter with abject evil. And of these moments, the dismembering of Olympia—a literal rending of body-borders and the life they carry—is the most uncanny. These incidents, delineated by encounters with one who tears out one's eyes, return Nathaniel and the reader to an abject abyss of being. There, a subject's effort to negotiate terms for an orderly existence on the plain of the Symbolic is no longer at issue; rather, in question is whether a subject will have access to the specular economy at all.

Far from being a side event in a Father-Son conflict, as Freud suggests, the dismembering of Olympia is the abject moment in the story on which the terror turns. From Olympia, Nathaniel and the reader of his tale do receive of course a lesson in sexual difference when they see materialized before them the feminine attitude (1955, 232, n. 1) and perceive its costs.[13] Even so, if they learn from Olympia how the Law produces and reinforces itself—she sees it, knows she is without it, and desires it—that is not the only instruction offered by her body. In the uncanny, abject moment when the truth of Olympia is revealed—as blood runs in rivers from eyes pulled from black holes—is unveiled the sacrifice of difference.

Interestingly, Freud cites only Nathaniel's observation of Olympia's bloody eyes as the cause of his madness and neglects to mention that Nathaniel glimpses the empty eye sockets before he sees the eyes. Freud may read in Olympia's eyes signs of a paternal economy: they are tiny, cut penises. But before Nathaniel's attention is drawn by Spalanzani (a father-figure) to the eyes, Nathaniel has first caught sight of Olympia: he "stood transfixed; he had only too clearly seen that in the deathly pale waxen face of Olympia there were no eyes, but merely black holes" (Hoffmann, 1982, 304). That these holes abjectly script the maternal body may account for Freud's omission of all reference to them from his account of "The Sandman."

That which is uncanny in the story of the Sandman is this glimpse of maternal alterity that neither Nathaniel nor the reader of Hoffmann's tale were to see. This alterity was to have been wholly replaced by signs of the Father's mechanical creation so that those who encountered Olympia might perceive themselves as fully self-possessed creations of their own efforts. Freud does readily recognize that wrapped up in the uncanny are experiences of doubleness: uncanny reflections in mirrors, shadows, guardian spirits (1955, 233–35). But that which is uncanny in Olympia's mimetic labor is not that she mirrors a castration threat for Nathaniel and the reader. An uncanny reaction to Olympia is not precipitated because they fear that, like her, they will lose the sign of the Law and be blinded (castrated) by it. The uncanny emerges because they dread that when life circumstances draw them to the edges of the signifying order they will be confronted with the fraudulent bases of their own death-work: the black hole of an abyss over which they have attempted to construct themselves.

Thus, in the shadow of a paternal play, is spied that which Freud sought to veil: the maternal markings of the uncanny. When Nathaniel catches sight of Coppola and Spalanzani fighting over Olympia, he identifies with her and against the Father-doubles (1955, 232, n. 1). But he does not fear only for his penis/eyes. His horrified gaze is not fixed on them. Rather, Nathaniel is maddeningly riveted on Olympia and the larger catastrophe her lifeless form with its gaping holes represents. In her, he encounters the abject, and so do we.

This reading of Freud is a cautionary tale: if we move with Kristeva to explore a familiar strangeness in which lessons garnered from reflections on maternal alterity no longer figure prominently, we should not imagine that we have left problematic territory behind. The story of the Sandman suggests the presence of diverse legacies of abjection in the narratives of human lives, in which maternal markings yet shadow emancipating human encounters with an uncanny strangeness. The maternal abject is with us always, even though she is always already veiled.

IV. In Quest of a Strange Politics: Religion, Feminism, Elsewhere?

Ethical inquiry, modeled on the invitation to an analytic encounter which Kristeva has located in her analysis of the stranger, suggests the possibility of new political engagements on behalf of emancipating agency. *Strangers to Ourselves* and *Nations without Nationalism* are Kristeva's initial contributions to such an effort. In these works, Kristeva traces a history of the foreigner in the West. Deconstructing identities, displacing categories, subverting her readers' ease of identity, and returning the uncanny from the ground of repression, Kristeva provokes in her readers, as Oliver astutely observes, "a transference to the place of the stranger" (1993, 151). Made strangers to ourselves by newly hazy categories of native/foreigner and citizen/noncitizen, Kristeva would position us at the signifying bar, there to "conjure the uncanny" (1993, 152). Phantasies of strangeness invite us to engage alterity at multiple levels rather than bound it from us as a known and necessarily refused entity. They invite us to acknowledge the strange and the alien, not as we locate and define it at a distant site, but rather as we claim "the stranger who is always already myself." In claiming that strangeness, Kristeva wagers, we can begin to chart anew the agency of our lives.

If analytic inquiry directs us by means of a politics of strangeness beyond the limits of a sacrificial economy toward forms of death-work that entail nonlethal engagements with the other, in what signifying practices—institutional, social, mythic—can its insights be deployed? Can religion, historically a master specialist in sacrifice, contribute to these new signifying ventures? Can feminists take up a discourse of the stranger and find that it promotes the free agency of women? Kristeva offers options for further inquiry rather than ready answers to these questions. For example, Kristeva makes observations about a tradition of the stranger in Judaism and Christianity which suggest that religion might be able to forward the work of a nonsacrificial economy. Kristeva offers insights also about a dialectic of uncanny strangeness that looks very much like the heretical ethic she previously has associated with a third-generation feminism. In the comments that follow, each of these options are looked at in turn.

In "A New Type of Intellectual: The Dissident," Kristeva observes in psychoanalysis and religion a mimetic bond: mirroring analytic inquiry, religion effects a like posture toward subject-shaping dynamics of negativity: "active dissidence in the face of an all-embracing rationality" (1977, 295). But, if religion is able to participate in those excesses of language which promise to articulate death-work and not submit it to the sacrificial sign or repress its force under the guise of Law, can religion do so with the same subversive acumen that Kristeva attributes to analytic inquiry?

In an interview with Clark and Hulley, Kristeva states that she does not see in the religion she observes around her a radical discourse of the stranger. Of course, Kristeva does allow that religious believers do demonstrate concern for others: for example, Roman Catholic aid organizations offer immigrants educational, moral, and material aid. But Kristeva does not observe that Christians encounter the foreigner as "the other *as other* in the same." Rather, they welcome the foreigner only as "other in the same": only if she or he accepts the moral and cultural codes that make it possible for Christians to say, "You are like us. We accept you" (1990, 164). Thus, Christians tend not to fully deconstruct the question of the other (1990, 163). Notwithstanding the well-meaning attention that they give to the stranger who sojourns in their midst, Christians bypass the uncanny moment in their encounters with others. Repressing labor that must be done at that juncture if they are to elaborate and integrate the uncanny in an analytic ethic, Christians assume an ethical stance that readily can be made to serve a sacrificial agenda. Encouraged to perceive the foreigner as a problem to be managed, Christians may find themselves summoning scapegoats.

Of course, the potential for a praxis of strangeness is never wholly missing from religion. Religion never functions as a pure discourse of sacrifice. Its narrative engagements with the work of negativity are diverse.[14] Indeed, in *Strangers to Ourselves* and *Nations without Nationalism,* Kristeva observes that Judaism and Christianity sometimes engage in a dialectic of strangeness and do not advance an assimilationist ethic that makes space only for the other as the same. At various points in past history, Judaism and Christianity have demonstrated a capacity to dwell in a discourse of radical strangeness which exhibits an attentiveness to the other who *is other* in the same.

Kristeva acknowledges that, in the alliance with God that makes of the Jews a "Chosen People," one can see an orientation toward a sacred nationalism. But choosing to emphasize a different moment in Judaism—a primal inscription of foreignness—Kristeva locates in the narratives of the Hebrew Bible attestations to universalism that elaborate an ethic of the stranger (1991, 66–68). Citing a variety of texts, including those of the prophets that assert the respect due the stranger in his or her intrinsic dignity (1991, 68),[15] Kristeva comments at greatest length on Ruth, the Moabite. Ruth's story, attesting to a time when Jews were forbidden to marry a foreigner (particularly a Moabite), details a period of distress in Judea that leads a Jew to settle in Moab and his sons to marry two Moabite princesses: Ruth and Orpah. After her husband dies, Ruth returns with her mother-in-law, Naomi, to Judea. Marrying again among strangers, Ruth has a child with Boaz. Curiously, the foreign mother—

Ruth—is missing from the story at its end: she is not mentioned in a recitation of the lineage that links Ruth's child, Obed, to David. Nevertheless, preserved in Ruth's story is its sacred strangeness. Ruth reminds us, Kristeva suggests, that "divine revelation requires a disparity, the welcoming of a radical otherness, the acknowledging of a foreignness that one would at first tend to consider the most degraded" (1993, 24).

The story of Ruth suggests an ethic of uncanny strangeness because God works through a Moabite to effect God's relationship with humanity. Moreover, God does not use this woman as a mindless incubator of faith: she is not a cipher or a mere tool of God. Rather, God works through Ruth's active agency: her wisdom, courage, and resourcefulness. All that is special to God about Ruth's distinct humanity are invoked in order that God's presence in the world be affirmed and furthered. Thus, in the uncanny moments of Ruth's life emerge a narrative of Jewish history whose very vitality is indebted to the other *as other* within. Notwithstanding the assimilating tendencies of Judaism—for whom the foreigner (*guer*) is identical with the proselyte (1991, 68)—Judaism may still dwell on moments of its history that Ruth typifies. Ruth's foreign difference preserves within Judaism a memory of an otherness that is other in the same. Her acts recall a sacred difference and a God who is revealed in an uncanny strangeness.

So also does Kristeva observe in the history of Christianity instances when it evinces a like openness to the stranger. She notices, for example, in narratives of Saul/Paul—a Jew and a Christian, a preeminent leader who is always also a stranger—attestations to the creation of *ecclesia* as a community of strangers: merchants, sailors, exiles, sectarian Jews, women. A community of those who reside in the margins—"neither Greek nor Jew, slave nor free, male nor female"—these Christian converts of an itinerant missionary are joined through identification with a new being forged in the passion and resurrection of Christ (1993, 22). If ecclesia accomplishes among its members a certain sameness—generative of an inquisitorial institution's later excesses—Kristeva yet commends Paul's spirit to us. The appeal of ecclesia for the early Christians is not that it becomes for them an alternative polis in which they can set aside prior marginalization and assume central roles. Rather, the constructive import of ecclesia may be traced in the "therapeutics of exile" constituted by Pauline myth (1991, 82). The journey of faith described by Paul, moving between death and life, body and soul, flesh and spirit, articulates the wanderings of a people whose very heterogeneity divides them within themselves before it divides them among others. Ecclesia is born and sustained because these wanderers recognize themselves in Christ, who is himself a stranger on this earth: the mythic codes of death and resurrection, conflict and victory, old self and new creation common to the Pauline narratives establish a space for death-work. Ultimately an analytic discourse, the Pauline journey to faith, undertaken by many, moves through the "splitting that is generative of catastrophic anguish" and reaches home by means of a sojourn with that other who is other in the same. A sacred strangeness—bound by the foreignness of a Jesus who is not of this world—is thus the basis of Paul's ecclesia (1991, 83).

Paul's legacy persists, Kristeva suggests, in the two cities of Augustine. Against a state of oppression, Augustine advocates a pilgrimage to a different space: "you are not from this world but from elsewhere" (1991, 84). Torn from every identity that would offer a resting point, the Christian pilgrim is drawn forward to the boundlessness of *caritas:* a love of the other that is capable of bringing foreigners together. In *caritas* Kristeva sees a new economy: not dependent on the ability of the participants to effect reciprocity in their affairs, it does not turn on the proper adjudication of debt. Instead, *caritas* is an infinite and uncanny currency. Embracing and going beyond every known exchange rate, the magnanimity of *caritas* welcomes foreigners who are joined in community in their very distinction (1991, 84–85).

Of course, the religious bond of which Augustine writes is to collide with the needs of a different economy. Christian hospitality will extend only to the Christian foreigner: wanderers, exiles, and aliens are to be made pilgrims of Christ or experience ostracism and, eventfully, a deadly Inquisition. However, Kristeva's musings do suggest that, were Christianity to dwell more often in the uncanny, to draw on subversive elements in its tradition to journey with the stranger, it might again generate emancipating practices evocative of Pauline ecclesia and Augustinian *caritas.*

That Kristeva locates in Christianity and Judaism an affinity for the politics of strangeness is most suggestive. To the extent that religious myth and ritual become a site for the generation of an analytic space, religion may contribute to an ethic of strangeness. Necessarily, in supporting that ethic, religion should not elaborate a triumphant discourse of Truth. Rather, it should hold to the ambiguities of the analytic stance. Sustaining and elaborating uncertainty, those who journey with strangeness by way of religion should remain attentive to an uncanny that eludes the grasp of a managing reason. For the history of religion has too often been a history of a master narrative that, presuming to know the Truth, has promoted an economy of sacrifice.

And what may be said of feminism? In what ways does analytic inquiry lend itself to feminism's interests? Clair Wills (1992) and Norma Claire Moruzzi (1993) argue that feminists are unwise to turn to Kristeva in the interest of advancing their emancipating goals. Wills doubts that the analytic structures to which Kristeva appeals can support viable challenges to sexism, racism, and colonialism. Indeed, she charges Kristeva with "wilful blindness to issues of racism and colonialism" (1992, 290). Wills asserts that, because Kristeva is attracted to "object-relations theory" (1992, 284), she is fixated on the "individual son's relation to his mother" (1992, 286) and cannot move away from the individual to "theorize the link between the individual and the social group" (1992, 287). As a consequence, she cannot articulate ways in which "my personal experience of separation from my mother" (1992, 285) informs relations with specific others in which difference is culturally particularized. For Kristeva, as Wills reads her, racial and ethnic tensions dissipate in a universal and transhistorical narrative of "individual and inner difference" (1992, 288).

That such differences are irrelevant for Kristeva, Wills argues, is confirmed by Kristeva's analysis of the actions of Meursault in Camus's *L'Etranger.* Mourning a dead mother, Meursault is a French colonial settler in Algeria who is wholly alienated from his surroundings: he takes no comfort in a motherland. When Meursault shoots an Arab, Wills submits that "Kristeva makes the astonishing claim that it is not a matter of importance whether he kills a Frenchman or Maghrebian"(1992, 289). In making this statement, Wills understands Kristeva to assert that it does not matter to her who Meursault kills: "since we are all foreigners, none are any more foreign than others" (1992, 289). Believing that Kristeva's perspective on the stranger is shaped by object-relations theory, Wills attributes to that theory Kristeva's inclination to "dissolve all differences of class, gender and ethnicity within an essential difference" (1992, 290). For Wills, Kristeva subsumes historical instances of alienation and uncanny strangeness under the universal rubric of mother-alienation, as formulated by object-relations theory. On Wills's interpretation, Kristeva believes that, having made that difference-dissolving move, she is exempt from any obligation to articulate an ethics that addresses questions of difference in specific social and historical practices of imperialism, colonialism, racism, and sexism.

Like Wills, Moruzzi is doubtful that a viable feminist political theory issues from Kristeva's work. Faulting Kristeva for her "blithely personal approach," Moruzzi suggests that Kristeva's "emphasis on the psychoanalytic elides the political" (1993, 138). As has Wills, Moruzzi cites Kristeva's commentary on Meursault as prime evidence of her case against Kristeva. According to Moruzzi, Kristeva asserts that, when Meursault shoots someone, the particularities of his target matter little (1993; 138, 140). She writes that the case of Meursault demonstrates that, when Kristeva is "faced with an estrangement that is social and racial, Kristeva resorts to the personal and the (formally) political" (1993, 140). For Moruzzi, Kristeva's effort to address the question of foreigners consequently issues in "soothing mottoes of humanism" (1993, 143) from which are absent considerations of particular differences: specific instances of racism and racial estrangement which mark persons as strangers.

Wills and Moruzzi misread Kristeva. As a consequence, they misjudge the significance of her analytic method for feminist theory and politics. Wills errs when she treats Kristeva's analytic method as a species of object-relations theory, for Kristeva is not interested in patterns of child development on which object-relations theorists focus their attention. As is argued in Chapter 2, where Kristeva's work is distinguished from Chodorow's, the maternal body on which Kristeva focuses is not the "mother" of the Western, capitalist family nor are processes of subject formation that she identifies those that accrue to the "individual" within that family. Kristeva is attuned, instead, to economies of representation, to signifying practices that produce and support specific political, religious, and familial structures. Kristeva directs her analytic method toward these economies in order to attend to moments of crisis within them. She considers the pretensions of those who invest in specific signifying practices as well as the possibilities and risks that accrue to them.

In evaluating these practices, Kristeva is not nor does she claim to be "one who is supposed to know" the truth or untruth of the representations promoted by these investment strategies. Rather, in attending to moments of tension, violence, and conflict that emerge within signifying practices, she exposes as fraudulent and without position the stances of those who purport, on the basis of the status they secure within an economy of representation, to possess the truth. Like Judith Butler, Kristeva intends by this critical gesture a thoroughgoing challenge to identity politics out of which are constructed exclusionary practices, such as racism, sexism, and colonialism. In observing relations of power, Kristeva would concur with Butler's assessment that, notwithstanding the claims of the powerful, "there is no self-identical subject who houses or bears these relations" (Butler, 1993, 230). Identity categories simply do not do the work their advocates expect them to do: the identity they seek is radically uninhabitable (1993, 235).

Kristeva's political engagement with analysis centers on this critical function of exposing the logic of identity that drives economies of representation and historically has established and sustained oppression within them. She wants to acknowledge and protect evocations of difference that are closed off and made unrepresentable within signifying practices. She seeks to challenge mechanisms of exclusion so as to enable subjects to embrace an excess of difference that previously has been bounded off in economies of representation. She believes that evocations of that excess may open these economies to an uncanny difference productive of social change.

Kristeva's analytic method, invoking productive alterity, is oriented toward creating and sustaining conditions that can shelter and support radical strangeness within human community: an other that is an other in the same. Drawing on analysis, Kristeva does not distort difference, treating it in an essentialist or dichotomous manner. Nor is she oblivious to difference. Kristeva understands that the signifying practices she cites in her work are multileveled and complex: they are born of/in/through diverse economic arrangements. Kristeva intends to interrogate these practices in a manner that acknowledges that humans practice absence even as they historically have contested that practice. She hopes to honor the radical uninhabitability of the human habitat so as to preserve its difference and make space within it for strangers. Therefore, notwithstanding Wills and Moruzzi's protests against Kristeva's indifference, Kristeva does maintain interest in diverse exclusions of difference in human society—sexual, religious, national, racial—though not in terms that Wills and Moruzzi would ascribe to her.

For instance, in writing of Kristeva's theory, Moruzzi repeatedly juxtaposes key categories that she assigns to Kristeva. According to Moruzzi, Kristeva contrasts "personal estrangement" with "political and social structures," "personal identity" with "public, political signification," and "private self" with "national, political identity" (1993; 137, 138, 143, 144). But this dichotomizing schema is Moruzzi's, not Kristeva's. Kristeva does not endorse the autonomous subject of humanism in which an other and its social world is always embraced as an afterthought or an addendum in the subject's life. Because, as Oliver rightly notes (1993, 186), the other for Kristeva is always in the subject and original to it—the subject *is* in difference—Kristeva's theory lies at the furthest distance from the solipsistic humanism to which Moruzzi consigns her. Precisely because an otherness of social relation is proper to the subject, Kristeva does not pose political questions dualistically. Kristeva's subject—always, already political—is permanently outside the "self" which is the focus of Moruzzi's concern. As a consequence, in discussing the politics of strangeness, Kristeva evinces a cognizance of a systemic otherness that characterizes the signifying practices of human subjects. Working on that basis, Kristeva attends to socially productive and destructive expressions of that systemic otherness. She considers, in particular, whether the sociality that is constitutive of subjects is invested in sacrificial or nonsacrificial signifying traditions. She assesses the place of the stranger and the hospitality or inhospitality extended to the stranger within these traditions.

Kristeva's treatment of the figure of Meursault offers key evidence for reading her views on the politics of alterity along lines advanced here. Kristeva writes that Meursault is dead to himself: a cold orphan, he is indifferent toward everything (1991, 25, 26). Moreover, his indifference can become criminal because "otherness crystallizes as pure ostracism" (1991, 24) without remainder. Meursault is dangerous because he invests in "a 'we' that is purely Symbolic; lacking a soil it becomes rooted in ritual until it reaches its essence, which is sacrifice" (1991, 24). Whereas Wills and Moruzzi claim that the ethnic identity of the person Meursault murders makes no difference *to Kristeva,* Kristeva actually says that it makes no difference *to Meursault* whom he kills: his "anesthetized indifference to the stranger exploded in the murder of an other" (1991, 26). Kristeva most definitely is not indifferent toward Meursault's indifference. She wants to know what has produced indifference in Meursault. She observes his words: clean, metallic in their accuracy, catching nothing, objects without relief, without shadow (1991, 27). Rather than look inside Meursault for that which might have led him to murder (in order to cite an interiorized problem of the "individual," as Wills has claimed of Kristeva), Kristeva recognizes that Meursault "does not really have an inside" (1991, 26, 28). Meursault resides at the borders of the Symbolic order, invested in its economy but without desire, without memory, without excess, without a feeling for that other which has been bounded off so that he might exist. A creature of the "pure Symbolic," he is a sacrificial machine.

In reflecting on Meursault's anesthetized indifference, Kristeva does not bypass the political; to the contrary, she makes observations with profound political implications. She wonders not only about the constituting conditions for Meursault's indifference, but also about where and how he could be led to assume a stance from which he might be able to consider the particularities of difference anew. A long-time student of signifying practices, Kristeva approaches the case of Meursault as one well versed in the traditional options for meaning that societies have offered their subjects: sacrifice and melancholia. Meursault has the option of a sacrificial stance that recognizes difference because and as it sacrifices it or a melancholic posture that acknowledges difference precisely because it refuses to accept the mechanism for managing difference offered by the Symbolic. But Meursault evidences no engagement with difference in either of these traditional modes. Instead, Kristeva observes a foray by Meursault into a permutation of the sacrificial economy: a signifying venture that produces one who is wholly indifferent to difference. Kristeva's examination of the case of Meursault leads her to ponder the wholly chilling prospect of political engagements undertaken in the absence of an excess of difference that was to bound the sacrificial economy. Kristeva's commentary on Meursault may be "formally political," as Moruzzi has suggested; however, it is nonetheless riveting. With her observations, Kristeva invites her reader to ponder strategies for confronting one who is constitutionally indifferent to difference: how is a sacrificial machine like Meursault to be stopped?

Judith Butler, for one, would remain skeptical about the existence of Meursault outside the pages of literature. She would remind Kristeva that signifying practices, if forcibly produced, are not fully determined by the economies that produce them. The particular differences (race, gender, class) of humans, if assigned to them, are only imperfectly embodied by them. Taking gender as her example, Butler would observe, "to the extent that gender is an assignment, it is an assignment which is never quite carried out according to expectations, whose addressee never quite inhabits the idea s/he is compelled to approximate" (1993, 231). The excess of the norm—its abject—becomes "a site of resistance, the possibility of an enabling social and political resignification" (1993, 231). In general, Kristeva would concur fully with Butler: in *Revolution in Poetic Language,* for example, Kristeva champions that excess of difference and inassimilable alterity—the jouissance and rejection of negativity—that promises social change. But Kristeva recognizes that the case of Meursault represents a sinister disturbance in the portrait of difference that she advances in *Revolution.*

Confronted with Meursault's violence, Kristeva considers implications for society if a space of difference traditionally harbored within the signifying practices of humans is erased. She ponders how one generates an emancipatory politics if economic structures of society are so violated. What if sacrificial machines do exist not only in literature, but also in human experience? The case of Meursault raises as an issue whether colonial economies and other contemporary rites of indifference transpose the work of sacrifice to a new plane, a place from which all reference to difference is absent. It brings to mind Girard's troubling evocation of a world from which are absent persons capable of recognizing a witch hunt as a witch hunt.

Admittedly, Kristeva's own reflections on Meursault are preliminary and incomplete. She does not address why the language of colonialism has so perfectly accommodated the signifying practices of "a pure symbolic." Not investigating these perversely productive possibilities of colonial discourse, she does not discuss how that discourse may have functioned sacrificially, but without remainder, without an excess of the other that would make murder the death of a difference which, to its credit, it previously has acknowledged. But her analysis does not preclude future investigations into the etiology of colonial indifference and the specific virulence of its investments.

Kristeva does successfully highlight a key issue: the alienation of Meursault testifies to prospects for a metamorphosis in the sacrificial economy. That this system, in Meursault's experience, no longer can authenticate its own limits, makes Meursault the negative of the uncanny that announces limits (1991, 26). The case of Meursault leads Kristeva to ponder strategies for the practice of political intervention in a society from which the uncanny is absent. On that count, Kristeva's efforts are a significant contribution to critical reflection on the politics of alterity.

If Kristeva falls short of offering a full explication of the issues she raises, she yet can be credited for framing reflections on the stranger with a series of parameter-marking questions: how are persons to intervene in economies that deny access to a difference that their very limits have previously announced? If colonialism, among other economies, can produce itself so perfectly as to leave no remainder, what means exist to reconnoiter its margins in the interests of subversion? What are the implications for social change in societies populated by Meursaults, the quintessentially dead-ones, whose death-work is wholly mechanical? If no space exists in their feelingless existence for movement, distance, and alterity, will only periodic explosions of violence remain to point to the bulkhead of their "walled in violence" (1991, 29) that, when breached, may momentarily throw a wrench into the workings of these sacrificial machines?

Although Meursault is strangeness carried to its extreme, the uncanny turned outward to become its negative, Kristeva rightly recognizes that the questions posed by his life are endemic to critical analytic work concerning signifying practices of strangeness. She well articulates disturbingly sinister aspects in the life of Meursault which merit further attention. Neither bypassing the political nor addressing the political from a perspective grounded in naive humanism or object-relations theory, as her critics have claimed, Kristeva's probing analysis is altogether disquieting. Rather than dismiss Kristeva, feminist theorists would do well to consider her questions and to seek answers to the provocative questions she has posed.

At the same time, if feminist theorists wish to assess adequately the relation between feminist politics and Kristeva's ethics of alterity, they not only should review the political implications for feminism of Kristeva's analysis of strangeness, they also should assess feminism in light of a Kristevan critique. Can feminism generate a strange politics evocative of a difference that might nurture negativity in all its openness and potential? Should it? Interestingly, that Kristeva poses a challenge to feminism is more likely and more suggestive for feminist theory than that feminism poses a challenge for her.

Kristeva submits that woman, the irrecuperable stranger (1990, 168), the paradigmatic dissident, is always an exile (1977, 296). But, if feminism, in the name of woman, is to generate an emancipating ethic, Kristeva suggests, it must aim at the dissolution of every identity, including its own. If feminism does not root its truth in an open system and clings instead to identity politics, its truth will be abstract and increasingly distant from a political praxis productive of social change. Kristeva submits that, in insisting on the dissolution of feminist identity on behalf of a feminist ethic of emancipation, she is not recommending a politics of sacrifice. An ethics of strangeness is not a sacrificial social code that subjects women to deathly paralysis, scapegoating, or murder. Rather, Kristeva describes the strangeness that she would have feminism embrace as necessarily vital and dynamic. On behalf of that vitality, a strange feminism mandates a "separate vigilance," always "on guard and contestatory" (1990, 168). The productive marginality that Kristeva commends to feminism enables women to explore oppression lucidly, to articulate it analytically, to live the crises of every Imaginative construction rather than to deny them and, as a consequence, become paralyzed by hegemonic investments in a few of them (1990, 169).[16]

Just as Kristeva's deconstructive analysis of religion has attested to a mythos of the stranger in Judaism and Christianity from which they may yet draw an emancipating ethic, so also does Kristeva offer feminism a new myth. For Kristeva, the Greek myth of Io, moon goddess and sacred cow, articulates a narrative of strangeness that may stoke the vigilance of those who sojourn in patriarchy (1990: 169, 171). According to one version of the myth,[17] Io falls in love with Zeus, making an enemy of Hera, his wife, who sends a fly to craze Io and turn her into a cow. Chased from her native land, she becomes foreign, condemned to wander until Zeus decides to touch her (1990, 17). Finding her in Egypt, Zeus soothes her and her madness is eliminated. Among her descendants are the Danaïdes. To the Danaïdes belong a complex history of foreignness and violence. Born outside of Greece, they do not speak the language and, to the Greeks, their customs are unknown (1991, 44). Refusing to marry their cousins, in the most dramatic renderings of the myth, they murder them. These murders mark, in the Greek mind, a transition from endogamous to exogamous social relations: a transition underlain by violence (1991, 45). The Danaïdes articulate the violence that underlies the marriage bond, preserving its history as a pact between strangers. Thus, the Danaïdes carry water for Hera—symbolizing the domestic household—and participate in the cultic ceremonies of Demeter, during which blood, not water, is poured.

Kristeva includes this story in her book of the stranger, she suggests, because elaborated in the Greek mythical consciousness at the very intersection of political strangeness and estrangement between men and women is both the work of sacrifice—generative of political and social bonds—and the uncanny strangeness that precipitates it (1990, 171): Io, cow and moon; the Danaïdes, water and blood. In Greek myth, Kristeva sees retained the structure of an analytic inquiry. In myth, she detects an effort to articulate the violence and abject strangeness that is at the very heart of human origins. In attesting to that which is *unheimlich,* in and among us, myth facilitates the catharsis rather than repression of that consciousness (1990, 171).

On one level, the myth of Io does speak of sacrifice. But on another, the myth of Io is evocative of a "lunar identity" that Kristeva attributes to women and on which she suggests that women may draw, so as to preserve within every community that part which is essentially unreconcilable, that which "keeps groups from closing up, from becoming homogeneous and oppressive" (1990, 168). According to Robert Graves, Io, in the tradition of the Argives, is both a cow and the moon goddess. Changing her colors—as do the new moon, harvest moon, and waning moon (white, red, black)—Io, the cow, is also the moon goddess in her three stages: maiden, nymph, and crone (1955, 192). To Io, the moon goddess, change and transformation are intrinsic, in contrast to the Sun of identity. Io brings to expression both an inevitable foreignness—common to those who always will wander far from home and among strangers—and the uncanny within. In her mythic persona is glimpsed the persistent temporal displacement of one who never *is* but who appears only in process and to whom absence from the position in which she is to be found is intrinsic to her very existence.

If to a sacrificial economy belongs the myth of Oedipus, so too to an analytic economy of strangeness belongs the myth of Io. Each myth preserves a story of origins. Each serves to frame the vicissitudes of the human journey. Each attests to the necessary death-work that shapes human experience. In notable contrast to the investment strategies of a sacrificial economy, the discursive labor to which the myth of Io and analysis attest points toward a nonprojective engagement with the vicissitudes of one's life: one's life-sentences. By means of such a labor one may build expressive spaces in which to embrace an otherness that is both one's own and that of one's cultural heritage. Constructing such open, undecidable spoken spaces (1987a, 380–82), one may act in ways that elaborate one's history nonviolently. Conceiving one's life as a "work in progress" (1987a, 380) and embracing the foreigner that one always already is, one may cease to create scapegoats. One may invest in politics as a practice of strangeness.

In contributing to this praxis, feminists need to record the division in being that humans are and to reject as symptoms all totalizing interpretations that would remove human subjects from the crisis of being: their strangeness to themselves. Thus, the vigilance Kristeva would commend to feminism and to other forms of emancipatory politics entails a resolution to "dissolve and displace indefinitely all claims to self-mastery temporarily and for a lifetime" (1981, 319). Recording the crisis, holding to the questions rather than to the answers, persisting with the interrogative stance in order to displace all suppositions in favor of an uncanny experience of dispossession from oneself and one's truths, welcoming an other who is other in the same, these tasks of analytic inquiry may also be the tasks of feminists.

But, if women are permanent strangers, feminists will not acknowledge the appellation most fruitfully if they embrace it as the summa of a feminist truth; rather, they may bear the appellation best if they welcome irrecuperable strangeness as an unexpected provision to carry with them on their journey to emancipation. Not resting easily on their shoulders, the uncanny words that make them strangers to themselves are not properly theirs as feminists. Indeed, they may seem incongruous to feminists who are accustomed to seeking ready answers to their inquiries on behalf of women's emancipation. Even so, the ingathering of strangeness in an uncanny discourse yet may be found, Kristeva wagers, not to burden women, as has the sacrificial contract of patriarchy, but to move them forward on their journey. The practices of uncanny strangeness that Kristeva commends to others, perceived by feminists who receive them as problematic provisions precisely because they cannot be purchased with a currency recognized by any existing political economy, do not necessarily constitute starvation wages. Rather, their very strangeness may serve as testimony to the nourishment feminists can find in them: after all, they seek, in questing for emancipation, a world whose mores, culinary customs, and economy are now foreign. Uncanny—somehow also familiar—the provisions of analytic inquiry and a practice of strangeness which Kristeva would offer feminists may yet prove sustaining.

Moreover, the practice Kristeva describes can be commended to all who wish to embark on a journey to a less violent world. Undertaking such a venture, we would turn toward the uncanny. Neither suppressing nor exiling it, we would articulate its strangeness. Of course, our efforts would not promise to establish us in the truth. Nevertheless, in invoking an ethic of uncanny strangeness, we yet might find ourselves more able to reside as strangers among strangers and to do so less violently.

NOTES

1. Introduction

1. News accounts regularly inform us of a global landscape of violence inclusive of women murdered by partners and spouses, women killed in war zone rape camps, and women victimized by Internet pornography. However, that women are victims of violence *as women* often is ignored. Newspaper accounts of the 1989 Montreal massacre of 14 female students at the Ecole Polytechnique are a most telling example. Although Marc Lépine separated men from women before shooting and shouted, "the women here are a bunch of feminists," no news accounts described his actions as a crime against women. By contrast, the massacre of Israeli athletes at the Olympic Games in 1972 was treated as a deliberate act of terrorism against the Israeli people. In Montreal, Lépine's motives were wholly removed from a social context. Because he was "mad," his actions were senseless, and, in the absence of sense, those who possessed reason (reporters and their public) would find no grounds for his choice of victims (Bertrand, 1991).

2. A greater clarity in feminist conversations about psychoanalytic feminism is called for also in respect to the frequent charge of class and race bias. When feminist theorists address sociohistorical behaviors, they surely are remiss if their accounts privilege white, middle-class women of European descent. However, that psychoanalytic feminists appeal to transhistorical structures to advance claims about oppression which are distinct from those focused on the sociohistorical circumstances of women's lives does not immediately make them vulnerable to the charge of bias. Rather, only if psychoanalytic feminists fail to forge links between these structures and the diversity of women's lives should the criticism stand. Too often, critics of psychoanalytic feminism conflate these two foci, dismissing psychoanalytic feminists' claims out of hand. Critics would pursue a more constructive approach were they to ask that the proponents of psychoanalytic feminism initially defend these structures in their own right and subsequently indicate how they establish links between the transhistorical structures they invoke and the diverse social and cultural circumstances of women's lives.

3. This reading of Kristeva is aligned with the new Kristeva criticism exemplified by Oliver (1993, 1993a) and articulated also by Chanter (1993), Crownfield (1992), Elliot (1991), Kearns (1993), McAfee (1993), Prosser MacDonald (1995), and Ziarek (1992, 1993). These readers persuasively counter a received feminist tradition on Kristeva developed in the previous decade, which, in the majority, saw in her work an essentialist theory of a precultural feminine to be dismissed. By contrast, these newly appreciative readers offer a *nonessentialist* reading of Kristeva that reestablishes her significance for feminist theory. Readers wholly unfamiliar with the category of sexual difference employed by the new Kristeva critics, which they take to be nondichotomous, may find that Moira Gatens's "A Critique of the Sex/Gender Distinction" (1991)

is a most helpful introduction. Although Gatens does not speak of Kristeva, she refutes charges of a politically problematic essentialism directed against feminist theorists of sexual difference and offers a particularly succinct and clear explanation of why the sex/gender distinction favored by feminist theorists such as Nancy Chodorow leads to agency-effacing dualism.

4. Kristeva assigns a similar role to art. Because my scholarship is in the field of religion, religion is emphasized in this project. However, in *Over Her Dead Body: Death, Femininity, and the Aesthetic,* Elisabeth Bronfen engages Kristeva to pursue objectives that, paralleling those of this project, focus on art rather than religion.

5. Notable exceptions include Daly (1978), Carlson Brown and Bohn (1990), Nakashima Brock (1991,1990), Fortune (1990), and Williams (1993).

2. Kristeva in Context

1. A jumbled chaos of sensory experience, the Imaginary of human infancy is framed in terms of a maternal/infant dyad. The Imaginary does not end with the accession of that infant to the world of language and ordered experience, for it both precedes and coexists with the organized world of language. The term *Imaginary* rightly brings to mind phantasmatic elements. For the human infant, the tumult of sensory images comprises these elements. In the wake of the human infant's development of language, the Imaginary is phantasmatic in a different sense. The Imaginary enables the human subject to mark imagined alternatives to relations in the world produced by language, relations that, among other things, promise a unity of being. Lacan and Kristeva concur that the subject's access to that unity is forever precluded by the alienating structures of language.

2. Lacan notes that this Law is inscribed in the social order in the *name of the Father.* This concept is associated with Freud's *Totem and Taboo,* which tells of the initiation of subjects to the Symbolic order. The Father of the Law is not known empirically nor by means of the Imaginary. Rather, the *name of the Father* functions within the signifying economy to signify the binding of subjects to lack, which is the Father's (1968, 41).

3. To illustrate his point, Lacan describes a train arriving at a station, in which a little boy and girl are seated face to face next to the window. Observing the buildings along the station platform as the train pulls to a stop, the boy says, "Look, we're at Ladies." The girl says, "Idiot, can't you see we're at Gentlemen" (1977, 152). Their immediate situation depicts the metaphysics of representation: a word signifies a thing. Their confidence in their location and in its meaning marks the confidence of classic correspondence theories of truth. Even so, through the material given that they are seated on one side of the train compartment or the other, limiting and shaping their respective visions, each child is placed in a structure that dictates what will count as meaning for each. This story reminds us that the meaning of sexual difference is constituted in a signifying chain and that we are "held in train" to the culture created by that process prior to our arrival at any of the stations of our lives.

4. Under the sign of Oedipus, as interpreted by Lacan, heterosexual men give meaning to the phallus when they play the role of appearing to *have* the phallus (they mirror the other's desire for completion and accept that the desire ends with them). Heterosexual women play a role of *being* the phallus: in their own mirroring role, they

constitute the end toward which male desire has aimed. This dialectic of sexual difference circles having and being: I have myself (my desire finds its goal) when the other says "you are" (Kearney, 1986, 275; Lechte, 1994, 69).

5. Kristeva's notion of negativity is influenced by Derrida's *grammé*. Meaning—as a function of literary texts or intertextual practices of human lives (1990, 175)—is understood by Kristeva as an act of creative dissolution. Just as, on Derrida's account of *grammé,* that which is not marked is implicated in the act of inscription, so also is meaning that accrues in our acts linked inseparably with that which is absent or refused. In subverting the logic of identity, the *grammé* is the analog of a subject always already in process whose agency is harbored in acts of productive dissolution.

6. I discuss the association of negativity with culture-producing and community-building labor in Chapter 3 and in Sections III and IV of Chapter 7.

7. Not every crisis precipitates boundary failure as described by Kristeva. However, violence against women is symptomatic of boundary failure. Violence against women mandates assessment not only in terms of economic, political, and social factors, which contribute to the victimization of women, but also in terms of transhistorical processes on which Kristeva focuses in her account of boundary-failure.

8. Marks are distinguished from signs. Marks are associated with Kristeva's notions of negativity and alterity, and with the semiotic traces that found signs. Abject marks are traced to the maternal body (e.g., bodily fluids, alimentary motifs, refuse). Signs are associated with the world of the Symbolic order and its language system. Although this distinction may initially appear forced, in the course of the extended presentation of Kristeva's theory in Chapters 3 and 4, its saliency is demonstrated.

9. Patriarchy has disappeared from the lexicons of many feminist theorists. It is condemned as a falsely universalizing concept that, as Judith Butler observes, "overrides or reduces distinct articulations of gender asymmetry in different cultural contexts" (1990, 35). But, when this term is employed here, only one articulation of gender asymmetry is referenced: that associated with a sacrificial economy. When human societies inscribe sexual difference as a resolution of the crisis of an original separation and loss that accompanies the human apprenticeship to language and culture *and* under threat of loss and renewed crisis, draw on that difference once again, preferentially invoking women's bodies in violent resolution of that crisis, they create patriarchy.

10. Notwithstanding limits on our field of vision, we can muse about links between sexual difference and death-work. Is sexual difference exclusive to the sacrificial economy or would subjects in a nonsacrificial economy signify it also? If they did, what would be its features? The historical centrality of sexual difference to articulations of human subjectivity suggests that sexual difference would persist in a nonsacrificial economy. Subjects would continue to find in articulations of sexual difference a means to express living-at-a-loss. Nevertheless, sameness and difference among subjects would no longer be read in terms of threat, as they have been in the sacrificial economy that is patriarchy. Enacting death-work—jouissance *and* rejection—across the breadth of the economic continuum of negativity rather than ossifying on one aspect of that continuum, subjects could sustain, elaborate, and celebrate increasingly fluid and diverse modes of sexual difference.

Anticipating such a future, in *Tales of Love,* Kristeva offers a radically historicized treatment of sexual difference. She associates patterns of erotic expression that have been dominant in Western history with the construction of a particular form of psychic space "at the waning of the Ancient world with the advent of the Christian era" (1987a, 376). Observing that this psychic space has been the prison of the body for two millennia and that its warden, Christianity, is now enfeebled, Kristeva recommends against the permanent institutionalization of erotic histories which that order promoted. Rather than "repair the father" and "soothe the mother," she advises persons to depart from the traditional enclosure of the psyche (known since Freud as the house of Oedipus). In a new place, subjects would articulate the possibilities of difference, rather than the threat, and learn to "speak and write themselves in unstable, open, undecidable, polyvalent spaces" (1987a, 379–80).

11. Kristeva can justify her decision to typify the space of origin as maternal on heuristic grounds as well. The movement of subject-differentiation is misconstrued if the matrix in which that movement transpires is primarily associated with a subject. Were Kristeva to have spoken of a "matrix of origin" or a "presubject matrix," she might have misrepresented the place of the subject in her account, granting credence to the very phantasy of being she would expose. By contrast, the "maternal matrix" all but renders invisible the subject and its pretenses. Therefore, it nicely underscores one of Kristeva's major themes: the founding dispossession of the subject from itself. Anticipated also by this term is the subject's fear of an annihilating submersion in the other, which Kristeva's narrative will render in acute relief.

12. Alternatives to the sacrificial economy are explored in Chapters 3 and 7. However, brief reflections on the limits of the sacrificial economy in respect to maternity are appropriate at this juncture. Would the maternal matrix still be maternal if death-work did not transpire in a sacrificial economy? This reading of Kristeva suggests that, in a nonsacrificial economy, subjects would continue to reference the maternal matrix, but would do so differently. Because death-work is *the* human task, uncertainty, ambiguity, and threat of loss always shadow the subject. Perpetually at risk, subjects are likely always to have reason to recall the abject material circumstances of their origin. But in a nonsacrificial economy subjects could undertake boundary work with a new flexibility and tolerance before the ambiguity of their circumstances. Pursuant to their efforts to secure and resecure position in the world, they could attest in nonlethal ways to the matrix of origin. After all, within the sacrificial economy, subjects' escalating rage correlates with increasing threats to their phantasmatic investments: believing that they *possess the solution* to death-work in the person of the Mother, they become ever more fixed and unyielding in that belief to the extent that the circumstances of life give the lie to their claims on Her. In a nonsacrificial economy, subjects could release their death-grip on the Mother. Articulating and bearing the loss that they are, they would not deny it by virulently projecting it elsewhere. The mechanism for projection, which patriarchy has sustained and elaborated, could be retooled, breaking the links between death-work, sacrifice, and maternally marked victims.

On a different count, the reading of Kristeva advanced here suggests a flexibility on her part toward that which would count as maternal in the maternal matrix of a future economy. Alimentary motifs predominate among markings of the maternal as a matter of human history: the mouth always has been central to nascent subjects' acquisition of a world. If modes of primary, material commerce with the world among humans were to change (e.g., if evolutionary mutations made the mouth an extraneous orifice; if innovations in medical technology such as nutritional patches rendered the mouth obsolete as a pathway for nourishment), alimentary patterns would fade from prominence in evocations of the maternal matrix. *Marks* of the maternal vary with human history; *basic movements* in the corporeal mapping of the maternal matrix do not: the human subject always comes to be where it is not.

13. Critics of Kristeva who treat her as a social constructionist include Meyers (1992), Jones (1985), Doane and Hodges (1992), and Grosz (1994). Critics who believe that Kristeva consigns resources for human agency to a region wholly outside culture include Butler (1990), Cornell/Thurschwell (1987), and Fraser (1992).

14. At first glance, Grosz's description of Kristeva as a social constructionist is puzzling, for, in *Sexual Subversions* (1989), Grosz attends carefully to Kristeva's notions of drive theory, the semiotic, and the abject. Grosz notes the "chaotic, libidinally oriented semiotic" that has a capacity to "overflow its symbolic boundaries and transform the character of the symbolic unities themselves" (1989, 68). These themes should suggest to Grosz a species of "embodied subjectivity" or "psychical corporeality" that Grosz herself advocates in *Volatile Bodies* (1994, 22). Even so, neither in *Volatile Bodies* nor in *Sexual Subversions* does Grosz acknowledge that Kristeva challenges the sex/gender dichotomy. Instead, she construes Kristeva's work in polarized terms.

15. Continuing and broadening her criticism of Kristeva in *Bodies that Matter,* Butler similarly objects to Kristeva's strategy for enhancing emancipating agency. Because "sex" is always a reiteration of hegemonic norms produced by specific cultural configurations of power, "the radical divide" from which theorists such as Kristeva would attempt to mount political resistance unwittingly protects the Law (1993, 106–107).

16. Butler also cites Kristeva's comments on poetry as evidence of Kristeva's association of agency with a precultural, maternally oriented, libidinal economy of the body. But, Butler misreads Kristeva. For example, when Kristeva looks at the poetry of Mallarmé and Lautréamont, she does not observe in their poetry appeals to an archaic, libidinous process of jouissance that, predating the Law and its power, brokers subversion from without. Their poetry does not evince a prepaternal utopia organized by dictates of a maternal law of the body. In the state-dominated, bourgeois society that is home to these poets, maternity is fully contained within its borders *as a determinant category of its own creation.* The only maternal presence is phallic. Therefore, Kristeva views their work as a fetish-exposing permutation of the Symbolic from within, not dissimilar to a performativity that Butler commends as a practice of agency. Radically decentering and shattering all claims to mastery, their poetry is *a site of struggle* between heterogeneity and mastery and an act of creative dissolution (1984c, 216).

17. Differences between Kristeva and Butler are illustrated when a Kristeva-inspired account of Nella Larsen's *Passing* is contrasted with Butler's. In this story, Irene and Clare are "light-skinned Negroes" (1969, iv). Irene has built a solidly upper-middle-class life with her husband and sons in 1920s New York and has projected all risks outside the boundaries of her world and onto the figure of Clare, who is playing a dangerous game of passing as white. Notwithstanding Irene's self-possessed stance within the text, the fragility of her world is repeatedly attested to by Clare's mirroring-function within the text. As a consequence, the violent conclusion of the story—Clare plunges to her death from a window in a Harlem apartment, on her white husband's discovery of her deception—is enacted at several levels of meaning. On the one hand, within the Symbolic order, Clare's death signifies the reassertion of the white Law in all its violent hegemony. But another level of meaning in the text is enacted by Larsen's deathly allusions to Irene. The lethally violent denouement of the story is expressed not only by Clare's death, but also by Irene's mental breakdown: they are mimetic doubles

to the end. If Clare loses everything to the policeman (object-warden) of the Symbolic order, Irene loses everything to its vandal (the abject). Of the two threats, the latter may be more menacing. For Clare is killed by that which she knows and knowingly rejects: white racism implicated in heterosexual marriage bonds. But Irene's "death" takes her wholly by surprise: when the world Clare and Irene have shared collapses, an abject darkness wells up to envelop and drown Irene (1969, 216).

18. For example, in one of Butler's most extended commentaries on violence—a discussion of the mutilation and murder of Venus Xtravaganza, a Latino man who passes as a light-skinned woman in *Paris Is Burning* (1993, 129–33)—violence is displaced from a perpetrator onto a linguistic order, rendering him all but invisible. Venus's killing "is performed by a symbolic that would eradicate those phenomena that require an opening up of the possibilities for the resignification of sex" (1993, 131). Although Venus crosses gender, sexuality, and race—"talking back" to those discourses that proclaim hegemony over her, normative discourses of femininity and whiteness "cross out that prior crossing," becoming "an erasure that is her death" (1993, 133). In the absence of references to a material agent of violence, Butler's commentary is uncomfortably reminiscent of police reports that state a woman was battered "by a lead pipe" or hit on the head "by a stick with a nail in it" (Jones, 1994).

3. The Subject of Psychoanalysis

1. These images are not privileged examples, for nothing in Kristeva's writing warrants treating these cases as "essential" markers of negativity. Instead, each example should be evaluated on its pedagogical merits: they are valuable to the extent that reflection on them facilitates our efforts to attend to a broad expanse of materiality as it is spied in a moment of turning to become bound space. These examples enable us to affirm, with Kristeva, that, *in the very marking of a bounded space, an "I" is born.*

2. Kristeva does not privilege or treat the female breast as essential. Any marking, interruption, scission, or movement in the undifferentiated buccal space of the human infant which establishes that buccal space as social can teach the lessons of mimesis. Consequently, that aspect of her discussion of orality which is crucial to her theory is not its historically and culturally specific content, but its dynamic, which displays in rudimentary form the pathway the human subject takes in its acclimation to the world. That these two aspects—the path and its historically and culturally specific contours—are, from the vantage point of the Symbolic, perceived as one (with pernicious consequences for those whose bodies are marked in culture as Mother), is addressed in detail in the chapters to follow.

3. Irigaray claims that her account of emerging subjectivity applies only to the male child. However, such a restricted field of application is not intended here. For Kristeva, the fort/da game draws our attention to the context of the Imaginary, to an emerging subjectivity in transition to the Symbolic. The dynamics cited here move the subject toward sexual differentiation which is proper to the Symbolic; however, they do not presuppose sexual difference, as Irigaray's comments suggest.

4. Among feminist theorists, Teresa Brennan is notable for joining Kristeva in attending closely to drive theory. In *The Interpretation of the Flesh* (1992), Brennan advances a theory of psychical energy which has strong affinities with Kristeva's drive theory. Her argument is offered in its richest from in that work. A more accessible

summary of Brennan's theory of the "fleshly logic" of the drives is found in Chapter 3 of her *History after Lacan* (1993, especially 102–13).

4. In Search of the Mother in Mimesis

1. Indeed, the direction of Kristeva's thought in *Revolution in Poetic Language* underscores her contention. There, Kristeva's comments on sacrifice precede her extended theoretical commentary on negativity and drive theory. Kristeva's theory of the drives and her nuanced exploration of the forces of negativity in a signifying economy represent an effort to analyze something which previously has come to light for Kristeva in the course of examining cultural practices in the Symbolic order: a widespread human fascination by and ambivalent regard for the status of their origins.

2. Significantly, although Kristeva claims that human interest in returning to the site of the thetic break to interrogate and resecure the boundaries of the Symbolic order is not specific to either sex, she does observe that the commitment to focus one's research so intently on this human interest may be found most often among women analysts such as Melanie Klein and herself (1987a, 373). I attribute Kristeva's claim to her concern about the prominent role played by the female body when parties to the Symbolic are forced, under threat of loss, to reiterate exercises in bounding and mastery that brought them to the Symbolic. Consequently, in distinction from their male colleagues' relative disinterest in subject-bounding exercises, when women analysts make the sexual difference that marks this exercise the focus of their reflective inquiries, they are motivated, as Patricia Elliot cogently observes, by a "deeply rooted desire to refuse victimization" (1991, 208).

3. In pursuing a conversation between Girard and Kristeva, I draw on and extend Kristeva's own commentary on Girard. Although John Lechte has attributed the theme of sacrifice in Kristeva's work to the influence of Bataille (1990, 74), Girard figures prominently, and not only in *Revolution in Poetic Language* (1984c; 249, n. 91; 250, n. 100). His work is cited also in *Powers of Horror* (1982; 213, n. 4; 215, n. 17) and in "Women's Time" (1981a, 213, n. 21). The consistency with which Kristeva invokes the name of Girard when she is talking about sacrificial theory and her detailed knowledge of his work suggests the position I am advancing here has strong precedents in Kristeva's work. Michael Payne confirms my assessment in citing Girard's influence on Kristeva's sacrificial theory (1993, 182). At the same time, I do not disavow Bataille's influence on Kristeva. I find suggestive Suzanne Guerlac's observation that Kristeva draws on Bataille in her formulation of negativity. In describing the mechanism of agency (*signifiance*) that accrues to the subject who performs death-work, Kristeva notes that it entails both the production and pulverization of signifying positions in which the subject has previously found itself. Her description is indebted to Bataille's economy of expenditure (1993, 246–47).

4. Mimesis in the first instance is acquisitive, in the second conflictual. Acquisitive mimesis is contagious: if a number of individuals polarize around a single object, in the wake of intensifying mimesis, the object will disappear. It will be replaced by conflictual mimesis, which will snowball in its effects (1987, 26).

5. Kristeva (1984c, 177; 1987a, 375) and Girard (1977, 188) agree that the familial drama which scripts object-desire is not only secondary to prerepresentational mimeticism, but also historically specific. Far from being a universal drama, patterns

of erotic rivalry of which Freud wrote (and hypostatized in the Oedipal complex) are a peculiar product of Western European patterns of social differentiation, which were most acute at their point of breakdown in the late nineteenth century (Webb, 1988, 188). Girard and Kristeva concur that, by contrast, mimetic conflict remains a pervasive phenomenon in human experience which still mandates our attention.

6. As Hamerton-Kelly observes, Girard stands within the tradition of Durkheim in his understanding of religion as "the primary expression of the power that forms society, and ritual as the essence of religion" (1994, 15). The power of religion derives from "what it has said in real terms to human beings concerning what must and must not be done in a given cultural context, in order to preserve tolerable human relations within the community" (Girard, 1987, 42). As a consequence, Girard does not make the exchange of gifts central to his theory of sacrifice; instead, he locates substitutionary violence at its core. His thought contrasts also with Eliade, who makes myth rather than ritual central to religion and believes that "the word precedes the deed and myth goes before ritual" (1994, 16).

7. Akin to the engram cited by Kristeva, the victim as signifier stands at the margins of the Symbolic order. Not contained within a signifying system of differential opposition (a and not-a), the iterative practice of the victim, as Girard describes it, is "uniquely dynamic and genetic. . . . It offers itself as . . . the single trait that stands out against a confused mass or still unsorted multiplicity" (1987, 100). As in games of chance (e.g., drawing straws or finding a bean in the Epiphany cake), this primal sign distinguishes only *one* (the straw or bean); *the rest remain indeterminate* (1987, 101). Although in her discussion of the engram, Kristeva does not invoke its connection with the sacred, on all other counts, Kristeva's commentary on the initial bounding work of subjects which opens up a space to be (the one . . . the rest remaining indeterminate) could not more closely parallel Girard's.

8. Heretofore, we have seen that Kristeva describes the primary referent in the archaic experience of the subject as the maternal body or matrix. Now, she speaks of the Imaginary Father and the parents of prehistory. With all of these terms, Kristeva directs her attention toward a common phenomenon. Not intending to speak of fathers and mothers named in signs and known empirically, Kristeva wishes to highlight a process of emergent subjectivity undertaken at the borders of language which, if subject to language, is not coterminous with it. Admittedly, Kristeva's vocabulary can be confusing. Some wonder whether they can locate the maternal body in culture or if it falls wholly outside of culture. Others are confounded by distinctions between parents of prehistory and parents of culture (e.g., their own moms and dads). I suggest that puzzlement before Kristeva's terminology actually is instructive. That we are uncertain where we stand with Kristeva's terms reminds us that all language about negativity associated with emergent subjectivity is only approximate. We truly have no access to a site that would position us to grasp that to which these terms allude: the death-work by which we come to be in the world.

9. Kristeva and Girard share a notion of positive mimesis or the constructive aspects of death-work. Because I focus only on that aspect of Girard's work that illuminates Kristeva's sacrificial theory, I do not elaborate on these parallels. However, Girard does describe mimesis as a cohesive force (1987, 17) and "the basis of heroism, devotion to others and . . . some kind of divine grace" (1993, 23–25). Also, Girard's notion of interindividuality may be likened to Kristeva's intertextual practices. His appeal to a nonsacrificial ethic (e.g., 1986, 1987) in the Christian gospels has affinities with Kristeva's ethic of strangeness (see Chapter 7 below) and helpfully augments her

relatively brief comments on a nonsacrificial ethic and Christianity (1991). Readers with interests in feminist theory may find suggestive Nowak's comments on the implications of positive mimesis in Girard for feminist theory (1994). They may also find Teresa Brennan's work insightful. In discussing ego formation in *The Interpretation of the Flesh* (1992, 202–206), Brennan offers a portrait which has strong affinities with the notion of positive mimesis sketched here. Brennan's concept of the "protective shield," which exists from the earliest period of psychical life, parallels Kristeva's concept of the Imaginary Father. So also does Brennan's notion of an "affectional current," which she associates with the protective shield and distinguishes from erotic desire ordered by the phallus, appear quite similar to Kristeva's notion of the "gift of love."

10. Girard cites also as a factor in human violence the role of adrenaline, "which is necessary at a critical moment in the hunt." Were this adrenaline to be released within the human community, on occasions other than hunting, it would account for the introduction of lethal forms of violence into that community (1987, 85). But high-energy hunting is not unique to humans. Animals expend adrenaline when they hunt (perhaps more so than humans who can rely on traps and lures to capture prey); yet, they do not regularly attack their own kind. Another explanation of the human propensity for murder appears necessary.

11. These distinctions are illustrated in Kristeva's and Girard's commentaries on the fort/da game. Against Lacan, they share a view that the nascent subject's struggle is sacrificial. But only Kristeva makes central to her vision of sacrifice *the way* in which Ernst, the subject of the fort/da game, enacts sacrifice, invoking not only his body but that of the Mother. Although, like any small child, Ernst certainly is capable of adrenaline-driven rage, he does not quickly dispense with the Mother/reel. Lingering over its "death," his contest is deliberate and prolonged. He relishes with his mouth the metaphorical dismemberment—in sounds that reverberate between his teeth—of his mimetic foe.

12. The reader may note my qualification of Kelly Oliver's assertion (1993, 61) that the subject of *Powers of Horror* is always male. Kristeva states in an interview (1980a, 136) that "the abject is a category which cuts across the two sexes." Even so, *Powers* does offer compelling evidence that men, more than women, have availed themselves of opportunities to mobilize the vast resources of cultural institutions to battle the abject; by contrast, although Kristeva does express concern, in her essay on Duras in *Black Sun* (1989), that the West is shaped increasingly by a discourse of suicide, the narrative of implosive violence, more common to women's lives, does not seem to have been "writ large" in culture on a scale as massive as that of the narrative of sacrifice. That the implosive violence of melancholia leads to a withdrawal from the Symbolic may account for the predominance of sacrificial rather than suicidal themes in cultural institutions and for the virtual impunity with which the sign of sacrifice is inscribed on women against their will (*à leur corps défendant* [1981a; 212, n. 17]). More detailed feminist analyses of *Black Sun* are needed, especially those that, in tracing the work in culture and on women's bodies of the narrative of suicide, thematize power. Perhaps the narrative of melancholia is a permutation of the narrative of sacrifice. Were the latter narrative to be weakened and broken open, would the former persist?

13. Girard indicates that alimentary and sexual prohibitions featured in *Totem and Taboo* are in some sense identical, even though the banned objects differ. Dissenting from Marxist, psychoanalytic, and structuralist accounts of these prohibitions, he

suggests that they reflect mimetic rivalries (1987, 75–76). Overall, Kristeva would concur with Girard's assessment; however, she would assert that the mimetic context these prohibitions share is shaped by an abject maternal referent. Indeed, alimentary markers are prime indicators of the maternal abject (1982, 76).

14. Kristeva's attention to ritual underscores her recognition that sacrifice is among the most extreme and visceral of gestures by means of which humans would subject the conditions of their existence to representation, order, and control when the extant thetic resources of the Symbolic order prove inadequate. Less drastic, but still more compelling than are the interdictory edicts offered on behalf of social order by the Symbolic, are the many sacrificial substitutes (e.g., pollution rituals) which provide for the ritual replication of human origins and consequently enable humans to manage the legacy of violence deeded to them by their birth. Humans turn consistently to ritual—often marked with alimentary themes—to bound their communities and themselves against the threat posed by an order-defying and polluting menace.

15. Although situated in a culture in which the religion of Christianity was a dominant force, the instances cited here have a significance for sacrificial theory not restricted to that context. The women discussed here have not been selected because their experiences witness to unique events in history nor because a sacrificial theory of sexually differentiated violence can be traced only in those societies in which the discursive practices that feature a sacrificial pattern are proper to religion. These women and their tragic circumstances do not exhibit a singular quality as instances of sacrifice. Rather, they have been selected because, when we set out to learn how to recognize patterns of sacrifice, we may more readily trace those patterns in times and cultures which are not our own: our own lived investment in contemporary culture may preclude us from detecting patterns of sacrifice that we could observe more readily were we to approach them at a distance. The cases cited here have been selected also because, in those societies in which religion functions as a dominant cultural discourse, religion promotes a more direct and honest engagement with the cultural work of sacrifice than is the case when the work of sacrifice is transposed elsewhere. As Kristeva has recognized, few discourses in the West speak of sacrifice with the clarity that Christianity did when it was a dominant discourse of that culture. Finally, these instances have been chosen because we are able to make a case for a sacrificial theory, most economically and succinctly, when we refer to those historical moments when a sacrificial pattern is most unambiguously present in women's lives. In fact, if a sacrificial theory does not appear credible on that count, sacrificial analyses of more complex discursive practices will prove even more daunting.

5. "This Is My Body"

1. This section is indebted to Caroline Walker Bynum's research on late-medieval holy women. The constructive position advanced here complements hers. However, the reader should note that Bynum, as a historian, stands at some distance from the kind of theoretical reflections that frame this discussion of the late-medieval mystics.

2. These criteria, as summarized by Bell, include: 1) onset prior to age twenty-five; 2) lack of appetite accompanied by loss of at least 25 percent of original body weight; 3) a distorted, implacable attitude toward eating that overrides hunger, admonitions, reassurance, and threats. This attitude may include denial of illness, apparent enjoyment of losing weight with overt manifestation that refusing food is a pleasurable

indulgence, and an unusual handling or hoarding of food; 4) no known medical illness that could account for weight loss; 5) no other known psychiatric disorder; 6) at least two of the following: amenorrhea, lanugo, bradycardia, periods of overactivity, bulimia, and vomiting (1985, 2–3). As indicated in Section III of this chapter, although these criteria are rightly descriptive of self-imposed starvation, Bell's psychoanalytic framework of explanation is inadequate to the complexity of women's asceticism and its social role.

3. Turner's coining of the word "psychosemantic" as a play on "psychosomatic" wonderfully captures the work of the drives in Kristeva's theory of negativity. In emphasizing the implication of the drives within a linguistic economy, "psychosemantic" does maintain continuity with "psychosomatic" truth: we are reminded by the play on words that the action of death-work is effected at the boundary of the psychic and the somatic. Even so, the novel aspects of the word appropriately and helpfully distance us from notions of a mute body energetics: "psychosemantic" reminds us that death-work, above all, signifies.

4. Rudolph Bell's work holds suggestive possibilities for efforts to correlate late medieval Christendom's battle to maintain the integrity of its borders against outside attack with holy women's struggles for ascetic control over their bodies. According to Bell, severe asceticism, including self-imposed starvation, featured more prominently in the lives of Dominican women than it did in the lives of the Poor Clares (the Franciscans) (1985, 132–33). Bell chronicles differences between the two groups: the Poor Clares were centered in the Umbria and Marche regions; the Dominicans were clustered in Tuscany or the northeast (Florence and Venice), which were centers of opposition to the Papacy. The region was beset by conflict: both the Avignon papacy and, later, the Protestant Reformation threatened societal order. Dominican women were more likely to have struggled against parents who opposed their religious vocations. Their devotion was more likely to have included visions and direct communication with God. Bell roots the differences between the Dominicans and Franciscans in a "rich psychological portrait" that reveals an "intense struggle for autonomy" among the Dominican women (1985, 133). But the different positions of the Dominicans and Franciscans suggest an alternative explanation focused on a conflict-ridden social body. On that account, the social unrest described by Bell was reproduced on the bodies of Dominican women whose struggle for autonomy and escape from bodily and social constraints—detailed in their hagiographies—matched on a smaller scale the response of the society to the tensions of the day.

5. Parallelism between Christ's wounded breast and a woman's lactating breast, indicated by paintings such as that done by Quirizio for the monastery of St. Clare on the island of Murano, is underscored by paintings of the double intercession published in *Holy Feast and Holy Fast.* In mirror gestures of each other, Mary and Christ offer their breasts: just as Mary nurses the hungry so also does Christ (Bynum, 1987, 270–72, Plates 25–30).

6. Nancy Jay offers a helpful synopsis of the history of the Eucharist as sacrifice. She emphasizes that the ritual of sacrifice is not found among Christians in the Biblical period. Its origins can be traced to a priesthood that emerges later. Jay submits that the sacrificial cult in Christianity reached its peak in the thirteenth century (1992, 116–18).

7. The reader may be cautioned against reductionistic interpretations of the somatic productivity of the mystics' body practices that would cite hormonal dysfunction, self-mutilating desire (the product of mental illness), or self-conscious deception. As Bynum notes (1987, 194–207), medieval society itself applied a nuanced herme-

neutic to the endeavors of its holy women: it discriminated between ascetic practices that were the product of a physiological condition, illness, or fraud and those that demonstrated the conformation of the body to the work of faith. The mystics' asceticism constituted a complex discursive practice which cannot be examined adequately if interpretations of these women's actions offered by their contemporaries and by themselves are treated as epiphenomenal. Thus, the narrative structure of the medieval world which allowed the physical suffering of the mystics to be experienced as sacrificially productive should be taken most seriously by its interpreters.

8. Although this discussion of the medieval mystics and themes of mimetic violence and surrogate victimization draws on Girard, relying on him to sustain a sacrificial thesis proves more difficult. After all, holy women did not die in the wake of a frenzied attack, which Girard has cited as an earmark of sacrifice. Moreover, using Girard as a primary resource on this point is problematic because he associates an accelerated and increasingly homicidal mimeticism among humans with their enhanced intellectual powers. Of examples one might cite to show that humans employ their intellectual acumen to transpose lethal violence into nonlethal signs, the Eucharist appears among the strongest. Rather than victimize a neighbor, medieval Christians made Christ—present in bread and wine—their victim and killed him/it. On that count, the deaths of the mystics would appear to be socially unnecessary. Although their ascetic labors wonderfully conveyed to others the symbolic richness of the Eucharist, their deaths appear to have served no purpose that a ritual invocation of bread and wine had not already served. However, as stated in Chapter 4, the weak link in Girard's theory—his inadequate explanation for why surrogate victims must not only suffer but also die—is very well addressed by Kristeva. Her insights sustain the sacrificial thesis advanced here.

9. As stated in Chapter 4, future feminist analyses of melancholia may facilitate a more precise adjudication of whether and how the discursive practices Kristeva cites in her discussion of melancholia function as permutations of a sacrificial narrative and its shaping power. This study of the mystics lends support to a thesis that treats melancholia as such a permutation. Bynum's persuasive account of the social significance of the medieval mystics' ascetic practices implies that more careful consideration should be given to analyses of contemporary melancholia and depression that explain how these forms of death-work function within a signifying economy and for what purposes. That jouissance, set in play by a sacrificial economy, is always already in its debt—and does not direct women who invest in it toward an alternative economy—is attested to also by Kristeva in her critique of second-generation feminism, which is discussed in Chapter 7.

6. "The Devils Are Come Down Upon Us"

1. The quote in the title is attributed to Cotton Mather in 1693, as cited in John Demos's *Entertaining Satan: Witchcraft and the Culture of Early New England* (313).

2. The majority of victims were women. Of the 20 percent of victims who were male, most were charged with additional crimes (e.g., heresy) and not exclusively with witchcraft, or they were relatives of women accused of witchcraft and were guilty by "contagion" or association (Larner, 1981, 91–94; Midelfort, 1972, 95; Demos, 1982, 60–62). Demos devotes one chapter (36–56) to the case of John Godfrey who, as an exception to the general rule, was accused of being a witch for reasons similar to those

cited in the cases of females accused of witchcraft. Godfrey's life was characterized by extreme rootlessness: no parents, no spouse, no children, no property. Demos speculates that homosexual behavior may have been a factor in his persecution, as indeed it probably was for other marginalized males accused of witchcraft (marginality was defined both in terms of property-holding and marital status). Although some research has been done on the persecution of persons accused of engaging in homosexual acts during this time period (e.g., a summary of research may be found in Greenberg, 1988, 301–46), more work needs to be done to produce an integrated analysis of persecution that accounts for multiple dimensions of scapegoating during the time of the witch hunts.

3. Bynum's research on medieval views about gender suggests that a late medieval qualification of misogynistic dualism, visible in the lives of the mystics, anticipates the Reformation changes cited by Karlsen and Larner. Bynum's observations indicate that changes in gender role expectations in the Reformation era do not introduce within the society wholly novel expectations about gender; however, the state's interest in adjudicating the parameters of gender role expectations is new.

4. Interestingly, Larner finds the lull inexplicable; others, noting that plague and famine years often alternated with witch hunting years and that the latter provided a scapegoat mechanism for the tragedies of the former, would find the lull quite explicable (Demos, 1982, 386; Midelfort, 1972, 70–73).

5. Girard's paradigmatic scapegoat is not the witch of the sixteenth and seventeenth centuries but a Jew persecuted for causing the plague in the fourteenth century. Girard's text cites the accusation of Guillaume de Machaut, in a fourteenth-century text, whereas this chapter invokes the image of a woman in a subsequent century accused of a similar crime. Nevertheless, the thesis of this chapter is advanced by insights located in Girard's work.

6. The third stereotype of persecution—the lack of difference of the victim from his or her accusers—identifies an important element in anti-Semitism. The dynamics of anti-Jewish prejudice, stemming from the first century of the Christian era, as recorded in the New Testament, are highlighted by this typology. The differentiation of Christianity, as a separate religion, from Judaism, was very much an intrafamilial debate: Judaism and Christianity were two children, born of the same parent: prerabbinic religion (Ruether, 1974, 62). Thus, in the story of the Jewish woman cited here, the dynamics of her persecution are traced, not to her "alienness," but to her lack of difference from those who would secure the boundaries of their altogether fragile world at her expense.

7. Supporting this analysis is Larner's own observation (1981, 113) that witch executions were preceded by a day or days of fasting and sermons. Prior to the modern era and the ascendance of medical discourse, fasting was meaningful within the context of religious practices. That, apart from her brief observation, Larner has remained silent about the meaning of fasting suggests that she may have recognized the inadequacy of her mode of analysis to this phenomenon. Were she to have integrated fasting into her theory—witch hunting was the instrument of ideological education of a state bent on legitimating itself—she might have said that "a hungry stomach is a stomach attentive to the state's message." By contrast to that impoverished analysis, in the context of Christian myth, for centuries, communal fasting had united a people before God. Partaking of a ritual of communal penitence and invoking divine power, in fasting, a people made themselves vulnerable before God in order that, through suffering and loss, they might induce God's blessings. Fasting thus served the

drama of witch execution by preparing people for the sacrificial act that would banish evil and return God's people to their covenanted order with God.

8. Foucault is a notable exception to this trend. He acknowledges the social productivity of violence when he emphasizes that the work and meaning of torture lie in its public display (Foucault, 1979, 34). A generative instrument of control and discipline, the tortured body functions as a social imperative: the body of the condemned is "the place where the vengeance of the sovereign is applied, the anchoring point for a manifestation of power, an opportunity of affirming the dissymmetry of forces" (1979, 55). However, Foucault's treatment of violence and torture is inadequate on two counts. First, he reads only the truth of a persecutor on the body of a victim. But an adequate analysis must seek to understand what the persecutor claimed: history records that persecutors believed that they did not inscribe on the broken flesh of the accused lessons of their own creation; instead the tortured body exhibited a truth that came from elsewhere (the Devil or God). Sacrificial theory facilitates an inquiry into the distinct truth of torture to which mythic language points. Second, Foucault reductionistically addresses the question of why instruments of torture were designed to ensure a slow and painful death (1979, 45). Interestingly, he does not argue initially that a political power which killed slowly was more able to impress itself on the body-politic than was a power that killed quickly. Rather, he invokes a sacred mythology (1979, 46–47): in the age of torture, the slow and deliberate pace of torture enabled all observers to see that "the eternal game" had already begun and God was prepared to adjudicate the final destiny of the condemned. The cries that accompanied the extended agony of the tortured were a narrative of sacred truth which functioned as an "ultimate proof" to conjoin the "judgement of men with that of God" (1979, 46). But Foucault subsumes this penal liturgy to politics when he claims that the mythic language of torture is only another form of political discourse. It always is in full possession of the sovereign. By contrast, sacrificial theory distinguishes the mythic language that punctuated the protracted course of torture from political discourse. Not mandating that the narrative structure of the former be collapsed into the latter, sacrificial theory facilitates a nuanced account of the social work of violence and torture.

9. Among her many examples, duBois cites a speech of Lykourgos in a court case against Leokrates in which torture is crucial to the legal debate. Demanding that the slaves of Leokrates be tortured, Lykourgos argues, "Which people could not have been misled by cunning or a deceptive argument? The male and female slaves. Naturally [*kata physin*], when tortured, they would have told the whole truth [*pasan tên alêtheian*] about the offenses" (Lycurgus, *Against Leocrates,* as cited in duBois, [1991, 52]).

10. DuBois carefully documents in another work, *Sowing the Body: Psychoanalysis and Ancient Presentations of Women* (1988), links between woman and earth in ancient Greece. Key representations of the female body treat it as a field and stone. As a field, woman is a site for plowing, which, when implanted with seeds or sperm, will be productive. As stone, she is a latent potentiality, a buried power and a sacred threshold.

11. Girard would affirm duBois's move to link myth with actual incidents of violence. As noted in Chapter 4, Girard argues most persuasively against Lacan and Lévi-Strauss that myths attest to real violence. When duBois finds common motifs in myth and torture, she underscores Girard's point. Victim marks in myth (physical peculiarities, odors, elements of contagion, and menacing encounters with strangers)

are not mere window-dressing on lessons in cultural linguistics. They attest to cultural memories of actual violence.

12. Athena's story likewise attempts to speak, under the auspices of the sign, of the sacrificial roots of the Symbolic, which mythic memory would preserve. Graves reminds us that Athena's first mother, the abject, maternal entity known as Metis, is devoured by Zeus (1955, 9d). So also is Athena's aegis sometimes said to be the skin of the archaic maternal entity, Medusa (1955, 33b). The ascendence of the Symbolic order is then represented by the emergence of the Father's Law when, in the wake of matricide, Athena is born of Zeus.

13. The work of feminist theologians, as represented by the contributors to the anthology *Christianity, Patriarchy, and Abuse* (Brown and Bohn, 1990) and by theologians such as Brock (1990, 1991), Daly (1978), Fortune (1990), and Williams (1993), indicates that sacrificial language remains endemic in Christian theology and ritual, with troubling implications for women who experience abuse. Although Christianity no longer functions as a broad cultural and political force, as it once did, the continuing investment of its ethical codes in a sacrificial logic suggest a remnant power of an earlier time, with a potentially devastating impact on the individual lives of women.

7. Life-Sentences

1. The phallic mother is born of a child's fantasy of an omnipotent and absolutely powerful figure. She is able to grant the child everything: not only is she its object of desire, but also she is perceived by the child to desire it as her object (Kristeva, 1984c, 47). Under the Law, the phallic mother is castrated, but her lack is not coded as irretrievable loss. Rather, loss is managed when, within the oppositional coding of phallic signification, a woman gives to a man the phallus that she does not have (Lacan, 1985a, 84). Appearing in the Symbolic as the object of man's gratification, woman recalls for him the Imaginary promise the child once read in the mother: "her replete body, the receptacle and guarantor of demands, is . . . in other words, the phallus" (1984c, 47).

2. By "generation" Kristeva does not refer to chronological phases in the history of feminism; rather she intends distinct signifying practices (1981a, 209), both material and psychic, which are subject to simultaneous deployment. As specific configurations of temporal difference, each signifying practice promises expanded agency to the feminists who claim it.

3. Kristeva likens the logic of first-generation feminism to the Hegelian dialectic in its idealist mode. In *Revolution in Poetic Language* (1984c), Kristeva criticizes the idealist aspects of Hegel's work because genuine creativity and social change is excluded when negativity is subsumed to a Self-Consciousness fully in possession of itself. For Kristeva, feminists need to sustain an investment in the creative work of negativity, where Hegelian idealism does not. Such work functions by means of the displacement and dispossession of received positions to sustain revolutionary openness.

4. The translator of "Motherhood According to Giovanni Bellini" (1975a, 269–70, n. 2), has not translated *enceinte*. So also is it not translated here in order that the French pun may be preserved: *enceinte* is a protective wall bordering a town; *la femme enceinte* is a pregnant woman.

5. Edelstein argues that Kristeva should not draw on the figure of the mother in her emancipatory project because her words exclude any reader who is not "a heterosexual Christian woman who has borne at least one son and who knows something about theoretical and literary avant-gardes" (39). Contrary to Edelstein, Kristeva's commentary on becoming a mother can be likened to Merleau-Ponty's appeal to Schneider in the *Phenomenology of Perception* (1962). One need not have had one's life altered by a shrapnel wound in the occipital region of the brain, as did Schneider, to perceive that Merleau-Ponty's comments about Schneider illuminate his theory of embodiment. So also can one find Kristeva's references to motherhood insightful, even if one's life has not been shaped by heterosexual relationships, the birth of a male child, or exposure to French intellectual culture. That Kristeva refers to her own experience, whereas Merleau-Ponty refers to Schneider, attests to Kristeva's openness to forms of self-disclosure that are uncommon among philosophers. That a feminist critic should find Kristeva's references to her own life problematic, rather than refreshing, is disappointing.

6. Throughout this chapter, the mark of difference within every maternal identity that retains "the other *as other* in the same" (Ziarek, 1992, 98) is treated as a key paradigm of nonsacrificial alterity. Although it describes a trinitarian schema of child, Imaginary Father and archaic Mother, because it is set forth in afamilial language, this paradigm clarifies Kristeva's objectives. Kristeva's use of familial terminology has confused some readers (e.g., Rose, 1986, 154), who have perceived that Kristeva "races back into the arms of the Law" when she summons an Imaginary Father to counterbalance the archaic mother. By contrast, this formula, which Ziarek likens to the Derridean "trace," sets Kristeva's constructive position on a broad plain, unconstrained by what some perceive to be the distractions of familial language.

7. In a revised version of "Women's Time," published in *New Maladies of the Soul* in France in 1993 and in the United States in 1995, Kristeva states, "I strongly support" ("je revendique") a third-generation feminism which is now taking shape (1995, 222; 1993a, 328). Her comments reiterate her advocacy of feminism published initially in the 1979 version of "Women's Time."

8. When Kristeva describes an analytic method or practice she does have in mind as a model encounters between a psychoanalyst and her client. However, she does not imagine that an analytic practice is restricted to that context. Virtually any environment exhibits a potential for analytic engagements among persons. Directly suggested by Kristeva as possible sites for analytic encounters are the family unit, religious institutions, and art (experienced in literature, poetry, and graphic art). Through such diverse encounters, persons can articulate an ethics of analysis.

9. Oliver helpfully interprets a potential difficulty in Kristeva's assertion that analysis maintains a thoroughgoing skepticism before all truth-claims. Oliver recognizes that psychoanalysis must also be analyzed as a symptom or raise itself to a master discourse. She suggests that this apparent paradox—an antifoundational theory advances a foundational claim—is resolved when we note that psychoanalysis never stops analyzing any representations, including its own. Open to continual modifications, analytic inquiry remains aligned with heterogenous rather than hegemonic meaning: the analyst is always also an analysand (1993, 147).

10. The difficulties of speaking about sexual difference in new ways are well illustrated by the critical reception of Kristeva's writings on maternity among feminist scholars. As Elliot perspicaciously observes, notwithstanding Kristeva's explicit commitment to an analytic discourse of sexual difference, her feminist critics have

consistently misread her position and have labeled it an essentialist metaphysics of sexual difference (1991, 192–200).

11. For another feminist reading of Freud's essay on the uncanny, see Jane Marie Todd's 1986 essay, "The Veiled Woman in Freud's *Das Unheimliche.*" Todd's essay initially suggested to me the merits of looking again at Freud's essay on the uncanny. Her commentary is particularly intriguing when she notes that Freud, in dissenting from arguments that would associate the uncanny with any maternally marked death-work, betrays himself. Intending to attribute his definition of the uncanny to Schelling, Freud errs and credits Schleiermacher—the veil-maker—instead (521–22). That which Freud seeks to veil, Todd and I hope to glimpse, however indirectly.

12. Olympia's eyes are bloody from a cut Spalanzani received in his struggle with Coppola.

13. Freud imagines only a male gaze directed toward Olympia's body and her penis/eyes. Feminist readers, attuned to the dynamics of the sacrificial economy, would restate Freud's object-lesson. When Olympia does teach women about the Symbolic order, she emphasizes that, under the conditions of patriarchy, women are paralyzed: they are constrained by the economy of sexual difference to play the roles of mechanical dolls or phallic women. Feminist readers will find chilling in this story not only the prescription for their lives exacted by the Law of the phallus, but also the price they pay when that Law breaks down. At the borders of the Law, those who confront the uncanny may preferentially extract from women the bloody price of death-work: patriarchy will augment the force of its object-work by undertaking abject-work with their bodies.

14. This diversity is attested to in Kristeva's thoughtful comments on religion in *Tales of Love* (1987a) and *In the Beginning was Love: Psychoanalysis and Faith* (1987). Essays in *Body/Text in Julia Kristeva: Religion, Women, and Psychoanalysis,* edited by David Crownfield (1992), especially "The Sublimation of Narcissism in Christian Love and Faith," by Crownfield, also speak of Kristeva's positive assessment of the work of religion in culture.

15. In traditional Middle Eastern society, the foreigner or stranger marked the line between human community and that which was excluded from it. Strangers were not owed justice, care, or concern. Those who traveled outside clan and village boundaries deserved whatever befell them. Early on, the people of Israel set a different ethical standard: hospitality was owed the stranger. The prophets underscored and uplifted this ethic, elaborating the parameters of a circle of justice. Within the circle were persons owed care and concern; outside the circle were strangers who were owed nothing. When the prophets were asked to name those who fell outside the circle, they stated that even orphans and widows, the most abandoned of the abandoned in Middle Eastern society, were to be included. Through the mouth of Isaiah, God set forth necessary terms for a relationship: "Cease to do evil, learn to do good; seek justice, correct oppression, defend the fatherless, plead for the widow" (Isa. 1:17). The prophets' ethic made an ongoing relationship with God contingent on the people's inclusion of the refuse of refuse—*the abject*—within their community.

16. On this reading of Kristeva's ethics of strangeness, Madelon Sprengnether's criticism of Kristeva is unfounded (1996). Sprengnether writes that Kristeva "seems to feel that women have made such significant gains toward equality that further efforts in this direction are misguided, even dangerous." Sprengnether condemns Kristeva for being oblivious to "women's worldwide vulnerability to poverty and violence" and for being hostile to the creation of "'marginal groups of sex, age, religion, ethnic origin

and ideology.'" Rather than perceive that organizing such groups is necessary for effective political strategizing, Sprengnether reads Kristeva to denounce them as "merely a mechanism for denying castration and hence refusing one's place in the social order" (20). But Kristeva does not dismiss the political goals advanced by groups organized around specific categories of difference; instead, she means to enhance their ability to achieve their goals by suggesting new grounds for activism. Not meaning to silence the voices of the marginalized, she instead wants to challenge the identity politics they have embraced because that politics restricts their ability to effect social change. Kristeva wants to expose the sacrificial logic that drives identity politics and to open politics up by challenging the dynamics of representation that create margins in the first place. Kristeva does not want those who have been relegated to the margins of history by the exclusionary politics of representation to exhaust themselves scrabbling for the right to turn the tables on their masters. On behalf of political visions that are larger and more powerful than those now held by political activists, Kristeva wants them to make a creative claim on an excess of being that the sacrificial logic has attempted to thwart. This excess partakes of what we might call an economy of plenty instead of an economy of scarcity (Brennan, 1992, 75). Kristeva does not invoke castration in order to teach compliance with the political status quo; she mentions it in order to expose the pretense of the status quo. *The* lesson of castration that Kristeva wants to cite—the subject comes to be in a place where it is not—teaches us that otherness is installed at the heart of the subject. Because we *are* in difference, we always are outside the selves that the politics of identity have constructed for us (Oliver, 1993, 186). Rather than invest in them, we should move forward to articulate networks of difference that "allow change and surprise, that is, that will allow life" (Kristeva, 1995, 44).

17. Graves cites another version of the myth which ascribes to Io more emphatically than does the version Kristeva cites the role of a stranger. Io is residing in Argos when Zeus Picus sends his servants to capture her. Raped and made pregnant by him, Io escapes after the birth of her daughter and wanders in Egypt and later among the cities of Syria until she dies in grief and shame (1955, 191).

REFERENCES

I. Julia Kristeva

1966 "Word, Dialogue, and Novel." Trans. Thomas Gora and Alice Jardine. In *Desire in Language,* 1980, 64–91.
1971 "How Does One Speak to Literature." Trans. Thomas Gora and Alice Jardine. In *Desire in Language,* 1980, 92–123.
1972 "Four Types of Signifying Practice." *Semiotext(e)* 1, 65–74.
1973 "The System and the Speaking Subject." Trans. Toril Moi. In *The Kristeva Reader,* 1986, 24–33.
1974 *About Chinese Women.* Trans. Seán Hand. In *The Kristeva Reader,* 1986, 139–59.
1974a "The Ethics of Linguistics." Trans. Thomas Gora and Alice Jardine. In *Desire in Language,* 1980, 23–35.
1974b "The Novel as Polylogue." Trans. Thomas Gora and Alice Jardine. In *Desire in Language,* 1980, 159–209.
1974c "Phonetics, Phonology and Impulsional Bases." Trans. Caren Greenberg. *Diacritics* 4, no. 3, 33–37.
1974d "Pratique signifiante et mode de production." *Tel Quel* 60, 21–33.
1975 "From One Identity to Another." Trans. Thomas Gora and Alice Jardine. In *Desire in Language,* 1980, 124–47.
1975a "Motherhood According to Giovanni Bellini." Trans. Thomas Gora and Alice Jardine. In *Desire in Language,* 1980, 237–70.
1975b "The Subject in Signifying Practice." *Semiotext(e)* 1, no. 3, 19–34.
1976 "Stabat Mater." Trans. Leon S. Roudiez. In *The Kristeva Reader,* 1986, 160–86.
1977 "A New Type of Intellectual: The Dissident." Trans. Seán Hand. In *The Kristeva Reader,* 1986, 292–300.
1977a "Place Names." Trans. Thomas Gora and Alice Jardine. In *Desire in Language,* 1980, 271–91.
1980 *Desire in Language: A Semiotic Approach to Literature and Art.* Trans. Thomas Gora and Alice Jardine. Ed. Leon S. Roudiez. New York: Columbia University Press.
1980a "Interview with Julia Kristeva." In *Women Analyze Women.* Ed. Elaine Baruch and Lucienne Serrano. New York: New York University Press, 1988, 130–45.
1980b "Warnings." In *New French Feminisms.* Ed. Elaine Marks and Isabelle de Courtivron. Amherst: University of Massachusetts, 137–41.
1981 "Psychoanalysis and the Polis." Trans. Margaret Waller. In *The Kristeva Reader,* 1986, 302–20.
1981a "Women's Time." Trans. Alice Jardine and Harry Blake. In *The Kristeva Reader,* 1986, 188–213.
1982 *Powers of Horror: An Essay on Abjection.* Trans. Leon S. Roudiez. New York: Columbia University Press (1980).

1983 "Within the Microcosm of the 'Talking Cure.'" Trans. T. Gora and M. Waller. In *Psychiatry and the Humanities.* Ed. Joseph H. Smith and William Kerrigan, Vol. 6. New Haven: Yale University Press, 33–48.

1984 "Histoires d'amour—Love Stories." *ICA Documents 1: Desire.* London: Institute of Contemporary Arts, 18–21.

1984a "Julia Kristeva in Conversation with Rosalind Coward." *ICA Documents 1: Desire.* London: Institute of Contemporary Arts, 22–27.

1984b "My Memory's Hyperbole." Trans. Athena Viscusi. In *The Female Autograph.* Ed. Domna C. Stanton. A special issue of *New York Literary Forum,* nos. 12–13, 261–76.

1984c *Revolution in Poetic Language.* Trans. Margaret Waller. New York: Columbia University Press (1974).

1984d "Two Interviews with Julia Kristeva," with Elaine Hoffman Baruch and Perry Meisel. *Partisan Review* 51, no. 2, 120–32.

1985 *Au commencement était l'amour: Psychanalyse et foi.* Paris: Hachette. Trans. David Crownfield (unpublished).

1985a "The Speaking Subject." In *On Signs.* Ed. M. Blonsky. Baltimore: Johns Hopkins University Press, 210–20.

1986 *The Kristeva Reader.* Ed. Toril Moi. New York, Columbia University Press (1986).

1986a "An Interview with Julia Kristeva," with Edith Kurzweil. *Partisan Review* 53, no. 2, 216–29.

1986b "An Interview with Julia Kristeva," with I. Lipkowitz and A. Loselle. *Critical Texts* 3, no. 3, 3–13.

1987 *In the Beginning Was Love: Psychoanalysis and Faith.* Trans. Arthur Goldhammer. New York: Columbia University Press (1985).

1987a *Tales of Love.* Trans. Leon S. Roudiez. New York: Columbia University Press (1983).

1989 *Black Sun: Depression and Melancholia.* Trans. Leon S. Roudiez. New York: Columbia University Press (1987).

1989a *Language: The Unknown.* Trans. Anne M. Menke. New York: Columbia University Press (1981).

1990 "An Interview with Julia Kristeva: Cultural Strangeness and the Subject in Crisis," with Suzanne Clark and Kathleen Hulley. *Discourse,* 13, no. 1, 149–80.

1991 *Strangers to Ourselves.* Trans. Leon S. Roudiez. New York: Columbia University Press.

1993 *Nations without Nationalism.* Trans. Leon S. Roudiez. New York: Columbia University Press (1990).

1993a *Les Nouvelles Maladies De L'âme.* Paris: Librairie Arthème Fayard.

1995 *New Maladies of the Soul.* Trans. Ross Guberman. New York: Columbia University Press (1993).

II. Secondary Sources

Abel, Elizabeth. "Race, Class, and Psychoanalysis? Opening Questions." In *Conflicts in Feminism.* Ed. Marianne Hirsch and Evelyn Fox Keller. New York and London: Routledge, 1990, 184–204.

Alcoff, Linda. "Cultural Feminism versus Poststructuralism: The Identity Crisis in Feminist Theory." *Signs* 13, no. 3 (1988): 405–36.

Althusser, Louis. "Freud and Lacan." In *Lenin and Philosophy and Other Essays.* Trans. Ben Brewster. New York: Monthly Review Press, 1971, 195–219.

Barstow, Anne. "On Studying Witchcraft as Women's History: A Historiography of the European Witch Persecutions." *Journal of Feminist Studies in Religion* 4 (1988): 7–19.

Barzilai, Shuli. "Borders of Language: Kristeva's Critique of Lacan." *PMLA: Publications of the Modern Language Association of America* 102, 2 (1991): 294–305.

Bell, Rudolph M. *Holy Anorexia.* Chicago: University of Chicago Press, 1985.

Benhabib, Seyla, and Drucilla Cornell, eds. *Feminism as Critique.* Minneapolis: University of Minnesota Press, 1987.

Bertrand, Marie-Andrée. "Feminists Targeted for Murder: Montreal 1989." *Feminist Issues* 11, 2 (1991): 3–10.

Boothby, Richard. *Death and Desire: Psychoanalytic Theory in Lacan's Return to Freud.* New York and London: Routledge, 1991.

Bordo, Susan. "Anorexia Nervosa: Psychopathology as the Crystallization of Culture." *The Philosophical Forum* 17, 2 (1985): 73–104.

———. 1992. "Postmodern Subjects, Postmodern Bodies." *Feminist Studies* 18, 1: 159–75.

Braidotti, Rosi. "Embodiment, Sexual Difference, and the Nomadic Subject." *Hypatia* 8, 1 (1993): 1–13.

Brennan, Teresa. "An Impasse in Psychoanalysis and Feminism." In *A Reader in Feminist Knowledge.* Ed. Sneja Gunew. New York and London: Routledge, 1991, 114–38.

———. 1992. *The Interpretation of the Flesh: Freud and Femininity.* London and New York: Routledge.

———. 1993. *History after Lacan.* London and New York: Routledge.

Brock, Rita Nakashima. "And a Little Child Will Lead Us: Christology and Child Abuse." In *Christianity, Patriarchy, and Abuse: A Feminist Critique.* Ed. Joanne Carlson Brown and Carole R. Bohn. New York: Pilgrim Press, 1990, 42–61.

———. 1991. *Journeys by Heart: A Christology of Erotic Power.* New York: Crossroad.

Bronfen, Elisabeth. *Over Her Dead Body: Death, Femininity, and the Aesthetic.* New York and London: Routledge, 1992.

Brown, Joanne Carlson, and Carole R. Bohn, eds. *Christianity, Patriarchy, and Abuse: A Feminist Critique.* New York: Pilgrim Press, 1990.

Brown, Joanne Carlson, and Rebecca Parker. "For God So Loved the World?" In *Christianity, Patriarchy, and Abuse: A Feminist Critique.* Ed. Joanne Carlson Brown and Carole R. Bohn. New York: Pilgrim Press, 1990, 1–30.

Brown, Peter. "Sorcery, Demons and the Rise of Christianity: From Late Antiquity into the Middle Ages." In *Religion and Society in the Age of Augustine.* By Peter Brown. New York: Harper and Row, 1972, 119–46.

Burke, Carolyn Walker. "Irigaray through the Looking Glass." *Feminist Studies* 7, 2 (1981): 288–306.

Butler, Judith P. *Subjects of Desire: Hegelian Reflections in Twentieth-Century France.* New York: Columbia University Press, 1987.

———. 1990. *Gender Trouble: Feminism and the Subversion of Identity.* New York and London: Routledge.

———. 1992. "Response to Bordo's Feminist Skepticism and the 'Maleness' of Philosophy." *Hypatia* 7, 3: 162–65.

———. 1993. *Bodies that Matter: On the Discursive Limits of "Sex."* New York and London: Routledge.

Bynum, Caroline Walker. "Fast, Feast, and Flesh: The Religious Significance of Food to Medieval Women." *Representations* 11 (1985): 1–25.

———. 1987. *Holy Feast and Holy Fast: The Religious Significance of Food to Medieval Women.* Berkeley: University of California Press.

Chanter, Tina. "Kristeva's Politics of Change: Tracking Essentialism with the Help of a Sex/Gender Map." In *Ethics, Politics, and Difference in Julia Kristeva's Writing.* Ed. Kelly Oliver. New York and London: Routledge (1993), 179–95.

Chodorow, Nancy. *The Reproduction of Mothering: Psychoanalysis and the Sociology of Gender.* Berkeley: University of California Press, 1978.

———. 1989. *Feminism and Psychoanalytic Theory.* New Haven: Yale University Press.

Chopp, Rebecca S. *The Power to Speak: Feminism, Language, God.* New York: Crossroad, 1989.

Cixous, Hélène, and Catherine Clément. *The Newly Born Woman.* Trans. Betsy Wing. Minneapolis: University of Minnesota Press, 1986 (1975).

Clark, Suzanne, and Kathleen Hulley. "An Interview with Julia Kristeva: Cultural Strangeness and the Subject in Crisis." *Discourse* 13, 1 (1990): 149–80.

Cornell, Drucilla, and Adam Thurschwell. "Feminism, Negativity, Intersubjectivity." In *Feminism as Critique.* Ed. Seyla Benhabib and Drucilla Cornell. Minneapolis: University of Minnesota Press, 1987, 143–62.

Coward, Rosalind, and John Ellis. *Language and Materialism.* London: Routledge and Kegan Paul, 1977.

Cowie, Elizabeth. "Woman as Sign." *m/f* 1 (1978): 49–63.

Crownfield, David, ed. *Body/Text in Julia Kristeva: Religion, Women, and Psychoanalysis.* Albany: State University of New York Press, 1992.

———. 1992a. "The Sublimation of Narcissism in Christian Love and Faith." In *Body/Text in Julia Kristeva,* 57–64.

Daly, Mary. *Gyn/Ecology: The Metaethics of Radical Feminism.* Boston: Beacon Press, 1978.

Demos, John Putnam. *Entertaining Satan: Witchcraft and the Culture of Early New England.* New York: Oxford University Press, 1982.

Diamond, Irene, and Lee Quinby, eds. *Feminism and Foucault.* Boston: Northeastern University Press, 1988.

Doane, Janice, and Devon Hodges. *From Klein to Kristeva.* Ann Arbor: University of Michigan Press, 1992.

Douglas, Mary. *Purity and Danger: An Analysis of the Concepts of Pollution and Taboo.* Boston: Ark Paperbacks, 1966.

duBois, Page. *Sowing the Body: Psychoanalysis and Ancient Representations of Women.* Chicago: University of Chicago Press, 1988.

———. 1991. *Torture and Truth.* New York and London: Routledge.

Duchen, Claire. *Feminism in France: From May '68 to Mitterrand.* New York: Methuen, 1986.

Edelstein, Marilyn. "Metaphor, Meta-Narrative, and Mater-Narrative in Kristeva's 'Stabat Mater.'" In *Body/Text in Julia Kristeva: Religion, Women, and Psychoanalysis.* Ed. David Crownfield. Albany: State University of New York Press, 1992, 27–52.

Elliot, Patricia. *From Mastery to Analysis: Theories of Gender in Psychoanalytic Feminism.* Ithaca: Cornell University Press, 1991.

———. 1995. "Politics, Identity, and Social Change: Contested Grounds in Psychoanalytic Feminism." *Hypatia* 10, 2: 41–55.

Fletcher, John, and Andrew Benjamin, eds. *Abjection, Melancholia and Love.* New York and London: Routledge, 1990.

Fortune, Marie F. "The Transformation of Suffering: A Biblical and Theological Perspective." In *Christianity, Patriarchy, and Abuse.* Ed. Joanne Carlson Brown and Carole R. Bohn. New York: Pilgrim Press, 1990, 139–47.

Foucault, Michel. *The History of Sexuality. Vol. I, An Introduction.* Trans. Robert Hurley. New York: Pantheon Books, 1978.

———. 1979. *Discipline and Punish: The Birth of Prison.* Trans. Alan Sheridan. New York: Vintage Books.

Fraser, Nancy. "The Uses and Abuses of French Discourse Theories for Feminist Politics." In *Revaluing French Feminism: Critical Essays on Difference, Agency, and Culture.* Ed. Nancy Fraser and Sandra Lee Bartky. Bloomington: Indiana University Press, 1992, 177–94.

Fraser, Nancy, and Linda Nicholson. "Social Criticism without Philosophy: An Encounter between Feminism and Postmodernism." In *Universal Abandon? The Poetics of Postmodernism.* Ed. Andrew Ross. Minneapolis: University of Minnesota Press, 1988, 83–104.

Freud, Sigmund. "The 'Uncanny.'" In *The Standard Edition of the Complete Psychological Works of Sigmund Freud,* Vol. XVII. London: Hogarth Press, 1955, 218–56.

Fuss, Diana. *Essentially Speaking: Feminism, Nature and Difference.* New York and London: Routledge, 1989.

Gallop, Jane. *The Daughter's Seduction: Feminism and Psychoanalysis.* Ithaca: Cornell University Press, 1982.

———. 1985. *Reading Lacan.* New York: Cornell University Press.

Gallop, Jane, and Carolyn Burke. "Psychoanalysis and Feminism in France." In *The Future of Difference.* Ed. Hester Eisenstein and Alice Jardine. Boston: G. K. Hall, 1980, 106–21.

Gatens, Moira. "A Critique of the Sex/Gender Distinction." In *A Reader in Feminist Knowledge.* Ed. Sneja Gunew. New York and London: Routledge, 1991. 139–57.

Gelfand, Elissa D., and Virginia Thorndike Holes. "A Topography of Difference," *French Feminist Criticism: Women, Language, Literature.* New York: Garland, 1985, xv–lii.

Girard, René. *Violence and the Sacred.* Trans. Patrick Gregory. Baltimore: Johns Hopkins University Press, 1977.

———. 1986. *The Scapegoat.* Trans. Yvonne Freccero. Baltimore: Johns Hopkins University Press.

———. 1987. *Things Hidden Since the Foundation of the World.* Trans. Stephen Bann and Michael Metteer. Stanford: Stanford University Press.

———. 1987a. "Discussion." In *Violent Origins: Walter Burkert, René Girard, and Jonathan Z. Smith on Ritual Killing and Cultural Formation.* Ed. Robert G. Hamerton-Kelly. Stanford: Stanford University Press.

———. 1993. "Violence, Difference, Sacrifice: A Conversation with René Girard," with Rebecca Adams. *Religion and Literature.* 25, 2: 9–34.

———. 1993a. "An Interview with René Girard," with Richard J. Golsan. In *René Girard and Myth: An Introduction.* Ed. Richard J. Golsan. New York: Garland, 129–49.

Graves, Robert. *The Greek Myths.* Two Volumes. New York: Penguin Books, 1955.

Greenberg, David F. *The Construction of Homosexuality.* Chicago: University of Chicago Press, 1988.

Grosz, Elizabeth. *Sexual Subversions: Three French Feminists.* Boston and London: Allen & Unwin, 1989.

———. 1990. "The Body of Signification." In *Abjection, Melancholia, and Love.* Ed. John Fletcher and Andrew Benjamin. London and New York: Routledge.

———. 1994. *Volatile Bodies: Toward a Corporeal Feminism.* Bloomington: Indiana University Press.

Guerlac, Suzanne. "Transgression in Theory: Genius and the Subject of *La Révolution du langage poétique.*" In *Ethics, Politics, and Difference in Julia Kristeva's Writing.* Ed. Kelly Oliver. New York and London: Routledge, 1993, 238–59.

Hadewijch. *The Complete Works.* Trans. Columbia Hart. New York: Paulist Press, 1980.

Hajnal, John. "European Marriage Patterns in Perspective." In *Population in History.* Ed. D. V. Glass and D. E. C. Eversley. Chicago: Aldine, 1965, 101–47.

Hamerton-Kelly, Robert G. "Religion and the Thought of René Girard: An Introduction." In *Curing Violence.* Ed. Mark I. Wallace and Theophus H. Smith. Sonoma, CA: Polebridge Press, 1994, 3–20.

Hoffmann, E. T. A. "The Sandman." Trans. L. J. Kent and E. C. Knight. In *Tales.* Ed. Victor Lange. New York: Continuum, 1982, 277–308.

Irigaray, Luce. *Speculum of the Other Woman.* Trans. Gillian Gill. Ithaca: Cornell University Press, 1985.

———. 1985a. "La Mysterique." In *Speculum of the Other Woman,* 191–202.

———. 1985b. *This Sex Which Is Not One.* Trans. Catherine Porter with Carolyn Burke. Ithaca: Cornell University Press.

———. 1985c. "The Power of Discourse and the Subordination of the Feminine." In *This Sex Which Is Not One,* 68–85.

———. 1986. "Women, the Sacred and Money." *Paragraph* 8, 6–18.

———. 1989. "The Gesture in Psychoanalysis." In *Between Feminism and Psychoanalysis.* Ed. Teresa Brennan. New York and London: Routledge, 127–38.

Jaggar, Alison M., and Paula S. Rothenberg. *Feminist Frameworks.* New York: McGraw-Hill, 1993.

Jardine, Alice. "Theories of the Feminine: Kristeva." *Enclitic* 4, 2 (1980): 5–15.

———. 1981. "Introduction to Julia Kristeva's 'Woman's Time.'" *Signs* 7, 1: 5–12.

———. 1981a. "Pre-Texts for the Transatlantic Feminist." *Yale French Studies* 62: 220–36.

———. 1985. *Gynesis: Configurations of Woman and Modernity.* Ithaca: Cornell University Press.

———. 1986. "Opaque Texts and Transparent Contexts: The Political Difference of Julia Kristeva." In *The Poetics of Gender.* Ed. Nancy K. Miller. New York: Columbia University Press.

Jay, Nancy. *Throughout Your Generations Forever: Sacrifice, Religion, and Paternity.* Chicago: University of Chicago Press, 1992.

Jones, Ann. *Next Time She'll Be Dead: Battering and How to Stop It.* Boston: Beacon Press, 1994.

Jones, Ann Rosalind. "Writing the Body: Toward an Understanding of l'Écriture Féminine." *Feminist Studies* 7, 2 (1978): 247–63.

———. 1984. "Julia Kristeva on Femininity: The Limits of a Semiotic Politics." *Feminist Review* 18: 56–73.

———. 1985. "Inscribing Femininity: French Theories of the Feminine." In *Making a Difference: Feminist Literary Criticism.* Ed. Gayle Greene and Coppélia Kahn. New York: Methuen, 80–112.

Karlsen, Carol F. *The Devil in the Shape of a Woman: Witchcraft in Colonial New England.* New York: W. W. Norton, 1987.
Kearney, Richard. *Modern Movements in Philosophy.* Manchester: Manchester University Press, 1986, 268–82.
Kearns, Cleo. *Kristeva and Feminist Theology.* In *Transfigurations: Theology and the French Feminists.* Ed. C. W. Maggie Kim, Susan M. St. Ville, and Susan M. Simonaitis. Minneapolis: Fortress Press, 1993, 49–80.
Kieckhefer, Richard. *European Witch Trials: Their Foundations in Popular and Learned Culture, 1300–1500.* Berkeley: University of California Press, 1976.
Kipnis, Laura. "Feminism: The Political Conscience of Postmodernism?" In *Universal Abandon? The Politics of Postmodernism.* Ed. Andrew Ross. University of Minnesota, 1988. 149–66.
Klaits, Joseph. *Servants of Satan: The Age of the Witch Hunts.* Bloomington: Indiana University Press, 1985.
Kuykendall, Eléanor H. "Subverting Essentialisms." *Hypatia* 6, 3 (1991): 208–17.
Lacan, Jacques. *Écrits.* Paris: Éditions du Seuil, 1966.
———. 1968. *Speech and Language in Psychoanalysis.* Trans. Anthony Wilden. Baltimore: Johns Hopkins University Press.
———. 1977. *Écrits.* Trans. Alan Sheridan. New York: W. W. Norton.
———. 1981. *The Four Fundamental Concepts of Psycho-Analysis.* Ed. Jacques-Alain Miller. Trans. Alan Sheridan. New York: W. W. Norton.
———. 1985. *Feminine Sexuality: Jacques Lacan and the école freudienne.* Ed. Juliet Mitchell and Jacqueline Rose. Trans. Jacqueline Rose. New York: W. W. Norton.
———. 1985a. "The Meaning of the Phallus." In *Feminine Sexuality: Jacques Lacan and the école freudienne.* New York: W. W. Norton, 74–85.
Larner, Christina. *Enemies of God: The Witch Hunt in Scotland.* Baltimore: Johns Hopkins University Press, 1981.
———. 1984. *Witchcraft and Religion: The Politics of Popular Belief.* Ed. Alan Macfarlane. Oxford: Basil Blackwell.
Larsen, Nella. *Passing.* New York: Arno Press, 1969.
Lechte, John. *Julia Kristeva.* New York and London: Routledge, 1990.
———. 1994. *Fifty Key Contemporary Thinkers.* New York and London: Routledge.
Livingston, Paisley. *Models of Desire: René Girard and the Psychology of Mimesis.* Baltimore: Johns Hopkins University Press, 1992.
Lorde, Audre. "The Master's Tools Will Never Dismantle the Master's House." In *This Bridge Called My Back: Writings by Radical Women of Color.* Ed. Cherríe Moraga and Gloria Anzaldúa. Watertown, MA: Persephone Press, 1981.
Macfarlane, Alan. *Witchcraft in Tudor and Stuart England.* New York: Harper and Row, 1970.
Marks, Elaine. "Women and Literature in France." *Signs* 3, 4 (1978): 832–42.
McAfee, Noëlle. "Abject Strangers: Toward an Ethics of Respect." In *Ethics, Politics, and Difference in Julia Kristeva's Writing.* Ed. Kelly Oliver. New York and London: Routledge, 1993, 116–35.
McKenna, Andrew J. *Violence and Difference: Girard, Derrida, and Deconstruction.* Urbana: University of Illinois Press, 1992.
Merleau-Ponty, Maurice. *Phenomenology of Perception.* Trans. Colin Smith. London: Routledge and Kegan Paul, 1962.
Meyers, Diana T. "Subversion of Women's Agency in Psychoanalytic Feminism." In *Revaluing French Feminism: Critical Essays on Difference, Agency, and Culture.* Ed. Nancy Fraser and Sandra Lee Bartky. Indiana University Press, 1992, 140–61.

Midelfort, H. C. Erik. *Witch Hunting in Southwestern Germany, 1562–1684.* Stanford: Stanford University Press, 1972.
Mitchell, Juliet, and Jacqueline Rose. "Feminine Sexuality: Interview with Juliet Mitchell and Jacqueline Rose." With Parveen Adams and Elizabeth Cowie. *m/f* 8 (1982): 3–16.
Moi, Toril. "The Missing Mother: The Oedipal Rivalries of René Girard." *Diacritics* 12 (1982): 21–31.
———. 1985. *Sexual/Textual Politics: Feminist Literary Theory.* New York: Methuen.
———. 1986. *The Kristeva Reader.* New York: Columbia University Press.
———. 1987. *French Feminist Thought: A Reader.* New York: Blackwell.
Moore, R. I. *The Formation of a Persecuting Society: Power and Deviance in Western Europe, 950–1250.* Oxford: Basil Blackwell, 1987.
Moruzzi, Norma Claire. "National Abjects: Julia Kristeva on the Process of Political Self-Identification." In *Ethics, Politics, and Difference in Julia Kristeva's Writing.* Ed. Kelly Oliver. New York and London: Routledge, 1993, 135–50.
Nicholson, Linda J., ed. *Feminism/Postmodernism.* New York and London: Routledge, 1990.
Nowak, Susan. "The Girardian Theory and Feminism: Critique and Appropriation." *Contagion: Journal of Violence, Mimesis, and Culture* 1 (1994), 19–30.
Nye, Andrea. "Woman Clothed with the Sun: Julia Kristeva and the Escape from/to Language." *Signs* 12, 4 (1987): 664–86.
Oliver, Kelly. "Kristeva's Imaginary Father and the Crisis in the Paternal Function." *Diacritics* 21, 2–3 (1991): 43–63.
———. 1993. *Reading Kristeva: Unraveling the Double Bind.* Bloomington: Indiana University Press.
———. 1993a. *Ethics, Politics, and Difference in Julia Kristeva's Writing.* Ed. Kelly Oliver. New York and London: Routledge, 1993.
Pajaczkowska, Claire. "Introduction to Kristeva." *m/f* 5 and 6 (1981): 149–57.
Payne, Michael. *Reading Theory: An Introduction to Lacan, Derrida, and Kristeva.* Oxford and Cambridge: Blackwell, 1993.
Poovey, Mary L. 1988, "Feminism and Deconstruction." *Feminist Studies* 14 (1988): 51–65.
Prosser MacDonald, Diane L. *Transgressive Corporeality: The Body, Poststructuralism, and the Theological Imagination.* New York: State University of New York Press, 1995.
Rabine, Leslie Wahl. "A Feminist Politics of Non-Identity." *Feminist Studies* 14, 1 (1988): 11–31.
Ragland-Sullivan, Ellie. *Jacques Lacan and the Philosophy of Psychoanalysis.* Chicago: University of Chicago Press, 1986.
Rathbone, Perry Townsend. "Giovanni Battista Tiepolo." In *Museum of Fine Arts: Boston.* New York: Newsweek and Arnoldo Mondadori Editore, 1969, 124–27.
Reineke, Martha J. "Lacan, Merleau-Ponty, and Irigaray: Reflections on a Specular Drama." *Auslegung,* XIV, 1 (1987): 67–85.
———. 1988. "Life-Sentences: Kristeva and the Limits of Modernity." *Soundings* 71, 4: 439–61.
———. 1990. "'The Devils Are Come Down Upon Us': Myth, History, and the Witch as Scapegoat." *Union Seminary Quarterly Review* 44 (1990): 55–83. Published also in *The Pleasure of Her Text.* Ed. Alice Bach. Philadelphia: Trinity Press, 117–45.

———. 1990a. "'This Is My Body': Reflections on Abjection, Anorexia, and Medieval Women Mystics." *Journal of the American Academy of Religion* 58, 2: 245–65.

———. 1992. "The Mother in Mimesis: Kristeva and Girard on Violence and the Sacred." In *Body/Text in Julia Kristeva: Religion, Woman, Psychoanalysis.* Ed. David Crownfield. New York: State University of New York Press, 67–85.

Rich, Adrienne. "Resisting Amnesia: History and Personal Life." In *Blood, Bread, and Poetry: Selected Prose 1979–1985.* New York: W. W. Norton, 1986.

Richardson, William. "Lacan and Non-Philosophy." *Continental Philosophy I: Philosophy and Non-Philosophy Since Merleau-Ponty.* Ed. Hugh J. Silverman. New York and London: Routledge, 1988, 120–35.

Rose, Jacqueline. "Femininity and Its Discontents." *Feminist Review* 14 (1983): 5–21.

———. 1986. *Sexuality in the Field of Vision.* London: Verso.

———. 1989. "Julia Kristeva: Take Two." In *Coming to Terms: Feminism, Theory, Politics.* Ed. Elizabeth Weed. New York: Routledge, Chapman, and Hall, 17–33.

Ruether, Rosemary Radford. *Faith and Fratricide: The Theological Roots of Antisemitism.* New York: Seabury Press.

Sayers, Janet. "For Engels: Psychoanalytic Perspectives." In *Engels Revisited: New Feminist Essays.* Ed. Janet Sayers, Mary Evans, and Ranneke Redclift. New York: Tavistock, 1987, 57–80.

Schwager, Raymund. *Must There Be Scapegoats? Violence and Redemption in the Bible.* Trans. Maria L. Assad. New York: Harper and Row, 1987.

Spivak, Gayatri Chakravorty. "French Feminism in an International Frame." *Yale French Studies* 62 (1981): 154–84.

Sprengnether, Madelon. "Freudian Slaps." In *Women's Review of Books* 8, 4 (1996): 19–20.

Stanton, Domna. "Language and Revolution: The Franco-American Dis-Connection." In *The Future of Difference.* Ed. Hester Eisenstein and Alice Jardine. Boston: G. K. Hall, 1980, 73–121.

———. 1986. "Difference on Trial: A Critique of the Maternal Metaphor in Cixous, Irigaray and Kristeva." In *The Poetics of Gender.* Ed. Nancy K. Miller. New York: Columbia University Press.

Taylor, Mark. *Altarity.* Chicago and London: University of Chicago Press, 1987.

Thomas, Keith. *Religion and the Decline of Magic.* New York: Scribner, 1971.

Todd, Jane Marie. "The Veiled Woman in Freud's *Das Unheimliche.*" *Signs* 11, 3 (1986): 519–41.

Trevor-Roper, H. R. "The European Witch-Craze of the Sixteenth and Seventeenth Centuries." In *The European Witch-Craze of the Sixteenth and Seventeenth Centuries and Other Essays.* New York: Harper and Row, 1967.

Trible, Phyllis. *Texts of Terror: Literary-Feminist Readings of Biblical Narratives.* Philadelphia: Fortress Press, 1984.

Turner, Bryan S. *The Body and Society.* Oxford: Basil Blackwell, 1984.

Wallace, Mark I., and Theophus H. Smith. *Curing Violence.* Sonoma, CA: Polebridge Press, 1994.

Webb, Eugene. "René Girard: Consciousness and the Dynamics of Desire." In *Philosophers of Consciousness* by Eugene Webb. Seattle: University of Washington Press, 1988, 183–225.

Weedon, Chris. *Feminist Practice and Poststructuralist Theory.* Oxford: Basil Blackwell, 1987.

Weinstein, Donald, and Rudolph M. Bell. *Saints and Society: The Two Worlds of Western Christendom, 1000–1700.* Chicago: University of Chicago Press, 1982.

Weir, Allison. "Identification with the Divided Mother." In *Ethics, Politics, and Difference in Julia Kristeva's Writing.* Ed. Kelly Oliver. New York and London: Routledge, 1993, 79–92.

Williams, Delores S. "Black Women's Surrogacy Experience and the Christian Notion of Redemption." In *After Patriarchy: Feminist Transformations of the World Religions.* Ed. Paula M. Cooey, William R. Eakin, and Jay B. McDaniel. New York: Maryknoll, 1993, 1–14.

Wills, Clair. "Mothers and Other Strangers." *Women: A Cultural Review,* 3, 3 (1992): 281–91.

Ziarek, Ewa. "At the Limits of Discourse: Heterogeneity, Alterity, and the Maternal Body in Kristeva's Thought." *Hypatia* 7, 2 (1992): 91–108.

———. 1993. "Kristeva and Levinas: Mourning, Ethics, and the Feminine." In *Ethics, Politics, and Difference in Julia Kristeva's Writing.* Ed. Kelly Oliver. New York and London: Routledge, 62–79.

INDEX

abject, 32, 43, 44, 48, 86, 173
  and crises of late medieval Christendom, 125
  and Eucharist, 120
  and late medieval mystics, 119, 122, 126
  and melancholia, 93
  and witch hunts, 153
  Butler's critique of, 42
  defined, 21
  marks, 201
agency, human, 166
  and drive theory, 51, 64
alêtheia
  and torture, 154
anality, 54
  and language, 56
analysis
  as a feminist strategy, 166, 176
  as inquiry into death-work, 178
  contrasted with sacrifice, 178
anorexia
  clinical symptoms, 208
  interpreted by Bell, 124
  interpreted by Turner, 110, 118
  strengths of Kristeva's analysis of, 125
anti-Semitism, 211
asceticism
  as instance of sacrifice, 126
  cultural meanings of, 113
  discussed by Kristeva, 119
  men's and women's compared, 122
  psychological analysis of, 124
Athena, 213
Augustine, 190

Barstow, Anne, 127
Barzilai, Shuli, 61
Bataille, 205
Baudelaire, 60
Bell, Rudolph, 112, 114, 124, 127, 208–209
Bellini, Giovanni, 167–71, 173
Bertrand, Marie-Andrée, 199
Black Sun (Kristeva), 91, 207
Bohn, Carole R., 200, 213
Bordo, Susan, 43, 109
borderline discourse, 62
boundary failure
  defined, 27
boundary-work, 68, 95, 98
  by late medieval mystics, 120, 124
Brennan, Teresa, 5, 8, 204, 207, 216
Bronfen, Elisabeth, 70, 200
Brown, Peter, 136
Butler, Judith, 192, 194, 203, 204
  compared with Girard, 85
  criticism of Kristeva, 42
  feminist objectives furthered by Kristeva, 42–45
  inadequate treatment of violence, 46
Bynum, Caroline Walker, 111–15, 126, 129, 209, 211

caritas, 190
Carlson Brown, Joanne, 200, 213
castration, 66, 84, 91, 92, 165, 173
  and limitations of Symbolic order, 95
Céline, 61
Chanter, Tina, 199
Chodorow, Nancy, 35
  views of distinguished from Kristeva's, 36
chora, 23
Christ, 116, 120
  as Mother, 126
  importance of body, 114
Christianity, 99, 166, 187
  and defilement, 98
  as religion of sacrifice, 149
Chrysostom, John, 175
colonialism, 195
condensation, 63
Cornell, Drucilla, 203
Coward, Rosalind, 172
Crownfield, David, 172, 199, 215

da Vinci, Leonardo, 168
Daly, Mary, 200, 213
Danaïdes, 196
death-drive
  defined, 25
death-work, 41, 59, 98, 119, 121, 202

and defilement, 97
and feminist goals, 166
and late medieval mystics, 123
and melancholia, 93
and sacrifice, 28, 69, 71, 90
and the maternal body, 28
and the Mother in late medieval Christendom, 125
and the nascent subject, 28
and witch hunts, 157–58
defined, 25
differential impact on women, 38
distinguished from sacrifice, 25, 50
interrogated by analysis, 178
defilement, 93
and the Mother, 97
defined, 96
demonology, 139
Demos, John, 134, 210, 211
diabolism, 138
Doane, Janice, 203
Douglas, Mary, 96, 105, 106–10, 117–18
contribution to Kristeva's sacrificial theory, 96
drives, the, 52. *See* death-work
duBois, Page, 153–57, 212
Durkheim, Émile, 206
Dyer, Mary, 135

ecclesia, 189
Edelstein, Marilyn, 214
Eliade, Mirca, 206
Elliot, Patricia, 6, 7, 40, 165, 176, 178, 199, 205, 214
engram, 62, 206
Eucharist, 99
and abject, 120
and food, 111
and men's spirituality, 112
and sacrifice, 123
and women's spirituality, 112
as rite of eating God, 114
cultural meanings of, 113, 115
observance as death-work, 120

fascinated rejection
and sacrifice, 40
and the maternal body, 39
defined, 39
father of individual prehistory. *See* father, Imaginary
father, Imaginary, 82, 91, 94, 206, 207, 214
feminism
and the myth of Io, 196
need for a theory of sacrifice, 6
psychoanalytic, 7
radical, 3, 164
three generations of, 163–66
femme enceinte, 167, 213
food
meaning in late Middle Ages, 111
special meaning for women, 112
fort/da game, 56, 57, 69, 71, 204, 207
and Girard, 75
and Irigaray, 58
Lacan and Kristeva compared, 57
Fortune, Marie, 200, 213
Foucault, Michel, 107, 109, 212
Fraser, Nancy, 203
Freud, 50, 52–53, 56, 61–62, 72, 74–77, 85, 92, 95, 181, 183–84, 215
and "The Sandman," 184–87
the sign in, 61
views of on melancholia contrasted with Kristeva's, 92

Gasché, Rodolphe, 174
Gatens, Moira, 199
Girard, René, 69, 195
and mimetic desire, 74
and witch hunts as sacrifice, 142–46
compared with Butler, 85
compared with Eliade, 206
compared with Kristeva, 74, 80, 102
criticisms of Lacan, 75
criticisms of historical analyses of witch hunts, 130
influence on Kristeva, 205
limitations of his sacrificial theory, 87
on violence and sexual difference, 84
sacred defined by, 80
grammé, 201
Graves, Robert, 197, 216
Greenberg, David F., 211
Grosz, Elizabeth, 33–36, 203
Guerlac, Suzanne, 51

Hajnal, John, 133
Hamerton-Kelly, Robert G., 78, 206
Hegel, 61
Hegelian dialectic, 213
heimlich and *unheimlich,* 181
heterosexuality
compulsory, 42
Hodges, Devon, 203
Hoffmann, E. T. A.
"The Sandman," 184–87
Hutchinson, Ann, 135

Imaginary, 18, 82, 83, 177, 200, 204
  failure to create bridge to Symbolic, 94
In the Beginning Was Love: Psychoanalysis and Faith (Kristeva), 215
incest, 95
interdividual relations, 78
intertextual practice, 39
  defined, 19
Io
  myth of, 196, 216
Irigaray, Luce, 2, 3, 116, 126, 204

Jay, Nancy, 209
Jerome, 175
Jones, Ann Rosalind, 203
jouissance, 24–26, 38–39, 46, 52, 56, 58, 71, 83, 98, 119, 123, 125, 126, 157, 159, 169
  defined, 19
Judaism, 99, 187
  and defilement, 98

Karlsen, Carol, 133, 211
Kearns, Cleo, 6, 199
Kieckhefer, Richard, 138
Klaits, Joseph, 132, 134, 138, 141, 147
Klein, Melanie, 67, 205
Kristeva, Julia
  advocate of women's agency, 38, 41, 47
  analytic method of, 192
  and antifeminism, 7
  and social constructionism, 34
  and three feminist generations, 163–66
  as a theorist of sacrifice, 6
  attention to soma in sacrificial theory, 88
  compared with Girard, 74, 80
  compared with Lacan, 20
  concerns linked with identity as a woman, 68
  critique of Tiepolo, 163
  feminist criticisms of, 33, 176, 191
  importance of unconscious for, 26
  influence of Girard on, 72
  on violence and sexual difference, 84
  reflections on love, 83
  relevance to feminism's concerns, 196
  sacrificial perspective on the mystics, 119–24
  typology of matricide, 93

Lacan, Jacques, 9, 18, 69, 200
  views of myth criticized by Girard, 79
Larner, Christina, 132, 136–38, 141, 147, 210, 211
  persuasiveness of research, 141
Larsen, Nella, 203
laughter, 59
Lautréamont, Isidore, 203
Law, 20, 25, 29, 32, 40, 42, 56, 63, 79, 86, 92, 97, 100, 101, 123–24, 126, 165, 167, 173–74, 177, 184, 188, 200
  Butler's views on distinguished from Kristeva's, 46
  of the Symbolic order, 19
L'Etranger, 191
Lechte, John, 6, 205
Lévi-Strauss, Claude, 79

Macfarlane, Alan, 134
Madonna
  representations by Bellini, 167–71
Mallarmé, Stéphane, 203
maternal body, 22–24, 27–30, 37–38, 40, 42, 48, 53, 59, 92
  abject marks of, 30
  analogy to Derridean trace, 24
  and fascinated rejection, 39
  and the sacred, 96
  as defined by Lacan, 24
  defined, 23
  implicated in mimetic violence, 86
maternal matrix, 59, 98, 202
  and late medieval mystics, 120, 124
  and matricide, 91
  and sexual difference, 31
  and witch hunts, 153, 158
  defined. *See* maternal body
maternal Thing, 91
matricide, 84, 90, 92, 174, 180
  as founding strategy of human subject, 28
McAfee, Nöelle, 45, 182, 199
mé-connaissance, 19, 28, 30
melancholia, 91, 92, 207, 210
  and abjection, 93
  and late medieval mystics, 120, 122
Merleau-Ponty, Maurice, 214
metaphoric object, 82
metonymy of desire, 83
Meyers, Diana T., 203
Midelfort, Erik, 132, 136, 141, 147, 210, 211
mimesis, 169
  acquisitive compared with conflictual, 205
  and late medieval mystics, 120, 123
  described by Kristeva, 82
  dynamics of, 53, 74
  role of language in intensification of, 89
mimetic crisis
  and anality, 55

defined, 27
described by Girard, 76
role of sexual difference in, 85
mimetic violence, 95
and late medieval mystics, 120, 122
and melancholia, 91
and witch hunts, 150
centrality of somatic work to, 89
miracles, 112, 115, 120, 126
mirror stage
and thetic crisis, 28
defined, 18
Moi, Toril, 165
Moore, R. I., 136
Moruzzi, Norma, 190–94
Mother, 86, 92, 93, 97, 125, 127, 168, 202, 204, 214
and death-work of late medieval mystics, 125
and melancholia, 92
and witch hunts, 153, 158
as Christ, 126
as primary site of abjection, 94
defined, 32
mother, phallic, 213
mystics, late medieval
and abjection, 122
and mimesis, 120
and surrogate victimization, 121
asceticism as sacrifice, 119–24
compared with witches, 127
cultural meanings of bodies, 116
miracles of, 115
myth
and sacrifice according to Girard, 79
compared with history, 149
contemporary resistance to, 145, 148
significance according to duBois, 155

Nakashima Brock, Rita, 200, 213
narcissism, 82, 96
Nations without Nationalism (Kristeva), 187
negation, 61
negativity, 21, 24–26, 29, 34, 37–41, 43, 46–47, 67, 71, 91, 98, 119, 120, 123–25, 166, 204
and analysis, 178
and orality or anality, 54
and origin of language, 58
and the Mother, 92
and witch hunts, 157–58
defined, 24
"A New Type of Intellectual: The Dissident" (Kristeva), 187
nonsacrificial representation by Bellini, 169
Nowak, Susan, 207

Odysseus, 155, 157
Oedipal stage, 82
Oedipus, 145
and a sacrificial economy, 197
Oedipus complex, 74
Oliver, Kelly, 6, 10, 40, 169, 171, 173, 176, 180, 187, 193, 199, 207, 214
orality, 53, 83, 94, 204
and language, 56

Paganism, 98
Pajaczkowska, Claire, 45
patriarchy, 29, 38, 41, 116, 166, 198, 201
predominance of women as victims of violence in, 86
Paul
and a community of strangers, 189
persecution
stereotypes of, 143, 150
phallic mother, 173
phallus, 171, 200
defined, 20
pharmakos and *pharmakon,* 70, 124
Powers of Horror (Kristeva), 42, 91, 93, 205
pollution, 97
primary repression
and mimesis, 86
and the uncanny, 181
distinguished from secondary repression, 86
Prosser MacDonald, Diane, 174, 199
psychoanalytic theory
potential contribution to feminist theory, 8
psychosemantic fallacy, 113, 117–19, 209

Rathbone, Perry Townsend, 162
Reformation
and witch hunts, 135
Reilly, Peter, 148
rejection, 52, 56, 58, 62, 71, 98, 113, 119, 125–26, 157, 159
defined, 24
relics, 114
religion
as humanizer of violence according to Girard, 79
contribution to analysis, 187
potential for a praxis of strangeness, 188
role of in sacrifice according to Girard, 78
upholder of sacrificial economy, 12
repression

primary and secondary defined, 45
Revolution in Poetic Language (Kristeva), 60, 62, 71, 194, 205, 213
inadequacy of treatment of religion in, 72
Rich, Adrienne, 129
ritual, 208
and sacrifice, 78
rituals
and defilement, 97
Rose, Jacqueline, 214
Ruth, 188

sacrifice
and analysis, 178
and art, 72
and founding of the Symbolic order, 69
and myth, 79
and patriarchy, 29
as rite of scapegoating, 146
centrality of somatic work to, 89
Girard on witch hunts as case of, 142–46
matricidal pattern of, 90
mystics' asceticism as, 119–24
witch hunts as instance of, 158
sacrificial contract, 26
sacrificial economy
contrasted with analytic economy, 179
learning to recognize, 9
viable interventions in, 177
sacrificial theory
as key to witch hunts, 149
centrality of soma to, 88
importance of *Totem and Taboo* for, 95
origin of Kristeva's, 26, 40
three tasks of, 87, 119, 150
Saussure, Ferdinand de, 61
The Scapegoat (Girard), 142–46
scapegoat mechanism
defined by Girard, 76
scapegoats, 177
contemporary incapacity to recognize, 159
poor women treated as, 139
power of, 146
Schwager, Raymund, 85
semiotic, 21–26, 35, 37, 39, 40–42, 44, 67, 168
and defilement, 97
defined, 22
sexual difference, 39, 93, 201, 214
and mimetic violence, 85
and truth, 181
construction of, 20
Kristeva's theory of, 20
Kristeva's and Girard's views compared, 84
Lacan's theory of, 19
slaves
truth tellers under torture, 154
social constructionism
defined, 35
soma, 3, 118, 125, 127, 174
and defilement, 96
centrality to sacrificial theory, 88
defined, 3
meaning for late medieval mystics, 112
meaning in witch hunts, 158
sorcery, 138
compared with demonology, 139
Sprengnether, Madelon, 215
"Stabat Mater," 170–75
strangeness
praxis of, 180
the stranger, 178
Strangers to Ourselves (Kristeva), 187
subject, human
agency of, 8, 52
and castration, 66
and split identity, 19
boundary-work. *See* boundary-work
formed by drives, 51
most archaic boundaries of, 96
suicide, 92
surrogate victimization, 76, 90, 151
and late medieval mystics, 121
Symbolic, 18, 48, 63, 83, 91, 94, 123, 204
and fascinated rejection, 39
confinement of subject to, 40
limitations of, 98
Symbolic order, 42, 46, 66, 174
and late medieval mystics, 126
and sacrifice, 29
and witch hunts, 157
melancholic refusal of, 92
replicating founding of, 68
subversion of, 165

Tales of Love (Kristeva), 53, 81, 201, 215
thetic crisis, 26, 28, 84, 92
and the abject, 91
defined, 27
Kristeva's views distinguished from Girard's, 84
thetic phase, 66
Thing, the maternal, 91
and castration, 92
Thomas, Keith, 134
Thurschwell, Adam, 203
Tiepolo, Giovanni Battista, 162
Time

disrobing Truth, 162
Todd, Jane Marie, 215
torture, 90
meaning of in witch hunts, 153–56
sacred role in witch hunts, 151
Totem and Taboo (Freud)
interpreted by Girard, 77
interpreted by Kristeva, 94
transference, 179
Trevor-Roper, H. R., 147
Turner, Brian, 105, 107–10, 113, 117–19, 127, 142

uncanny, 87, 123, 181–83, 198, 215
and primary repression, 182
as work of mimesis, 181
maternal markings of, 184–87
unconscious, 37, 42, 46, 47
defined, 21
feminist criticism of, 33
radical politics of, 48

violence
abject pattern of, 94
and soma, 11
implosive and explosive compared, 91, 125
paralyzing continuum of, 11
silence about in contemporary witch scholarship, 146
social productivity of, 151
substitutionary pattern of, 11, 32
Violence and the Sacred (Girard), 73
Virgin Mary, 166, 170, 175

Webb, Eugene, 87
Weir, Allison, 56
Williams, Delores, 200, 213
Wills, Clair, 190
witch hunts
and death-work, 157, 158
and economic pressures among Puritans, 133
and marriage patterns, 133
and negativity, 157, 158
and new social ethic, 134
and Reformation ideology, 135
and Symbolic order, 157
and the abject, 153
and the Mother, 153, 158
as mimetic violence, 150
as one of last direct instances of sacrifice, 159
as surrogate victimization, 151
factors contributing to, 131–36
historians' treatments of violence in, 147
inadequacies of current accounts, 142
reasons for decline, 141
sacred role of torture, 151
special vulnerability of women, 132
three sacrificial functions of, 158
women as majority of victims, 210
witches
as scapegoats of elite and peasant cultures, 138
as scapegoats of the peasant class, 136
as scapegoats of the ruling class, 136–38
persecution of in mythic perspective, 143
"Within the Microcosm of the 'Talking Cure'" (Kristeva), 61
women
life-sentences of, 6
as irrecuperable strangers, 196
women's bodies
and the thetic crisis, 68
use by religions, 108

Xtravaganda, Venus, 204

Ziarek, Ewa, 23, 92, 126, 171, 174, 199, 214

MARTHA J. REINEKE is Associate Professor of Religion and Director of the Graduate Program in Women's Studies at the University of Northern Iowa.